KIDS

KIDS

CHILD PROTECTION IN BRITAIN:
THE TRUTH

CAMILA BATMANGHELIDJH
WITH TIM RAYMENT

Biteback Publishing

First published in Great Britain in 2017 by
Biteback Publishing Ltd
Westminster Tower
3 Albert Embankment
London SE1 7SP
Copyright © Camila Batmanghelidjh and Tim Rayment 2017

ISBN 978-1-78590-119-5

10 9 8 7 6 5 4 3 2 1

A CIP catalogue record for this book is available from the British Library.

Printed and bound in Great Britain by
CPI Group (UK) Ltd, Croydon CR0 4YY

CONTENTS

INTRODUCTION

On 5 August 2015, Kids Company had to close its doors, depriving some 36,000 children and families of a resilience-enhancing charity. Desperate children were clinging onto staff, both weeping. Mothers were rummaging through the kitchens, gathering potatoes because they knew they would be left without food. For the reporters, it was another day of news. For vulnerable children and families, it was the last day of a lifeline. For many, Kids Company had been their second home; a source of comfort and hope in the shadow of an unforgiving, violent urban environment.

False sexual abuse allegations made public through the media, before the charity knew about them, led to the closure of the organisation.

After seven months of rigorous police investigations, the charity was cleared. The allegations were deemed by the police not to present a child protection failure or risk. In fact, the investigating team stated they 'found no fault with Kids Company's safeguarding of children and vulnerable adults'. For nearly two decades the organisation had had no child protection failings. The charity was exonerated of any crime or malpractice. However, it was too late. Thousands of children, families, workers, donors and supporters felt perplexed and betrayed.

Who took these allegations to the media and why?

If safeguarding was their primary intention, they could have taken their concerns to the police first, the local safeguarding boards, the Charity Commission, the NSPCC, the government, local MPs, the Care Quality Commission or Ofsted, if they had lost faith in Kids Company's ability to keep children safe. Instead, their first port of call was the media. BBC *Newsnight* sat on these allegations for some time, during which they identified contributors to their programmes and those of their online media outlet partners, in preparation for mass release.

Had Kids Company been abusing children throughout this period, while the media were creating content, more children could have come to harm. Protecting abused children was neither the alleged whistle-blowers' nor the media's priority.

Kids Company would have survived without the false sexual abuse allegations, because we had raised a year's money ahead for 2015/16 and we could meet all our liabilities.

Post closure of the charity, elements of the media and some civil servants suggested that the government did Kids Company 'a favour' by giving the charity grants. In fact, it was the other way around: Kids Company was doing the work the state should have done in protecting vulnerable children and families and we were not properly funded for it because children and families were self-referring for help. No one would take financial responsibility for them, leaving the charity to raise £123 million to supplement the £41 million in grants the government gave it over twelve years.

Conflict arose between the Cabinet Office and Kids Company when I insisted that an independent firm of auditors should count and cost the number of children in our care who were the state's responsibility. We wanted government to step up, rather than use a charity to avoid their statutory duties to protect vulnerable children.

The political system's response was to 'lose' reports and documents which demonstrated the charity's efficacy, so that an impression could be created of Kids Company as an inefficient and failing organisation. This was a strategy to weaken Kids Company's message – too many maltreated children are being failed by their government.

Subsequent inquiries into the charity's efficacy colluded with this agenda by not taking available evidence which would have both proven the charity's capabilities and the government's distorting narratives. All inquiries avoided scrutiny of why Kids Company was systematically disrupted through a partnership between elements of the state, some members of the media and a handful of staff they co-opted into the agenda.

One care-leaver watching me be interviewed by MPs during the parliamentary inquiry apologised profusely, saying it was his fault, because he had asked for too much help. Children and young people who had already experienced unforgiving devastation in their lives did not deserve the public humiliation.

Over two decades, among the most vulnerable, Kids Company had acquired a reputation for being powerful advocates with an unwavering agenda: to see children and young people become safe and able to realise their potential. Most of the time, this agenda was achieved through partnerships. Generous and kind social workers, health practitioners, teachers, business leaders and the general public collaborated with us to generate a safety net for the most vulnerable and reconnect them to the centre of society.

We were profoundly moved by the kindness of strangers: members of the public who would walk onto our premises with cash and goods, as well as philanthropists who would sign million-pound cheques. Companies embraced our young people for work experience and gave goods-in-kind to improve their lives. Kids Company was enriched by the generosity of people irrespective of their wealth.

For some children and young people, the path to recovery was much harder than some decision makers were prepared to acknowledge, because they struggled with the dark repercussions of childhood maltreatment. Instead of being able to focus on achievements, they were condemned to surviving not only the abuse they were exposed to, but also the haunting memories of it which replayed in body and mind, creating lifelong battles.

Perhaps the most painful part of our families' journeys was the way society resolved the complexities of inequality by attributing to struggling individuals a kind of moral flaw, making them responsible for their unhappiness. It was a cultural and systemic defence in the service of sustaining the delusion that life is predictable and follows rules. Therefore, those who fall foul of it must have broken the rules and were being rightly punished.

Maybe what has been hard and unpalatable for all to acknowledge is that a mere throw of the dice renders one child secure and another devastated. It's called chance.

Of course, in the context of the arbitrariness of life, there are better choices to make than others. However, fundamentally the children and families Kids Company cared for were citizens whose quality of life was radically affected by psychosocial toxicity. Their mountain was much higher and harder to climb than for those whose citizenship had been better resourced, both psychologically and economically.

How does society reconcile such extreme divides between the rich and the poor, the safe and the unsafe, the psychologically stable and the unstable? As lives have become more individualistic, and our politics more about personal competencies, we have bought into the delusion that we only need to succeed personally.

People have been forced to turn themselves into commodities for sale. Working has ceased to be about earning a living and contributing to the wider community. Work has now become about 'selling' the self and our children as desirable products.

It is survival behaviour, forcing the belief that unless personal attributes and characteristics are enticing enough, the individual will be dispensed with, rendered worthless. It is in this context that even the securest is still a prisoner to being a brand.

In selling the self as an object to others, we sit in judgement, not only of our own identity but also the identities of others. Over time, human beings lose touch with their emotional frailties and the need to be nurtured. As personal psychological maps become distorted, negating our emotional landscape, it becomes easy to deny the needs of others. In the service of survival, the best of us are becoming lethal. We murder vulnerability within ourselves and kill it in others through negation.

The message to the poor and the destitute has become one of 'pull up your socks, turn yourselves into "desirables", otherwise there's no point to your living'. So the disadvantaged are doubly burdened – not only do they have to struggle with personal pain, but they also have to cope with a societal message letting them know that they are not welcome. This intrinsic lack of welcome has been at the heart of the challenges faced by maltreated children over decades in Britain. Cattle in Britain were protected under the Cruel Treatment of Cattle Act before children were.[1]

At first the child experiences a lack of welcome at home, if their parents are struggling with the legacy of their own childhood maltreatment. The mind of a perturbed parent only has space for the damaged child within themselves. They are preoccupied with the survival of their own hurting and underdeveloped self. There is no room mentally to accommodate the needs of another, even if it is their own offspring. It's not about poor morality – I have rarely seen a parent who didn't want to look after their child, but I have seen many who couldn't because their emotional life was too polluted. The parental lack of welcome is then extended into wider societal approaches to maltreated children. Institutionally, the survival preoccupations of professionals lead unwittingly to the rejection of the vulnerable child.

I believe Kids Company was closed down malevolently and abruptly because Britain was unable to tolerate seeing its lack of welcome for vulnerable children reflected back at it. A psychological dual had been set up. As a charity, we kept highlighting the need to generate more meaningful structures in order to protect vulnerable children. In return, the political system refused the advocacy because it was preoccupied predominantly with its own survival.

Meeting the needs of maltreated and mentally ill children was not going, as the politicians saw it, to enhance their own abilities to survive.

Most politicians' survival is, on the whole, driven by the promotion of a shallow brand. It is about brand leadership as opposed to moral leadership.

The difference between these two styles of leadership is that in moral leadership, there is an understanding that the world is built on systems but the energy that propels it is primarily emotional, because its inhabitants are people. We delude ourselves into thinking that the origins of our choices are objective and rational. The truth is that our motivations, the reasons we live and work hard, are always emotional. We modify our drives by rationally adjusting them so that we can exist in community.

Instinctively we know that our survival as a species is entirely dependent on being able to honour the life forces of another, with equity to generate harmony. It's about love. We live for it and we are made by it. Kids Company was built brick on brick by the compassion of strangers who shared our philosophy that maltreated children will recover with *unrelenting love*. Unrelenting because it is tough and the journey is painful, but ultimately love is the life force.

So why write this book? It's not about clearing my name, although the sullying of it prohibits my ability to fundraise and continue the work. Neither is it in revenge, to show up the people who caused this damage. Our staff and trustees deserve better than the malevolence generated against them. Our children and families exercised great courage in sharing their pain – they taught us everything we know about how best to help traumatised children. This learning must be shared.

This book is also not an attack on the hard-working clinicians, social workers and teachers who are giving their best to children in their care. In describing systemic difficulties, I am not devaluing their work, for which I have always had enormous respect. I am just questioning the way the children's workforce has bought into the false government narrative, keeping services impoverished and struggling. I am attacking a culture of subservience, which has enabled repeated governments to place an unfair burden on dedicated workers. Maltreated children do not vote and therefore politicians do not feel accountable to them. But their workers' advocacy is being paralysed and that is what I am raising the alarm about, because both workers and children are betrayed.

I love our staff and volunteers. They helped make Kids Company an amazing place for children. The charity was enriched by the contribution of some 650 staff and 10,000 volunteers in 2014/15, as well as 500 clinical and social work students who did their work experience with us. Along with the trustees, I did my best to shield them from harm. It would be impossible to acknowledge adequately the thousands who have contributed to the organisation over the years. The book has focused on my experience of running Kids Company, but it is important to emphasise that the organisation was a team effort and thousands of staff helped change lives for the better, giving children hope.

We have changed the names of the children to protect their identities, but the stories we will share with you are factual. Young people have been actively involved in creating the book. Every chapter has been reviewed by at least three senior scientists and clinicians. Ex-Kids Company staff have also been given a draft to comment on so that we can be sure that the content is reflective of their experience. Throughout the book, we refer to 'children', 'young people' or 'kids' interchangeably. Some of them would have come to Kids Company as five-year-olds and stayed with us for many years. We helped young people beyond their thirtieth birthday because severely traumatised children experience discrepant development. Elements of their personality become stunted by the trauma of abuse while in other areas they are highly competent. Our care for young people into their thirties, where appropriate, is also reflective of the latest findings in neurodevelopmental science, suggesting that the adolescent brain does not complete development until the late twenties or early thirties. Kids Company continued work with a young person until the developmental assault was ameliorated.

We have left out the names of individual donors and companies to respect their privacy apart from those who were and some who remain content to publicise their involvement with or connection to Kids Company.

The aim of this book is to explore the barriers which have, since the Victorian times, prohibited effective protection of vulnerable children. We need a brave and meaningful redesign of children's services, informed by cutting-edge understanding of the psychological and physical implications of trauma. Child abuse is destroying our society.

Science confirms the protective and healing power of love. The challenge is to turn love into political action. Informed by intelligent tenderness, we can create effective structures for protecting and healing children who are hurting.

When an organisation closes, many questions are asked. Everyone frames their perception according to their world view: so for the financial people, it was about alleged accounting problems; for the managers, it was about perceived lack of delegation; for the politicians, it was because I had 'mesmerised' the Prime Minister; for the civil servants, it was a perceived dearth of measurable outcomes and outputs; for the charity world, it was the absence of reserves. There was no shortage of people to get on individual bandwagons. Even a comedian on her way to the Edinburgh Fringe Festival wrote in *The Guardian* with pride that having an assistant to organise her schedule would ensure her success and that Kids Company had failed because I didn't have such an assistant! Poor timetabling was not the reason Kids Company closed.

This book is not being written to answer false allegations, because in truth they are 'side stories', taking the scrutiny away from the real story. I appreciate that for some, those details are important and it is in this context that I have asked the forensic journalist Tim Rayment to collaborate with me. He was sent by the *Sunday Times* to investigate Kids Company in 2015. In a climate of hysteria, he was the first journalist to approach the task with an open mind, seeking the truth. His and his colleagues' rigour in investigating us generated a sense of trust. I respected him for his fairness.

As Rowan Williams, the previous Archbishop of Canterbury, said to me: 'Kids Company is forever in the eyes of the children who benefited from it.'

Kids Company was a sanctuary and a place of hope. A safety net where reparation was possible and the imagination could create new dreams, making life worth living for children whose despair drew them to death. For desperate families, we were a secure base and through ordinary kindness we reduced the deleterious impact of maltreatment.

Through our partnerships with the business, media, fashion, arts, sports and scientific outlets, we opened doors of opportunity to young people who by virtue of their poverty would have been denied them. Thousands of young people went on to achieve and contribute to their communities.

There are undoubtedly many things we could have done better, but our failures were not the ones the 2015 media frenzy howled about. I would not apologise in the context of their pseudo-narratives, because in doing so, they would have had me confirming their 'side story', racism, xenophobia and misogyny, as representative of the truth. I am grateful for all those journalists who, as far as I am concerned, exercised integrity and did not jump on the destructive bandwagon. I felt deeply saddened by the fact that our self-employed staff and creditors were not paid. We left £2.1 million in the Kids Company bank account. They could have been paid, but the Cabinet Office's false assertion that we had misspent their £3 million grant, ignoring the conditions attached to it, meant the trustees felt legally obliged to withhold payment. In 2017, as I understand it, a judge ruled that Kids Company did not have to pay the Cabinet Office back as the charity had spent the money in accordance with the contract. I was deeply sorry for the difficulties caused in some people's lives as a result of the delayed payment.

The upset I felt is nothing compared to the pain the children in our care had endured. Their courage has remained my inspiration. But I am sorry for the pain caused to all who were involved with Kids Company.

The sight of a weeping mother putting her pleading hands on the metal mesh of the gates of Kids Company while her small children stared shocked and vacantly into space will always for me remain one of the most painful legacies of the organisation's closure.

This book is an attempt to understand what happened, and to learn from it, so that we can protect vulnerable children more meaningfully. Their courage deserves this reflection and I hope good will come from it.

CHAPTER 1

MEET THE KIDS

It is dusk, and a man is walking along a dual carriageway. He is a young adult – not what you'd normally call a kid. He has broken glasses held together by Sellotape, and is wearing some kind of uniform. Nobody offers him a lift; but then, nobody ever notices this man, even in normal circumstances, on the streets of London in daylight. Something about his body language makes him invisible.

If you had also been out for a walk at dusk that day on the dual carriageway – with no hard shoulder and no footpath – you might have seen the sweat on his forehead, the battered black bag over his shoulder, and the black, tired-looking trainers he would later change for blue Crocs at the start of his shift. He is of mixed race and his face wears no expression. Close up in the gloom, the uniform is now recognisable: this is a student nurse walking to hospital, a black jumper over his white shirt and blue clinical trousers.

Meet Kevin. He is a former client of Kids Company, the children's charity that imploded in spectacular fashion in 2015. Unless you were also a client, it is almost certain that in his twenty years of life he has seen more hardship than you. He would never tell you this. He walks calmly alongside the traffic after being chucked off a train for having no ticket. He knew that this would happen; he had planned for it. He left home at 5 p.m. to allow time to catch the train, be ejected from it, walk along the A21 and not be late for his 8 p.m. work placement in Tunbridge Wells. He is embarrassed by the fare-dodging, but is determined to get his degree.

If you have ever wondered where the stiff upper lip went, consider this man. You might even think he embodies the best of being British, after absorbing some of the worst of being human. The same is true of his partner, Luciana. Her voice is soft as she describes her hopes for their baby daughter. 'I don't mind if she's poor,' Luciana says. 'I just hope she's stronger and more self-dependent than me' – Luciana cannot sleep on her own at night – 'and that she could meet someone like her dad that genuinely cares about her, because a lot of my friends are in horrible "domestic" relationships. And that she outlives me. I want her to outlive her parents.'

It is an unusual wish, but then Luciana has just buried a friend who committed suicide at the age of nineteen. He looked like he was coping and then he was gone. Now she fears a second friend might kill herself. Luciana, too, is a former client of Kids Company.

You have heard of Kids Company. It was a charity that grew and grew for nearly twenty years, because so many children and families turned to it for help. Everyone praised it and tried to be associated with it, even though it dealt with the dark underbelly of life and the children who have to exist there. Academics visited from business schools. Child protection officials from other countries flew in for advice and inspiration. In 2009, the charity's founder, Camila Batmanghelidjh, was named Business Woman of the Year at the Women in Public Life Awards. Her portrait hung in the National Portrait Gallery and her clothes in the Design Museum. Celebrities, big companies, charitable trusts and thousands of people funded Kids Company to the tune of £123 million to 2015, on top of the £41.8 million it received from central government between 2003 and 2015. In addition, Kids Company competed for money from lottery funds and other statutory sources and received £2.6 million over fifteen years.[1]

Then, over a few months in 2015, everything changed. The veneration vanished, evaporating in the heat of a series of media stories until people believed the whole thing was a fraud. There were reports of money being spent on spa treatments, £150 shoes and a mansion with a private swimming pool. Batmanghelidjh was said to have 'mesmerised' the Prime Minister into handing over millions for no good reason. She went from 'Britain's most colourful and inspirational charity leader' (*GQ* and Editorial Intelligence's 100 Most Connected Women 2014) to disgrace. By 2016, Kate Hoey, a Labour MP, was asking the authorities to consider stripping her of her CBE.[2] As Wikipedia summarised it in 2017, 'Amid allegations of mismanagement and the squandering of funds, Batmanghelidjh was forced to step down as the charity's chief executive, and Kids Company was closed, by now insolvent, despite millions of pounds in government funding.'

In one of the most extraordinary reversals of sentiment in modern times, some people even started to doubt whether the thousands of vulnerable children cared for by the former 'Angel of Peckham', her 650 staff and 10,000 volunteers, clinical staff and social work trainees ever existed. 'Mysteriously, they were not there,' is how Tim Loughton, the former children's minister, described a visit to Kids Company.[3] 'What I saw was very, very few children using those services,' Sue Berelowitz, the former deputy children's commissioner, told a parliamentary committee.[4]

'We have spoken privately to two journalists who very courageously and with great skill did put this issue into the public domain,' Paul Flynn, a veteran Labour MP on the same committee, asked Berelowitz, 'but shouldn't you or some other person have alerted us to the fact that they were not doing the job? They didn't have 36,000 children, they probably didn't have 2,000 children and they were getting money on false pretences, and the children in great need were not getting any services at all?'

Others asked whether Kids Company, which by the end raised and spent £2 million a month, had any real purpose. 'How do you account for this very strong evidence from a very credible witness that, in fact, when social services looked [into] many of these cases, they simply said you were servicing clients where the need did not exist?' Oliver Dowden, a Conservative MP and former deputy chief of staff to then Prime Minister David Cameron, asked Batmanghelidjh. 'So, again, it is taxpayers and charitable funds being used for clients where there simply is not the need for it.'[5]

It could be a case study for a 21st-century version of *Extraordinary Popular Delusions and the Madness of Crowds*, the enduring history of witch trials, financial bubbles and other collective follies by the Victorian journalist Charles Mackay. 'Men, it has been well said, think in herds; it will be seen that they go mad in herds, while they only recover their senses slowly, and one by one,' he wrote.[6] But which was the delusion? Was the deification built on madness, or the denunciation? Or both?

Now, it sometimes happens that honest people say the exact opposite of the truth without realising it, and that is the fate that befell Oliver Dowden. Social services – meaning David Quirke-Thornton, the head of children's services in the London borough of Southwark, who had given written evidence to the select committee – had conveyed to MPs an understanding that it is deluded to think that large numbers of children are being failed by statutory services.

This book will show the reverse. Britain has a crisis in child protection, and another in child mental health. The two scandals are hidden behind a fragile edifice of denial and muddling through. Despite the efforts of a few campaigners, the crises receive so little attention that when Kids Company closed, it was seriously suggested that ministers had done the charity favours by allowing it grants. In fact, Kids Company carried out work the state should have done with vulnerable children, and it was mostly private funders that paid the bill.

• • •

Even if you do not recall these controversies, you are likely to recognise Kids Company's colourful founder and former CEO. That's me. I am the fat beggar who persuaded people, possibly including you, to part with money to keep Kids Company going for nineteen years. Since the change of sentiment, I have been described as 'that garishly-dressed lard-mountain of Persian self-regard' (*The Spectator*), 'an explosion in a Nigerian sofa factory' (the *Sunday Times*), 'a pile of Aladdin's laundry' (the *Telegraph*) and 'a bowl of fruit salad' (*Daily Mail*). 'She arrived at Parliament yesterday wrapped in textiles of 100 colours,' wrote Quentin Letts in the *Mail*.

Yellows, pinks, scarlets, greens, indigos, and more tartan than they use in the carpets at Balmoral. She's as tall and wide as a heavyweight wrestler, with Ronnie Barker spectacles and a Robbie Coltrane chin. Her accent is what a chef might call fusion: West Country by way of Tehran, Brick Lane and the Caribbean.[7]

I do not mind these descriptions; the kids say worse, and I find the inventiveness of the insults funny. But they add to a perception that a person of my size and dress cannot possibly have ordered thinking. The assumption is that a 'charismatic leader' runs her organisation on whim. It is another inversion of the truth, which leads us to the second purpose of this book.

Emotional wounds have a profound logic, and require logic in response. At Kids Company, we created structures that brought not just love to deeply troubled children but science. Love provided the secure base that allowed young people to face emotional and developmental disturbances with less loneliness and more control. We helped them lead healthier emotional lives and to be less dangerous. Everything we learnt is set out in these pages for anyone who is interested, whether parent, teacher, social worker, policy maker or researcher.

Because they did exist, the 36,000 children, young adults and family members for whom Kids Company offered sanctuary and solutions. In the United Kingdom as a whole, they number many hundreds of thousands – abused, neglected, their pain denied by a country that cannot bring itself to acknowledge a scale of need with which it fears it cannot cope.

Consider Kevin. Kids Company knew him as an infant. We became aware of him after one of his brothers, who was then fourteen, turned to street crime to survive. He was trying to rob bus passengers when he was stopped by a member of our staff, who told him about our services. The boy showed up the next day, taking advantage of a model that was our systemic weakness and our great strength. No one paid for the children who arrived at our centres, because they referred themselves, like people turning up at Accident & Emergency. We had to raise most of the money privately. I later made a home visit.

The family of eight shared three plates; the entire household was depleted. Rat holes were stuffed with old clothing and shoes. There were no sofas, chairs or tables. Francis, the man performing the role of Kevin's father even if this was not biologically true, cooked some rice; he put it on a single plate, with a single fork, and the kids formed a circle in the little kitchen before taking turns to ingest a forkful of food, then pass the plate and implement to the next child. With no furniture available, the group stood for its nourishment as an intimate circle. This was in 21st-century Britain.

Everyone slept on a mattress on the floor except for two of the younger boys, whose beds were broken; one rat had got into a broken cot and bitten the baby's ear. Social services should have known about this family's circumstances: they had placed an extra child in the house, a disturbed fifteen-year-old girl in local authority care, and were paying the mother £50 a week to look after her. The decision had been taken without bothering to visit.[8] After pressure from Kids Company, the girl was removed and the rest of the family offered a new home, where we helped with bedding, towels, kitchen resources and furniture.

It is worth spending a little time with Kevin and considering his official classification as a child who was never in need of state protection except for one, brief period in response to chivvying from Kids

Company. Many equally troubled families are hidden behind the fragile screen of denial.

His mother, Diane, has a history of emotional and mental trouble and addictions to prescription drugs and crack cocaine. She was in love with two men who lived with the family. It was a set-up that caused Kevin and his siblings to witness extreme violence.

On the day of the rice dinner, I had called round after finding Michael, one of Kevin's older brothers, in a bloody state in the Kids Company shed. He had tried to intervene when Francis, the man he regarded as his dad, and Donald, the drug dealer trying to replace Francis in his mother's affections, fought with knives. Kevin was seven years old at the time.

The children described the general violence. Mum hit Dad 'all the time ... she stabbed him, put a cup in his face, dashed him in the skull with rollerblades ... I used to go to school and when I came back I always used to see blood – on the wall or on my dad's face,' Michael told us.[9]

The violence was so frequent that Michael stopped going to school for fear of what might happen if he were not there to protect his father. 'I think I went ten times in Year Seven,' Michael says now. 'A few times in Year Eight ... probably my whole attendance was sixty days, maximum, from Year Seven to Year Eleven, when I finished.' He took up weed and became violent himself. He would pick up a knife and stab someone, or pick up a chair and hit Donald.

Social care placed the children on the child protection register but failed to carry out the required assessments. Michael's school was recorded as not co-operating with the child protection process. The violence continued. Kids Company made a further referral, reporting that the fights and stabbings were making the children very disturbed. It was decided to refer Michael to mental health services for therapeutic counselling, but there was no follow-up. A social worker is recorded, nine months later, as having spoken to him about counselling, and being told that he did not want to attend it.

Against Kids Company's advice, Michael and his siblings were removed from the child protection register after just over a year (except for one sibling who had been removed earlier). His mother then threw him out. Aged fourteen, Michael moved in with squatters. Kids Company advised that a child protection investigation should be reinstated to look into the welfare of his younger siblings, including Kevin. We believed the children were not safe, were not getting enough to eat, and that older children were looking after younger ones. The local authority declined.

Now and again, the mother disappeared. Even when present, she was not always conscious. 'When she knocks out, she really knocks out,' says Luciana, who once had an accident in the house as she was looking after Kevin's youngest siblings, and could not rouse her. 'She was in the room when it happened. But we couldn't wake her. Even when the ambulance came she was unconscious. Everyone was jumping on her and she's still flat cold.'

I was so used to the pattern of referral and denial that in 2012, after years of being unable to get social care and mental health services to pick up our most serious cases, I decided to bring in independent evaluators to capture what was happening. I hoped that with a powerful partner I could get the government to take responsibility for these vulnerable children and compel local authorities to protect them properly instead of faking it. I would no longer be an unsupported voice calling for change.

Too many kids were being considered children in need, an official category that means they get much less scrutiny, when they should have been child protection cases. Then the deprived and vulnerable children who should have been identified as 'in need' were being overlooked because the thresholds of intake were too high.

We chose the Centre for Social Justice (CSJ), a Conservative think tank founded by Iain Duncan Smith and Tim Montgomerie. I believed in Iain's commitment to the welfare of vulnerable kids. He seemed to understand how depleted the neighbourhoods were and the depth of the families' struggles. A visit to Easterhouse in Scotland had taught him the debilitating impact of drugs. I knew that as Secretary of State for Work and Pensions in David Cameron's government, his vision of helping families was being compromised as he battled it out with the Treasury. But I had seen the thoroughness of the CSJ when I sat on a judging panel with Theresa May, then the Home Secretary, to consider charities for an award. I also had faith in Adele Eastman, a lawyer who was a policy specialist there. She had shown great moral courage when her fiancé, Tom ap Rhys Pryce, was murdered for his watch by two teenagers. Instead of seeking revenge, she and Tom's family sought to understand the factors that had brought the boys to stab him. The government would find it hard to dismiss a report from the CSJ. Who could deny the truth now?

I gave Eastman and her researchers access to everything. They met young people and key workers and read the files. Among the cases scrutinised was that of Kevin's family. The report, 'Enough Is Enough', tells the story of their interactions with social care through the eyes of his brother Michael.

'Social care decided to work with the children on a child in need basis, but later no longer even considered them to be children in need,' the CSJ found. The report also records that Kids Company described an alleged attempt by Diane to stab Michael, and continuing concern for the younger children, including Kevin. According to Michael, social workers never spoke to him about the alleged stabbing. When he needed to get away, he slept on the beach in Brighton.

At sixteen, when his mother threw him out a second time over his fights with Donald, Michael was placed by the local housing department in a B&B where other residents reportedly used crack cocaine. Only after solicitors instructed by Kids Company threatened a judicial review did social care offer to make an assessment.

The CSJ found, among other lapses, a 'failure to undertake a child protection investigation … or issue care proceedings, despite clear and repeated evidence of all the children in the family witnessing or being involved in violence within the home, including stabbings, and the mother's frequent absences from the home due to suspected drug misuse'. It also found a 'failure by social care to treat Michael as a child in need and to accommodate him under S.20 [of the Children Act 1989], which also thereby deprived him of necessary support under the leaving care provisions' and a 'failure to adequately investigate or give sufficient weight to information provided by the voluntary sector' – meaning Kids Company.

The report adds:

> We have been astounded by the number and nature of legal failings and missed opportunities which were identified by the legal professionals' review of Kids Company cases ... Michael did not have a childhood. Kids Company tried for years to shed a critical light on the reality of the home environment – to secure social care's intervention to ensure the safety of the children. However, despite the gravity of its concerns, Michael and his younger siblings remained in Diane's care – exposed to continuing chaos, danger, neglect, emotional abuse and trauma.[10]

All this happened in David Quirke-Thornton's borough. In his evidence to Parliament, Quirke-Thornton was able to assure MPs that when Kids Company referred children and young people for help when the charity closed, 'none of the 299 Southwark cases were escalated to Child Protection'.[11]

Four of the 299 cases not referred to child protection are siblings of Michael.

Only as an adult has it occurred to Michael that he was not, in fact, a child criminal – his arrests were for stealing milk and nappies for Kevin, not sweets for himself. 'I used to be so kind and good,' he says of his young self. He told the researchers for 'Enough Is Enough' that he would have opened up to a social worker, but that no one spoke to him on his own.

I put a mask on but was crying underneath, begging for someone to give me a hug or help me. Only my dad and Camila gave me a hug. When I was 10, 11, 12, 13 or even 14, I would have talked; it would have burst out and I would have cried. But no one had the time to look into me, although they could have seen the pain in my eyes. After that, I hated the system.[12]

The 'dad' is Francis, the father figure Michael tried to protect; his biological dad had killed himself.

Kevin was also affected. He lost a month of school when Diane became upset at her partner's long hours in the betting shop. She vanished, leaving her son with no money and four younger siblings. Luciana did not have it easy either. She became part of Kevin's household after a member of her family started creeping to her bed at night, a 'cringe' over which her mother was unsupportive. When threats from a gang meant that Kevin, Luciana and Michael had to relocate – after Kevin had refused on principle to start dealing drugs for the people who supplied weed and crack to his mum – they squatted in a place where one room was for a crack dealer, another for a weed dealer and there were prostitutes 'just flowing through the house'. Luciana was approaching GCSEs; she was fifteen years old, and embarrassed to be a homeless school prefect who smelt.

Luciana reported herself to social services. She says that after two days' investigation, they told her to return to her mother and closed the case.

So it was back to the crack house. I got really skinny. My head teacher noticed it. She'd buy me food and stuff, but it got really bad, because my exams were coming up and I'd be in class and pass out. And one time – two times – they had to call the ambulance.

It was soon after that that Kevin and Luciana asked Kids Company for help.

• • •

In Parliament after the charity closed, MPs seemed extraordinarily naive about inner-city life. Some suggested that Kids Company only had clients because it handed out cash that was then spent on drugs. (For the most part, it handed out Tesco vouchers.) Told that in the two months since the closure there had been several stabbings and four suicide attempts, Bernard Jenkin, a Conservative MP in one of the safest seats in the country and chair of the committee examining the government's dealings with Kids Company, responded: 'We have been advised that these incidents occurred because kids no longer had money to pay their drug pushers, and the breakdown in the flow of funds on to the streets has led to that violence – your clients no longer being able to pay for drugs.'[13]

This sounds plausible, but only if you have never met people such as Kevin and Luciana. When the two teenagers finally asked for help, they were in a sorry state. For years we had glimpsed Kevin only at special events such as the Christmas lunch, or at one of our centres when he and Luciana ran out of food. It was desperation that brought the couple to my office.

'I was thinking when I walked in, in all honesty, this woman's crazy,' says Luciana. 'She's a big, fat white woman that's dealing with poor black kids, wearing a multicoloured turban with a tree in her office. I just looked at him like – this is a movie scenario. But by the time we left I already loved her. She gave me a hug.'

Kevin and Luciana had walked to central London. They had no money for travel or to feed the siblings or themselves. As Luciana was taking GCSEs, she was not entitled to benefits: the pair had no income at all. Luciana was pregnant. They were homeless. Kevin had to glue his shoes together on the journey.

What Luciana really wanted was a parent. As this book will show, the key to recovery for traumatised children is re-parenting. Or, to put it in simple language, love.

She found one in Jackie, the red-haired key worker Kids Company assigned to her. We also introduced her to a midwife. 'My labour was through the night,' says Luciana. 'She didn't take a phone call; she didn't leave; she cuddled me, she put me in the bath and took me out of the bath. She stayed the whole labour. The whole labour.' She says this as if it were the most amazing thing in the world. As for her key worker: 'Jackie was my mum … I don't have another mum like that. I have a breathing parent, but she's my mum. I miss her.'

Jackie bought Luciana her first plates and cutlery. She went with her to the park, to be quietly present when Luciana was overcome by depression.

Luciana says now:

I had a lot of people [say]: do you want to come and do your CV? I already had my CV. I need someone to cuddle me; I need someone to say, 'You've done well.' I need someone to say, this is how you spend money, not just, here's money.

She found that having a Kids Company worker had an effect on social services; we also found her a lawyer. 'I went into meetings before, without Jackie, and they were like, so which case is this? They're reading the case in the meeting. But when Jackie was there, they spoke to you a little bit more like a human being.' She adds: 'Why did I need a lawyer to argue as a fifteen-year-old that I should be in care? When I'm in the crackhead house and you've come to assess it? Why am I fighting to prove that I'm worthy of living? It shouldn't be like that. It shouldn't.'

Luciana is now at university. Her ambition is to be a diplomat. Kevin has qualified as a nurse. All his work placements were out of London, and there was no money for fares after Kids Company closed. Sometimes he left home at 4 a.m. and came back eighteen hours later. He never missed a placement and never complained. He holds his daughter in the same way: quietly, without drama.

Like Kevin and Luciana, Michael broke the cycle. With Kids Company's help, he gave up drugs, qualified in his chosen occupation and became a very good dad. Of the charity, he has said: 'Without Kids Company, I would have been dying out there – living like a tramp – and would have gone into the crime world and worked my way up the ladder.'[14]

They are all worried about another brother – thirteen when we closed, and soon in a deteriorating state. Luciana believes he will end up in prison or dead. 'When Kids Company stopped working with him, it was a bit of a shock because he was so used to them being his parent,' she says. 'He looks dirty. He has never been in a class. He had a court case last week. He sleeps at different addresses, and he's, like, fourteen. Two days ago his friend got stabbed in this park thing. And it nearly was him.'

He can be lovely, Luciana says; if there is money on offer, he hustles and works hard. But he is angry. No one cuddles him; no one even notices when he goes missing. 'Before, Kids [Company] would give us some money,' says Luciana.

> Therefore he was at mine all the time eating. I can't feed him any more, so he's losing weight. He's smoking weed. He's gone a bit skinny. And he doesn't get money for clothes. All his friends are looking nice, they're looking sharp, and – it sounds petty, but in our area that's what it's about. If you don't look good and your friends do, you're gonna want to get money, so how?

Even before we closed, he held up a shop with a fake firearm. He has also dealt class-A drugs.

I have referred him so many times to Quirke-Thornton. Nothing seems to happen.

• • •

On the day Kids Company closed, children clung to staff, both parties weeping. Mothers rummaged through our kitchens, gathering potatoes because they knew they were going to be short of food. For them, it was the end of a lifeline. Kids Company had been a second home, a source of comfort and hope in an unforgiving urban environment.

The end was abrupt, and it was not because of money. I had been under intense pressure to raise just over £11 million, a task for which I was given three weeks. This was a requirement for the release of a £3 million government grant, with a further £3 million to come from philanthropists who would restructure Kids Company into a smaller charity. Without the first £11 million, all £17 million would be lost.

I fell short by £350,000, for which I put up my flat as a surety with the Cabinet Office. The deal done, the government's £3 million arrived. But within half an hour, news broke that Kids Company faced allegations concerning sexual and physical abuse. The claims, passed to the police by the BBC's *Newsnight*, shut us down. For a children's charity, a scandal over systemic safeguarding lapses can be fatal.

In nineteen years we had not had a single child protection failure, an extraordinary achievement given the levels of vulnerability and disturbance on our premises. The allegations spanned seven years. The Metropolitan Police gave them to its serious complex case team, part of the Sexual Offences, Exploitation and Child Abuse Command. The investigation took six months.

They were unfounded, as the Met revealed in an 'update' after six months. 'These reports concerned allegations or information relating to children and staff based at the charity. However, the majority were third party reports which were vague in detail,' the Met said in a statement.

Officers carried out detailed and extensive inquiries to establish the veracity of the information ... to date the Met has identified no evidence of criminality within the 32 reports which would reach the threshold to justify a referral to the Crown Prosecution Service. Nor have we identified any failings by the charity in respect of them carrying out their duty to safeguard children or vulnerable adults.[15]

In short, Kids Company shut in a blizzard of accusations for which there was no case to answer. There was no victim and no perpetrator. There was nobody to arrest, or even to interview under caution. When the police told me, I burst into tears. They had called me to the police station, but would not say why until I got there. The no. 2 on the investigating team read out the statement. When she got to the line on safeguarding, I started crying, because we had worked so hard to keep the kids safe.

The fact that police could find no evidence of any crime or safeguarding failure was announced on 28 January 2016. Three weeks later, *Newsnight* won an award from the Royal Television Society. The award is listed on the RTS website as 'Scoop of the Year: The Closure of Kids Company'.

I believe Kids Company closed as the result of a malicious campaign driven by Britain's inability to tolerate a mirror reflecting back its lack of care for vulnerable children. We kept highlighting the need for meaningful structures. The political system refused the advocacy because it was preoccupied predominantly with its own survival. *Newsnight* was used to undermine us. The BBC programme helped generate a hostile climate for which the sexual abuse allegations were the deadly pinnacle. As an unwitting participant in the campaign, it missed the bigger story because it was part of it.

There were exceptions to the intolerance. 'We are calling on all political parties to commit to the establishment of a Royal Commission to advise on the wholesale redesign of social care and statutory mental health services for vulnerable children and young people,' said the CSJ in its 2014 report. The commission 'should report by the end of 2017, and, most importantly, ask how best to recreate parental support for these children and young people in the public space'.

Needless to say, it did not happen. The children's landscape is rich with guilt-inducing reports that are filed away or addressed by pseudo-initiative, and a commission would take too long. I urged a bolder plan, called 'See the Child. Change the System'. The children's sector would work together to propose a new structure for child mental health and social care. We would redesign the delivery of provision throughout the United Kingdom, and pilot the result in two local authorities before campaigning for its adoption in a fifteen-year recovery plan for children's services.

Sir Keir Starmer, the former director of public prosecutions and now the shadow Brexit Secretary, agreed to chair the taskforce. With £3 million from a philanthropist, the project was fully funded. Among the advisers were Maggie Atkinson, the then children's commissioner for England; Javed Khan, the chief executive of Barnardo's; Lisa Harker, the director of policy for the NSPCC; Derrick Anderson, the then chief executive of Lambeth Council; and Andrew Webb, a past president of the Association of Directors of Children's Services. There were professors from top universities throughout England. Other partners included the Royal College of Paediatrics and Child Health, the Royal College of Psychiatrists, the Health and Care Professions Council, the Royal College of General Practitioners, the Royal Society for Public Health, the National Youth Agency, the Royal College of Nursing, the National Association of Head Teachers, the British Association of Social Workers, the British Association for Community Child Health, the National Association of Social Workers in Education, Unison, Childline, Action for Children, the Children's Society and the National Children's Bureau.

When Keir and I announced the venture at a social work conference in June 2014, one could sense the trepidation in the room at the audacity of it, but also the support. See the Child. Change the System was to be independent of Kids Company, to exercise neutrality and champion the best ideas. The charity was no longer a maverick organisation, as some in the government saw us. It was mobilising a serious group of institutions. Recruitment for the project started just before we closed. Modelling the new services was to take eighteen months, followed by the pilots.

I turned up at the Department for Education to invite Sir Tom

Jeffery, the director general for children, young people and families, to join the project. His response was aggressive: 'I don't want you doing this and criticising us.' Criticism was not the aim: I wanted all of us to work together to bring about improvements for the children's sector.

Then came the first straws of scandal, and soon Kids Company closed.

This is the story of what was lost, and why I think it happened.

CHAPTER 2

SUZY

At boarding school in England, my reputation was as an out-spoken, creative daredevil. Everyone called me Batman and if there was anything adventurous going on, I was at the centre of it. At Sherborne Girls, the assembly hall on the first floor had an impressive hammer-beam roof resting on carved stone supports, as if it were the work of a medieval carpenter (in fact it is twentieth-century). The oak-panelled walls bore the names of award winners and old head teachers in gold. I would often sit there on the creaking chairs attempting to keep up with hymns. I could never follow the hymn book, so I would mime to minimise the fury of Gusy, who was God's gift to music, and whom I grew to love and respect. Years later I found out she was actu-ally scared of me, just in case I cracked a joke and engaged the other pupils in disrupting hymn practice. I love music, but even the piano teacher threw me out of her class in frustration. Thanks to my learning difficulties, I couldn't read a note. I was so aware of how much she tried not to hit me over the head. The first day I arrived at Sherborne, I burst into tears in this hall. I had never seen a priest, so I couldn't understand why this man dressed in black was shouting and making everyone sit, kneel and stand up! I later realised he was giving a sermon. I had been used to the mullahs in Iran bellowing Friday prayer, and I had got good at mimicking them, but the priest in black was a shock to my system. It was my first introduction to Britain, a country I grew to love very much.

My experience of children's social services and mental health comes from thirty years of working in the inner cities. In my early twenties, when I was training as a psychotherapist at Regent's College, the London extension of an American university, I was asked by Westminster City Council to work with boys who had been sexually abused. I also worked at Women's Aid supporting women and children who had fled domestic violence. Another aspect of my work involved therapeutic support for children who came from extremely wealthy backgrounds. I would discreetly go to their homes, using a suitcase of toys, puppets and art materials to work with them. And, in partnership with the Royal Free Hospital and Cruse, the bereavement charity, I ran groups for children whose fathers had died.

I loved running these groups. Using the arts, we would try to help the children come to terms with grief. Since they were very young and distressed, they struggled to sit down and talk about their loss. So, we used to try to think of creative ways to enable them to express pain and process the abandonment. I remember covering the floors of the room we worked in with bags and bags of marshmallows. We had sprayed Evian bottles silver and dressed the kids in silver freezer bags, which looked like a padded space suit. A white builder's mask was connected to the Evian bottles by tube. It was our trip to the moon. The marshmallows were sufficiently squashable beneath their feet to generate the feeling of loss of gravity.

Through this symbolic adventure, the children were given a chance to explore the idea of death and transitions.

Two weeks earlier, I had made a giant aeroplane with Nini, my co-worker, big enough for all twelve kids to fit in it. The kids created passports, and all of them got into the aeroplane, which travelled down the pavement at the venue. We were exploring how your life could change while also considering what the children may have thought about where their fathers had gone to in death and where they could go with their lives.

The group was full of characters. Ginger-haired Tommy would shriek randomly, while Peter barely spoke a word or even looked up at anyone. At all times, I was aware of the other two co-workers who were holding groups with the mothers in the same room. My marshmallow and aeroplane trips were stretching their patience! However, for some reason, the kids were getting better, so they tolerated me with great generosity.

I trained in infant and child observation at the Tavistock and Portman NHS Trust, a specialist mental health trust; taught psychology part-time at one American university in London, and therapeutic studies at another; and have had twenty-seven years of psychoanalysis, five days a week. This began as a requirement of my training. It helps to keep clinical work to a high standard. In my late twenties, I worked part-time with Family Service Units, a charity that supported vulnerable families referred by local authorities. My role was to run groups for sexually abused girls and boys with behavioural difficulties. This is when I founded the Place2Be, which is now a programme offering counselling to children in schools across the country. At the time, I was working with family service units as a therapeutic worker for children. My post was funded by BBC Children in Need. The team leader at Family Service Units was very generous as a manager and allowed innovation.

I soon realised that for some children the model of offering therapy in a clinic is flawed, as it relies on parents making a commitment to take them there. Most of the carers we dealt with were busy surviving their own disturbances and struggled to achieve the consistency needed for therapy. Some children were disappointed if they missed sessions, while others came but found it a burden, because a parent told them what to say or questioned them afterwards. Most professionals will admit that one in three children from backgrounds of abuse or neglect drops out of therapy.

Family Service Units offered some group work, but I could see that something much more substantial was needed. So, by ceasing to pay the mortgage on my ground-floor flat in north London and by using the psychotherapy students I was teaching at university, I had the financial and human resources to start work in a primary school in south London.

As I did up the play room, I knew I did not want the support programme to have some miserable, therapeutic name. It needed to suggest help, twinned with joy. Sweeping the floor of the broom cupboard that would be our counselling room, I decided to call it the Place2Be. In a lunch break from teaching at the university, I drew the logo that to this day carries its cheerful history.

I stood before the primary school in assembly to say that my team and I were there to listen and the children could bring us all their troubles, but also, if they wanted fun, we had arts, sports and play groups. I knew that we had to offer a non-stigmatising environment so that vulnerable children would not feel ashamed and cared-for children would feel included. I was also aware that it might take some time before a child trusted us enough to talk, and they might want to try us out with an activity before any counselling.

All our team wore the yellow-and-red Place2Be badge. The broom cupboard, a fine example that was blessed with a window, could accommodate thirty-six children a week in one-to-one sessions that were fifty minutes long. As time went on, we created more rooms as well as running the activity groups.

I started this project because of a little girl who had been referred to Family Service Units. I remember the call from the local educational psychologist. He told me he was worried that Suzy would kill herself on school premises. She had tried to suffocate herself with a plastic reading folder, had thrown herself in front of a car and had stood on the roof of a building. She was seven years old.

I shall never forget the bolt of shock when I realised that for the psychologist, the thought of where Suzy might kill herself, on local authority premises, was more alarming than the question of why a seven-year-old would want to end her short life. I do not judge his anxiety. It is typical of what goes wrong in our care institutions, leaving staff more frightened than concerned.

I visited Suzy at the family home. Her mother was barely coping as her younger child was very ill. Suzy stared at me through her long blonde fringe and did not utter a word. There was no way this mother was going to bring her child to weekly therapy sessions; I had to rethink it. So, I took the suitcase of toys and art materials I used for therapeutic work in my small private practice with wealthy families, and went to see Suzy in the school library. She sat on a chair, tight with resolve not to speak.

The school believed she had a low IQ as she was not reading or writing at an age-appropriate level. It did not seem low to me. She was too determined to defeat me, and not to let me discover anything.

I decided to make no inquiries. Finding anything out from her was precisely what I was not going to do. I would just sit with her and use art materials to function alongside her as a compassionate companion.

Tentatively, she began picking up the felt tips. I drew and she followed me on the page. Eventually, her drawings started the communication. She would draw big gorilla bodies with a child's head on top. Or a bird head with a child's body. It was clear that she wanted to convey some kind of split between the head and the body propelled by grotesqueness. She still did not say a word. I did the talking, reflecting back at her what I felt about her drawings. Then eventually, on the back of my language, she reclaimed her ability to speak and in tiny whispers told me what had happened.

Three men who lived in a tower block opposite her home had taken her in. Her mother was preoccupied with the care of her sick sibling. Suzy was a cute and curious five-year-old the men found easy to entice. Over two years, this child was in their flat experiencing adult sexual activity which, in her innocence, she perceived as 'games with special toys'.

For me, the most striking part of the narrative was that a five-year-old had not felt able to speak about what had happened to her. No one at the school or home, no neighbour, doctor or family member knew what was happening to her as she withdrew by degrees into an angry silence.

Child protection protocols demand that neglect or abuse, whether emotional, physical or sexual, is reported to a school's safeguarding officers, who tell the local child protection department (social services), which in turn can involve the police. Before long, all the professionals were round a table deciding what to do with Suzy.

I was asked to take her to a police interview. The cameras were up on the walls. Two kindly officers sat ready to question her while I went to another room to watch on closed-circuit television.

Suzy's little legs could not reach the floor and she was swinging and twisting them with nervousness. I recall her little white socks, neatly pulled up as if this were the one thing she could control. The interview took hours, until they decided that she could not sequence events robustly enough for the narrative to withstand the adversarial criminal justice system.

It was obvious she did not understand the police officers. At one point they asked, 'When the men befriended you...' and I urged a police officer sitting with me to pass on a message to her colleagues. 'She doesn't understand the word befriend!' Sure enough, she spun in confusion. When it was concluded that she was not a suitable witness, the professionals withdrew and we were left with Suzy, who had to tolerate one of the men delivering the post to her home. Despite what he had done, he remained the postman for the block. To Suzy, it was evidence of his supreme power in the face of her powerlessness. So, aged eight, she began cutting herself as a way of managing complex feelings.

Eventually her mother and I agreed that the family had to move, and through a house swap they went to another city and I never saw her again. The three men reoffended, and as I understand it, the twelve-year-old they chose next was a suitable witness to make prosecution a success.

This little girl stuck in my head and my heart. She was the reason I wanted children to be able to ask for help directly. I wanted a service that was not reliant on adults noticing what children needed, but enabled children to say when they could not cope.

They were too brilliant at it. Within months we had a waiting list and had to bring in more therapists. Children were referring children to the Place2Be and the programme uncovered the under life of the school. The teachers and support staff were incredibly caring. The head of the school was visionary. But no one knew what the children did about their own lives. When we got some more money, I brought in child psychotherapists to supervise our growing number of trainees.

If a school file described a mother as living on her own with the kids, a child would inform us otherwise. We would hear of the drunken partner and the drug dealings at home. Once, I had to laugh when a child psychotherapist, acting as clinical supervisor for a student, launched into a long, psychoanalytic interpretation about the meanings of firearms in the home. A child had spoken of a gun while playing in the doll's house in the therapy room.

A product of the middle classes, the supervisor had not for a second thought the child was talking about a real firearm. When we checked, the child's father had one.

The beginnings of the Place2Be were challenging, not because of the children but because the established structures perceived me as an impostor taking therapeutic programmes away from their clinics into the community on an unprecedented scale.

My understanding is that meetings were held to decide how to stop me. Rather than fight them, I invited them all to be supervisors. And so we came to collaborate, with some of the best child psychotherapists overseeing the work of trainees at the Place2Be.

• • •

Even as a child in Iran, I was interested in the mind. When I was nine, I asked my mother why, among her thousands of books, she did not have any that explained how people think and feel. She tried to tease out of me what I was looking for, as I did not know the word 'psychology'. I said I wanted to understand children and how their minds work. By then I was quite interested in the fact that my little brother was hyperactive. He did not pick up the atmosphere in a room, whereas I felt it intensely. My mother was partly surprised, partly bemused. She ordered a child development journal. It was called *Child and Life* and arrived every Wednesday. I never read a novel or a story book; what I wanted was theory about children – in fact, anything about children. The journal, which was in Farsi, began to scaffold a vocabulary for what I was observing.

The nursery teachers at my school used to leave me in charge of the little kids at lunchtime. It is hard to imagine in modern Britain, with its strict ratios of carers to children, but there were at least seventy infants and me, just nine years old myself. I organised them into small circles of activity for the first half of the lunch break and then, in the second half, brought them together for singing, dancing and showcasing their talents: they would jump or pull faces. I felt like the conductor of an orchestra, fine-tuning the atmosphere to stop them getting bored.

Set against this was my absolute and total cluelessness about what was going on in my own class. I could not take in academic work at all. Concepts would not stay in my head, although pictures did; I made myself copy out the text in science books in an effort to break down the themes into something I could draw. I have almost no recollection of the classroom, the teachers or my peers, because I was on another planet. It is not until I reached adulthood and had lots of assessments that I realised I can produce and communicate very sophisticated material based on observations but I cannot decode material somebody else produces unless I have ended up sitting with them, going through it and then memorising it. The child development journal was easy to comprehend because it was giving words to what I was observing, but I struggled to decode the science material in the textbooks at school until I turned them into drawings and they were internalised.

The other kids knew I was different. I had been born more than two months premature, and was sent home to die, weighing one kilogramme, without the birth being registered. As a result, I do not know my birthday. They didn't think it was worth putting me in an incubator. The birth had been really traumatic. I had been starving because I was on top of the placenta and it was coiled around my neck. It took more than twenty hours before I came out. A combination of these challenges and the premature birth has resulted in my having a range of health problems and learning difficulties, impacting my writing, sequencing and the processing of complex information. The worst of my learning difficulties cluster around visual processing, so I can't coordinate to use a keyboard, and stairs look flat. As a child, I used to tumble down them regularly until I worked out it wasn't worth it and took to sliding down the bannister on my stomach. So I try to avoid the stairs as much as possible. People have got used to me knocking into door posts because I misjudge the space. I am not allowed to drive, and I didn't learn to tie my shoelaces or tell the time until I was twelve. This is not an exhaustive list, but it gives you a sense.

I do have two memories from primary school. One is of a teacher, her breath smelling of alcohol, congratulating me on getting zero for my spelling test. I remember thinking it was wrong that she was happy, but at least it wasn't minus fifty, which was where my marks would normally be. The other memory is of a boy called Babak who was vomiting violently. I worried about who was going to take care of him, as he lived in an orphanage. Was it this boy, the only child I remember from school in Iran, who made me want to open an orphanage? That was my ambition when I was nine. I told my mother that I wanted to dedicate my life to helping children. Perplexed, she looked at me with a mixture of humour and surprise, and wondered what she'd given birth to. My mother looked like a cross between Sophia Loren and Elizabeth Taylor. She was very artistic and had great flair. I don't think she thought her daughter would be running an orphanage, but she gave me the biggest gift a mother could give her child, which was to allow me to follow my dream even though it wasn't hers.

My brothers used to tease me, telling me to shut up and go and run my orphanage. They also used to regularly tell their friends that I was plugged into a different socket and not to mind me. I felt great love from them and they tolerated my inability to do a whole lot of things with generosity and patience. Consequently, I didn't develop the emotional difficulties most people acquire when they're continuously failing to achieve in school. To my dad, I was very un-Persian. I didn't care about convention and didn't worry about what people thought of me. He found my emancipation baffling, but we would play chess and backgammon. The chess he won, the backgammon I won.

As children, we were very protected. Wealthy or influential families were very worried about kidnapping, so I never stepped foot in a shop except for the newsagent's right next to our house. I did not go to the homes of my peers, but we spent every day we had free at the sports centre my father had built. It had ice skating rinks, swimming pools, dodgem cars, a cinema, a dry ski slope and a shooting range. We used to be given passes for activities and food. Then we would run around the centre with our friends. I was very good at shooting, which served me well when I got to Peckham! But the figure skating was an ask too far.

The Persian culture, as I perceived it, was hospitable and thought children should be cherished. All around me there was a sense of opulence and a readiness to share that with others. However, in the spirit of not offending the guests, there was a tendency to prioritise other people and in the process exercise too much compromise. So people wouldn't always say what they were thinking, and yet they would worry what other people were thinking about them. I was a touch oblivious to it all. I would wear what I wanted and endeavoured to be kind but say it as I saw it. My mother appreciated the drop in atmosphere my honesty would often create, but my father would silently shake his head, defeated by the fact that following convention wasn't my trip.

When I applied in my late teens to universities in England, my writing age was seven. Every university said no except Warwick, which offered an unconditional place to read Theatre and the Dramatic Arts. The interviewers at Bristol wanted to offer a place on the English and Drama course, but were told they could not by their Senate. The university didn't believe that I would be able to achieve academically, despite having done really well in the interviews. The other universities wouldn't even interview me because I hadn't managed to get a pass in English or Maths GCSE. I was touched to learn that the lecturers from Bristol who had interviewed me still remembered me three years later, and contacted Warwick to ask how I did in my degree. I got a First.

I was so grateful to Warwick University for giving me a place. They taught me to look at people through their strengths, and not through their disabilities. It was a gift I was able to pass on to the young people in the care of Kids Company, as we encouraged them to access university despite their difficulties. Warwick were also brilliant in helping me manage my health problems. A year prior, I had ended up at the research hospital National Institute of Health in Washington because my endocrine difficulties had become complicated. I wasn't allowed to start university and had to stay in the hospital until the doctors could work out how to manage the crisis.

While at the hospital in America, I absorbed an important life message. I shared a room with other patients who didn't survive their illness. Some of them had to have brain surgery, which completely changed their character. Others died. So, aged seventeen, one minute I'd be acting out the menu for a Spanish-speaking patient who didn't understand English, giggling at my chicken and Coca-Cola imitations. The next minute, I'd see the curtain drawn round a patient's bed, knowing that this was a sign she had died. It made me think that the bottom line is they draw a curtain round you when you're gone. It was, while deeply sad, peculiarly liberating, because I understood that none of us are that important, but we can do important things, and there's limited time to do them. My motto became, when worried, 'Is it going to kill you?' If it is going to kill you, there's nothing you can do about it, and if it's not going to kill you, then it's not worth worrying about.'

When I was seven, I had an operation. There were complications with my reaction to the anaesthetic and I nearly died. I remember experiencing what is often described by people who have had near-death experiences as being a kind of 'tunnel of light' one travels through. I believe this was a key experience in helping me tune into a more spiritual dimension to life. Even though I was surrounded by people with diverse religions, I did not follow a particular faith. But I was acutely aware of energetic forces beyond concrete experiences. This in part has informed a more vocational approach in my life.

I started regaining the ability to write more legibly in my late twenties, and by the age of thirty I could write in the opposite direction to normal, with individual letters reversed, so that the result is best read using a mirror. But I still cannot write and think at the same time and cannot decide which hand to use for writing. I can copy legibly from my own scribbles if I really concentrate.

I cannot use a keyboard. This book reaches you via personal assistants who typed thousands of words of dictation a day into laptops. I can dictate 10,000 words in one go, in clear sentences which seem to emerge in a state of flow. But if someone clicks a pen near me, or unwraps a sweet, then I will completely forget what I have just dictated, and have to ask my PA to repeat the last line before I can resume the dictation. Until recently I was lost without my personal assistants, but voice recognition software, such as the Apple app Siri, now makes email possible even though I still can't type documents. During the disruption of Kids Company, my needing help and therefore having personal assistants was presented as a symbol of my allegedly indulgent, luxury-seeking behaviour.

I grew up in a sheltered environment in a wealthy family, though my life has had its share of trauma: my sister killed herself after our father was imprisoned in the Iranian Revolution in 1979. This is not the reason I work with troubled children, however. That decision came much earlier. I have not changed since childhood. I think now like I did at that age; I have just learnt more. At night, before I went to sleep, the maid used to sit with me, and I was preoccupied with how to organise her room to make a larger living space for her and her sons. I had never been inside the room, since my parents' fear of kidnapping meant that I was not allowed anywhere without the police drivers or the cook.

I loved abstract things: visual images, sounds and philosophical concepts. I could never understand why an abstract painting would reduce me to tears, and I didn't feel I could really explain it to anyone else; as already I had exceeded the abnormality scale! I painted for hours on canvas, always from my imagination. The cook would go out and buy the oils and the brushes for me.

After I won an international award for painting, the Minister of Culture advised my parents to send me abroad, as I was 'too unusual for Iranian education'. At ten, I was sent to school in Switzerland. Two years later I could write English like a child of about five, but I passed the entrance paper for Sherborne by dictating an essay to my mother and copying her writing. I ended up in the bottom set with five other common entrance mistakes: it was obvious there was something major wrong with all of us. I was the error with a passion for learning. By the age of twelve I could read widely, even if I could not write well. I read Bertrand Russell and philosophers such as Jean-Paul Sartre, George Santayana and Karl Popper. Popper became infatuated with my mother and used to visit our flat at Lancaster Gate in London, where we lived after the Iranian Revolution. I do not claim to have understood it all, but I was trying to find a language for what I felt I understood intuitively.

By the second year at Sherborne, I was bored. I was struggling with the school work, but I still wanted some kind of philosophical exchange. I asked to go into the senior library to find books on aesthetics. Mr Hall, who was in charge of the library, told me I was too young. I thought this was outrageous and we had an argument. What has age got to do with it?

I was saved by the bookshop owner in the town, who used to get me books every Saturday. He was a quiet man with no small talk. But he got books he thought I would like, and when I collected them he would comment on an aspect of them. He also helped with any words I could not read. By fourteen, I was familiar with Freud and Jung. The bookshop owner never asked questions or probed. It was an intellectual exchange, and he let me choose any book I wanted.

By this time, I could write like a primary pupil. Then I regressed and lost the ability to write altogether. I started running in the wrong direction on the lacrosse and hockey pitches. I also stopped being able to do the high jump or long jump. To this day I struggle to work out how to step over an electrical wire on the floor.

I now realise that significant changes were taking place in my brain, making my visual processing difficulties worse, and impacting my endocrine and immune systems. By the end of secondary school, I had become very ill and had to be hospitalised for what they believed was a tumour on my adrenal glands.

When I let in twenty goals on the lacrosse field, they realised something was wrong. An optician tested my eyes and reported back to the school that I had read the clock the wrong way round. I was sent to Macdonald Critchley at the National Hospital for Neurology and Neurosurgery in Queen Square, who thought I was joking when I could not put together the puzzle on his table. He was shocked when he realised I was serious. He stopped the IQ tests and we started talking about whether I saw people in colours, as I did with music and poetry. At the time I was surprised that he had asked me this question because my senses did seem to merge. I now realise it is called synaesthesia.

Critchley advised the school to halt all remedial lessons and to get an extra teacher to help me learn at an intensified rate. He also contacted the examining boards so that I could sit my A-levels at Senate House in London by dictating to a secretary. The teacher brought in by Sherborne was excellent. We studied the Greek tragedies and the French philosophers, and for the first time I was happy being educated. The school became a loyal supporter of Kids Company, too: years later it give a number of our kids free places. Sherborne had the courage to adapt and gave me the support I needed to be able to realise my potential despite the difficulties I was experiencing. They encouraged my artistic life and for that I will always be grateful.

For as long as I can remember, children and adults have told me their problems. Even strangers would open up if they sat next to me at my father's sports centre in Iran, or at the home of one of the ambassadors who made up our social circle. At Sherborne, I noticed that the girls were depressed at weekends, so I set up the jelly club. I trekked around the school with a lunch trolley, collecting board games from all the houses before setting up a games room with jelly babies scattered on the tables. On Sunday afternoons, the girls could come to play games and eat jelly babies. I also wrote shows, as school plays at the time seemed scripted and dated. I looked at every girl's ability – some danced, some cartwheeled; one called Sally pulled amazing faces – and wrote their talents into the shows. It reached a point where none of the girls wanted to go to lunch because they were so busy rehearsing, and the school locked me in the sanatorium to get control back.

By the age of sixteen, I had written the model for what I believed was my future project. It would be a street-level centre to give children therapeutic use of the arts. This is why I read drama at university, as I was interested in the therapeutic use of puppetry. The model emerged as part of my remedial classes. My first remedial teacher used to make me write Bs in the births column of the newspaper and Ds in the deaths column until the letters were the right way round. I thought she was crazy and fantasised about cutting her hair net in defiance. My second remedial teacher asked me to write something that interested me, so I wrote the model. The school then entered it for an award.

It won a prize called the Spooner Award, including £250 to put towards the project. When I started the Place2Be, I put in £250 to honour the promise. At the Hay Literary Festival in 2014, the woman who had created the award walked up to me when I was with Jon Snow, to say that I had ended up doing what I said I would.

I was ferocious about protecting the vulnerable. At eight, I got into a fight, rolling on the asphalt with a big boy who was beating up a smaller one. As he would not listen, I wrestled him to the ground. At Sherborne, there was a girl who had been placed at the school by social services. She was the classic withdrawn, nail-biting, knuckle-chewing, crying, constantly upset little girl. When I arrived at one of the houses to find girls trying to drown her in the bath, I went crazy. First I pulled her out, then I pushed them out of the bathroom.

The girls at Sherborne had to wash their clothes by hand in the 1970s: there was no washing machine. People brought bags of washing, usually on a Sunday, and queued to use one of the big Victorian sinks. Then they put the clothes on racks to dry, as there was no dryer either. So, as a message of protest, as the school would not listen when I kept telling them we needed washing machines, I sent out a message to all the girls.

I said Sherborne now had washing machines and told everyone to leave their clothes in labelled bags in the prayer room next to the big hall, so that the laundry people could pick them up and put them in the new machines. Of course, the girls brought their washing. At the Sunday-night service in the hall, Miss Coulter, the head teacher, who wore silver moon boots that glinted as she stood on the stage, was astounded to discover the prayer room full of laundry bags. I was made to wash the clothes myself, by hand.

I was also made to stand in a circle chalked on the floor of the entrance hall as punishment for my attitude to school uniform. I had painted my brown school shoes in all the colours I wear now, and stretched my jumper over a wooden chest at night to make it baggy.

Eventually, the school bought washing machines.

• • •

A gold-toothed bailiff was standing outside my home with his mate. I thought they were chirpy workmen, and as I left my flat I gave them my usual cheery hello. One of them responded by asking if I was Camila, and told me that they were waiting to repossess my flat in an hour. I was stunned.

It transpired that my mortgage lender was taking me to court. For some reason, I had received no warning letter. But for the glinting tooth of the bailiff, it might have been too late. But the men gave me the address of the hearing and I found myself in front of a judge next to a man from Abbey National holding my file.

The judge asked why I had not paid my mortgage. I explained that I needed the monthly payments to get the Place2Be going, because no one would listen to me until I could show that it worked.

Everyone else in the courtroom was asked to leave. It was just the judge and me. I thought, 'He's going to take my flat away.' After a long silence he said, 'Do you realise you could lose your home?' I said yes. He said, 'You've prioritised this project over your own home.' I confirmed this was the case. Then he asked if I was for real.

I said I was.

There was a silence. The judge asked everyone to come back in. By now my heart was thumping, as I thought he was about to announce that they could take my flat. Instead, he told Abbey National that I would pay them back when I was ready. Turning to me, he asked for evidence. Benita Refson, who went on to lead the Place2Be after I left, wrote to the judge to confirm that I had used the money to found the charity. I hope one day to find this judge again, because he was an amazingly far-sighted man and because of his generosity the Place2Be was allowed to thrive.

I left the Place2Be when I thought the model I had created could carry on without me. I left them with a giant manual of how to run the project, including a document for teachers on how they would feel when the Place2Be came into their schools. It predicted that they would initially sabotage the project. They would be furious with the trainee therapists for using the tea and coffee in the staff room, and would envy the children for receiving therapy and the therapists because the children looked forward to seeing them. This used to make the teachers laugh, because it was true.

Within a year of starting, we had sixty trainee therapists in five

London schools; it was to become a national provision. Benita made a big commitment to spread the programme, which now serves 282 schools. At its heart was a structure co-created with the children and the original volunteers. We were helped by a few charitable trusts and the Department of Health, which contributed a substantial grant just before I left.

I still remember turning up at the health department with a roll of wallpaper on which I had laid out, in multicolour felt-tips, the structure of the Place2Be and how it would work. One of the doctors present took me by surprise when she asked my trustees if they were brave enough to follow the vision I had just shared.

When I was supervising the therapists at the Place2Be, I would hear about children's lives. They were primary school pupils of extraordinary courage. There was the boy who would not sleep for fear that his mother, a sex worker, would be attacked by a client; the children who hid under the bed when their mother was out of control and drunk; a ten-year-old girl who could only watch as her dad battered her mum and blood dripped down the staircase. This last child would use dolls to show us what had happened and then weep at the guilt of not having intervened. Then there was the seven-year-old whose mother had died of cancer, who would carry her bag from house to house to sleep on people's floors, knowing that she was the unwanted leftover.

Belinda stuck in my head. Her older sister had disclosed sexual abuse; the perpetrator had wired her up to the mains in revenge and electrocuted her. I worked with Belinda after she stopped speaking because of the trauma. We went to the park and I would spin her on the roundabouts. It was as if she were looking for things that moved so that she could find some kind of movement in her voice and eventually speak.

For these children and others, the holidays brought a sense of horror as they meant losing the protection of school as well as its guaranteed lunches. The likelihood of being hit or abused is higher during holidays, as there is no teacher to notice a bruise.

The kids watched their peers from more stable homes walk down the road with their parents, delighting in being close. These were the children who would go back to school with lovely stories to write in their exercise books, making the vulnerable kids feel further marginalised and bereaved.

Some children became good at faking stories of their holidays, with fictitious ice cream-fuelled trips to Disneyland or London Zoo. For them, the contrasting loneliness inside was inescapable, and this is what made me want to set up what I thought would be a holiday programme for vulnerable children, whom we would identify via their schools. We would be their beautiful play room, a project offering activities, trips and healthy food. This was the original vision for Kids Company.

To this day, I wonder at the madness of governments in seeing that some children need state-funded school dinners without considering the unmet need during the holidays, when we know that some 3 million children suffer from food poverty.[1]

We found some railway arches in Camberwell, cleaned them and created a child oasis filled with toys and art materials. I was hugely helped in the early days by Sue, who generously donated funds as well as working hard alongside me. The Abbey National man became a supporter. He came to the railway arches with Abbey National pens and notepads for the kids. My next lender knew what I did, and when Kids Company had no money, it remortgaged me quickly so that I could pay the staff. Sometimes I used credit cards and store cards to buy food and other essentials for the arches. I had developed a fantastic begging strategy. I would stand in the queue at Harrods and Hamleys with my basket of toys for our kids and ask each passing parent to buy one for us as they bought toys for their own children. I was onto a good one until Harrods marched me out.

Of course, my oasis of calm never happened. It was invaded by a gang of adolescent boys from the local criminal networks. As the police soon put it, every child they were looking for was on Kids Company premises. One hundred boys would arrive at my new project at 3 p.m. and rampage through the place, setting fire to the curtains, gouging out the eyes of the dolls, and rolling their spliffs in defiance. They had self-referred!

I was terrified. The psychotherapy I had learnt in the training schools of Hampstead had not prepared me for the gangs of Peckham and Brixton, armed with scorn and knives.

CHAPTER 3

GHETTO BRITAIN V. LEGITIMATE BRITAIN

I understand and agree that society needs rules to maintain cohesion and stability. The question is, whose rules should we follow and how do we decide which rules are appropriate? I really struggled with this when running Kids Company. I felt like a bridge, with one half grounded in the ghettos and the other in what I used to call in my head 'Legitimate Britain'.

It felt as if the kids we worked with were denied access to Legitimate Britain and all its possibilities. I could visualise what I needed to do to create a chance for them to cross the divide, play a part in the economy and benefit from it. But that meant understanding and respecting their rules as well as those of 'legitimate' society.

I know both sides of this divide. I was born into one of the wealthiest families in Iran, with police drivers as bodyguards, with chandeliers, rich carpets, parties, exquisite earrings, kings and queens coming and going, refined protocols, diverse foods and fruits and the hierarchy of royals and maids. Persian wealth was so opulent that Buckingham Palace seemed somewhat understated in comparison. As a child, I was skiing, shooting, driving dodgem cars, ice skating and watching international performances as well as Disney movies in our private cinema in the sports centre my father built, which was rare in the 1960s. I popped from our house to my grandfather's hotels with their many swimming pools and then over to my dad's sports centre with every activity a child could dream of.

We met ambassadors from other countries, but I had never seen a black person until I got to Britain when I was twelve years old. She became one of my closest friends at Sherborne, but was from one of the chief families in Nigeria.

I was so sheltered I knew nothing about criminality, gangsters or the underworld, except when it involved the British spies my brother and I found transmitting messages in our gardens as ambassadors came and went from a party at our holiday home by the Caspian Sea.

In 1996, in some railway arches in Camberwell, I had my first encounter with Ghetto Britain. It is an extraordinary space with its own rules, rarely understood by Legitimate Britain because it is outside most people's experience. Teenagers can imitate it with the pulling down of trousers and a bit of rapping, but the imitation is a stereotype. I am not saying an entire neighbourhood is ghettoised, because in Peckham and Brixton there are ample examples of Legitimate Britain. Hidden among them is an underworld you only get to see if you have to deal with it.

Within a few weeks of starting our work in the railway arches we had about 100 adolescent black boys, with one ginger-haired, Irish white boy in the midst of them. The blood used to drain from my cheeks with fear at 3 p.m. as the gates opened and all these kids poured in.

We had intended to offer vulnerable under-11s a secure base during the school holidays, but the arches became a secure base for the most insecurity-inducing teenagers. They were incredibly aggressive. I couldn't work out a word they said and it took me a while to realise that 'bad' meant 'good', 'bling' was 'gold', 'wagwan' was 'hello' and that the vocabulary kept changing.

Soon I learnt the ground rules. These boys had a need to appear powerful. They achieved this by having a reputation for violence, showing no emotion and wearing designer outfits. The unspoken statement was that the expensive clothes could not have been bought, as their families were too poor to pay for them. They must have been acquired by crime.

Immediately, people would think twice about attacking such a well-dressed individual because the impression would be that their criminal backing was powerful and therefore the revenge would be swift. 'Rep', or reputation, was very important. At the centre of it was the notion that you should never appear to be a victim, or stay in the role of victim. If you were attacked, you had to deliver revenge, otherwise the neighbourhood would know you were 'trashed goods', and in that diminished state you stood no chance because you would invite further attacks.

The kids kept telling me, when we were in a room on our own, that they trusted no one. So, even though they described gang members as 'family' and would have each other's backs when it came to the enemy outside, they understood that each man is a 'lone soldier'. They used the term as if they were in some kind of war.

Girls started coming to us a little later. The first was incredibly loud and difficult. Her brother was one of the boys accused of killing Damilola Taylor, the ten-year-old seen on CCTV hopping and skipping his way home from the public library before bleeding to death in a stairwell fifteen minutes later. A jury found him not guilty. The second was a girl whose mother was prostituting her to support the mother's drug habit; she was also the child carer for her younger siblings.

Speaking years later, a detective on the south London murder squad explained why the killing of Damilola caused such shock. 'It was kids that were accused of doing it,' said Nick Ephgrave, who is now the acting chief constable of Surrey Police. 'Those who killed him were well known to the police and were out of control. That all added to the sense of outrage. How could we as a society have let a child like that be picked on and killed by these kids, when everyone knew they were bad kids?'

It did feel like a war. We were never safe. We would get strangers coming onto the premises to shoot the kids and to run us over. There would always be a rival gang in search of one of the children. They would pile into the premises with knives and we would have mayhem as we tried to protect everyone. One day when I heard gunshots, I had to ask Baron Hastings of Scarisbrick to get under the table during a meeting we were having to talk about funding while I went outside to calm the boy with the firearm. I didn't know him. But I told him he was too good to be a killer and he ran off.

The police were after the kids and the local authority was after us. A planning officer in Southwark Council told me, in front of the black architect David Adjaye, that we had too many black children and would cause the price of nearby property to fall. It did not help that the children played us off against the Youth Offending Team, which is part of the council, telling them they were crap and we were better. The Youth Offending Team thought we were 'colluding' with the kids and tried to get rid of us by talking to the Youth Justice Board, which oversees youth justice services in England and Wales.

When the Youth Justice Board paid a visit and realised we were a really good programme, it awarded us a grant via the council. We never saw the money. My understanding is that Southwark sent it back without telling us, claiming we did not need it. It was a substantial grant at the time.

It felt like a job from hell, and yet the kids were courageous and dignified, and exquisite in the emotional subtleties they displayed.

As I got to know them, the first dilemmas arose. A thirteen-year-old boy who was selling drugs at school was in debt to a dealer who wanted to kill him. As a matter of principle I don't like paying drug debts because it is a road to nowhere. But this boy was going to die, and it is human life versus the law. When I called the police for advice and named the dealer, they told me to pay the debt and asked if I needed undercover support at the café where the cash was to be handed over. The police will deny it happened. But the people who understood these children best, and who had the greatest compassion for them, were the police officers they so hated.

The officers knew just how brutal these children's lives were. They had walked into their homes and seen the lack of furniture, the missing toys, the desperate sheets that looked unwashed for years, the urine-soaked mattresses on the floor. They saw how there would be no food in the cupboard and yet, in a disgusting corner, were the 'crisp trainers', a pair of shoes that looked clean and new for public display. The trainers were a symbol the child could take out of the home and show without being ashamed.

Few of these children would invite friends round, because they portrayed themselves as clean-cut, expensively dressed young men when the truth might be that their stomachs were empty and there was no food in the house. Some slept on park benches and in the dustbin enclosures of estates.

Very quickly I saw that it would be difficult to explain their lives and get the right kind of help from Legitimate Britain. I couldn't put in a request to a charitable trust for 300 pairs of Nike trainers. Most people's idea of a poor child is an Oliver Twist type, sweet and begging, whereas these kids were ferocious and denying. You see their tears only if you reach the cowering little child within, frozen in development because terror has deviated the course of it.

This dramatic discrepancy in the 'rules' about poverty and how to address it was not the only chasm. The same division presented itself in measuring the value of our work. We would be visited by charitable trusts and bank officials who were considering us for donations. Their 'due diligence' checks terrified me, because these tidy thinkers were coming into an environment where the kids were unpredictable.

They stole the Comic Relief woman's bike and used petrol to set fire to the tea bags for our visitors from Deutsche Bank. The meeting had to be interrupted and Deutsche Bank never gave us the money. Luckily, the ghetto network returned the Comic Relief bike and we won a grant.

Every visitor looked for outcomes. The list seemed so Legitimate Britain: to acquire qualifications, refrain from drug use – 84 per cent of the kids at the railway arches where we worked initially were addicted to drugs, of whom 90 per cent had been given them by family members – get a job and be housed.

If we achieved these outcomes, we were deemed effective. If we did not then we were 'failing'. All the organisations that funded us employed these measures, including the government. What is the best use of £100 for one of our children? Legitimate Britain says it is education, perhaps a course. The kids would say shoes. I begged funds from people whose value system prizes education, because they assume basic needs such as shelter and food are in place. If I spent it on trainers, they would be horrified. But the trainers are a necessary step to education. They give a kid the dignity to tolerate the shame of not reading and writing, then walk into college to learn. What Legitimate Britain didn't seem to understand is that designer clothes were the only things the deprived kids could use to fake being equal to their well-cared-for middle-class counterparts. When they wore them, it was the only time they got to feel included, even if that inclusion was achieved through shallow means.

Every community has a uniform: business leaders wear suits to work; chefs have their hats and aprons; teenagers have their fashion statements. Sadly, teenage fashion choices are predominately driven by brand marketing. Our teenagers were compelled by sophisticated advertising to believe that if they had the right kind of trainers and branded clothing, that they would be accepted. For children who were pained by exclusion, it looked like a hopeful strategy.

It wasn't just inclusion they were seeking. In the neighbourhoods we worked in, children would be beaten up, and young people stabbed, often for not wearing designer goods. It had become, for many kids, a matter of survival.

Often, Legitimate Britain was so sure of its own perspective that it failed to see the world from the viewpoint of a deprived teenager. Dave was a white boy whose dimples and long eyelashes should have suggested innocence. He came to the arches as an eleven-year-old in 1998, after being excluded from every school he had attended. We were doing a play about kids who are misunderstood. The children had designed a programme cover. It showed kids behind bars in prison, with a portrait of Tony Blair on the wall inside the cell. They thought it was very funny that the Prime Minister at the time could be in a cell with them.

In one scene, Dave was to be arrested by the police, and I saw a flash of his ferociousness, a visceral rage that came from somewhere deep within. When we had a moment together behind closed doors, we peeled the defensive layers in search of that little boy. That is when he told us he was being beaten with belts and kicked by his dad. A little later he explained that his older sister was using him sexually, while his younger brother was ill and had locked his mother into an emotional bond that left no room for Dave. Aged eleven, he saw no choice but to run away. At nights, he and his friends used to sleep on the night buses, or creep into Camberwell bus station. Then he graduated to trains, which is how a paedophile got him.

He could not cope with the flashbacks and found that drugs gave him relief. To support his habit, he started stealing and became very good at it. Between the ages of thirteen and twenty-six he was in prison every year. I tried to get him picked up by social services, but they put him in a children's home in Lambeth where kids were being sexually abused. Dave knew it and kept running away.

When he was twenty-six, and was again in court, I sent the judge a letter. 'You have had him all these years in your system and nothing has got better. Why don't you let me have a go?' The judge, who had a reputation for ill temper but was nevertheless far-sighted, responded. Dave was given a suspended sentence.

Recovery is not tidy or nice; it is ugly and painful, and has many ups and downs. It is a fallacy to think you can make a plan and implement it. Clinicians who work with desperate people know this, but are forced to describe what they do in a linear way because Legitimate Britain requires a tidy thought to go into the tidy drawer of the tidy outcome cabinet. Clinical truth is often rewritten in polite, evasive language to make it seem sequentially clear. The result is silly phrases such as 'treatment plan', 'intervention' and 'outcome' as clinicians try to please their purse-holders.

The approved treatment models are evidence-based, but most of the research is in clinics on patients who are capable of turning up for the length of the study. The children we worked with had so much complexity and emotional volatility that if you wanted to break it down into psychopathology, you would need a directory; they had it all. They displayed nearly everything in DSM-IV, the fourth edition of the Diagnostic and Statistical Manual of Mental Disorders, and yet the manual did not describe them.

I met one of the psychiatrists who was on the board of the DSM. We were sitting in my office and I said, 'You know, you left a syndrome out of your manual which describes these kids,' and explained the characteristics. The inability to hold eye contact. The exceptional violence juxtaposed with extraordinary timidity. The sadism coupled with an absolute disregard for themselves; the inability to sit still, coupled with extreme apathy; the sleep disorders and impaired learning capacities. He leant over to me and said, 'Years ago, a group of psychiatrists came to us to suggest that there was a condition just as you describe it. We didn't get it registered because we felt society wouldn't be able to accept it.' The idea that environmental adversity could create a psychiatric disorder was too controversial.[1]

Dave tried to cross the bridge to present his complexity to the legitimate world. By his mid-twenties he was a high-risk, volatile individual who could bake a beautiful Barbie cake for his daughter, creating a stunning visual piece, but was also capable of using a car to ram someone into a fence when in an altered state. He was one of the kindest and most gentle people I had come across when he was well. His intelligence was ferocious, and yet he was so compassionate towards children and other vulnerable individuals. He could be described as having flair; whatever he did, he did it to the best of his ability. He loved a job well done.

It was his considerable intelligence that helped him work out exactly how to carry out the most effective crime. His analysis of buildings and how to get into them would have left the SAS drooling with envy; however, he would not rob the elderly, mothers with children, or the disabled. He was a thief with a code of ethics, and what he wanted more than anything else was to 'be legit': have a job, be able to stick to it, and support his family. He did not like being a criminal.

As part of his recovery, our first encounter was with a drug rehabilitation centre. Clients spent hours in group therapy, sitting in a circle while men broke down as they recounted how they were violated as children. Dave was passionate about it and wanted to believe it would help. But as good as the therapy was, it could reach only part of him. He also needed a lot of physical activity. He required risk and challenge, because for years his biology had been driven by terror and weaning him off it could not be abrupt. He was diagnosed with attention deficit hyperactivity disorder, depression, obsessive compulsive disorder and post-traumatic stress disorder. It's hard to tell whether he was born with these challenges, and that caused his difficulties, or whether the abuse he was exposed to generated the inability to be calm and concentrate. It was probably a mixture of genetic vulnerabilities and adverse environmental triggers. Either way, it was causing havoc in his life and he struggled to manage it.

The ordered life of rehab was bizarre to someone who was marinated in fright. The placement broke down with one of his rages, an explosion of energy that had no other outlet. He ended up sleeping in the park as we rushed around to find an alternative. Going to his parents was not an option; they had not called him for years, missing birthdays and Christmases. He had no other relatives. His partner was afraid of him even though he adored his children. Psychiatric hospitals would not take him because he was not sick enough. There was no place for Dave in Legitimate Britain.

What he needed was a therapeutic village where he could work, contribute to the community, have his own space and be re-parented in a safe environment, so that the developmentally stunted child could grow into a man, rather than be a man in body only, using adult strength to protect the damaged child within.

We thought he could move outside London, take a carpentry course and start to earn a living. A woman he had met when she visited the rehab offered to find him a place in her town. She fancied him, however, and in Dave's head the dynamic of the older woman wanting sex with the younger child started up again, repeating the trauma of his sister abusing him. This placement, too, broke down, and now the police wanted Dave for his old offences. He did what he always had – ran away, this time in a car. But the motto at Kids Company was never to give up. So we waited until he made contact again and could decide what to do next.

On the day he turned up at my office, he brought a wood carving of the word 'love' and hung it from a nail above my sofa. Tears welled in his eyes as he tried to express gratitude for the fact that I had not given up. He told everyone I was his mum; I never asked him to do this, but neither would I decline the use he needed to make of me. These moments of tenderness would alternate with hatred as he experienced me falling short if I could not respond to him straight away. Then I became his hated biological mother, paying attention to other siblings.

Although I'm describing Dave based on my personal experience of him, I didn't make decisions about his treatment or welfare on my own. We worked with him as a team and discussed his needs in our Right to Health meeting, where a range of professionals made up of social workers, psychotherapists, psychiatrists and key workers would come together to look at solutions for him, and at the impact of his difficulties on his partner and his two children. These discussions were often heated, because there was so much complexity to deal with, not only his but also his partner's. There was healthy debate chaired by an independent specialist, who was brought in to ensure appropriate clinical scrutiny. We agreed that he had to come off drugs. Simultaneously, his partner and children were looked after by another Kids Company key worker, who prioritised their needs. So, our next attempt at change was a halfway house belonging to another drug rehab, but he clashed with a client and ran away.

Finally, Dave and I ended up in the middle of Edgware Road in west London. He had called my office to say that he had gone for help to St Mary's Hospital but had been turned away. I found him in a very unstable state, part going for my throat, part wanting to throw himself under a car. I knew that if I did nothing he might kill himself or someone else. I rang my clinical PA and asked her to phone private hospitals to find a bed, all while trying to calm him as the London traffic went past. We knew the private sector well, because so many of our high-risk clients were rejected by the NHS. I could write the directory of what each hospital is willing to do and how much it costs. The catch is that they cannot section a patient; that has to be done by the NHS. But the health service often refuses, because it is an admission that the patient is ill and should be taken in.

Eventually, a call came through that a private hospital could take him. One of the men from our team went with him, as I had to be at a fundraising event. I would often go from the crack den to the palace, relieved that I did not have to change outfits! It took days for the psychiatric team to stabilise him with anti-psychotic medication. We were lucky that our long-term relationship with Dave encouraged him to cooperate without being sectioned. With nobody else visiting, we took turns to see him with art materials and things he could paint for his children.

Then he and another patient played a practical joke on the nurses and put the result on YouTube. The 'joke' involved having to clean up pretend plastic faeces. The staff felt humiliated and I was told to remove him within twenty-four hours. He had not been an easy patient.

No rehab would take Dave because of his challenging history, no other private hospital would take him because of his violence, the NHS would not take him and he had no home. I came up with the plan, which seemed a stroke of genius, to buy a little thinking time by sending him to Champneys Spa, a health spa outside London, one of the few places where a nurse is on call and a doctor is at hand. It solved the problem of not leaving Dave unsupervised while he was still stabilising on anti-psychotic medication. I believed that the doctor and the nurse would have been able to intervene and call specialist services if Dave became unstable. It was something Champneys were used to, because they would often have clients from wealthy backgrounds who were detoxing.

The spa was remote enough for him not to access street drugs, and the availability of treatments throughout the day meant that someone would be seeing Dave at regular intervals, not only giving him the human contact needed but also noticing if he was unwell. We were transparent with the medical team there, and he was drug tested during his stay to ensure that he was not taking anything besides his psychiatric medication. It wasn't ideal, but it was the best we could find for him at short notice and, paradoxically, the cheapest.

Two years later in my inbox arrives the question from *Newsnight* – did we send Kids Company clients to Champneys for beauty treatments? I have one hour to answer before it goes live as evidence of my failures. What can I say? Dave's history is confidential. But if I offer no explanation, it will look like we sent kids for pampering. Such were the dilemmas that generated much of the critical media coverage of Kids Company.

Dave started work and gave up all Class A drugs. He was starting to get his life together until a family setback led to a second breakdown, in which he tried to jump from a bridge onto a dual carriageway. Police grabbed him as he jumped from the parapet and took him to hospital. When the mental health team arrived, they brought a pre-signed form confirming that they would not take him as an in-patient, even before they had assessed him.

In Legitimate Britain, it has reached a point that even if you launch yourself from a road bridge there is no support to keep you safe. Dave was released with no package and only our staff to oversee his care, pleading with the mental health team to intervene. When asked why they had not sectioned him, the reply off the record was: 'We had no beds.' But on his record, it says, 'He was well enough to cope.' Often, for patients like Dave, the community psychiatric team are asked to keep an eye on them in their own home. However, this assumes that the patient is going to stay at home waiting for the team to visit. It also assumes that the patient will be able to raise the alarm if they become very ill. For Dave, the arrangements were not adequate, and this left him in desperation, drawing intensively on our team for support.

As part of the Charity Commission investigation of Kids Company, I was asked about Dave, who was one of our most expensive clients. The Commission wanted to know if, while standing in Edgware Road as my PA called around frantically for help, I had recorded the hospitals that had turned him down. As a charity, did we make the best procurement decision to get the best value for money? The Charity Commission man on this occasion was kind and rigorous, but Dave is on the wrong side of the bridge to fit his remit. I had to balance Ghetto Britain with Legitimate Britain, and in the balance was a precarious and complex human life. Someone too disturbed to withstand the long and often impossible wait in hospital casualty departments so that he could receive assessments for mental health. Even when he did turn up and lasted the four-hour wait, he wouldn't be offered a bed, not because he didn't need one but because there wasn't one to give.

To top it all, I cannot give anyone a fairy-tale ending that makes all of this worthwhile and presents Kids Company in a triumphant way. Dave is still struggling. He is so much better, but he will need support for the rest of his life as he tries to gain some mastery over his damaged being. At least I can tell you that for the first time in his life he has not been in prison for four consecutive years. He is contributing to the community, and living with a partner whom he loves very much and who loves him back. They're working together to buy a home. Dave has crossed over to Legitimate Britain, but it took decades to make this a possibility.

As for the boy with the drug debt, he now works for the ambulance service and is in his final year of his degree at a Russell Group university. An extraordinary achievement when both your parents were drug addicts on the street, and one of them died from their habit, while the other is barely alive.

CHAPTER 4

THE ORIGINS
OF VIOLENCE

Michael is in a frenzy. His pupils are dilated and he is threatening to kill the staff in the safeguarding department. He has pulled down the ceiling tiles, leaving thick cables hanging in the room. Every piece of furniture is his weapon. He throws chairs into the walls, kicks filing cabinets and hurls computer monitors as if they are frisbees. This sixteen-year-old cannot stop.

Charisma's teacher calls in a state of breakdown. The fourteen-year-old schoolgirl in her charge keeps goading her and has pushed her down the stairs. The teacher can take no more.

Just as I am considering how to handle these violent incidents involving our young people, emails arrive calling me a 'fucking paedophile like Jimmy Savile'. I follow protocol and call the police, asking them to investigate the allegations against me like any other. The accuser, a client aged twenty-five, calms down and withdraws her claim. It was not uncommon for maltreated kids to confuse our workers with the adults who first harmed them.

It is a normal week at Kids Company. Every centre had a version of these behaviours every day that we were open.

When I started Kids Company in 1996, I thought violence was what it said on the tin – a selfish, immoral, outrageous exercise of

53

personal power. I believed punishment could redress the balance. Spending time with the children in those early days led me to a different understanding.

When the kids came into my room for a chat, they shared their worries. Connor curled up in the big armchair. Even at fifteen he looked like a skinny eleven-year-old whose blood did not reach his cheeks. His skin was pale and unhealthy. His eyes were tired, as if he had had enough of living.

His mother was struggling with depression and alcoholism. He did not know his father, or even his father's name. Connor saw himself as the one person who could save his mum. He was preoccupied with how much she needed a washing machine and he was determined to get her one.

It would not be by working legitimately. He delivered drugs for a dealer who worked by remote control. Such people had the appearance of legitimate lives, sitting on often black leather sofas flicking through television channels while directing drug deliveries using several mobile phones. Sometimes they would give one of the mobiles to a child such as Connor, and customers would call the number for their drugs.

These desperate little boys, and increasingly girls, were delivering illegal substances to members of the elite. Politicians, bankers, owners of television production companies, judges, barristers. I marvelled at the kids' integrity. They were reluctant to identify their clients, but from the descriptions I sometimes worked it out. I did find it hypocritical when our children were publicly criticised for drug dealing, sometimes by the very people who were buying from them.

I did not behave illegally and didn't want members of the public to be put at risk. The children had understood that, so if they had already committed a crime, they would not give me any names or venues so that I wouldn't be put in a position where I would have to report the crime. They knew I could not break the law. For my part, I did my best to try to dissuade them from committing crimes and to give themselves up when they had. We would often take young people to police stations so that they could take responsibility for the offences that they had committed. Kids Company would support kids through the criminal justice system, including visiting them regularly in prison. We were often the only people visiting them.

We also left it to staff to decide if they wanted to press charges against young people who may have assaulted them. We would support staff if they chose to do so, whilst also supporting the young person. Barely any staff over two decades chose to press charges, and incidents were increasingly infrequent, as we understood how to prevent them.

Connor looked up at me. 'Camila, I have stabbed this man and I just couldn't stop. I don't know what came over me. I just couldn't stop. I kept stabbing him and stabbing him.'

He was so shocked by what he had done, and bewildered by the fact that he could not control it. The kids referred to this type of uninhibited violence as 'switching'. When Michael pulled down the ceiling and smashed up the office, he had had a 'switching' moment. Such episodes usually lasted about forty-five minutes before the child either burst into tears or fell asleep as if the violence had depleted them. As more and more children described similar sequences and we saw them lose control in front of us, we began to understand how it works.

At night, I used to go home and review my encounters with the kids like a painful film. I wanted to know why they were so violent and how Kids Company could help them. Eventually I asked a young woman to go to the British Library to find clinical papers on child development and the brain. I was sure our young people were communicating a clinical theory about the effects of early maltreatment, as so many of them showed similarities.

Over time she returned with about 300 studies, which curled with damp in the railway arches; the rest of the team subsequently gathered a further 200. The papers were not specifically about neglected children in deprived urban settings, as there were practically none available, but helpful themes emerged.

It was evident that the brain had a mechanism to calm itself down, and another to rev itself up. One American paper suggested that abused children can experience a form of seizure in the limbic system, the emotional centre of the brain, until violence calms them.[1]

At the time this information was like being struck by lightning. Our boys had described feelings of relief, and even a sense of soothing, after getting into fights. Beating someone up, or being beaten up, calmed them. 'Oh my God,' I thought, 'they are using violence as a substitute maternal soother.' They can't use their frontal lobes to calm down; they don't have the attachment relationships to be able to regulate their own emotions and energy. But violence, horrible as it is, helps them achieve some calm. The exhaustion after violence was their version of the maternal experience. Now a scientific paper was laying out the brain processes that might be involved.[2]

The brain can be divided into three. The part behind the forehead, closest to the skull, is called the prefrontal cortex. It controls our impulses and encourages us to act in ways that society finds agreeable. Its capacity to manage our emotions depends on the care we receive, ideally from a mother who has bonded with her baby. Close relationships with extended family members and other significant carers can also help a child develop the prefrontal cortex.

Deep inside the brain is the limbic system. This is the seat of the emotions. The system is a collection of brain structures, including two that have central roles in the genesis of violence. One is the hippocampus, which looks like a seahorse and stores our memories. The other is the amygdala, which has the appearance of an almond and processes our fears. The limbic group also features the corpus callosum, which is structured like a chilli pepper. It is the central transit of the brain, connecting the right and left sides. The corpus callosum, the amygdala and the hippocampus, along with a few other areas, coordinate our reactions to fear. Together they make up the limbic system.

The third part of the brain is the most primitive, called the brain stem. It joins the bottom of the skull to the top of the spine. This area holds our primitive repertoire. It does not think. It expresses a programmed set of reactions handed down by evolution. It is the space that drives procreation. It may also be the space from which murders are made, because it houses the 'fight, flight or freeze' survival mechanism that is shared by all animals.

As the emotionally driven parts of the brain react, the prefrontal cortex lights up and modifies the response, keeping us appropriate so that we do not slap the old man who irritates us in Costa Coffee. The prefrontal cortex tells the limbic system, 'You have no right to be critical of the elderly. You will be old one day and unable to lift a cup because of arthritis, and you too will slurp your coffee. In any event if you slap a member of the public you are committing a crime and you could be prosecuted. It will do your reputation a great deal of damage.'

The prefrontal cortex is developed by good-quality care in childhood. It exercises rational control. When a mother tells her child, 'You are hungry, that's why you're upset, let's give you some food and you'll feel better,' the network of neurons in the child's brain memorises the mother's voice. It also memorises her actions and the consequences of those actions, so that eventually the child learns how to deal with the sensation called 'hunger' or the distressed feelings attached to it. When the child becomes more independent, they can deal with hunger irrespective of the mother's presence.

Gradually, the prefrontal cortex learns to regulate emotion and energy and to generate decisions which are protective, pro-social and life-affirming. This is referred to as 'self-regulation'.

If you've refrained from hitting the old man in Costa Coffee then your prefrontal cortex has managed to calm your limbic system down; you have self-regulated.

Most people decide that evacuating their irritation with an act of bodily harm is not worthwhile. Sometimes, however, the prefrontal cortex ceases to have power over the emotionally revved-up limbic system. The emotional group wins and a tantrum follows. You start to shout, then throw a mobile phone at your line manager by way of resignation. This is referred to as 'losing it'.

People who were well cared for as children tend not to go to extremes when they lose it. Those who end up in a stabbing frenzy, as Connor did, have a different brain pathway generating their extreme violence. Over the years at Kids Company, with the help of the children and scientists, we began to understand how this works and what we have to do to help maltreated children manage it.

This applies even to Connor, who started stabbing a man and could not stop. When 'switching' violence happens, the prefrontal cortex pathways, which should intervene to keep Connor appropriate, shut down. Believing he is at risk, he starts fighting for survival. Once he starts stabbing, nothing in his brain can stop him. He is just as overwhelmed by violent internal forces as his victim was by the external blows of the knife.

The process of 'switching' is so powerful that those who experience it feel they have been spun out of control by a tornado, and it is only after the whirlwind has passed that they regain a state of conscious awareness and realise what a terrible thing they have done.

As a baby, Connor was hard to calm. He smiled little, cried a lot and his mother began to experience herself as a failure. She did not enjoy spending time with him. She started to behave in a functional way towards him. She patted his back after a feed, but did not respond to his attempts to engage her. When he made gurgling sounds and sought her glance, she was often unable to come back with an appropriate and delighted response.[3]

Realising that his mother was out of sync, Connor became further distressed. At first he tried to engage her by crying a little louder and more often, hoping this would summon her to become attuned to his needs. The more he cried, the worse his mother felt and eventually a disruption in attachment was generated between them. Understanding that his mother could not help him, Connor decided that the best way to preserve his emotional energy was not to engage with her unless it was absolutely necessary. In some ways, he became precociously self-reliant, but at the same time desperate for maternal love. So, an ambivalent attachment developed in which he moved towards his mother and then recoiled, confused by her position as care giver and care refuser.

Everything changed for Connor when his stepfather walked into his life. He remembered being beaten by this man, even as a toddler. His stepfather called him the 'shit at the bottom of his shoe' and bit him, drawing blood. Connor never knew when the moment of violence would be, as the man he was forced to call Dad would 'lose it' and attack him without warning.

As Connor got older, he realised that he was not the only victim. His mother was also being attacked by this man. Sometimes Connor would get on top of 'Dad' to try to pull him off his mum, but he was not strong enough and could never save her. It was left to the child to find the dishcloth when her lip was cracked open and chunks of her hair had been pulled out and were on the kitchen floor. The inability to save his mother left him with a powerful sense of guilt and a need to rescue her, seen in his preoccupation with buying her the washing machine.

To survive the violence, Connor hid away and kept as quiet as possible. Everyone used to say how well behaved he was, but he struggled to learn in school. He just could not remember anything, except the terrible scenes of violence at home that kept playing in his head. To get rid of the images he would do something dramatic to distract himself: he would tip the table over in class, pour milk over his classmate's head – anything to get people to rescue him from the nightmarish images that had taken over his brain. As he was normally quiet and compliant, no one could understand why every now and then he did something crazy. It was his way of making himself feel safer.

Children who have been exposed to extreme violence may not show significant changes in behaviour for a long time. In fact, the repercussions might not be evident in brain development for several years.[4] Reactions to violence can have a lengthy incubation period, and children may also dissociate, or become detached, when their limbic system is in turmoil. These facts combined can disguise the consequences of maltreatment. However, child abuse has repercussions throughout life. What happens to a child aged two is relevant when they are forty-five.[5]

Scientists group the abuse symptoms that emerge from limbic dysregulation into clusters.[6] One cluster is called paroxysmal somatic disturbances. These include headaches, dizziness, sensations of things crawling under the skin, irregular heartbeat, a rising or sinking feeling in the stomach almost as if you are in a lift, and feelings of nausea. The symptoms come from extra and irregular electrical activities in the limbic system pathways, which then seem to cascade into the physical realm of the head, heart and stomach.

When he was at primary school, Connor suffered inexplicable aches of the head and stomach. He also refused to wear long-sleeved shirts or jumpers because it felt as if things were crawling under his skin. This was significant, as the arms were the areas his mother's boyfriend would bite.

For other traumatised children, the effects of maltreatment would show up as visual disturbances. Some saw people as smaller or further away than they were. Or people looked larger, all of a sudden, as if they were towering over you. These visual distortions were flashes that came seemingly out of nowhere. Many of the teenagers we cared for would get into fights because they thought someone had 'looked at them funny', leaving victims shocked because they had not noticed their teenage attacker, let alone looked at them in a strange or challenging way.

As well as visual disturbances there is a hallucinatory cluster, with effects such as experiencing disgusting smells that are not related to what is in the room, tasting metal in the mouth, hearing voices or a ringing or buzzing, and seeing patterns or geometric shapes or flashing lights.

I worked with a seven-year-old who had been sexually abused. At night she would wake up with metallic tastes in her mouth, some so powerful they made her vomit. During the day she would look at a person and sometimes the entire belly area would look as if it were metal and melting away. She would find these visual intrusions very disturbing. As she had been penetrated from an early age, she would also see flashes of male genitals with metallic distortions.

One of our most difficult and dangerous young people used to hallucinate an orange cat on his shoulder, which instructed him to do bad things.

A maltreated individual who has been severely traumatised can experience a combination of these bodily, visual and auditory responses suddenly intruding into their daily life, either randomly because the parts of the brain that have memorised the patterns of abuse become dysregulated, or because something in the outside world triggers the stored memory pattern. Memories of traumatic events stored in the brain are not subjected to modifications based on the passing of time. The brain thinks the trauma is 'now', hence some individuals may have flashbacks of traumatic memories even though those events may have happened months, years or decades ago.

Some children experience the opposite of these intrusions, suffering a cluster of dissociative disturbances. The child experiences a sensation of being unreal. They experience their limbs as being rubber-like. They feel that what they are looking at is unreal. Some feel as if they are possessed or have different personalities. The same seven-year-old would wake up from time to time thinking she was her grandmother, the mother of the father who had harmed her. We learnt later that the father hated his mother, and the child may have picked this up. She may even have concluded that she was being abused because the father really wanted to hurt and have sex with his mother, and had transferred the hatred to his daughter.

Of course these processes and thoughts are not conscious on the child's part. Even so, they reward analysis: they are not just biological manifestations of abuse. The symptoms described by a child have a purpose. They not only express the pain but help to organise her defence against it, perhaps by offering the brain some unconscious meaning to explain what is happening.

Some maltreated individuals describe their mind separating from their body, as if they are looking at themselves from above. This is common among rape victims, who can be so overwhelmed that they seem to rise above the perpetrator in their mind while physically still under him, giving the sensation that they are watching themselves being raped. This is the brain's defence against a consuming sense of terror. It also serves to detach the victim so that they experience less pain as they disconnect mind and body during the assault. Similarly, children who are sexually abused receive the erotic experience through a pathway that can trigger changes to compensate for early arousal. Genital sensations are shut down as a way of protecting the child from pain, but with implications for gratification and reward as an adult.[7]

The final cluster of repercussions linked to limbic system dysregulation are called automatisms. This is involuntary behaviour, as if the child is not fully in charge of it, such as staring into space, purposelessly running in circles, picking bits off their clothes, twitching arms or legs, feeling sudden weakness in their limbs, or briefly losing the ability to speak. At a secondary school in north London, they did not know what to do with a teenage boy who refused to remove his woolly hat and spent hours walking in the squares of a dining room floor.

Autistic children can engage in repetitive actions, but when maltreated children do this it calms them down, because the repetitive movement releases some of the tension that builds up with limbic dysregulation. The repetitive action gives the brain, through its physical pathways, a sense of rhythm it can use to help regulate the agitated emotional system. Repetitive behaviour gives the child a feeling of mastery. As the chaos of their lives becomes unmanageable, these children try to generate order by carrying out repetitive tasks.

Much the same is achieved by wearing a particular item of clothing. Hats are a favourite among maltreated kids. They are a comforting cocoon, a place to hide, a substitute maternal container. Without realising it, schools with strict uniform policies take comfort objects away from troubled children by force. The children resist and hostility follows, perhaps because teachers are unaware of the psychological service performed by a piece of clothing. Most of the kids at the railway arches wore hats, either woolly ones or caps. It was rare to find a boy or girl without one.

Elizabeth illustrates the effects of a dysregulated limbic system. She came from a rural English county, where she was in the care of the local authority after years of sexual abuse by a family member who had threatened her with knives. She had the added problem of disturbed and dysfunctional parents who struggled with addictions. After hearing about Kids Company, she made her way to London.

She arrived at Paddington Station unannounced and since she had dodged fares, she was arrested by the British Transport Police. Although she was eighteen years old she presented as a fourteen-year-old. In her bag, she had a picture of me that she had found in a magazine and framed. She showed this to the British Transport Police, who then managed to track me down with her help.

It was late at night when I arrived at Paddington. I tried to get the local authority to come and pick her up, but they were unable to do so and it was agreed that she would stay the night at Kids Company's north London house. At the time, she was living in a flat which she shared with another psychiatric patient in the south of England. Neither received visits from mental health professionals or social care providers. She had been permanently excluded from school after failing to control her anxiety. She burst into tears frequently and could not hold eye contact.

Initially we tried to get her the right kind of help where she lived, but she ran away several times and returned to us. Eventually it was agreed that she needed a proper mental health assessment, as she had never had one. The process of disclosing abuse was so traumatic for her that she developed a stomach ache of such severity she was admitted to hospital. The conversion of emotional pain to physical symptoms is common, especially in traumatised individuals who struggle with too much anxiety to express in speech the nature of what they have endured. As a way of regulating her own limbic system and evacuating the stress, Elizabeth used to pull her hair out in large chunks and cut her arms. She described the bleeding as substitute tears. After harming herself she felt relief.

She also rocked backwards and forwards to soothe herself, much like the Romanian orphans of the early 1990s. The orphans had nobody to love them; their frontal lobes were not developed enough to offer soothing for the limbic system. Instead, the young children left in cots rocked and hurt themselves as a way of finding comfort. Elizabeth stayed at Kids Company's White House, which in the frenzy of 2015 was wrongly described as my personal mansion. In fact, we used it to accommodate some of our most vulnerable young people. She was transferred from there to hospital, where she spent nearly three years. After we closed, I had no way of finding out how she was doing. I feared she may have taken her own life, but her call came through via a hospital payphone. She wanted a bag like mine, a giant colourful one, and she told me she missed me.

The child cannot be left at the mercy of a dysregulated limbic system. If they cannot find a way to discharge the tension, they have no choice but to evacuate it, usually through violence to others or the self. For maltreated children who are without appropriate care, it becomes a perverted maternal substitute. If there is no mother who can soothe, peace can be achieved by a dramatic evacuation of stress.

Charisma, in tormenting her teacher and pushing her down the staircase, found a way of getting rid of the tension building up in her limbic system without completely exploding, or 'switching', as Connor tends to do. Of course, her choice of teacher is not a coincidence.

The teacher reminds Charisma of her mother. Her mother was detached, unavailable and cold. The English teacher is shy and not very expressive. She has the perfect characteristics to be used by Charisma to project the hatred she feels for her mum. By persecuting her, Charisma not only gets rid of limbic stress but is returned to childhood traumas. All the provocations are an attempt to bring to life her emotionally dead mum.

In turn, through a process called countertransference, the teacher is forced to enact Charisma's disassociated parent. She withdraws more and more, rendering herself emotionally unavailable to Charisma. She ends up behaving like Charisma's mother, and for that she is hated more and attacked anew.

Connor is too compliant to carry out such low-level violence. This was not his experience. He has had more dramatic intrusions than Charisma, so the violence he needs in order to regulate his limbic system and evacuate tension is more explosive.

He does not sit in a chair and decide to explode. Something has to trigger him into 'switching'. This is what happened in the case of the man he stabbed so ferociously.

They were outside a nightclub. The man was slightly drunk. He started teasing Connor, telling him he looked a bit gay, but that his genitals looked too small for a decent fuck. When the man then burst out laughing, he had no reason to know that he had rekindled memories of abuse lodged in Connor's hippocampus.

Connor's stepfather laughing loudly when drunk. Connor could also remember the smell of the drink on his breath. He had heard the comment about being too small too many times as he tried to pull his dad off his mother.

The link between the man outside the club and his stepfather is not conscious. But the amygdala, the fear centre of the brain, can recall and act on frightening patterns. It is like a shuttle arrangement between the hippocampus, which is the brain's memory bank, and the amygdala, its fear processor, under which primitive and recognisable patterns are transmitted in a fast-response emergency messaging system. In situations of extreme fear there is no time for long stories. Responses have to be quick, because the pituitary gland, part of the limbic system at the base of the brain, needs to signal the adrenal glands on top of the kidneys to release adrenaline, a hormone involved in the fright process, in case fight, flight or freezing are required.

Not all traumatised individuals are the same. But all traumatised individuals have difficulties in the areas of the brain responsible for managing fear. Once Connor has been triggered by the smell of alcohol in conjunction with abuse followed by laughter, his fear becomes so great that the limbic system overreacts. This is the moment when the prefrontal cortex shuts down, ready for lower brain functioning to take over.

Connor turns to the man, gets out his knife and starts stabbing. Deep inside the brain, the patterns he remembers tell him that when a grown man is drunk and abusive, the next thing he will do is hit and bite you. This time Connor is strong enough to give harm before he receives it, and to deliver the revenge he has always wanted. Ten years' worth of revenge, which as a child he had been too weak to generate, but which now, as a teenager, he has the testosterone and muscle strength to make real. He stabs the drunken man as he wished to assault his stepfather. The man was lucky to survive.

What could help maltreated children such as Connor? Enter the Prince of Wales.

CHAPTER 5

PRINCE OF INTUITION

In 1998, the Prince of Wales came to the railway arches. Unlike most of his visits, which are planned six weeks in advance, it was sudden. I told the kids that if they had hidden anything, it had better not be there when the dogs arrived. I had no reason to expect concealed drugs, but you could never be certain.

The prince had heard about us through one of his charities, Business in the Community. I loved Julia Cleverdon, its chief executive for sixteen years. Energetic and genuine, she brought groups of business leaders to us to give them an insight into inner-city lives. I knew Julia thanks to Jane Tewson, who co-founded Comic Relief. These two women started the network of contacts I built up over the years. Without them, I would not have known anyone. I went to a girls' boarding school that has the odd princess among its pupils. But I was an outsider – a refugee.

Like me, Jane is dyslexic. She left school without qualifications, but went to lectures at Oxford University when she worked in the city as a cleaner. She founded a homelessness charity at the age of twenty-three. By now she was turning forty, and she introduced us to Gordon Brown, Chancellor of the Exchequer in Tony Blair's government, and visited us in the early days with Alan Yentob and Michael Jackson, who was head of Channel 4. That is how Alan came to chair our trustees.

There is nothing fake about Prince Charles. He is empathetic and good at teenage banter. He talked to the children, played pool with them and cried several times at their circumstances. He also seemed to have real insight, even though his world was so remote. His attitude was respectful curiosity, always wanting to know more about the concerns young people shared with him.

At the time, many of the kids were anxious about shelter. Councils had no duty to house them after the age of sixteen, when they were deemed old enough to look after themselves. At Kids Company we worked to change this through judicial review, making local authorities responsible for housing homeless young people up to the age of eighteen.

At the end of his time with us, Charles asked me to get into the car with him. It was a surprise not only for me but for his minders. He had to go to the City to give a speech and wanted me there too. Some 600 business people were waiting.

In the back of the car, he asked me why I did it. I explained that these children were victims of chronic abuse and institutional neglect. They needed help, but there was a widespread denial of how severe their needs were and therefore an unwillingness to help them appropriately. I also said that I thought the number of abused children being left without support was much larger than acknowledged.

He turned his head to look out of the car window and said quietly, 'I always knew it, but people tend not to tell me the truth.' He meant that he was not given the full story by his advisers. Then he turned back to face me and said, 'What do you want to do? How can I help you?' I asked if we could set up a commission to assess the true scale of need and to offer new models for intervening in the lives of mistreated children. He thought it was a really good idea and promised to help.

By now we had arrived at the venue, where he insisted I speak alongside him. He first made the business audience laugh, saying, 'I have just had a lovely time with Camila under the arches.' When the conference ended, he called one of his officials and explained that he wanted to set up a commission, instructing the official to meet me as soon as possible. I have never told the prince what happened next, but it shocked me. The official and I did meet. His exact words were, 'This is too hot a potato.' A senior figure, trusted by the prince, did not want to get involved in systemic problems in child mental health and social care. Instead, he asked me to take £10,000 and never mention the commission again. I refused.

In 1999, Charles came back to the arches, this time to see a musical that the kids had written in collaboration with some West End performers and a songwriter who later became a psychoanalyst. The work was based on the life of one of the children. Her arm had been broken by her mother when she was four years old and she was put into foster care, where the son in her new family subjected her to sexual abuse. In the musical, she expressed her dreams and the challenges she faced. Once again the prince was moved to tears.

Before the performance began, I saw the ugliness that royalty can attract. A few of our donors were fighting to sit next to Charles. One in particular, the female half of a London power couple who had millions in their bank account, became an implacable enemy after I insisted that the children sit next to him, as they were the people he had come to see. After that she tried to frustrate our fundraising.

The musical was called *Kids Need Friends*. The actors who worked with us were generous, but they were shocked at how disturbed the kids were. Some of our young people would explode in rehearsals, their violent outbursts triggered by moments of humiliation that are part of the rehearsal process. By the end, the artists felt sorry for our workers and marvelled at how we could do this job every day. The real rewards came later. One of the lead kids is now a social worker, another is in a high-earning job in education and the third is at university.

The next time we heard from the Prince of Wales's office was a request to host a visit in 2002 for the then seventeen-year-old Prince Harry. He had got himself into a spot of bother smoking weed at Highgrove, and his dad wanted him to understand the lives of disadvantaged young people. Harry was like his father: he was brilliant with our kids. He played a bit of table tennis and pool, bantered with the boys and listened to his peers. To my embarrassment, one of the girls shouted out, 'He's good looking for a white boy!' She had suffered the most horrific childhood, often being sexually abused or left without food while acting as the main carer from the age of nine for three smaller siblings; her parents were addicts who were out of control. Harry responded with a beautiful smile. He was cool, even then, yet it was obvious he was struggling, five years after the loss of his mother. The kids reacted instinctively. Despite the vast gap in privilege, they appreciated him.

Prince Charles and I kept in touch. He came back when we moved to our Kenbury Street site after being evicted from the arches in 2003. As he and Camilla walked around, they were both genuinely engaged in what they were doing. You could also feel the love the young kids had for him. Everyone knows he has kept faith with these communities and has not abandoned them. For many poor black adolescents, the Prince of Wales and his charity for 13–30-year-olds, the Prince's Trust, are transformative. Thousands have benefited from his programmes to help young people find their confidence, develop new skills and stabilise their lives. I came to an arrangement with Martina Milburn, the trust's chief executive from 2004, that Kids Company would take anyone who was too disturbed for her courses, while we sent our young people to her when they were well enough.

When I next met the prince, I had read those 500 or so clinical papers we had gathered in the early days. By now we had a doctor working with us, and a young neuroscientist. The three of us started logging the papers and trying to work out how best we could help the children.

For at least five years, since the turn of the millennium, I had been trying to rethink the kids' negative behaviours. Society saw our teenagers as deviant. I saw them as exquisitely logical, because they had adapted to abuse. Their negative strategies, experienced by the rest of us as aggression, were an attempt to achieve some kind of equilibrium.

Realising this gave me deeper compassion for them, and an admiration for how paradoxically intelligent they were in finding ways to cope with violence, albeit with anti-social consequences. 'Violence adapting disorder' is the name I thought we should give to this reframing of the kids' bad behaviours.

The sometimes violent and disruptive behaviour of these kids seemed to be functional in some way, frustrated attempts at managing or expressing literally unbearable feelings or experiences. Something was causing them to re-enact deep patterns of neglect and abuse, driving them to both relive and relieve what they most wanted to forget. Now, with the benefit of the scientific papers, intuitive clinical pondering turned into a much more confident vision. Kids Company had to deliver a service that took the children's anti-social behaviours and interpreted them as strategies to survive. We must take the blame out of it, and partner with the kids to find a solution for their difficulties that was less anti-social. It would be about love and respect combined. Respect for how they were trying to survive by violently acting out, and love because ultimately that was what was missing in their lives, driving them towards perversions as a substitute for it.

I shared with the Prince of Wales that I was planning to give Kids Company a new dimension. I would try to get scientists to research what was happening in our children's brains. To my amazement, Martina then handed over twenty-five clinical papers the prince had gathered. Apparently, seven years before she joined the Prince's Trust, he had tried to have his team initiate similar research. They had dismissed him, believing he was off the mark. This would have been in about 1997. The prince's thinking was not only ahead of theirs; it had been ahead of mine.

My interest in the science came from observation. When we were at the railway arches, I noticed kids hugging staff a lot and seeking them out. Even the difficult ones would do it through play-fighting. Some bonded well with foster carers: we supervised one woman who fostered many difficult cases, and the children loved her. Then there were the babies who calmed down when breast-fed. Sometime in the year 2000, I noticed the doe-like quality that comes into the mother's and baby's eyes. Our kids' eyes, by contrast, were electrified. What was it between the mother and baby that gave them those eyes? That was what we needed to reproduce to calm down the boys' frenzied eye quality.

I also thought science had a problem. Like the rest of society, researchers often saw bad behaviour as a moral question. I saw it as a symptom of dysregulation. I could see that children use violence to soothe themselves and it is their attempt to adapt to environments they cannot control. I described to researchers the problems the kids had with eye contact. I also said that punishment does not work, because it reinforces humiliation and power loss for the offender.

The scientific world tends to be insular, chasing fashionable themes, with much of their research being driven by the type of funding that is available. At the time, it did not study young people such as ours, because science did not come to the street. From the start, I had two central theories. One was that violence is the children's attempt to regain an equilibrium. Love was the legitimate route to it. If we could offer love, they would give up their violence, because love was going to achieve what they were attempting to achieve biologically using violence.

I did find some of the people around the Prince of Wales condescending. They had less intuitive intelligence than their employer, and referred to him in a derogatory way. 'Oh, here he goes talking to the plants again.' This was said by the same senior official who had offered me the £10,000 'shut up money' years earlier. Charles's private office and communications staff were really decent, though, and respected his interest. When he made his third visit to Kids Company, his private secretary emphasised, as the prince was being rushed by a crowd of kids, that his boss wanted an update on our research.

Inspired by him, a number of business leaders came together to fund the investigations. Over the years the biggest contribution was from Alannah Weston, whose father, the British-Canadian billionaire Galen Weston, bought Selfridges in 2003 for £628 million. Alannah was creative director of Selfridges, credited with reinvigorating the store group. Later she became deputy chairman. Even so, she took our child protection training, and came to read with children in one of our street-level centres until just before the closure. Her charitable trust paid for the Institute of Psychiatry at King's College London to investigate the effects of maltreatment on traumatised children's ability to control their behaviour.[1]

The last time I saw the Prince of Wales was when he hosted an event for Kids Company that brought more than 1,000 guests to a marquee in Battersea Park. We sat side by side at dinner. The conversation started with sacred geometry and other patterns that hold an intelligent order. He expressed a fondness for Islamic art and we talked about the designs on mosques. He also spoke about the importance of farming using the rhythms of nature. I begged him to write a book, as I felt his intuitive knowledge should be given a voice. In 2010, he sent me a copy of *Harmony*, his book with Ian Skelly, the classical music expert, and Tony Juniper, of Friends of the Earth. It sets out how human activities as diverse as architecture, farming and medicine have abandoned a classical sense of balance and proportion.

People under-estimate the Prince of Wales. He was very much in touch with the challenges faced by vulnerable young people. His intuitions are astute, but as he lacks a broad life experience he looks to his officials to help him articulate what he picks up. They are often so sure their cleverness is greater than his that they dismiss an intuition ahead of its time.

We kept in contact by letter as the scientific research progressed. Unknown to me, someone sent him recordings of a lecture I gave, bringing together the findings related to childhood trauma. The prince wrote a two-page letter, excited by the research and its implications.

Prince Charles visited Kids Company four times. By contrast, local authority chief executives, who are enshrined in law as the corporate parents for the most vulnerable children, visited once in two decades. I think that says a lot about their respective priorities.

By 2010, I was ready to campaign for formal recognition of violence adapting disorder. I walked into the Royal Society of Medicine to try to persuade the doctor in charge that a new diagnosis was justified. The kids were changing in biology and psychology to cope with the violence to which they were exposed.[2] They were not flawed as individuals; it was an intelligent set of adaptations for which they were paying a price.

The security guard recognised me straight away. He was from Peckham. I often had this experience with men and women at the reception desks of posh buildings. They usually helped me find the powerful people upstairs, giving me access when normally it was denied.

As I sat down in the meeting room with David Misselbrook, the dean of the Royal Society of Medicine, he gave me a look I had come to know well. 'What is this mad woman doing here in her funny outfit?' I talked about the kids and their behaviour. He confirmed that family doctors were seeing young people with the set of symptoms I described, and were at a loss as to how to respond.

We persuaded him to hold a symposium at which we could explore the characteristics and needs of these children. I am grateful for his moral courage in holding the event, which took place in May 2010. Some of the best scientists and practitioners were in the room. I presented my observations and shared what the kids had said. Three professors – Eamon McCrory, Essi Viding and Sarah-Jayne Blakemore – from UCL, and Dr Mirza from the Institute of Psychiatry, King's College London, brought everyone up to date with international research. It was evident that little work had been done with maltreated urban children. None of us could find more than a handful of papers on the impact of trauma on urban children across the world.

After a few hours of discussion, it was agreed that the scientists would collaborate in new research to examine the effects of maltreatment. It was also agreed that they would not compete. Our aim was to generate a collective portfolio of work, and we divided the tasks for investigation among the institutions.

The Institute of Psychiatry at King's College London carried out a study to find out the impact of error correction on young people who had been abused. When the scientists scanned three sets of young adults, they found that a control group corrected its behaviour when sanctioned. A second group, whose members were psychiatrically ill but had not been mistreated as children, also corrected its behaviour when punished for making errors playing video games. But the young people who had been mistreated early in life became 'stuck' when punished and could not correct their actions. This showed up in brain scans taken as the young adults were sanctioned while playing the games. The research pointed to the inefficacy of punishment for maltreated kids. Abused children seemed to have a disturbed relationship with making mistakes and correcting them, because when they made mistakes they froze, anticipating further abuse.

I felt relieved. Years earlier we had noticed that punishing the kids was ineffective. Of course, you had to use some sanctions to communicate to the rest of the group that bad behaviour was unacceptable. But I knew it brought no improvement in behaviour in children who had been abused.

It is not a surprise to learn that maltreated minds can go into a frozen state when punished. An adult who harms a child creates a power imbalance. The adult has the power and the child experiences a loss of it. Lost power equals humiliation. This, for maltreated children, is a primitive memory stored in the hippocampus. The imbalance can return, years later, when the child is disciplined by an adult whose intentions are benign. Messages are sent to the amygdala, triggering the fight/flight response through bringing back to life previous memories of being extremely frightened in an abusive situation.

An abused child who is being punished does not think: 'I was wrong. I can learn from this to do better in future.' Instead, they become preoccupied with survival. This is not on a conscious level. It is a rapid communication involving the limbic system and memories of maltreatment, changing how the child processes the fact of another human being applying sanctions. The dominant thought is, 'How can I save myself?' This is when maltreated children 'switch', becoming ruder and more challenging towards the adult who is trying to correct them.

David Misselbrook, the head of the academic department at the Royal Society of Medicine, felt a degree of conflict over my proposal for a new diagnosis of violence adapting disorder. If doctors recognised this as an illness, would people say they were lending medical justification to bad conduct? By the time invitations for our day of expert discussion went out, the condition had a different name: adaptive violence disorder.

It is a subtle change, but the original title ascribes less blame. It places violence in the environment. Misselbrook's version places it in the child. He recognised the implications for policy, though. 'If an adaptive violence disorder exists then any debate about society's response to violent juvenile crime and the "gang culture" must take this into account,' he wrote in the *Journal of the Royal Society of Medicine* after the London riots in 2011.

> We ... need to come to a richer understanding of the human condition. One which does not see damaged children as 'nothing but' the consequence of trauma. But a view that at the same time is grimly realistic about just how deep that trauma may be embedded in children's cognitions. If we better understand the complexity of this mix of neuroscience, genetics and common humanity then we will be better placed to find a way forward for our 'broken society'.[3]

If Kids Company were still open, I would ask the researchers to add another dimension to the tests. Does it make a difference if we praise maltreated children before explaining where they made the error in the video game? Praise reassures vulnerable children that the adult is not an enemy, weakening the defensive stress response. Perhaps the young people in the study would be better able to perceive correction as a constructive act and not an attack.

As a result of the 2010 symposium, University College London began looking at the traumatic experiences that many urban children experienced. Their peer-reviewed research focused on inner-city youth, many of whom were Kids Company clients. The levels of adversity the kids had endured, which were captured by the research, shocked us all. One in five (19.4 per cent) of Kids Company's young people in the study had been shot or stabbed. Nearly one in four (22.6 per cent) had seen a friend or relative being shot or stabbed in the past year. More than a third (36.6 per cent) had seen someone in their community being shot or stabbed in the previous twelve months. Levels of abuse and neglect were startling. The ninety-eight Kids Company clients, who were 16–24-year-olds from our Urban Academy, were six and a half times as likely to have experienced 'severe to extreme' emotional abuse when compared with 106 young people recruited from other sources (24.5 per cent at Kids Company versus 3.8 per cent of the control group). They were seventeen times as likely to have gone through severe to extreme physical neglect (15.3 per cent versus 0.9 per cent) and eleven times as likely to have experienced severe to extreme sexual abuse (10.2 per cent versus 0.9 per cent).[4]

The Anna Freud Centre and Professor Pasco Fearon, also of University College London, explored the importance of our key workers as additional parental figures. The preliminary results suggested that after nine months psychosocial intervention with Kids Company, teenagers showed significant improvements in emotional processing.[5] When they first came to us, their brains responded no differently when presented with unpleasant and neutral images. The emotionally driven parts of the brain were underactive, as you would expect in children who could come across as emotionally cold. If young people have muted emotional responses to cues signalling threat, they may be more prone to taking excessive risks or becoming aggressive. They may be less open, too, to feeling emotions or responding to distress in others.

Clients with an average of eighteen months' exposure to key workers reacted to the emotional content of the images like typical teenagers.

Their brain responses were normal, perhaps also indicating an increased ability to experience attachment and empathy. I was given the news in a phone call on my way to Wales and it was a magical moment. I believe the damage of neglect can be managed; if not fully, then to a life-affirming degree. However, recovery is slower after the age of twenty-seven.[6]

Adolescence may give those who work with vulnerable children a second opportunity to provide them with a greater ability to self-regulate, because the adolescent brain is restructuring. This is provided the child is given a consistent attachment opportunity, not unlike one provided for toddlers.

Most people gain the capacity for empathy from their mothers.[7] When a baby cries and a carer responds, the infant learns that they exist in another person's mind. It is through this process of 'need declaration' and 'need satisfaction' that the child develops the concept of another human being, starting with the mother who tries to imagine what the cause of her baby's distress might be and tries to resolve it. The Fearon research, although only a pilot study, suggested that children who are emotionally frozen by trauma can be helped to improve considerably. Even violent children – and even in their teens.

CHAPTER 6

NARCISSISTIC PHILANTHROPY

For me, the most painful part of running Kids Company was the fundraising. Of some £24 million a year, about £4 million came from the government; the rest we had to raise as we went along. We were never sure where it would come from.

We kept overheads low. We had a small fundraising department of about ten people. Two part-time designers created our campaigns and reports for individual donors. Lean administration allowed eighty-five pence in the pound to go to frontline services. In fact, it was better than the cold figures in the accounts suggested, because almost all our administrative staff spent some of their time working with the kids, and we calculated that ninety pence in the pound went to the front line. Some big charities spend a quarter of their revenue on income generation and governance; one, well known and comparable to ours in size, employed 250 fundraisers.

Despite the hard work of our fundraising department, most of the weight fell on me. The trustees tried fundraising consultancies, only to find the client group was too hard to sell. As a bank chief executive told me, 'Your kind of kids' – meaning kids with black faces, some with criminal records – 'don't look good on our annual report.' I realised early on that we needed to create a parallel brand to unlock money from donors who might not like our kids, but who wanted to be associated with Kids Company because it had grown into a desirable commodity.

I carried around a spreadsheet, divided into three. One column was for confirmed money, the second for potential donations and the third for new prospects. I treated these pieces of paper as if a child's life depended on them (which of course it did). Morning, noon and night I stared at the pages, terrified by the responsibility and hoping that by month end my prospects and potentials would fill the shortfall. I was oppressed by the burden and elated each time someone decided to give. Our income in 2014 came from 77,000 sources. A restaurant, sketch, added £1 to every bill unless customers opted out. We used the money to feed our kids.

We had wonderful supporters. One man used to repair chairs and give us the proceeds. Groups of women would knit socks and hats and sell them to raise funds. Each Christmas, a man who declined to give his name appeared with £600 and a message: 'Tell Camila this is for the kids.'

A secretary turned up with a cheque; she had saved the money over time. Thanks to her, we got a girl whose mother was ill, and whose father had died, through university. She left the London School of Economics with a master's degree and went straight to a £60,000-a-year job in the City. Only then did the pair meet. I fought back tears because their relationship symbolised Kids Company. A stranger had transformed the life of a vulnerable teenager, who seized the chance and then was able to help her disabled mother. As it happens, the two got on well, and started meeting to go to the theatre.

Nina Campbell, the designer with heart-shaped glasses, was another true philanthropist. She mentored a teenager who had grown up in care and who, aged fifteen, tried to kill himself by ramming his foster carer's car into a wall. His depression was so profound there were days he could not get out of bed. Nina stuck by him, and put him to work in her business.

It would take volumes to list the people who helped make Kids Company a place of safety and opportunity, and this book cannot begin to name them all. The founder of an insurance company turned up one day, watched the staff interact with the children and made a substantial donation. A financier gave millions. Stuart Roden, the chairman of a hedge fund, and John Frieda, the celebrity hairdresser, supported us until the final moments. They too gave millions. One of my favourites was a lady who had co-founded a satellite navigation company; she came to a music event organised by the kids and grooved to the beat. She had a soft spot for teenagers and I loved her for it, because so many people hate them. Her generosity transformed Kids Company from a smaller charity to one of medium size. J. K. Rowling, Coldplay, Sting and Trudie Styler, Joanna Lumley, Helen Mirren, Jamie Cullum, Sophie Dahl, John Bishop and Michael McIntyre, among others, all gave generously without asking for any public acknowledgement.

I saw the donors as partners and felt a profound love for them. Whether they were poor and sharing limited resources, or rich and giving through charitable trusts, they were united in reaching out to our courageous children to help them along. My role was to ask, and in doing so to represent the children.[1] They saw support of Kids Company as enabling a social experiment that in time would be funded differently. None of us viewed their contribution as endless. But as government after government failed to embrace the challenge of so many abandoned children, I valued their sustained commitment all the more.

I called the best of them 'creative philanthropists'. They combined deep emotional capacity with analysis. I enjoyed their scrutiny, which led to changes as I learnt from them. The first, right at the beginning, was an unassuming man in an overcoat who walked onto the premises when I was not there. The kids gave him a chilling welcome as they thought he was an undercover police officer. It was Peter Kindersley, publisher of the extraordinary reference books with 3D structures emerging from the page; he followed up by telephone and gave us £20,000. I put down the receiver and burst into tears, moved by his ability to see the children's plight and Kids Company's potential when we were a marginal project in some railway arches. Equally transformative in the early days were the contributions of charitable trusts: Henry Smith, Tudor Trust, Comic Relief, to name but a few.

What is philanthropy? Ruby Wax, the comedian and mental health campaigner, once said to me that I was 'cursed with empathy'. I laughed because it is true. In empathy, the emotionally driven parts of the brain experience another person's state as if it were our own. The prefrontal cortex then decides what to do.[2] This can happen even at a distance of thousands of miles.

We received *The Times* in Iran, and the terror of a Vietnamese girl photographed running naked after being hit by burning napalm was one of the defining moments of my childhood. She was nine and so was I. My father also imported English films to show in his sports centre. One was about a group of kids trying to survive in wartime. I did not understand a word of it as I spoke no English, but I was devastated by the children's aloneness. As Adam Smith put it in 1759, in his *Theory of Moral Sentiments*:

> As we have no immediate experience of what other men feel, we can form no idea of the manner in which they are affected but by conceiving what we ourselves should feel in the like situation. Though our brother is upon the rack, as long as we ourselves are at our ease, our senses will never inform us of what he suffers ... it is by the imagination only that we can form any conception of what are his sensations.[3]

For the philanthropists, my role was to make the plight of the kids visible by bringing it into the imagination. We tried to maintain an honourable approach to fundraising, because I felt we were creating a loving community and this should extend to every part of the organisation. All our fundraisers worked with at least one child so that they could keep alive the reason they were asking for money. I would not allow cold calling or the chasing of prospective donors. I would say, 'Put the offer on the table. If the other party wishes to take it up, they will.' I disliked the tricks of some charities, such as using pictures of miserable kids as if their pain were on sale. If we wanted to communicate the children's desperation we created art, or showed their living conditions.

We thanked our donors properly. I signed every letter, even for a gift of 50p. Some nights this meant signing 200, but I did it happily. I would focus on the name of the person to make the feeling of gratitude real. The kids expressed their appreciation through art, which our art department sent out. A publisher and champion of poetry was one of their favourites, because every Christmas he funded presents for young people who were on their own. The art they made for him was beautiful.

People think philanthropy is selfless. I disagree. We gain from helping others: it gives me a feeling of deep happiness. After years of watching people give to charity, I have decided that altruism exists on a spectrum. The highest philanthropy, I believe, is creative. At the other end of the spectrum from what I call creative philanthropists are narcissistic philanthropists, and in the middle are transactional philanthropists. The mechanisms of giving are different in each case.

When the help seeker comes into contact with the help giver, a rapid series of exchanges takes place. Some of it is through language, but the powerful part is unconscious. The seeker appraises the giver to confirm that they can offer support. They might even work out the giver's emotional typography to make the appeal more effective. The person who would like to help checks if the need is appropriate and whether they can meet it. An unconscious contract is created, allowing the pair to embark on the collaborative task of transforming a poor situation into a better one. The giver feels empowered after coming into contact with their own capacity to transform the world. They also receive an emotional reward from witnessing the seeker's happiness. This is what I believe a creative philanthropist gains from involvement with a charity.

It helps if you can bring donors nearer to recipients and indicate the need for collaboration, as a genuine philanthropist is more likely to give to an individual than to a group.[4] The reward, I believe, is biological. The billionaire is 'in community' with the child from the ghetto. He experiences a connectedness in the imagination, even if he has no other need to help the child.[5] The neuropeptides oxytocin and vasopressin, which engineer the release of the neurotransmitters dopamine and serotonin, then lift his mood.

Genuine philanthropists need a nuanced appreciation. If the gratitude comes from the excitement of transformation, it is received as an act of celebration. However, if the help seeker is over-grateful, the help giver feels burdened and uncomfortable. The equality implied by collaborating to effect change is lost, as the seeker makes the helper dominant by relinquishing power and attributing it to the aid giver. This makes the giver lonely, because they have no partner. Instead of doing a task *with* someone they have done it *to* them. People who enjoy having that power feel rewarded, but the creative philanthropist, who prefers a participatory model of help, feels loss. One of the most egalitarian donors we worked with was Sigrid Rausing, the anthropologist and publisher. Her only interest was to know that kids were helped.

The creative philanthropists I was privileged to work with were visionaries. It was as if their personal fright and anxieties had been ameliorated, allowing them to think of the world around them as an intimate space. As they came to understand the failures of social care, they wanted to solve them. The founder of an executive recruitment company was one. Just before we closed in 2015, he agreed to fund See the Child. Change the System, a project to design a new care system and pilot it in local authorities. He wanted to be closely involved in resolving the problems of the children's sector.

We found our kids benefited greatly from volunteering, because in the process they began to matter to someone. They felt they would be missed; being a volunteer enhanced their sense of identity and generated encouragement, connectedness and intimacy. Depressive symptoms began to lift as they ceased to perceive themselves as powerless and started to see themselves as agents of change. Young volunteers from harsh backgrounds often challenged their peers to make progress too.[6]

We had 10,000 volunteers, including students from social work, psychotherapy and NHS training programmes. One of my favourites came three times a week to file the children's notes in eighty cabinets. She was very stylish and sought nothing in return. Three hundred volunteers were mentors. The boss of a building firm showed limitless patience with a boy who had lost his mother and was difficult to handle. A designer used her drawing skills to connect with a depressed girl who refused to get out of bed. That girl is now at art college. *The Times* reported recently that 97 per cent of children in care are denied the mentors to which they are entitled by law, and that vetting, training and matching each volunteer costs councils about £40,000.[7] We trained our 300 at a total cost of £50,000, equivalent to saving the state nearly £12 million – half our budget.

Companies gave us stock, which we used to replenish depleted homes and clothe the kids. In three years, we received £40 million of goods and volunteering under our Poverty Busting programme, which Samantha Cameron launched in Downing Street.

I remember bumping into her husband at another No. 10 cocktail party. He always remarked on his wife's passion for our children, and she was certainly more committed than he was. When she visited us one afternoon, the children responded to her warmth by clambering around her to explain their activities. It was the same with Cherie Blair. When she came to Kids Company, one of our most disturbed teenagers, who had been horrifically sexually abused, started chasing her with vile and aggressive questions about her sex life with Tony. Cherie responded with kindness, telling her security team not to touch the girl and continuing with her tour under a barrage of verbal assaults. I could not believe it when she sent the child a Christmas card and then gave her housewarming presents when, as an eighteen-year-old care leaver, the girl got her own flat. Cherie Blair and Samantha Cameron are creative philanthropists. They could imagine a child's devastation and their interest was purely personal. At no time did either of them use us in a public way.

Queen Rania of Jordan was another of these genuine philanthropists. As I watched her play pool with boys from the gangs, I marvelled at the tenderness with which she listened to the kids. The sight disturbed her security men, who had been told to keep a distance. But her kindness brought out the best in our young men.

I did not want Kids Company to become a fish bowl of misery, offering quick tours to view the disadvantaged, and we insisted that visitors spend proper time with the kids. I stayed in the background while each side discovered respect for the other. Bankers were a hit. Our children liked them very much, and supposedly callous financiers were awed by the courage of the kids and the levels of adversity they had negotiated. Disturbed teenagers became the bankers' fans because they communicated.

The opposite of the creative philanthropists, with their genuine intentions, were the narcissistic philanthropists. I often felt enraged by them. I hated asking them for money and hated receiving it. But my role was to represent the children and to get the resources to give them a meaningful chance in life. So I did what I could to accommodate the narcissists.

They were a complex prospect. They said they wanted to help, yet showed little interest except in themselves. Some wanted a plaque, or a building that carried their name. Others included the 'I know better than you' donors, who attached conditions to a gift. A financial institution insisted we took our children to Shakespeare, undeterred by the argument that dysregulated teenagers are trouble in confined spaces. The kids would not sit still. They bothered the people around them and ran across the theatre as key workers chased after them. On the bus back, they produced the binoculars they had stolen in the dark, leading to new conflict as we insisted they give them up. The institution was able to show that it had helped inner-city children and supported a theatre company, but it was corporate veneer.

Some volunteers, told by their companies to help us, showed such disdain I asked them to leave. I also hated it when parents forced their kids to volunteer briefly to enhance a CV. It was such a destructive introduction to philanthropy, to use destitute kids to serve their own. Often we found that these young people reflected their parents' perception of poverty as moral failure.[8] I removed anyone who seemed not to have good intentions, including a music A-lister who visited us after a conviction. The camera she carried signalled motives that were not honourable, and to the kids' shock I escorted her out.

One might expect the greatest commitment to come from volunteers with comfortable backgrounds, but it came from those with tough ones. Perhaps they had resilience. They also realised what a lifeline these relationships were for vulnerable kids. The most beautiful transformation was when a young, white Jewish woman mentored one of our most challenging gang members, who was barely literate. She persuaded him to go to college and now he is training as a teacher. When Kids Company closed, they kept up contact because she got as much from being with him, which helped her confidence, as he did from her.[9]

For some families it was easier to be helped by a volunteer who was not from their community, avoiding comparison stress. They would not see themselves as failures next to their neighbour. However, they did not want the volunteer to be too posh or attractive, as they felt they would be perceived as 'low' in relative status and not worthy of help. They found it easier to ask for help with practical questions than psychological deficiencies, which are a bigger threat to self-esteem. The inability to reciprocate was painful. Our families wanted to feel morally equal to those who helped them.[10]

Some were terrified, as they associated accepting help with losing control. When they had higher self-esteem, they could use the help better because they believed themselves worthy of receiving it. When they were low, they saw the volunteer as a witness to their failings, and shame trumped the reward of being assisted.[11] It can be humiliating to ask for help; our young men found it especially difficult, as they felt they could not show vulnerability in case it was perceived as weak, a fact that has been recognised in research.[12]

The grovel-for-me donor was especially hard to take. Some enjoyed humiliating and almost playing with you. 'I may or may not give' would be their phrase as they asked lots of questions and had us running everywhere. They would invite us to speak at events, or to do something for them, with the incentive that it 'may' lead to a donation. They loved pointing out where else we could get money. One said that if I turned away maltreated children they would go to social services, which would send them back to us with a payment attached to the child. This was logical, except that social services were overwhelmed. The kids who made their way to Kids Company had no one to pay for them.

If you react truthfully, this type of donor can become angry. It was as if wealth proved to the narcissistic philanthropist that they also have superior knowledge. Similar were the 'let me sort you out' brigade, which consists of young men who are clever but not wise and briefcase-carrying females with discreet strings of pearls around their necks. Often they came from charity evaluation groups or clever think tanks. These are small organisations that might come up with a single management theory and try to apply it everywhere. Charities tolerate them for fear of being described as 'difficult', which can deter a donor from parting with the pounds. I would often wonder why people think that charities lack expertise.

As a strong female, I knew my role was to shut up and get the money for the kids. I shut up more than was good for me. Had I had a handbag, I would have knocked it over their heads. Instead, I survived by imagining the evil deed and giggling to myself.

Narcissistic donors are from every class and background. The final sub-category of narcissists is the give-me-a-graph donor. They were not greatly interested in the life transformations their donations made possible. Instead they wanted 'value for money' comparison studies. I always thought it was a disturbing concept.[13] How do you measure the worth of the changes that are possible in a child's life? For Juliet, having a room with a bed and proper covers was more important than GCSEs. All her life she had been in smelly bed-and-breakfasts where she was too scared of the other residents to go to the toilet. In the bath, as a seven-year-old, she would remove syringes and condoms before getting washed and ready for school. Rats competed for her breakfast as they ran across the dining room and climbed the tables.

Who has the right, or the skill, to determine the value of what she receives? She is the expert on that. No comparison study could capture the importance of the dignity she yearned for. Instead, the give-me-a-graph donor wanted an analysis of the cost of her poor education versus the economic benefit of qualifications. If an equation showed the potency of his donation and we agreed to be measured against it, we got the money.

I am in favour of measurement and evaluation, including value-for-money studies. But children's charities do not have the resources to produce meaningful analysis because the national and local data for comparison do not exist. Until very recently, no local authority captured the cost of a vulnerable child. If Juliet goes for help with health, social care, education and leisure, she is considered a new child by each provision.

I believe that unconsciously, such donors are seeking reasons not to give. Some look for risks in the charity or its client group. Others blame the disadvantaged, as if poverty is the result of personality. This is a version of what social scientists call 'self-serving attribution bias', which is the understandable habit of attributing achievements to our own efforts while setbacks are the fault of events. The narcissist attributes success to personal excellence even if luck is involved, while failure is considered the result of a flaw.[14] I would sit in meetings and defend children against donors who dealt with feelings of guilt by presenting the world as just, making our kids responsible for their diminished state.[15]

Narcissistic philanthropists tended to avoid contact with the people they helped, as they were not greatly interested in them. Their desire was to see the potency of their actions reflected back at them, preferably in public. Often, they delegated the giving decision to others. Representatives would come and review the charity. After a while, the representatives came to believe they were donating their own funds, and acquired the same, distasteful approach. If the charity passed the test, the donor asked for the gift to be publicised.

The narcissistic philanthropist has a different motivational path from the creative philanthropist. They are not seeking a joint project with the help seeker. Instead, they want power over the seeker, and to turn the individual into an object to satisfy their needs. I saw it happen so often. Some wanted designer poor people; they knew what need should look like. They would ask, 'If they are poor, why do they have a plasma TV?' It is a perfectly legitimate question, but the subtext is that some people fake being poor. This can be a useful assumption: it is a defence against guilt and against failures of giving, as true giving requires the handing over of the gift without seeking to control it further. The narcissistic philanthropist, however, wants to make the contribution and stay in control of it, because the act of altruism is about what he wants and not what the recipient needs.

Turning to charity is an indignity. Receiving help is a humiliating and disempowering experience. Faking need is rare. A television is a window to the world; it allows children to be distracted from turmoil and can be a shared family experience. In communities where it is not safe to wander down the block, the virtual world of the TV is their walk in the park. Our kids could not participate in PlayStation or Xbox because consoles and games were too expensive, but they could talk about TV programmes with their peers. Someone always had an uncle or a friend who worked in a warehouse and 'lent' the family a television. Lorry drivers would sell them at low cost, or give them willingly or unwillingly from the back of the lorries. But the most common method was hire purchase, with a monthly payment of no more than £15.

Then the question becomes, why could it not be a little TV as opposed to a big one? This is about dignity. Families perceived a 'posh-looking' TV as a way to be as good as their neighbours. They could not pay for a car or a kitchen, but a TV on credit was possible.

One narcissist, a partner in one of the world's biggest consultancy firms, wanted to hear about the gratitude of the family who benefited from his £500 donation. In a thirty-minute meeting, this man did not ask at all about the transformation his generosity had made possible. The conversation was about the degree of gratitude the family felt and how his name would appear in our literature. He wanted a prominent place, and to ensure that we did not state the actual amount. This was a multi-millionaire. If it were not for the kids, I would have given back his £500 and marched him out of the door.

The position of donors in annual reports is a tool some charities manipulate. Our policy was to identify donors, rich and poor, alphabetically. We could not include them all, but tried to generate a mix. I often had to debate with narcissistic donors over their prominence. I came under pressure from advisers to create 'patrons', whose status would be elevated by the sums they gave as if they belonged to an elite club. I resisted, because some people who give less money share a higher proportion of what they have. Certain charities create bands, with donors who give £500–£999 going into that category.[16] I resisted that too. On one occasion a donor said he was willing to contribute to our summer scheme if no black children benefited. Nobody could say yes to that.

Then there would be the rent-a-poor-kid brigade. 'Could we have some lovely, poor-looking children for our photo shoot?' (Someone actually said that.) The subtext was that they should also be white. We protected the children: only a small group did media interviews, and that was because they had reached a point in their lives where they wanted to represent their peers by talking about their experiences. For the young people, some of these activities were exciting and they felt empowered. When the *Sunday Times* Style magazine ran a feature in which some kids modelled clothes, the boost in their confidence was significant and the public donated 5,000 coats for the children that winter.

I was stoic about the transactional philanthropists. These were companies that sought a partnership partly to do good but mainly to help their public relations. We often heard from them before share-holder dividends were announced. They also wanted to exhibit their pseudo-altruism.[17] At least, unlike the narcissistic philanthropists, we knew where we stood. They made it clear that they were supporting the charity because they wanted something in return.

We tried to work with them so that the transactions acquired sub-tlety and became more nuanced. Instead of saying, 'This is the number of children our donation fed,' next to a picture of their beautiful food products, we would ask them to fund research on food insecurity. As they came to understand the levels of need the children faced, often these transactional philanthropists became fully engaged and would delight in being involved. The more contact they had with the kids, the greater the chance there was of developing a creative philanthropic approach, the bedrock of which is the capacity to empathise.[18]

Some of our corporate partnerships were wonderful. John Lewis turned our kids' designs into a fashion range sold with labels describing their courage. Individual workers in other big entities were sincere in their dealings with us, forging links that led to creative philanthropy even if the starting point was transactional. Huge resources were mobilised for our families in these transactional exchanges, and all the while we never lost hope that we could ignite a love for the kids.

The most beautiful transformation was that of Ed Burstell at Liberty. His staff gave our teenagers the chance to pitch ideas, then sold their designs. The kids invented Christmas cards, soap packaging and 'hood-ies that hug'. These were hoods with a scarf attached so that someone could wrap themselves up in it as if they were being hugged. We also designed some of the Christmas windows at Selfridges with Alannah Weston and her team. At midnight, I finished work and asked the cab driver to stop by Selfridges. When I saw the exquisite window with all the amazing toys the kids had dreamt up – mad-looking little monster figures and houses, filling the store windows with colourful characters – I felt deep gratitude for being given the chance to bring the message of the children to such a space. In short, transactional philanthropy was not disturbing, and led to transformational encounters for the kids and the companies, out of which real commitment was born.

Some private donors were transactional philanthropists. The starting point was guilt and their focus was how they felt. They gained a glow of satisfaction from the fact of a gift rather than what it achieved. They were driven by a need to self-signal, attributing to themselves qualities of compassion they believed they should have but which they could not access as a genuine feeling. This is altruism to avoid shame.[19] They were pressured into charity by a culture that expects them to do good. They were not as aggressive as the narcissistic philanthropists, but their motivation was to be included with their peers in doing 'something charitable'.[20]

Some were rich wives who carried out their charitable duties alongside Botox and attendance at the tennis club. They would whisper in my ear, 'Could we organise a lunch with a celebrity?' (Their favourite was Gwyneth Paltrow.) There was nothing sinister about them, but their lack of commitment made a slight toy of us. We had to fit in with holidays, facials and marital crises and could expect to be dropped at any moment. At the same time, I was grateful.

Isadora was typical. She would turn up at my office in the latest sunglasses; I could not see her eyes. She wore a navy blue blazer with gold buttons on the sleeves, and a black handbag held on her shoulder by a chunky chain of gold. After sitting down, she would begin. 'I love doing good. I want to do something. You are so marvellous, you are so marvellous. Tell me, tell me, what should I do? I can't bear it, I might cry. Tell me, what should I do?'

Then she would offer an idea that she would enjoy and wanted the kids to share. 'I could take them to Fortnum and Mason for tea.' I would come in gently with a counter idea, as I knew this volunteer was going to be inconsistent and I must not put her long-term with the children. I would say, 'Our kids don't have any towels. Do you think you and other mums could get them some towels?' This is where my mind would blow. They were prepared to take the kids to Fortnum and Mason, but the towels they handed over would be second-hand. I would explain that for poor children who have been degraded, a used item sadly signifies that they are not good enough to have a new one. I would add that I personally do not mind having second-hand things and many rich kids think old clothes are retro and fun, but our kids see it differently. Then I would tell her how to find towel manufacturers and encourage her to see if she and her friends could strike a deal, raise funds and buy the towels.

I never understood why the cost of towels agitated people who would drop a couple of thousand on a Fendi bag. But that is how it was, and I appreciated their kindness. Of course, these women were a sought-after group for the fashion brands, and we would set up an event at a particularly desired shop to give the retailer a chance to show their goods. You had to be creative to work out everybody's needs and generate alliances that served the children. These partnerships worked, but I despaired that I had to sit among pairs of stilettos to raise money for desperate kids. It felt wrong, and it deepened my fury towards the government for abandoning maltreated children.

The surprises came from the women in this group who became committed and passionate. Their husbands would start to worry about their repeated trips to the ghetto. We saw quite a lot of husband jealousy as the charity engaged their wives. I think of Mariella, an incredibly bright woman who was trapped in a challenging marriage. She had a natural talent for social care, with emotional responses of the highest quality. Her husband, one of the wealthiest men in London, wanted to shoot my shadow.

He seemed disgusted by the fact that I had to beg for money. Sometimes I wanted to shake him and say, 'A charity is different from a major financial institution. We survive by begging.' I told him once that if he was so clever, perhaps he could solve Kids Company's sustainability problem by giving me the model.

Every day, however, someone would surprise us with kindness and disprove the idea that behind every act of altruism lies a motive. 'Scratch an altruist and watch a hypocrite bleed,' wrote the biologist Michael Ghiselin. I held onto the knowledge that there is something intrinsically good in human beings that promotes generosity towards those in need. Over two decades, I saw transformational philanthropy by thousands of people who became absolutely bitten by the 'helping bug'. Kids Company was built on the goodwill of people to whom our children mattered. For our kids, the kindness of strangers was the first step to being embraced by a society they felt had banished them.

CHAPTER 7

LOVE IN ACTION

Love is the most important force in our lives. But what is it? Poets have tried for millennia to express the experience of attachment, or how it feels to have it denied. Rarely has there been an analysis of love in action, showing how to create it as a matter of policy and what it does to the body and brain.

When Kids Company made a commitment to help maltreated children heal through unrelenting love, we were not being sentimental. Our workers negotiated the daily challenges disturbed children hurled at them by being resolute and kind. Over the years, we came to understand how to help children acquire mastery over their traumas. Each needed something different to achieve stability and flourish. However, all were the same in needing our actions to be framed by a loving attitude. It took Kids Company two decades to understand what love looks like in action and to be confident that it can lead to recovery.

The biggest mistake made by service providers is to assume that traumatised children are the same and a single intervention will work for all. It will work in some cases, which can be identified in advance. It is a waste of resources to expect it to work for all. How to tell which is which? You have to explore the young person's background.

Some children benefit from an appointment-based provision. They can present themselves for help and make a success of what they receive. In social care, this can be a young person who turns up needing somewhere to live; in mental health, it might be a bereft child. Both young people, if they have a sound emotional structure as a result of high-quality care in early childhood, will use the help and benefit from it. The appointment-based, single-intervention delivery model works well with this group.

The second group turns up with exactly the same sort of problem, yet help proves ineffective. When they are given housing, they cannot sustain their home: living alone in a flat, where they cannot regulate their moods or organise themselves, leads to trouble and they lose their accommodation. If they turn up at the mental health provision for help with bereavement, they are likely to return with another kind of emotional distress because the internal architecture of wellbeing is missing.

The second group, of people who are developmentally traumatised, needs a service that has embedded in it a source of parenting to help regulate the individual. The young person in the flat on their own needs a phone call every day and regular visits, until they are strong enough and have internalised the care sufficiently to need less external help. Huge sums are wasted and vulnerable young people are left bereft because there is a mismatch between service model and client need.

Children who have had good-quality care from their parents, but who go on to be traumatised through misfortune, require a different recovery path from children suffering developmental trauma generated by lack of love, ruptures of attachment or abuse.

You might remember a French father and son outside the Bataclan theatre in Paris, where 129 people were killed by terrorists in November 2015. The father tries to soothe the fears of the little boy. In a television interview that went viral, the boy says that because of the 'bad guys' they will have to move house.

Father: 'Oh, don't worry. We don't need to change houses. France is our home.'

Boy: 'But there's bad guys, Daddy.'

Father: 'Yes, but there are bad guys everywhere.'

Boy: 'They have guns. They can shoot us because they're really, really mean, Daddy.'

Father: 'It's OK. They might have guns but we have flowers.'

Boy: 'But flowers don't do anything, they're for, they're for...'

Father: 'Of course they do. Look, everyone is putting flowers down. It's to fight against the guns.'

Boy: 'It's to protect? And the candles too?'

Father: 'It's to remember the people who have gone.'

Boy: 'The flowers and the candles are here to protect us.'

Father: 'Yes.'

Reporter: 'Do you feel better now?'

Boy: 'Yes, I feel better.'

When abuse is a one-off and the child is otherwise well cared for, trauma is considered to be 'type 1'. This means that a single bad event has taken place, but protective factors such as a loving family are present and the prognosis for recovery is good. The child may have frightening memories, but there is no dramatic assault on their view of themselves or their perception of the world. He maintains a sense of personal agency and there is less likelihood of developing low self-esteem.

If we look inside the brain, we find that as the child is not being chronically terrorised, the stress response is not sustained. The mind is allowed to calm down after the traumatic event, and biological changes leading to dysfunctions in brain activity are not activated. The disease process is not triggered because the individual on the whole feels secure. After a type-1 trauma, children adjust. They may come to believe that the shocking event is an exception and a sense of security the norm.[1]

Children who suffer type-2 trauma have a bigger challenge, as they have endured a number of episodes of terror. They divide into two groups: those who had robust care at home and those who did not.

Unsurprisingly, the first recover better than the second. They also gain more from counselling services and recovery programmes, as a history of good-enough attachments equips them to calm down and manage distress. The inadequately cared-for child, however, has a weaker self-soothing repertoire and is more at the mercy of trauma.

An example of a child suffering from type-2 trauma with good attachments is Lily-Ann. She was close to her mother, who developed cancer and died when Lily-Ann was thirteen. Her father abandoned the children at the hospital on the day the mother died, and we had to take them into our care in a hotel room until we could stabilise them and find them somewhere to live. Years later, the father attacked one of Lily-Ann's little brothers with a knife, putting him in hospital. We provided key workers and therapeutic counselling for her as and when she needed it. She went through several traumas, but made it to university before repaying society for its faith and investment in her through her career.

Similarly, Daniel Rye, a young Danish hostage freed by Islamic State, was able to articulate why 408 days of torture, beatings and starvation left him unchanged. His family had done more than raise a ransom. 'Rye still has nightmares about Syria, but they are rare,' *The Times* reported in August 2016, two years after the photographer's release. He had been left dangling for days at a time from a ceiling hook, wetting himself with fear.

> He puts his recovery down to a happy childhood and points out that he knew all along his family were made of something special. 'I knew I could do it, and I knew they could do it as well.' His life, he believes, is very much as it was before, his ambition to document suffering with his camera undimmed.[2]

Recovery is possible from the most extreme abuse if the emotional scaffolding is there. Even Natascha Kampusch, who was snatched off the street at the age of ten and hidden in a basement until she was eighteen, emerged with a calm maturity at odds with the world around her. Ten years after her escape from Wolfgang Přiklopil, she spoke of feeling that she had replaced one enemy with many, as internet users reacted to her peaceful demeanour by accusing her of being complicit in her kidnapping. Society needed 'supposed monsters' such as Přiklopil to give the evil inside us a face, Kampusch said. 'They need pictures of cellar dungeons in order not to see all the violence hidden behind a bourgeois front and all those well-tended façades and front gardens.' She simply wanted to live as normal a life as possible, reuniting with her family, making friends and finishing school, travelling and learning languages.[3]

A type-2 trauma without a history of attachment has a much more negative outcome, requiring more intensive interventions. Norina was from a chaotic traveller family. Her parental attachments were poor. They never stayed in one place for long, and Norina had nowhere to feel connected. As a teenager, she developed a drink and drug problem and, although highly intelligent, could not manage in school.

She self-harmed because she could not regulate her emotions, a result of not having had anyone to help her calm down. When she found work she could not sustain it and would leave within six months. She joined Kids Company just before we closed, as a nineteen-year-old who seemed closer in age to fourteen. We were unable to finish the work we started with her, which was to provide substitute attachments through a key worker, and complementary health therapy such as head massage and foot reflexology to help her learn to calm herself. After we shut, we heard that she had a psychiatric crisis and tried to kill herself. What she needs is a daily care structure around her so that her mind can develop better coping strategies.

Type-3 trauma is the worst, because it is chronic and unending. Even if positive attachments are available, the individual is overwhelmed. An example is child refugees from war zones. They may have witnessed atrocities, the loss of family income and status, the destruction of homes and the deaths of friends or relatives. When they come to new countries, they often experience further violation in the form of bullying or taunts. The child then internalises his or her status as a degraded individual who is worth less than non-refugee or non-black counterparts. Accepting this leads to low self-esteem as well as a state of sometimes extreme anxiety in which the child develops the idea that they could be annihilated. This is logical, as there is no reason why anyone should act to save a worthless individual, which is how the child feels.

The horrific nature of type-3 trauma can exact a lifelong price.[4] Even a caring background offers limited protection, because the empathy that comes from good care can stop a child adding to the burden of an already-traumatised parent. Such children often cease asking for help and may even stop speaking, especially if they do not know the language on arrival in another country. They become lonely while also traumatised.

Ali's ordeal started when the Taliban raped his seven-year-old sister in Afghanistan. They returned to torture his father while the children were in the house. Ali went to school one day and came back in the afternoon to find his family had disappeared. He was then trafficked by his uncle's friends to England and left at a railway station. The trafficker connected him to an Afghan, himself only eighteen years old. The eighteen-year-old took him into his own family home, where Ali was cared for. As a ten-year-old in a new school, he could not speak English, did not recognise the food and was teased quite mercilessly by the other children. Kids Company stepped in with a key worker, an education worker and therapeutic support.

Slowly, he improved. But in adolescence, as his brain structure changed – a normal part of teenage development, as we'll see in later chapters – he began having night terrors and flashbacks, including scenes linked to the abduction of his family, the torture of his father and the sight of his raped little sister bleeding as she walked into the house. The flashbacks hit his confidence. Assailed by annihilation anxiety, he became preoccupied with being a famous actor, having worked out that if you are famous, people want you close.

Children who are catastrophically overwhelmed by abuse lose their sense of power. They come to realise that the world is not predictable or safe. They may begin to mistrust adults, believing them to have malign intentions. Some experience constant anxiety, affecting their ability to focus. They struggle to retain, organise and reproduce information. Without the delusion of stability, human beings do not invest in long-term goals. All these difficulties are caused by disruptions of the electrical and chemical processes in the brain.

In wanting to deny the precariousness of human life, often victims of trauma blame themselves. It is more palatable to assume bad events are the result of rational behaviour, even if this is inaccurate, than to accept the fundamental lack of control in our lives against the power of chance. Children may have also had to do things during a traumatic encounter that are abhorrent, hurting others to survive or giving in to an assailant to lessen the violence. The active engagement in harm can create unbearable guilt.[5] All these problems last longer than they should, because often the child does not receive the right kind of help and support.

Much of the therapeutic work with traumatised children is about rekindling the desire to live and the will to achieve, despite the terror of unpredictability and the realisation of catastrophic vulnerability. On a physiological level, the child may be stuck, after being unable to complete the cycle of terror. Sheer fright may have blocked their capacity to fight back. As a result, children often need to complete a cycle of action, usually involving aggression that could not be delivered at the time to those who caused the shocking event. A child who loses his parents in war will have feelings of rage but nowhere to direct them, and at times the incomplete response to shock is turned inwards, onto the self. In the process, the child is simultaneously victim and perpetrator, with their own anger attacking their own vulnerability. Therapy with shocked individuals is about coming to terms with a fundamental ambivalence towards life and death.

Most of us survive with delusions of security that have not been ruptured by traumatic events. A child's sense of security was evident in an exchange between a three-year-old and her father. Her mother wanted red curtains; her father wanted brown and cream. To get his own way, he shouts, 'It's my house!' meaning that everyone should listen because he is in charge. The three-year-old promptly asks, 'Where is your house, Daddy?' as she thinks her father is referring to another house. She then goes on to say, 'This is my house,' referring to the family home. At this point the father is paralysed by the reminder that the residence belongs to all three of them. The little girl's confidence that she is entitled to the house is a sign of a child with a secure sense of the world. At three, she absolutely believes that the family home is her possession. The foundations of good care drive the psychology of this group of children towards life.

Well-cared-for children want to live because they know love and want more of it. They need help only to assimilate a traumatic event, complete the shock cycle by expressing anger externally as opposed to internally, and then restructure their philosophical approach to life to take account of human vulnerability.

We worked with children like this, from the relatively 'easy' group that responds most readily to help, mostly in our schools programme. We had teams in inner-city schools to support more than 7,000 young people a year with therapy and another 900 in group work. (More than 9,000 other young people were supported in our street-level centres.) We offered strategies for coping with psychological distress and used dance and art therapies to help shocked bodies complete the blocked physiological fight/flight cycle. With some children we found yoga helpful, if we could calm them enough to benefit.[6] Sometimes we used body therapies or acupuncture. Eye movement desensitisation and reprocessing (EMDR) could be highly effective despite its simplicity. Who would have thought a move of the therapist's finger in front of a patient's eye as they process memories or thoughts could work? It helped shift the trauma from a frozen state to a more processed one.[7] This technique did not work so well with the developmentally traumatised.

We also helped children articulate their experiences.[8] Very neglected children lose this ability.[9] Normally, children learn they have a degree of power over mind and body from their mothers. This is how they learn to manage feelings. When a baby cannot explain what it feels, the mother puts it into words. 'Are you hungry? Are you tired? I think you might need a nap ... We're not in a good mood today.' She names and defines the feelings.

Eventually the child will internalise the mother's commentary, with two results. First, she turns nebulous experience into named experience. Then she suggests actions to address the feeling and bring back a state of balance. To say, 'You're hungry, shall I get you something to eat?' gives the child a name for the feeling of hunger and the technique to relieve it. Parents do this for psychological experiences, too: 'You are scared of going to school because of being bullied. When you are bullied, you must tell the teacher so that she can help you.'

Neglected children often have a poor response to the weather. You can find them in T-shirts even when snow is falling. In part this is because they stop recognising bodily reactions such as feeling cold, but it is also because they do not know how to react, which is to wear a coat. These are things a parent helps to instil.

Unfortunately, most of the young people even in our schools programme had suffered extreme experiences. We did not provide therapy for children whose pet rabbits had died. For example, two teenage brothers who were very quiet came with a group of kids to our street-level centre. We did not know much about them and they did not talk. A few months later I received a call to say that one of the brothers had been knifed to death. His mother then contacted me to ask for help.

I walked into an ordered but dark house in Peckham as she waited for the police. No one knew why this boy had been killed and the worry was that the assailants were going to get his brother. Officers from Operation Trident, a police unit set up two years earlier to tackle gang violence and gun crime after a series of shootings in the London boroughs of Lambeth and Brent, arrived to speak to the mother and to help us establish some sort of security protocol. All the way through this, I kept noticing an eight-year-old boy in the house who did not utter a word. I thought he might be in shock and somewhat bewildered by the traffic of people in and out. After connecting up a panic button, the police left and we began talking about the funeral arrangements. I said goodbye to the eight-year-old and left the house feeling uneasy about his silence.

I next heard from the mother a few weeks later. She was upset and said she could not cope. The eight-year-old was starting fires. So we began seeing him therapeutically, in school. Much of the time was spent working through his grief and shock. He partly wanted his brother back but also felt jealous that his dead sibling was preoccupying his mother, while he had been banished. His fire setting was an attempt to express the aggression and also to reclaim her attention. Young children are astute and honest in their observations. He told his worker that he believed his mother would have preferred him to be dead, as opposed to his brother.

What he did not know is that this is exactly what his mother had told me. It is common in grieving parents who lose a child. Unconsciously, some strike a bargain with destiny. 'Bring back the child who has died and I'll give you another.' Yet his relationship with his mother was good. She was caring, and as a result he made good use of the therapy. We also supported his mum by providing her with massage and counselling, because she became suicidal herself. Sadly, the other teenage brother was shot several times and eventually had to leave the country.

At the lighter end of the spectrum, I remember a girl, not in formal therapy in our schools programme, who used our therapeutic arts. She recreated her bedroom in a shoebox. What she wanted to express was that her grandmother's tissue was still in the bin in her room. She did not want to remove it because the grandmother had died and this, for her, was a way of holding on to her.

These children, who have robust functioning of the prefrontal cortex, can calm their limbic systems when they are older because they have learnt to do that, biologically and psychologically, from a maternal carer.[10] The 'securely attached' child has a gift for life. Even if they experience overwhelming trauma, their chance of mastery over it is very good.

Unlike children who have emotional scaffolding already in place, the traumatised and developmentally deprived child needs more than therapy designed for shocking events. Turning up for an appointment with a mental health professional is not enough. Before they can use help, they need to feel cherished and loved.

Our developmentally traumatised children struggled with feeling obliterated. Their parents could not hold them in mind and they saw that society did not want them either. This is why loving them was so important. Children need to feel welcomed into the world. They need to claim an emotional and physical citizenship and it can only be done in a dyad, or pair relationship, where someone takes responsibility as an adult to meet the needs of the child.

Think of it like a jigsaw puzzle. At first the child expresses a lack of something, which is turned into a need for it. There is a gap, a missing piece, in the puzzle. Responding to the need, the maternal carer recognises the piece is missing. She shares the child's world view and produces the piece. As it fits into the puzzle, a transformation takes place: the child has the need met, but also comes to understand that they are important enough and powerful enough to 'articulate' a need and to command its satisfaction. This is what gives children a sense of existing. Jean-Paul Sartre believed that thought is the proof of existence:

My thought is me: that's why I can't stop. I exist because I think ... and I can't stop myself from thinking. At this very moment – it's frightful – if I exist, it is because I am horrified at existing. I am the one who pulls myself from the nothingness to which I aspire.[11]

In developmental trauma, however, the missing piece of the puzzle does not arrive. The child is left with an unmet need and her sense of agency, and hence identity, is also rendered vacuous. In being invisible to others, she becomes invisible to herself. Then distortions take place to survive. The child gives up wanting and starts meeting the needs of others instead. This is a compromise with existence. The child discerns that she will not be helped to survive if she expresses want, but will receive help if she is needed.[12] The thinking that proves our existence becomes twisted.

Telling the developmentally traumatised child 'I love you' does not work. They often do not know what you are talking about, as they have no experience of it. They may even feel angry because they do not believe the words, and if they have an inkling of what love feels like, they will be furious that the offer is from professional and not biological carers.

Just as the maltreated child may be suspicious of love, so are professionals. They are trained not to be personal or emotional. Quality is equated with objectivity, even if tenderness is allowed to sneak in under the professional label of 'unconditional positive regard'. This was a concept developed in the 1950s by the psychologist Carl Rogers, who believed each of us 'has within him or her self vast resources for self-understanding, for altering her or his self-concept, attitudes, and self-directed behaviour', and that these resources can be tapped if therapists accept clients as they are.[13]

Unfortunately, care for vulnerable children has produced more failure than success. In Britain, the law protected cattle, through the Cruel Treatment of Cattle Act 1822, before children. The first legal framework for young humans came sixty-seven years later, shortly before the dawn of the twentieth century, when it became a crime to harm a child. That year, 1889, an Act of Parliament commonly known as the

Children's Charter allowed police to arrest anyone found ill-treating a child. However, it seems as if disturbed children present in exactly the same way now as they did then, with institutions failing to manage the destitute in their care.

The Victorian social reformer Mary Carpenter (1807–77) tried to reflect back at society a catastrophic institutional failure in managing the needs of 'destitute and juvenile offenders'. Her recommendation for turning around the lives of 'moral orphans' was to love them. In her book, *Juvenile Delinquents: Their Condition and Treatment*, she produced a rigorous analysis of what was wrong with education and youth custody and suggested a rethink of care structures. If Carpenter looked at Britain today, she would probably marvel at the fact that the rotten situation has not changed much.[14]

Today's neuroscientists should marvel at her insight, and her daring, to recommend love as the potent ingredient of healing in 1853.

These are called, perhaps are, delinquents, not only perishing from lack of knowledge, from lack of parental care, of all that should surround childhood, but they are positively become dangerous. Dangerous to society ... such a condition is one of grievous moral disease. It needs a moral hospital and requires a treatment guided by the highest wisdom of those who learnt the art of healing from the physician of souls.[15]

Christian men and Christian women must become the fathers and mothers of these 'moral orphans'. They must restore them to the true condition of childhood, give them a home, open their souls to good and holy influence. If need be, correct them but with a loving severity.[16]

At Kids Company, we developed a menu for 'love in action'. Each key worker and each child under their care could choose from the therapeutic possibilities according to need. The first and most important course on the menu was to facilitate a sense of belonging. We realised very early on that our most traumatised children could not risk attaching to an adult. Instead, they sought connection to our buildings and their routine. We used to refer to this phenomenon as 'Mother Brick'.

Alessandra Lemma, Professor of Psychological Therapies at the Tavistock and Portman NHS Foundation Trust, confirmed the importance of our buildings and the routine we provided in them as the first step of generating trust.[17] She called it the 'hanging out' phase of children's engagement. Young people would drop in to the street-level centres during the day. They were warm and colourful environments with books, sofas, rugs, and fruit on the tables. Staff would greet them and have a chat if the young person wanted, or observe discreetly as they played basketball, chess, football and snooker, or simply slouched around and dangled their legs from the sofas. The difference is that most of the staff were therapeutically trained. Some were qualified psychotherapists; others had received in-house development programmes.

Each centre had set meal times, with some delivering four cooked meals a day: breakfast, lunch and two dinners, the first for younger children and a second for older ones. We did not hurry the kids, or push them onto a conveyor belt of appointments and educational attendance, because we realised that a disturbed child needs help to calm down before being ready to trust and engage. To an untrained eye, they looked as if they were not doing anything. In fact, the kids were engaged in a dance of therapeutic contact, establishing the first steps towards deeper trust and disclosure of painful narratives.

The casual banter between staff and kids began the scaffolding of care. It did not require a fifty-minute appointment in a consulting room, because the accumulation of five-minute chats was more effective with a young person at the mercy of inner and outer turbulence. We used to call it 'corridor therapy'. As kids trusted us, they went on to use more conventional psychotherapeutic interventions. But they could not use these services without checking us out through seemingly casual encounters.

At the heart of Kids Company's 'love in action' agenda was the facilitation of attachment. Our children and families suffered from ruptures in attachment or disturbed relationships with parents. In some cases, the child was profoundly hurt because there had been barely any love in their lives. As a therapeutic community, the staff functioned collectively in a re-parenting capacity. We had to be the parent the child needed while respecting biological carers as primary and unique. Sometimes we were re-parenting not only a child but also the child's parent, because that was what was needed. If we could strengthen a parent, helping them care for their child, this became the priority. If this was not possible, we did not shy away from the responsibility of being a substitute parent.

Break down a parent's job and the list seems endless. Children need nourishment, medical interventions, help with schooling, leisure activities, and guidance to interpret and manage the world around them. It is about noticing nuanced changes in the child and adjusting care. When a parent is 'good enough', a child thrives.[18]

The children who sought out Kids Company at its street-level centres were often devastatingly alone. The parent may have been physically present, but mentally they could not carry their children sufficiently in mind to make the constant adjustments in care that define good-enough parents. We blamed no one for failures in care, because when you peeled away the layers of history it was always evident that the failing parent was a failed child. Often the roles were reversed, with a child living with worry for a parent's wellbeing.

It wasn't easy. Even when they were with us, young people were exposed to, and generated, significant harm until they developed the capacity to think about the consequences of their actions and want better for themselves. As one young person put it, 'I was in a wave of crime, a wave of bullying, a wave of … a lot of things which really made me an unhappy person. It's the trauma I experienced as a young person and stuff that I saw which made me go into that stuff.'

• • •

In interviews after we closed, former gang members gave their per-spective to the *Sunday Times*.

'You can go to a place like Kids Company and tell them, look, I am selling drugs but I want to stop. Can you help me?' said Daniel Barnes, a former gang member who was among Kids Company's first clients. 'And they'll say, what do you need to help? What do you like doing? "OK – I like mechanics." And they'll try and find you a mechanic's course.'[19]

Sometimes it went deeper than that. 'Seven, eight years ago I said to Camila, look, I've been stabbed up. My friend got shot in the neck,' said Barnes, now twenty-seven. Batmanghelidjh called him to her office.

'I would never tell anyone the truth of the little gang war we had, but I told her. I said that he done this after we done this to him, and this is what happened. In our world that's called snitching. You wouldn't tell no one. But you trust Camila ... Where else could we go to do that? Probation just lock you up. They're full of shit. But Camila – not just Camila; it's the team around her. She's got excellent people. They care. That's the difference.'

'She's like a second mum to people, innit?' said Shubiah Linton, who went to Kids Company after being kicked out of school. 'Ba-sically it's been my mum [Batmanghelidjh] just telling me: "Stop doing this. You'll help your destiny." When you're young it just goes through one ear out the other.'

It took three spells in prison, the last for a firearms offence, before he was ready to listen. Then he was reluctant to see Batmanghelidjh because he was embarrassed. 'I'm just wasting her time; wasting her money, basically. And I thought: I don't really want to see no one. But my brother in law, he said, "No, don't be silly. Camila loves you. She always loves us."' When he went, he was amazed how the charity had grown. 'I said this has been the fruit, the seed of what Camila planted all them years ago. It's like a beautiful tree that has just grown. I want to be a fruit to come off this tree still. I don't want to be a failure.' He was planning a new venture with Kids Company, to combine football coaching with mentoring, when the charity closed.

To change people takes years, said another former gang member in south London, who had started selling drugs at school at thirteen. 'Look at me. I'm a prodigy of Kids Company. If you ask people about me, I'm one of the worst. I'm connected to the worstest people, yeah? I'm now a student and I'm a working man.'

CHAPTER 8

INNOCENCE

When Kids Company opened its doors in 1996, I had no idea it would take six years to understand the kids streaming in. Who were they? It was a time of discovery, spent piecing together the children's complexities and how to get the staff to manage them. The unqualified staff would have taken the kids around the corner and beaten them up if they could, because that is what had happened to them.

We employed local people, mostly male but including some tough women, because the neighbourhood and its children were so high-risk that I needed a bridge between the street and the organisation. If people came in with knives or kids lost it, the white, middle-class staff would rarely intervene: they froze. This changed, of course, when they became more experienced. But the workers from the community jumped in instinctively to pull the kids off each other. Some were amazing. Others were a nightmare to manage: they were late, lacked respect for rules and had a desire to match the children's violence. Often, they competed with the kids, wanting clothes and trainers because so many of them had been deprived when they were young. But they helped us understand the children and their backgrounds, and in time, with therapeutic training, they became our best workers.

Some of the professional staff, by contrast, arrived expecting to use sanctions to control the kids and thought their colleagues from the community were uneducated. They exulted when they could punish, and felt furious when the kids sarcastically usurped their power. The unqualified staff thought the professionals were useless as they could not handle ghettoised kids. Also in the mix were the tensions between black and white and Africans and Jamaicans. I hoped everyone would learn from each other, and I knew the diversity they brought into Kids Company would enrich it.

As a leader, I had to create a moral and clinical framework that rose above these divisions, with an egalitarian structure that allowed everyone to organise themselves. It meant being uncompromising about standards, and refusing to allow any of the games that can overwhelm voluntary agencies. Charities are prone to destructive staff dynamics because they are powered by emotional commitment. People feel passionate and personal about their work, and passions collide. As organisations evolve, they need structures that channel the personal and emotional more constructively. I first saw this in my twenties, when I worked for Family Service Units. This was a social work department in the voluntary sector that had contracts with Lambeth and Southwark councils. It did some really excellent work but at times it could be hijacked by dark politics. Our centre manager and chief social worker were at war, and we were often called to sit in circles as the latest consultant attempted to solve the unit's problems. Everyone had an opinion and no one took control. The place became so crazy that one of the workers came up one day to accuse me of stealing her house keys. Our paths had never crossed.

Even the buildings seemed miserable, so I decided to put together a team of volunteers to paint them. As we brightened each unit, using fifty volunteers at weekends, I got to know the politics of the other places. Like our unit, they barely mentioned the kids and the talk was often of their own dynamics. This was when I realised that a different leadership style would be required.

At Kids Company, I also had to negotiate the hierarchies among the children, with their gang affiliations and leaderships. We were at the heart of the inner city and exposed to all its cruelty and goodwill. The kids were run by adult criminals who had the power to kill us off or let us thrive.[1] If the drug dealers saw us as a threat, our lives were at risk. If we colluded with them to survive, we would fail morally and the children would not trust Kids Company.

There was no textbook to follow because our work was clinically new. No one took therapy to the street in this way. I could not go to senior clinicians for advice, as the rules that apply in a clinic are redundant with a knife-wielding group at the gate. I had no business or management training, either. I learnt how to run Kids Company by trial and error, supported by trustees and advisers, while listening to the kids.

An early bid to the National Lottery exposed a weakness. The bid was a hit and we were shortlisted for interview. As the lottery representative sat opposite me in the damp railway arch, with kids kicking and boxing the door because they wanted me to go out and spend time with them, he asked for a financial spreadsheet. I had no idea what he was talking about and we did not get the grant. I would have to master spreadsheets and accounts, a task complicated by my learning difficulties as I could not follow a horizontal line across the page. (I used an opaque ruler to help me stay in the right place.) A few years later, we secured our first grant from the Lottery. By then, I knew what a spreadsheet was!

Soon a pattern emerged, with the kids sitting on a blue bench outside my office. I found it fascinating that they did not push or shove, but waited. I would start at 9 a.m. and not see the last child until nine or ten at night. After that, my PA and I would put on gloves to start our administrative work, it was so freezing. We could see our breath at night in the damp arches, and papers were limp with absorbed moisture. There was a peculiar damp smell on our clothes and every item of furniture as well as on our papers. The arches had no daylight and the only way to get fresh air was to open the heavy doors.

The routine we created meant the kids started to settle. We gave them meals at consistent times and they were all assigned jobs, for which they earned points to spend when we took them shopping. As the day ended, each child would pick up a duster, broom or mop to help the staff. It felt a bit like a home, with the kids trying to cheat over their points and argue. Some set up sub-businesses, getting other kids to clean for them at a cut rate, and if we caught them the disappointment would not be expressed as a few insults. Usually some chair or object was hurled, and that is when you saw how different they were from normal kids. The head of children's services at Southwark, our local authority, paid a fleeting visit in the early days. I remember her racing from arch to arch, not obviously interested, and never saw her again. By the turn of the millennium, however, I realised that Southwark was resisting our presence.

It was the 2000 killing of Damilola Taylor, a ten-year-old boy in the borough, that roused public concern over so-called feral children. He bled to death in a stairwell after being surrounded on his way home from an after-school club and stabbed in the thigh with a broken bottle. The two brothers eventually convicted of his manslaughter were twelve and thirteen at the time.

Until that year, my relationship with Southwark was straightforward. I tried to engage the council to help our children. I started out full of hope, believing the local authority to be as committed to protecting the vulnerable as we were. In my naiveté, I thought they had failed to notice the kids who turned to us for help, and that our job was to get the children into their systems. We had two qualified social workers, Yvette and Tom, who were outstanding practitioners. They spent their time calling council social workers, trying to build a bridge for the children to cross, to get the help they needed. When the collaboration worked, it was beautiful. Everyone involved felt elated, as the children were safeguarded against harm. There were so many hardworking and really committed social workers in the local authority, but increasingly, we watched them get tired and leave. As the years went on, it became more and more difficult to get the kids the help they needed from local statutory services. I never foresaw that we would need to create our own social work and child mental health provisions to act as a safety net because the one available was struggling to cope.

A child who is thought to be at risk of neglect or physical, emotional or sexual abuse must be referred to social care departments by law. But the system often does not want to take them because it cannot cope, and here resides a tension. We are told to refer and as professionals we fail if we do not. But there is no capacity for the referrals. Practitioners can experience despair if referrals are not picked up; as no one enjoys despair, the effect is to discourage future referrals, artificially depressing the level of reported concern. It is a form of self-censorship as subtly the barriers are raised. Official statistics show that more than 57,000 children were identified as needing protection from abuse last year.[2] In 2013, the NSPCC estimated that for every child on a register or subject to a child protection plan, another eight were suffering abuse and neglect and were not getting the support they need. The charity says there is no reason to imagine the gap has closed.[3] If this is accurate, there are more than half a million children who need safeguarding, including more than 450,000 who are left to manage on their own, because they don't have a functioning parent in their lives.

The scale of unseen suffering is hard to take in. About 300,000 children have a parent who is a problem drug user. More than 700,000 are cared for by an alcoholic, and up to 3.5 million have lived with a parent who was a binge-drinker. More than 800,000 children have a physical or mental impairment. Nearly 1.8 million have witnessed adult domestic violence. More than 2 million live with an adult with a mental health problem.[4]

When parents abuse alcohol or drugs, children are at the mercy of an adult whose mood fluctuates. Spending on substances often means the child is deprived of necessities. Some parents come into contact with criminals to get what they need. Many of the children who attended our street-level centres reported being sexually abused by their parents' dealers or being recruited into drug dealing. Children feel ashamed of their parents' often erratic behaviour. It can lead to the child feeling unsafe and can erode self-esteem. In short, the child may be living with a biological carer, but in effect they are alone. At Kids Company we used to refer to these children as 'lone children', whose carers are unable to parent them adequately. There is often a role reversal, with the child responsible for a vulnerable parent's wellbeing.

Inside the local authorities, the workers are in trenches to protect themselves against overwhelming demand. They cannot possibly cope. Somehow they have to reduce the voraciousness of need, and one defence is called 'thresholds of intake'. If you are lucky, and your referral hits one of the unspoken thresholds, the case gets into the system. For example, 'hitting a child with an implement' might qualify for an assessment while battering a child by hand does not, as I discovered with a girl called Harper. She was being beaten by her mother and we kept referring the case to social services. Then the mum hit the girl in the street, relatively lightly, using her shoe. The case got in.

With her parents addicted to heroin, Harper was responsible for feeding her three younger siblings. Social workers held a thick file of reports from the public, including a sighting of her at the age of seven, carrying a baby under her arm and scavenging in bins for food. When Harper was nine, that baby as a three-year-old overdosed on her mother's methadone before recovering. When Harper was twelve, her father took her house breaking and got himself arrested and imprisoned. This left four children with a single, drug-addicted parent. We referred the family again to social services. Harper's mum forced her into prostitution to support her drug habit. Social workers still did not act to protect her. Harper and her friend, both twelve, were lured into a neighbour's flat with a promise of food, and raped. With four children going unfed, two addicted parents, the dad taking Harper on burglaries only to be caught and imprisoned, a three-year-old's accidental overdose and two raped children, it took the council years to make all the children in this house safe, and that is because we were relentless about advocating on their behalf.

Sometimes Harper would scream at us in exasperation that she had no food for her siblings; we called social services. And then, it is true, a social worker would inform her mum of a home visit, turning up to find the fridge and freezer full of food. What no one saw is that the mother had borrowed the contents of a neighbour's fridge as preparation for the 'initial assessment' that dictates whether further investigation is needed. Harper was told off for 'lying'.

As the social worker shut the door and left, not only was the twelve-year-old battered but she had to watch all the food being taken back to the neighbour, then go shoplifting for that night's dinner. After being hit on the arm with a shoe, however, she qualified for intervention. Harper's three siblings were taken into foster care and she was sent to a children's home.

Unfortunately, Harper's difficulties did not end there. In the children's home, the punishment for transgressions was loss of pocket money. Drug suppliers knew this, and would wait outside to take the kids dealing at King's Cross.

Today, Harper is in her late twenties. She breaks down and weeps like a child if she runs out of money. It is as if lack of cash in the ATM takes her back to the responsibility of feeding her siblings. She used to call us as a young adult, crumpled on the pavement and gasping for air, and I would remind her gently that she is not nine and does not have to feed her family, meaning that we could solve the problem together. She now hoards food to be at peace.

Harper has grown into an exceptional carer for the elderly. She is a community leader and always on the lookout to protect vulnerable children in her neighbourhood. Despite the challenges, she has had a profound love for both her parents. Every year, she hoped that they would pull through and go into recovery from their drug addiction. Her stepfather managed it, but her mother didn't. Harper had to nurse her through her dying days in hospital. She describes the pain of this complex love as being beyond words. The three-year-old who overdosed has a child of her own. She has done better, because she was accepted into care younger.

Southwark could not understand why all these disturbed kids were making their way to Kids Company. Our practice of giving children training shoes, which drew a lot of attention when the charity closed in 2015, was a potent symbol even then. Since we bought shoes for kids who were shoeless, or whose shoes were falling apart, alongside our social work and mental health interventions, we were accused of bribing them to use us. That is how the youth offending teams in Southwark and Lambeth saw it, as well as individual workers in social services and some charities. Statutory agencies perceived the kids who chose to come to us as materialistic beings reacting to a source of freebies. In this stereotype was a denial of their real material and emotional needs. Soon there was extraordinary hostility from the council.

The animosity was compounded by the fact that we kept referring children at risk to the local authority, as we had to. I remember writing to the director of children's services at Southwark about the welfare of two boys, not yet in their teens, who were not safe at home because of family violence. They killed Damilola Taylor.

Then there was the twelve-year-old caught with rocks of crack cocaine while riding his bicycle, and a sexually abused thirteen-year-old being monitored by Southwark's youth offending team. The latter had not been to school for two years, despite the council's duty to educate him. I feared he was dangerous and raised the alarm with the head of children's services. A few weeks later, the child battered a man he believed was a paedophile, leaving the victim needing life support.

The youth offending team was not to blame. It looked after some of the most disturbed kids in the borough, but could not refer them for help with housing, mental health services or education because its partner agencies could not meet demand. I felt as if I had no power to challenge the local authority either. Despite the organisational challenges, both Southwark and Lambeth youth offending teams were using Kids Company to deal with some of the highest-risk cases, especially the children and young people they were too frightened to work with, who would assault their staff. This dynamic changed when the police arrived on the scene.

Detectives investigating the death of Damilola had been given the names of 200 kids. If they interviewed a child, others would be mentioned. Now they faced the challenge of deciphering the street names. Who were Titch, Ryder, Revolver, Rascal, Blinder? Just to add spice, there could be several Ryders and Titches. The officers arrived at the arches and realised that for the past four years we had been trying to get most of the vulnerable kids on their list picked up by social services, including the two brothers who were later convicted.

The media depicted me as the enemy of Damilola's father. In the dichotomy it created, I looked after murderous kids and Richard Taylor had lost a child to their violence. What no one knew is that Richard and I were meeting weekly as he tried to come to terms with the loss of his beautiful son. To comprehend Damilola's tragedy, he wanted to understand the tragedies of the disturbed and abandoned kids who were so dangerous to each other. The word was that Damilola had been attacked because the children wanted his jacket.

The killing was the first time I saw central and local government called to account. They had to explain who these children were and why the country knew nothing about them. For a while, there was a chance to consider whether the system was working, and to identify why local authorities could not cope. Instead, a fairy tale was generated. Damilola was the innocent, beautiful child of committed parents and his life had been taken by animals. I was struck by the wild-animal imagery, with kids being described as savage and feral, as packs of wolves.

The hostility towards Kids Company grew intense, and I believe Southwark engineered our eviction from the railway arches in 2003. In a period lasting mere days, a series of inspectors turned up. We were investigated for food hygiene, fire risks and health and safety compliance. HMRC paid a visit after being told, wrongly, that we employed illegal immigrants. Southwark's planning department arrived, six years after we had set up, to announce that it had come to their attention that we did not have the right planning permission.

All the inspectors who were independent of the council told us they had received anonymous calls. They could see the allegations were malicious, and we passed every inspection except one. We had not realised, when we rented the arches from Railtrack, that we needed a different kind of planning permission, and that is what Southwark used to get Kids Company out of the borough. Even the judge at the eviction hearing apologised.

Of course, it is possible that the descent of the inspectors was the work of unhappy residents, not the council. At the time, Southwark was promising to do 'everything in its power' to remove us after our neighbours on the Grosvenor estate complained of assaults and verbal abuse. But I believe the real agitators lay inside the council, and the underlying reason was our refusal to be quiet about the children's level of need.

David Blunkett, the Home Secretary at the time, was suspicious and sent Nick Pearce, his special adviser, to investigate. Sure enough, Nick reported back his perception that the local authority was making trouble for Kids Company. Blunkett asked Louise Casey, who ran the anti-social behaviour unit in the Home Office, to intervene. She organised a review of Kids Company by Crime Concern, which was led by Michael Hastings. The review concluded:

> Kids Company is pioneering a radically new approach to tackling social inclusion. The model is so powerful in its central philosophy and practice that the view could be taken that it merits more than a mention in the annals of social care. Kids Company's core philosophy has much to teach other initiatives and its experience has wider implications for the design and delivery of children's services. In an ideal world, every neighbourhood should have a Kids Company.

A consultancy firm, Cordis Bright, also reached positive conclusions when asked by the Home Office to evaluate us and they helped set up our system of accountability for the living allowances that we were giving to the kids at the time. So, as far back as 2002 and for some thirteen years, government and ministers as well as civil servants knew we gave the kids money and understood why we had to do it. In fact, I was told it inspired the creation of the Education Maintenance Allowance – the £30 a week given to students who were in education and came from poor backgrounds.

As we were facing eviction from the railway arches, we could not raise funds from philanthropists or charitable trusts. I tried really hard to fight when Southwark was saying the children's voices from 3 p.m. to 7 p.m. four afternoons a week were too loud for the neighbours. I brought in a sound measuring specialist to capture the volume of sound created by the trains which went past our premises. It was evident that the volume of sound created by the trains was higher, but Southwark claimed that the one created by the children was more irritating.

The local authority claimed it was showing us alternative sites, but offered us none. At this point the charity nearly closed because so much insecurity had been generated as a result of our funders not knowing whether we would have any premises. However, the government came up with grants of £383,000, HMRC agreed to write off a debt of £590,000 and a philanthropist put in funds. Neil Morrissey, an actor who had grown up in children's homes, stepped in with ITV, locating a building for us, which a construction company, now called ISG, renovated. Without their intervention, the children would have had nowhere to go.

You will have to take it on trust, then, when I say that the fictitious local authority I introduce later in this chapter is not Southwark. My intention is not to blame local authorities, as I recognise that they are grappling with demand outweighing resources and that includes Southwark. However, I will say that Southwark has failed consistently to tell the truth about its relationship with Kids Company. I attribute this to defences against overwhelming demand. Lambeth tells the truth about how much it is struggling to meet children's needs; they are left to fail.

From the day we opened until we closed, most of Kids Company's difficulties were caused by our self-referring model. Children would tell other children about us, and those who were hungry or abused would make their way to our premises. After our arrival in Lambeth we had thirty or more self-referrals a week at just one centre. A few came from outside the capital, arriving from as far as Devon, Birmingham, Nottingham and Manchester, but they were exceptions. Most were from inner London. Every child received an immediate, brief assessment. As many were child protection or 'child in need' cases for which local authorities were responsible, we had to refer them to social services.

Our referrals and advocacy caused problems for social work and child mental health departments, which often stay within budget by limiting the number of children they let through the doors. When we looked at the figures kept by the Office for National Statistics, we were startled to see that for a decade, until the Baby P scandal in 2008, local authorities assessed a consistent number of vulnerable children each year, with a set proportion ending up on child protection plans. How could this be? The answer is simple: gate-keeping. I began wondering whether some areas coped with high demand by measuring children's needs according to their capacity to deal with them. The problem is systemic.[5]

Collectively, however, caring workers in social services and mental health come to normalise evil, because they see the dysfunction of their agencies as inevitable. They often end up, as a result of extreme emotional exhaustion, objectifying almost as 'things' the children and families they work with. This is because they perceive them as demanding too much. The objectification of the vulnerable is often collectively justified by platitudes such as 'there's no money', 'they don't have a need', 'their families are conning it', 'this is the way it is' and 'nothing can be done'. Of course, there are powerful dynamics at play, such as who has the power to make the right decisions. Social workers would argue it's their managers, who in turn would describe the government as having tied their hands by not providing enough resources. There's professional collusion so that there can be personal survival.

Some will object to my use of the word 'evil'. I should emphasise that we came across dedicated and spiritually beautiful people in children's social work and mental health who wanted the very best for the families who turned to them and felt equally frustrated by the system. However, I perceive evil to be the causing of significant harm to others by people who have the power to help, and it is a fact that the social care and mental health structures of which they were a part failed vulnerable clients with a depressing consistency.

In 2016, Ofsted reported that three-quarters of local authorities' child protection services are inadequate or require improvement to be good, meaning that millions of children live in places where those entrusted by the state to keep them safe do not act appropriately to protect and look after them.[6] 'Once children are in the care system, they are often well cared for,' the report noted.[7] 'It is children who have not entered the system because their needs have not been recognised, or whose support has been too superficial and ineffective, who need our attention.'[8] This is a catastrophic national failing and it is not about money. The report found that being judged 'inadequate' by Ofsted is not related to size or to levels of deprivation or funding. The quality of local leadership is the most important factor in the help, care and protection given to children. A separate review of local safeguarding children boards (LSCBs, which ensure that children are being properly protected), found a 'widely held view' that they were 'not sufficiently effective' and in need of 'fundamental reform'.[9] This means that the people who are supposed to hold heads of children's services accountable are unable to do so.

It is worse than it looks. We had cases where children were taken into care, then placed in absurdly inappropriate settings. One mother, a sex worker and class-A drug addict, lived in a damp, boarded-up council house. Two of her older children had been taken away and we managed to get two more accepted into care, including a fifteen-year-old girl, leaving four younger children in the house. When the fifteen-year-old became pregnant and suffered domestic abuse, social workers took

127

away her baby and placed it with her mother, the infant's grandmother, even though she and three siblings had been removed from the same place. Kids Company continuously objected to this placement. When the baby was three years old, I was so concerned about his wellbeing that I rang the head of children's services. A few days later he wandered off from the house and ended up with the police, who did not know who he was because no one reported him missing. When they made a correct guess and called into the house, they found all the children aged nine and under at home alone.

Another local authority also placed a highly disturbed, sexually abused fifteen-year-old involved with drugs and prostitution from outside the family in this household, paying the mother £50 per week without even a social worker's visit. This meant that a social work department was paying a drug-addicted mother, whose own older children had been taken into care, money to look after a child who had been taken into care because of their extreme needs. Local authorities do this to save money on foster care, and the practice is not restricted to only one council. We also saw it in our schools programme. We would discover kids living with all sorts of dodgy people, classed by social services as 'friends and family'. Of course, it is desirable for a child to be kept within the neighbourhood with people they know, but not at the expense of their safety.

We pleaded over nearly two decades for the problems in this house to be addressed. The children were hungry and unkempt. The mother rented one of the rooms to a local drug dealer. Users were going in and out. There was sexual abuse. All we wanted was a sample hair test, revealing the mother's history of drug use. To this day, they have not done it. The children would steal, take drugs, torment the public on public transport. They wept when their thirteen-year-old friend was raped in a graveyard by a stranger they met on the beach in Brighton. He gave them all sweets afterwards; that is how cheap their lives had become.

Although I am pointing out the structural challenges, my intention is not to criticise social workers and their managers. They are all trapped in a complex whirlpool of dysfunction, rendering not only the children but also the workers as survivors.

Research commissioned and funded by Community Care as part of their campaign 'Stand Up for Social Work' engaged the school of social work at Queen's University, Belfast to carry out a review of social workers' level of burnout.[10] This survey demonstrated that 91 per cent of the social workers suffered from emotional exhaustion, while 61 per cent suffered from depersonalisation, which generated in them a lack of feeling and an uncaring response to service recipients. Burnout syndrome involves emotional exhaustion, disassociation which can manifest as cynicism and lack of satisfaction with personal accomplishment.

Imagine having one of these disassociated and exhausted workers making a decision about whether a child should receive a child protection assessment. However much we may wish it, these decisions are not objective: they are about workers using their feelings to drive their judgements. If you cannot feel, the decision-making process becomes flawed.

When social workers face overwhelming circumstances they cannot make better, an emotional immunity can develop. There is a shutting down of the capacity to feel, because the pain of seeing children harmed becomes unbearable. When social workers fail to respond in places such as Rochdale and Rotherham, where girls subjected to organised abuse were described by some as making 'lifestyle choices', this can be why. Overfamiliarity with abuse turns harmful behaviours into normal ones so that they become tolerable and reduce the social worker's emotional disturbance at being unable to deal with them.

A range of other institutional dynamics conspire to make circumstances more complicated. Sharon Shoesmith was in charge of children's services at Haringey Council when baby Peter Connelly was murdered in 2008.[11] This is a toddler who had a broken back, gashes to his head, a fractured shin bone, a ripped ear, blackened fingers and toes with a missing fingernail, skin torn from his nose and mouth, cuts on the neck and a tooth knocked out.[12]

The politicians avoided responsibility and conspired to put all the blame on Sharon Shoesmith. To make her and her department seem dysfunctional, reports which had previously described children's services in the borough as 'good' were massaged into presenting her and the department as failing. She was sacked, but a court of appeal in 2011 described her sacking as 'unfair scapegoating' and awarded her significant compensation.

Sharon wondered why the police and Great Ormond Street children's hospital, who had also dealt with baby Peter's case, were neither scapegoated nor held accountable. Shoesmith suggested that their 'cover-up machinery' was more sophisticated. She might be right; one of the doctors involved in the case, who also volunteered at Kids Company, courageously fought for Great Ormond Street to acknowledge their role in failing to safeguard Peter Connelly.

Sharon Shoesmith believed that the police released into the public domain pictures of how baby Peter had been harmed. She attributed this to the police's desire to deflect from their failure to safeguard him. However, I think an additional dynamic may have provoked their actions. Often in local authorities, health services and the police blame social services for failing to reduce their burden. This sort of professional infighting makes collaborative work challenging and scapegoating easy.

In any event, 'blaming' any agency for the death of a child doesn't get anyone anywhere, unless there is evidence that they did it wilfully. Society is unwilling to accept that parents can harm their kids. It becomes emotionally more manageable to blame workers.

Sharon was subjected to a national witch hunt which she described as the nation's 'guilty pleasure'. She wouldn't stand near the edge of a train platform for fear that a member of the public would push her under a moving train.

She remarked, 'If I'm seen as courageous for speaking up, it is only because it is contingent upon what happened to me and my colleagues. Had I not been so directly involved, the likelihood is, that I, too, would have remained silent.'

She continued, 'The task is to cease to allow the profession to be cast as the "lame duck" or "the psychic retreat" for society's lack of courage.'[13] Sharon had the courage not to placate the nation by apologising for a failure which ultimately was beyond her control, and set in the context of profound political failings. In the meantime, David Cameron and other politicians were vehemently advocating for social workers to be prosecuted when a child in their care died. This led to social workers generating a petition because they felt that with the threat of prosecution the focus of the workers would be on saving themselves rather than the children who needed their protection.[14] It was noticeable that the politicians didn't identify any sanctions for themselves as they continuously fail to provide adequate resources for social workers to do their job properly. Sharon Shoesmith was tried and condemned in the court of public opinion, with politicians facilitating her scapegoating, and the country was never given a chance to scrutinise the real problem. Why does Britain continuously fail to prioritise the welfare of vulnerable children?

In England, one child a week is a victim of family homicide and has been for over forty years. Between Victoria Climbié and Peter Connelly, both of whom were murdered by their carers, 400 other children were killed, but we never got to hear about them.[15]

In the 1930s, the NSPCC stopped publishing information about children's deaths in Britain, in an attempt to build trust in the social work profession. The government, to date, has colluded, by not holding this information in one place.

The coalition government nearly made it worse still. In 2011, I learnt that Tim Loughton, the children's minister, was planning to take away the 45-day time limit on child protection assessments. He dressed this up as a bonfire of bureaucracy to 'put vulnerable children first' by giving social workers flexibility after Professor Eileen Munro, in an influential review, said the child protection system was rigid, dependent on central prescription and overly focused on compliance. His plan was to replace national timescales with an approach 'focused on the needs of each child'.

It sounded laudable, but Loughton wanted to act without consulting the children's sector – and I saw trouble. If we used the law to challenge a local authority for failing to protect a child, in future the council could frustrate the challenge by claiming that the child's assessment was still in progress. Abolishing time limits would create an informal queue, just as delaying tactics had been introduced into the process for obtaining a statement of special educational needs.

I suggested to Loughton on the phone that he must consult the sector. He wanted to press ahead without delay, so we issued a pre-action legal letter that put a stop to his plan. Of course, this infuriated him. I was told by one of his civil servants that he was livid, and at a conference in the north of England he walked up to one of our workers.

'Are you from Kids Company?' Loughton asked David van Eeghen. 'Could you ask Camila to stop taking my department to judicial review? Because it's slowing everything down and wasting time.' Van Eeghen was taken aback. Why did the minister not write to his CEO, instead of passing a message informally? He had yet to learn that in politics the most important communications are rarely written down. 'If you expect Camila to stop defending the rights of the young people she represents, you're wasting your time,' he replied. 'But I will certainly ask.'

In September 2012, Loughton was sacked in David Cameron's first reshuffle. I had told the Prime Minister from the outset that Loughton was weak. When the charity ran into trouble three years later, he was one of the first politicians to the microphones. He claimed to have had 'serious concerns' as a minister about Kids Company, but had felt forced to approve its funding applications for fear of the 'uncomfortable press coverage' he feared I could generate with my 'veiled threats' and 'bullying attitude'. Only now, in 2015, did this government protector of children feel safe to speak out. Not only had he not shared any concerns with me, quite the reverse – he would often refer to Kids Company as an example of good practice.

To illustrate the challenges faced by local authorities, I am going to create for you a fictitious borough. It is called 'Lupton'. The facts are real and based on existing inner London local authorities.

Children's social care in Lupton has been given £60 million per annum, allowing 1,500 children to receive some kind of support. The sum must cover children in foster care and children's homes – the UK has more than 90,000 children in care, including 500 in Lupton – and those with disabilities, for whom spending can be estimated in advance. What cannot be predicted is the number of children referred to social services by other agencies and worried members of the public, or how complex their needs will turn out to be. This is a lottery, and so the first gate appears.

The overstretched local authority on the receiving end of a telephone referral will do everything they can not to take the case, once they realise that their resources are depleted. But they must not behave illegally. Some of the excuses the social work departments come up with are jaw-dropping. I remember a sixteen-year-old who disclosed that her father was stripping her naked and beating her with a belt. When the school and I referred her to social services, the initial assessment resulted in the social worker concluding that the father was using 'culturally appropriate sanctions'. The girl ended up running away to keep herself safe because the local child protection department failed her.

It can be a risk to make referrals. There could be reprisals from furious family members or action to silence the child. We noticed that social workers, wanting to align themselves with the family and minimise the threat of violence, often put the blame on the referring agency. They would tell the family who had made the referral, sometimes colluding with the family to make the referral seem unnecessary as a way of getting it off the books and the case closed. There are so many subtle dynamics in this process, with everyone worrying about their position in it.

So, our social work managers in Lupton try to keep the number of assessments to a minimum. A full assessment usually takes forty-five days, although frequent interruptions for emergencies can prolong the process. Of course, every social work department is sincere in trying to reduce the risks facing children. Risk is a relative concept, however. In challenging environments, the definition changes, because professionals and families become too familiar with high levels of harm. A household with a crack-addicted mother generating chaos for the children will be seen as high risk in a wealthy borough, but will go to the middle of the risk pile in a challenged one. The 'evil' this chapter describes is subtle.

Added to this picture is the need for social workers to keep some optimism in a bleak landscape. If parents lie to them about positive changes, some social workers can be so grateful for 'evidence' of results that they minimise their levels of suspicion and can end up unwittingly colluding.

Another level of gate-keeping comes next, which is to make what I call a 'silly billy referral'. This is when they send (for example) an extremely unwell young boy to a football club run by a charity and it is described as an 'intervention' that means the case can close. They know it is not enough, but the case has gone through the social care conveyor belt and the professionals can say it is 'being looked into and dealt with'. The lack of meaningful intervention will eventually cost Lupton a great deal more as well as generating harm for the child and those around them.

This leaves the most extreme cases, which end up with a child protection plan. Lupton's managers don't want too many of these, as the escape routes are minimal and the costs are high. Any child with a plan has to be monitored carefully with visits and reviews. Even in this situation, we would have a nine-year-old with six changes of social worker in a year. By the third, he has lost hope and will not communicate. For many children, Kids Company workers were the constant in their lives. Often we would brief the new social worker and help them establish a working relationship.

At times, overworked social workers would ask us to do their jobs. At 4 a.m. on Christmas Day, two children, aged eleven and nine, were taken into care as emergencies. Their father had walked out on them as their mother had years before. The Kids Company worker sat with them in the town hall and then in the cab (as there were no trains) to meet the bleary-eyed Kent foster carer who had been dragged out of bed to receive them. In the car, it was about consoling, preparing, distracting, promising we would not abandon them, then getting on the phone after leaving them to prove we had not disappeared. When one of the children eventually ran away, he made his way to Kids Company.

Here is another corporate madness: in the local authorities we worked with, there was only one social worker on duty after 5.30 p.m. and at weekends. This individual was responsible for dealing with all the phone calls and emergency assessments. That is why you find vulnerable children dangling their legs over metal seats at police stations waiting for a social worker to come and decide their fate. There are no toys, no books and no carers as desperate people queue up to report crimes and handcuffed suspects being taken in and out. The brutality, thoughtlessness and compromising of children's rights to dignity when they are distressed is very sad. They are too young to create pressure groups, so no one hears their voice. All it needs is a friendly emergency house in a local authority, or shared with neighbouring authorities, to receive children. Why don't they do it? No one thinks about it from the child's perspective.

Social workers in local authorities who were exasperated with their managers would tell the kids on the quiet to make their way to Kids Company, as they knew we would help them and argue on their behalf. We had a similar experience with mental health teams, who would tell families they could not treat a child but add that we could help. We have so many letters and emails evidencing this, yet none of the clinicians spoke up in 2015 to admit that they sent children to us, respecting our practice enough to do so. I have been told over and over that everything would have been solved if we had stopped helping kids directly and signposted them to statutory services. In fact, they were marching them back down the road to us!

Yet, when Lupton social workers call a child protection review meeting to make a decision about the child's welfare, professionals experience covert pressure to save money by removing children from protection plans. It becomes a game of snakes and ladders. The child comes off the plan, often prematurely, and reappears on a new plan within a year. Nationally, nearly a fifth go back onto child protection plans after being removed too soon.[16] This is just part of the background to the recent estimate we saw earlier by the NSPCC that 'for every child subject to a child protection plan or register, another eight children have suffered maltreatment'.[17]

Kids Company knew the law and would find children a solicitor if Lupton refused to intervene and we were unable to address the need ourselves. For example, it was illegal for us to house people aged under sixteen, even for a night. But Lupton would leave twelve-year-olds with nowhere to go, giving us no choice but to involve lawyers.

One young teenager was battered by her father. He got her on the bathroom floor and hammered his foot into her face, leaving her cheeks imprinted with the ridge of his shoes. Her mother stood at the door of the bathroom egging him on. For the girl, this was the final, intolerable act of betrayal after years of abuse. Her father was a known criminal with access to firearms. She eventually ran away. We tried to get social services to take her case, but they refused. Initially we managed to get a couple of nights in the only children's refuge in the country, which had a few beds.

But the refuge could not keep her because the local authority refused to pay. The child was homeless, with nowhere to sleep. She needed to be fostered or taken into a children's home, as she had no alternative provision. We went to judicial review to challenge the local authority's decision not to provide care for the child and the judge placed her temporarily in our care, in a local hotel, and ordered social services to carry out an assessment. When the investigation of her circumstances was brought to court, the judge asked me to identify a suitable provision for the girl and ordered social services to pay. We found a therapeutic private children's home. For the first time, she was happy.

After a minor altercation at the children's home, however, the local authority paid a visit and told the owner that she had to use this incident to ban the child from the house. When the proprietor of the children's home refused, the council threatened to end a contract, putting her business at risk. She had no choice but to ask the child to leave.

As it happens, we had a Conservative MP with us on two weeks' work experience. He is now a Cabinet minister. I took him to meet the children's home proprietor, as I wanted him to see how dysfunctional the system could be and how, if children's services were privatised and run on a commissioning basis, local authorities would exercise control by withdrawing contracts unfairly if care providers stood up for children. We also saw private children's homes exclude disturbed young people as unprofitable because they needed a costly ratio of staff to care for them. The privatisation of care for the vulnerable is a risky construct unless independent checks and balances are put in place.

In twenty years – twenty because we carried on even after we closed – every case in which we challenged local authorities and housing providers was either won in court or settled in favour of the children without a full hearing. We functioned like pushy, middle-class, additional parents on behalf of our children. I calculated that we spent £1 million a year to police the care failures of local authorities.

To be effective, we had to train our workers to be brave but calm at council offices. We taught them to handle what I called 'the vanilla moment', which is when everyone in a child protection meeting knows privately that a child should not be taken off a protection plan but no one says so for fear of becoming an outsider. Seeking a higher standard than the group's unspoken consensus can make colleagues who stay silent feel ashamed.

Our role, whenever a Kids Company worker turned up at a Lupton meeting, was to be blamed. From the moment the meeting began, there would be a collective drive to minimise the power of Kids Company for fear that we would upset the status quo. It was hard for our workers, because they went to meetings knowing they were likely to be cut down with sarcasm. It took discipline and courage not to lose sight of the child and to advocate calmly on their behalf.

People will distort themselves into any shape to avoid ejection from the group. What happens eventually is that you create a rupture in yourself, separating you from your own goodness. People shun personal and professional fulfilment for the sake of the vanilla moment, which is a delusion of connectedness. Even the children contributed to this, by trying to play one agency off against another. Some would complain to us about their social workers. Some told social workers Kids Company was dysfunctional. No doubt some did both. It was not unusual to hear children saying, 'Social services hate you.' We formed our own opinions and tried to keep good working relationships.

At Kids Company, in order to protect our workers against burnout and emotional coldness, we provided them with a weekly one-to-one therapeutic supervision. This was separate from their line management supervision. I felt this was really important because the supervisors were predominantly experienced psychotherapists, who met with the workers to ensure primarily their wellbeing and to explore with them the impact their own emotional challenges may be having on the work they did. I used to call it 'thera-vision': providing therapeutic support for the worker while keeping an eye on their approach to their cases.

To double check for burnout we would carry independent reviews of workers' wellbeing, especially those who were at the street level centres. We would make necessary adjustments to help restore resilience. This included changing our workers' jobs and removing them from frontline work to enable them to recuperate. In addition to annual statutory holiday allowance, we would give our workers extra days off which amounted to approximately fifty days a year.

At times, conflict arose because of how different our model was from social services. This was crystallised by David Quirke-Thornton, the strategic director of children and adult's services in Southwark, when he told the local safeguarding board:

Operating models in children's services purposefully seek to achieve a safe distance between vulnerable children and young people and adults … A model of 'surrogate family' for children and young people living with their families runs the risk of confusing children and young people, disempowering parents and inconsistency of approach … The model of 'surrogate family' rather ignores the fact that most of the children and young people that Kids Company worked with have a family.[18]

Just because children are living with families – and many Kids Company clients were not – it does not mean they are being parented appropriately or at all. We never saw a child who was confused. We saw them grieve and be angry because they wanted the care we gave them from their families and recognised, as we had, that it was not possible.

We never sought to replace children's biological carers, as that relationship was sacred. But there was no reason we could not function as an additional parenting resource in these children's lives. In fact, we often also parented the children's parents to strengthen them in their ability to care for their children. Our infant psychotherapy programme was popular, offering parents support with their babies to halt the cycle of harm.

For us, the excessive distance created between social services and vulnerable children may help to explain many chronic failures of care with more complex families. Lupton's logic, meanwhile, is captured by Quirke-Thornton, a man who specialises in delivering emotional messages about a parallel provider as if they were neutral, professional judgements:

The ethics of practice within Kids Company appears to me to have been compromised by a cult of personality; a wilful blindness to the consequences and impact of their model on children, young people and their families; and a lack of acceptance by the leadership of the organisation of their accessorial liability.[19]

These comments came from a man who never visited Kids Company until the week we closed, when I met him for three minutes.

The day after the charity closed, four solicitors and barristers wrote to *The Guardian*. Under the headline 'Kids Company's demise speaks volumes about how Britain is run', they wrote:

> As lawyers we have represented hundreds of children denied their basic rights to a safe and loving home. Despite the legal obligations that require local authorities to prevent child neglect and abuse, children's voices are ignored. The young people we represent are abandoned without food or shelter and sometimes turn to crime and gangs to meet their needs. Justifying inaction, authorities disbelieve these children and accuse them of 'not engaging with services'. The Children Act 1989 expresses the will of society that these conditions should be prevented and authorities should intervene to protect children. Despite this, local authorities ignore the law.
>
> Over many years, Kids Company has brought hundreds of extremely vulnerable children to our offices and the courts to fight for their basic rights. Many children have long histories of abuse recorded by social workers who appear inert, merely witnessing the distress and trauma. The authorities routinely blame the downtrodden child to save money and reveal a lack of appreciation that their lives are a consequence of the harm that they have suffered. The closure of Kids Company means thousands of children will be denied access to justice. These are the children who local authorities appear unable or unwilling to support and who it is now said will provide the support now that Kids Company is closed. This is pure fantasy.
> – Chris Callender *Steel & Shamash*, Oliver Studdert *Simpson Millar*, Ian Wise QC, Caoilfhionn Gallagher *Barrister, Doughty Street Chambers*

In 2007, William was two years old. His two older step-siblings were bringing him to Kids Company. We were already worried about the older children as they smelt and were neglected. It was clear their grandmother was struggling to care for them. We referred William to social services for extreme neglect, bruising, developmental delay, possible failure to thrive, and emotional abuse. I remember him clearly. He was pale, lethargic and rarely smiled. He was insatiably hungry and thirsty and his clothes were always soiled. The only time we managed to get a little grin was when we read him a book and did some art with him. For two years, we tried to have his case picked up and this child protected.

Eventually William was taken to hospital. By now he was four, and the doctor identified thirty-six injuries, plus malnourishment. He was kept in hospital for a week before being moved into care. We had referred this child, and his siblings, over and over again. We could not take any of the children into care ourselves because only social services can do that. To this day, I feel those two years were two too many for this little boy to endure that level of harm.

The children then told us about William's half-sister. When she was three, she was sitting in her high chair when her mother's boyfriend climbed through the window in a drugged state and smashed her teeth with a hammer. To save money, social services placed her in the care of her maternal grandfather, but the children told us that the grandfather had abused his daughter. Sure enough, we discovered that this little girl, William's half-sister, was also being abused. By now she had survived six years in the household.

Every day we heard these tragic stories, with children who had already been harmed being placed in unsafe environments. In 2010, some eighty-four reports were published recommending early intervention in the lives of children, but sadly we are still a nation that reacts only to extreme risk – and even then not reacting well – as opposed to predicting and preventing harm to children.[20]

In October 2016, I heard from a clinician. A mother had disclosed in therapy that she was hitting her children, aged ten and three; the older child was a carer for the younger one, and the younger child cared for the mother. The clinician's supervisor told her to refer the family to child protection.

At 4 p.m., she calls social care; no one answers. The following morning she gets through and is told to make a referral online. She writes a detailed referral, but when she tries to send it, the system informs her that she is allowed only 1,000 characters. She cuts the description, which is a problem in itself as it forces the referring individual to decide what matters, when this should be judged by a social worker. Important information and nuance are lost. After she cuts the referral to 1,000 characters, the system fails three times to save the report. If she had not been tenacious she would have given up.

This one referral takes all afternoon. No one responds. When the therapist follows up a couple of days later, a social worker says it will take too long to find the report in the system and can she send the information again? Then the social worker arranges a home visit six weeks after the referral was made. As the mother has been warned in advance, the child is coached and says nothing. They try to get the clinician into a three-way conversation with the mother on the phone, but by now the therapy has broken down and the client has made a complaint against the clinician about the referral. Result: no one is monitoring this family, and who knows what will happen next?

Not everyone who is worried about a child has the literacy or internet access to make an online referral. Some people are scared of being identified.

It is another form of gate-keeping. I discussed these things with three Prime Ministers. One was honourable enough to tell me after he left office: 'Camila, you always told the truth. We know children's social services are not fit for purpose, but none of us want to go near it.'

CHAPTER 9

VOICES

THE LAWYER

Warwick Norris, a solicitor specialising in community care, asked Kids Company to help a teenager who was sleeping in an underpass in freezing temperatures. The boy was eighteen but lacked the mental capacity to look after himself. This was the young man who threatened to throw himself onto a railway track as Kids Company closed in August 2015. At the charity's headquarters, Camila was handed a phone and went into a trance-like state to tune into the boy and talk him out of suicide; her side of the conversation was recorded by Alan Yentob on his mobile phone. Camila was not aware of Alan recording. In a BBC radio interview the next day, a disbelieving John Humphrys demanded to know the boy's identity. In the Telegraph *one day after that, the journalist Harriet Sergeant wrote: 'It seems strange that [a child in crisis] always happens to phone Camila when she needs it.' This is the lawyer's story.*

C are leavers are very vulnerable because once they're eighteen they are often not seen as a priority by local authorities. Their accommodation can suddenly terminate and they are left with nothing. Local authorities owe them a duty to ensure the transition to adulthood is smooth and everything is planned. But the reality is that often they see eighteen as an end to providing a full package, and it's basically, 'You go and struggle on your own and you can come to us for help.'

The first time I came into contact with Kids Company was when there was a crisis for a case of mine. This was someone who does not have the mental capacity to make decisions about where he lives, or about his care support, or to run litigation. He had no provision and the local authority would not budge.

I had heard of Kids Company and in desperation I got in touch by email. They were absolutely amazing. [My client] is a person who finds travelling very difficult; he was completely disorientated. Kids Company was really accommodating and said, 'If he just gets here, we'll see him.'

I think he got there at something like 5 p.m. They spent a whole evening with him, made him feel really comfortable, gave him food, did an assessment of his immediate needs, and prepared detailed letters about his circumstances that I could use as evidence in my case asking for support from the local authority. And pending it going to court, Kids Company filled a gap by providing him with accommodation, making sure he was safe, visiting him on a daily basis and basically saving him from a complete crisis.

This was a person who had been in care, that the local authority had known about for so long, and they were prepared to leave him in crisis. The most striking thing, and I think this is something I read about Kids Company, is that Camila says their model is to show love to children and young people. I saw a huge difference between the way my clients interact with social care professionals and the way they interacted with Kids Company. They trusted the Kids Company staff completely.

Something I thought about was, do they set boundaries? Or do they just give them what they want? Because the impression I got from social services was that kids liked them because Kids Company was giving them everything. But in the cases I was involved with, they were quite firm with people, saying, 'We're setting a limitation on this because we think it is in your interest.' Everything was within a context of caring about their welfare and showing love. And for the clients that I had experience of, what was quite heartbreaking was that Kids Company became their family. Social services should actually be fulfilling that role. Social services are the corporate parents.

In my experience, local authorities process things against a background of, 'We're going to give you the minimum and it is not our duty to do any more. You get by on that.' At Kids Company it was, 'We want the best for you; if there's a limitation, this is the reason why.' If there was a problem, they would try to work through it. They were so patient.

Since the closure of Kids Company, the qualified solicitor who worked as a legal adviser at Kids Company and supported this young man has continued to work with Warwick to try to get this boy the appropriate help. This work has been ongoing for two years, involving court cases, independent social workers and the provision of practical as well as emotional support. There were times when the boy was left without food, and arrangements were made by ex-Kids Company staff for a local restaurant to feed him. His despair and exasperation escalated because of the uncertainty and the absence of Kids Company as a daily safety net. At one point, he stabbed himself in the stomach with a knife. He was one of the cases Kids Company handed over to social services when the charity closed, and to date his circumstances remain unstable.

THE INSPECTOR

I work for CQC, the independent regulator of all health and social services in England, inspecting child and adolescent mental health services (CAMHS). And it is amazing that even now, I meet managers who have no idea about the impact on a young person of being told they will get help, only to find they have to wait fifty-three weeks before the service can see them.

They have built up the courage to ask for help, whether it's through a social worker, school, or the GP. They wait fifty-three weeks. And then, when they get to the service, they might have an initial assessment and go on a waiting list for intervention. And the intervention isn't always in consultation with the young person; it's what the service can provide, as opposed to what the family needs. It's quite sad, because when you speak to families you hear the anguish. They are desperate. But they're in a difficult situation, because if they complain, are they likely to get a service?

It's like managers are aliens from the perspective of the service user. I interviewed a manager a few weeks ago. I was trying to find out: 'From your perspective, what is the patient's journey like, through your system?' He says, 'I think we give a good service; we don't have any long waits, and we're told that we provide a very good service.' And I said, 'You know what? Obviously we have to test whatever you tell us, and do some telephone interviews with service users.'

They had waited for eighteen months from going to their GP to getting seen, and then when they did get that initial screening, they thought that after waiting so long they were going to be seen by somebody who was experienced, who could actually give some advice. Because the situation had deteriorated and the family had called several times. And then they saw somebody who said, 'Well, I'm relatively new, and all I'm going to do is a bit of a screening and then you'll go on a list,' and then they got a letter stating that they had a 28-week wait for the next appointment.

And I just thought, that isn't in the forefront of managers' minds. They are more occupied with: are they meeting their targets? Are they keeping within budget? The trend is to employ more and more inexperienced or newly qualified staff to do their gate-keeping, which is really poor practice, because they don't have the experience to understand sometimes what is being presented. And so, you know, they make mistakes.

Three months ago, I went on an inspection. A young medic saw this fourteen-year-old who had been expressing suicidal ideation and delusional beliefs. The medic told the family, 'You have the crisis [telephone] numbers; you should be able to manage him.' I remember the case so well because it was so shocking. He had been seen on the 24th and he killed himself on the 26th. And the entry that was made in his records was that the next appointment offered to him would have been five months later. The medic was a CT3, so he was in training. He didn't recognise how unwell this young person was.

But more interesting was reading the entry that the senior consultant put in following the incident. He didn't think the CT3 could have done anything else. That is very worrying. The needs of the family are lost in the system of bureaucracy, and the concern that is expressed most readily is not about whether the quality of the work is good or effective; it is about the number of people that you have seen.

Have you ticked all the right boxes? Have you completed this form? Have you completed that form? And it's very soul-destroying. For me, personally, I got to a point where I felt I was a really bad administrator. This was before I worked for CQC. I felt I was becoming chained to a computer. Had I completed the wrong form? Had I done the assessment tick-box? Had I put in the diagnosis? Was the ethnicity form completed? Did you get the parents to sign the form that says that you can speak to school? And then, you know, managers got into this naming and shaming. So, you'd go to a team meeting and they'd be handing out all these lists where you're in red because so many of 'X' had not been done.

All of that has an impact on how you feel about the work, because you feel as if you have become as much part of the whole sausage-grinding machinery as the patient. I got to the point where I was staying at work until half past eight to complete paperwork. In one role, I was working three days a week and had a caseload of sixty-four. I said, it's a virtual impossibility – the maths doesn't work! But there was the expectation that you would somehow make it work. And if people raised the fact that it was too much, you were almost made to feel as if you were a bit incompetent. 'Why can't you do that? Everybody else is doing it.' To the extent that, you know, people were going off sick. And that is reflected in the work I do for CQC. If you go to an organisation where they have high waiting lists, you look at the staff sickness rate, staff turnover, and their vacancy rate. And you *know*. The story is there.

I have had staff say to me, 'We were told that all we are allowed to say is good things about the organisation.' Staff they felt would say things that were not complimentary were told to take leave for the week that CQC was turning up. This happens all the time. Or you go and there's a new manager who has been in post three days. Or it's their first day – an acting manager, because the real manager would say exactly what was going on. Are staff able to raise concerns without fear of reprisal? If you are trying to do a staff focus group, it is amazing how often managers want to come and sit in.

Getting a CQC rating has huge implications for an organisation. If you get a poor rating, you will be open to being tendered out to another organisation that is doing a better job of that aspect of the service. Senior managers are then vulnerable to being unemployed. And the culture in the NHS at the moment is that CEOs and senior managers are not on very long contracts; they are on performance-related contracts.

I worked with one organisation for ten years, and in that time we had five CEOs. Everybody comes in with a different idea about how things are to be done, without thinking about the impact. And when you have an unsettled staff team, it filters down to the quality of service that can be provided.

There is recognition at very senior level that yes, when you make these changes, there will be some collateral damage. So, you know, a few patients might die, a few people might complain, a few staff might leave. But it's collateral damage, because they are on a performance-related pay base. So, if I'm coming in and I have to save some money, I'm not going to be thinking about the long-term implications. If I'm on a two-year contract, I won't be there. But on my CV, it would look good that I was able to turn around this organisation financially, or reduce the spend on a particular type of staff.

THE LOCUM

I'm doing locum cover in child and adolescent mental health. There was another locum before me, who stayed six months and had this case load. The way they treat locums is that you get some of the most challenging cases. The locum workers inherit them and you are supposed to work magic.

One particular girl, I have just reviewed the case. I made a timeline of this child through the service. She has been hanging around since 2014. And in that time nobody has done a comprehensive assessment. She has had six different social workers, all of them locum. She has had at least five different workers in CAMHS. So, she's just been moved around.

And this girl is quite shut down. She's smoking a lot of cannabis. She's been out of school for about eighteen months; she didn't do GCSEs. Both her parents are drug addicts. And the mother has a range of boyfriends who are violent: you know the story. It's repeated over and over.

When it was this child's sixteenth birthday, the mother went away with her boyfriend and left her at home alone, because she was going to be sixteen. And, you know, you phone social services and they don't answer. And this girl is drinking herself into oblivion every weekend. She's smoking a lot of dope. She's drinking so much that she's having the shakes, and I feel really bad that I'm going to hand over to somebody else and she's going to start the story all over again.

But when I told the managers I was leaving, nobody thought, well, we really need to look at these cases and see who would be the best person. It was, 'Oh well, yes, we need to meet and I'll look at it going to somebody else.' I think that is what the system does to you. From the manager's perspective, she's doing the best she can.

If I were the Prime Minister, I would break down these invisible silos between agencies that work with children. Education, health and social care all have different targets and they all have different drivers. They should just have one budget. Little Johnny might be anxious, and he might benefit from home tuition or something other than the normal education package. Who is going to pay for it? So they send him to CAMHS to say he needs a diagnosis before he can access that. Then the mother isn't coping, so social services get in the picture and say, well, you know, this child has mental health issues and funds need to be provided there. You have one budget; you look at the child's needs; the money goes to where the child needs it. Instead, it's an exceedingly mad system. Your child is left not being educated, because there is no decision about who is going to pay.

That was one of the reasons I decided to take early retirement. I was going to meetings where, even with domestic violence, people would say things like, 'The children weren't in the same room,' or 'They didn't witness it.' They don't seem to have the understanding that if a child is in a house where his mother is getting her head kicked in... or, as a nine-year-old explained to me four weeks ago, his mother was on drugs and the dealer came around to collect the money, and of course she didn't have it and he came with a claw hammer and gave her a fractured skull. Now, the mother sent them upstairs. But they're kids. So, they were looking to see what was going on.

And this child just kind of broke down when he talked about all the blood, and then he says, 'I don't like to think about that.' And he stopped talking. And of course, they referred him for ADHD [attention deficit hyperactivity disorder], and I'm thinking: this kid has no ADHD, he's traumatised.

I have no understanding why they put children on the register for neglect and risk of abuse and leave them in the same house with the same family. That one is mind-boggling; I cannot get my head around it. And I have seen over the years an increasing number of children who are on protection plans and are left living with the same parents.

I think, well, are we just going through a bureaucratic exercise? As a child you go through all of this, you tell everybody what's going on, and then you have this big meeting and they say, 'We're going to try and keep you safe.' And then they leave you with the same mother, who's still a drug addict, who's still using, and who has two men you don't know who sleep on the sofa in the house that you have to go home to every day. And you have a young, locum social worker who's just qualified who is the case manager and can't make any decisions – and has to say, 'I need to discuss it with my manager.' And you have a nine-year-old boy who is not coping in school, and the school are saying, 'We think he needs to have a label.' That's the reality of the situation at the moment, and it's not an isolated case.

The mother never turns up for appointments. She sends him with the grandfather because she's still using. I said, 'Is anybody monitoring her? Does she do any random drug testing?' The social worker said, 'Well, she says that she's not.' So nothing, in effect, is happening. And this child is just there suffering and nobody is paying any attention.

You know, over the years you learn that you have to adapt how you apply your passion, because I have seen first-hand what it can do to colleagues. One has to protect one's own mental health.

THE DOCTOR

Dr Peter Green is a consultant forensic physician who assesses injuries, sexual assaults and suspicious deaths for the Metropolitan Police. He has a lead role in child protection in south-west London. He also advises national bodies on the safeguarding of children.

Just today I finished drafting a paper with a colleague of mine about the values needed in child safeguarding. And the first one is love. It is such an important discussion.

I meet people who have spoken to Camila, and you know immediately the ones that get it and the ones that don't. This stuff is deeply personal; the wrong characters won't understand. That is why they need to be challenged and pushed.

I found it heartbreaking watching the scrutiny that she and Alan Yentob came under at the select committee [the Public Administration and Constitutional Affairs Committee, which took evidence in late 2015 on the collapse of Kids Company, much of it broadcast live]. I was sitting there saying, 'Go on, Camila! Keep fighting, girl!' She won't cave over anything, because she knows that somewhere one, two, or a hundred or a thousand children will be watching her being torn to shreds by these bastards, as they will see it. Why are you killing my mum? I knew she would never back down. Alan was trying his best to be similarly robust. But changing the discussion from the money to the needs of the children didn't happen.

To me, she represents a sort of Galileo Galilei of child safeguarding. What she is saying is an undeniable set of truths. It would be a monstrous injustice for that to be forgotten. Next week I'm probably going to the Department of Health and the Department for Education to comment on the next piece of safeguarding legislation. I've spent the past twenty-four hours deciding, how far am I going to push this? Well, you are going to push it all the bloody way, I keep telling myself.

THE LOCUM REVISITED

I worked with a really experienced senior nurse in child and adolescent mental health. He was a creative guy; always lots of ideas, very bright. He had a desire to provide the best service that he could. I mean, he always would complain to – he used to call them 'the Suits'. He would complain to the Suits that they were making decisions without thinking about the impact on the people they were really going to affect. He was very passionate.

And we didn't recognise how much the gap between what the clients need, and what the service should look like, and what we were actually able to deliver, affected him. He was sectioned and went to hospital and eventually committed suicide. And it was one of the saddest experiences of my career, because this was a guy I had worked with, that had become like a family friend. And you know, all of us who worked closely with him did not recognise how ill he was. We have often, as a group of friends and ex-colleagues, wondered if we didn't see it because it was too difficult to see. It was difficult to acknowledge that this is what the work can do to you.

He was forty-six.

CHAPTER 10

YEARNING FOR A LEADER

U nfortunately, political leaders in Britain share a handicap when it comes to imagining the lives of vulnerable kids. Most come from caring homes. Few senior politicians were once so afraid to go to the lavatory because of the violence between their parents that they used the bedroom floor, and it is an unusual leader who can recall going without food for days. Of course, it is possible to care passionately about neglect even if you come from a loving background – Tessa Jowell, Frank Field, Harriet Harman and Iain Duncan Smith are four names that come to mind. But the general difficulty in imagining desperate lives results in unwitting thoughtlessness when policies are created.

Many of our leaders have endured a different kind of childhood assault. Often, either they or their parents suffered premature separation when they were sent to boarding school. To address the pain, some have shut down their ability to feel. This is not a stereotype. Over the years, I have explored the effects not just with politicians but with civil servants, lawyers and business leaders.

I used to say that when the children of the rich are traumatised they end up in rehab, but the poor end up in prison. Abuse knows no social divide. Both sets of children are scarred and have to grapple with the consequences for the rest of their lives. Boarding schools have changed, but they were once brutal places. Cruelty was part of the structure. Masters beat kids, sometimes in a sexualised way.

A private client told me of a school where he was stripped naked as an eight-year-old and so badly smacked that the handprint of the proprietor flared red on his backside. To shame him further, he was made to stand unclothed in the corner so that other children could witness the consequence of misbehaviour. In the same school, two bereaved little boys who had lost their mother kept crying. Two teachers tried to toughen them up by mimicking their grief in a caricatured and whiny way. I shall never forget the bewildered glance of one of these brothers as an adult, his face child-like as he recalled their sarcasm.

A fifteen-year-old who was in therapy with me captured the subtlety of it, showing the effect even of smaller trespasses. He was fighting tears as he described how at his prep school there were communal showers and the master in charge was aroused. No physical boundary was crossed, yet he had felt violated. He could see as a young child that the master's interest came not from a parental perspective but from adult desire.

Children who are alone in these schools develop defences to cope with the potential boundary violations that are a by-product of communal living. There is also a lack of tenderness as parents are absent. The school has to show egalitarian treatment of pupils and cannot always personalise the care. Young children see themselves as part of a human conveyor belt, accessing education. At first the child yearns for warmth and misses the parent. When the mourning cannot be resolved, they resort to denial and start to tell themselves they do not care.

A collective strategy emerges of children having fun as a way of manically fending off depressive feelings. Some children redirect their psychological energy into creative achievements at school, growing into a task-focused approach to life which leaves their emotional lives starved. Other children cannot maintain the delusion of self-sufficiency. They remain acutely in touch with the emotional void and can become very sensitive, seeking some form of tenderness.

If they are lucky it will arrive in a secret attachment, which may lead to sexual contact with another pupil. If they are unlucky and more disturbed, they tune in to the emotional perversions of school life, becoming a perpetrator, victim or both in some form of sadomasochistic exchange. This is fuelled by guilt and wrapped in secrecy. Before long, a pathway of sexual desire is set up that links sexual arousal with children, secrecy and potential sadomasochism.

This is the businessman who makes his way to a brothel to be spanked. He is taking the little boy in himself to have a repeat encounter with his own history of desire. It is also sometimes, sadly, the man or woman who ends up abusing children.

Modern boarding schools are better. They have counsellors and child protection specialists. They are trying to generate a home atmosphere, and to give children time with thoughtful adults, with tutoring systems. The internet and the mobile phone have reduced separation and there are more chances for parents to visit and for children to go home. The best schools can be a sanctuary for kids whose homes are hostile places. Even so, children institutionalised and separated from their families will develop a different kind of psychology.

I have often wondered whether maltreated children are of low political priority because, when confronted with the vulnerable, the politician has to face the damage within themselves. This is a lot to ask of a minister under scrutiny. With 24-hour rolling news, the poor politician has even less time for introspection as they are condemned to being a performing puppet, pulled by the string for public voyeurism.

Children from high-achieving families are under pressure to perform. They are in an educational system that is competitive and establishes early on that human beings are packaged as commodities. So the child is not told, 'Follow your passion and strive for excellence, because delivering quality reflects back a beauty that will satisfy you too.' Instead, the communication is, 'If you don't get your GCSEs you are a failure, and admiration depends on achieving institutionally set goals.'

A psychology is often generated in our leaders which has at the heart of it a compromising of authentic emotional life. Ambition demands personal supremacy, operating at a high level of achievement and preferably better than anyone else. They are also required to be with other number ones, as anyone seen as below their standard of achievement could diminish their credit rating. The lifeblood of British politics is the career-enhancing personal manoeuvre. Allegiances are formed as other human beings are used to achieve the individual outcome. Colleagues form the steps of a ladder to promotion. Collaborations are kept if they are useful and binned if they are not. Human beings become dispensable.

A more collegiate political model could be generated if the leader led morally as opposed to through brand leadership. Brand leadership demands the commoditisation of human beings, whereas moral leadership requires a human being to use their humanity to create quality outside themselves through a task that helps others. It is a non-narcissistic approach. The politician makes personal, ego-driven desires subservient to a compassionate project. Compassion is realised when the decision-maker can feel the pain of others as if it were their own. The leader unlocks resources and works in partnership with the help-seeker to confront the challenge.

Moral political leadership is focused on the integrity of the task. For a Prime Minister, it means identifying policies, lining up resources, mobilising public goodwill to achieve the policy outcomes, and explaining and acknowledging failings.

The trouble with pseudo-superhero, brand-driven politics is that the superhero politician sets up a story of heroic intention, but when they cannot deliver it the public have an infantile response as they are disappointed by their rescuer. It also puts the public in a passive position, expecting the superhero politician to solve their problems without feeling a need to take equal responsibility and contribute. Since the superhero politician is not genuinely motivated and cannot achieve the exaggerated task, they end up creating the illusion of success. This is where brand leadership, as opposed to moral leadership, inevitably leads.

In brand leadership, a symbol representing the task is created and it acquires a life of its own, disguised as the task. For example, the 2012 Olympics was presented as Britain's cohesive, multicultural success. The political leadership affiliates itself with the event, generating through it the illusion of a united and efficient Britain. Meanwhile, real Britain is suffering the fissures of apartheid, splitting people up by class, race and geography, including the ghettos versus legitimate spaces. Eventually, brand leadership generates toxicity as the public become disillusioned with their superhero. Once the leader is seen to be a diminished commodity, other politicians organise to dispose of him because they cannot afford to carry human baggage that threatens their status. This is a terrifying prospect, as they have received the message throughout their lives that they have to be supreme or their survival is at risk.

The 2016 EU referendum made the artificial nature of brand politics unusually clear, revealing ugly divisions under the narrative of unity from four years earlier. At the same moment, a top official, Louise Casey, delivered a report on community cohesion after being commissioned by Cameron a year earlier. This was so damning that the Home Office tried to suppress it, delaying publication for months and reportedly insisting on a rewrite. Casey was not taking part in brand leadership: this was moral leadership, telling it as it is, and it did not suit the government. 'Don't ask an old big beast to write something if you don't want a big beast,' she was quoted as saying. 'Find yourself a puppet, find yourself a muppet if that's what you want.'[1]

Political movements are born with an aspiration to do good. Faced with a choice to stay focused on a moral task for the good of others or a survival task for the good of the self, adults who are products of commoditised childhoods have no option but to seek their own preservation. In the process, they relinquish the moral agenda they initially projected.

David Cameron was especially adept at brand leadership. His eleven years as leader of the Conservative Party, including six as Prime

Minister, were spent in a constant state of campaigning. He repackaged tasks as agendas and communicated them to the public as if offering a relentlessly aspirational menu. The follow-through of actually completing the task and reporting back on it is not made visible. In child protection, his big announcement, after five years in office, was a taskforce 'to help protect the most vulnerable children in our society and give them the opportunity to succeed'.[2] By early 2016 it had met four times and the next development was a ten-page report setting out a vision for change. 'Over the last six months,' said this paper, 'the cross-government taskforce on child protection has been working on a comprehensive new reform programme for children's social care, and this document outlines the vision and principles which underpin these reforms'.[3] The 'reforms' were restatements of existing ideas.

So, the voter relates to Cameron as a confident politician with good intentions. By narrating public priorities, he gives the impression that he is in charge. In his early years as Prime Minister he was photographed with the cooler celebrities: not wrinkled, life-informed stars but younger, yet uncontroversial, celebrities such as Laura Trott, the Olympic cyclist, and the boy band One Direction. This was important because he wanted to convey the notion of a modern government with a can-do attitude that is seen to show concern. David Cameron and his team were selling emotional politics wrapped in the appearance of efficiency.

Experts are often not consulted when policy is formulated, and neither are the destitute, the poor, or specialist groups. Sadly, many of the organisations who are supposed to represent vulnerable children are subtly threatened and effectively gagged by the manoeuvres that take place in relation to government grants. When I was acting as chief executive for Kids Company, we, along with other charities, would often be invited to consultations. It looked like our opinion was being sought, whereas in fact, often the civil servants and ministers had already made their own decision about the way ahead.

The civil servants I dealt with – whether at Education, the Department of Health, the Treasury or the Home Office – were, on the whole, dedicated individuals with a desire to arrive at what they perceived would be a positive outcome. The trouble is that their lack of expertise in childhood trauma and its developmental implications meant that they selected inappropriate measures of performance, favouring outcomes which were quicker to achieve, fitted within their department priorities and were measurable by their crude evaluation systems. Post-traumatic stress in children and its implications does not fit so tidily into a departmental administrative box. Working with disturbed children is chaos-inducing, unpredictable and tough and it requires long-term input, affected by constant hurdles. It is not what the orderly thinkers want to hear. Often, they made decisions about the care of children that were ill-informed.

Take, for example, the restraint of disturbed children in custody. In 2004, there were two harrowing cases. Gareth Myatt, fifteen, died from 'positional asphyxia' after choking on vomit while being restrained by guards. Adam Rickwood, a vulnerable fourteen-year-old, killed himself six hours after being forcibly separated from friends in a privatised child prison. An inquest heard that he was 'very attached to his home and his family' and this was his first time in custody. The two deaths triggered the Carlile Inquiry, led by Lord Carlile of Berriew QC, who recommended in 2006 that restraint should never be used as a punishment or to secure compliance.[4]

Across the world, numerous studies have identified restraint as risky. A 'head hold' – which the kids call a 'choke hold' – can cause haemorrhages or asphyxia.[5] It is also understood that deprived children sometimes provoke restraint as a way of getting physical contact and a feeling of safety.[6] Paradoxically, they tolerate violence to be touched by another human being, because they are yearning for that care.[7]

Ten years on from the Carlile Inquiry, however, the rate of restraint has more than doubled. In one incident in Cookham Wood Prison, Kent, a boy was restrained for refusing to leave the room after a review into whether he was at risk of harming himself. A new report condemned the 'illegal, systemic, physical abuse of children, sanctioned by the state'.[8]

The Ministry of Justice should have banned these practices. Instead, it went to the Court of Appeal, insisting that restraint was needed to 'achieve good order and discipline'. Lord Justice Buxton, rejecting the appeal in 2008, described the practice as 'inhuman and degrading'.[9]

Like David Cameron, Boris Johnson, as Mayor of London for eight years until 2016, also operated through branding for its own sake, compromising delivery to the vulnerable. His election victory in May 2008 was attributed in part to a promise to take knife crime and other violence involving young Londoners seriously. In November that year, he published his proposals. And then, in the words of the senior official who had drawn up his plans, 'virtually nothing'. To Ron Belgrave, his policy chief for community safety, the commitment to tackle youth violence 'seemed to end the day after the proposals were published' except for a hope that the problem 'would just go away'.[10] Boris benefited from a brilliant team around him; I found the civil servants and advisers in his office to be on the whole genuine people who wanted the best for the kids.

Of course, no one can attach a brand name to a kid and there is no money to follow a disturbed child. This is in contrast to ideas such as 'Boris Bikes', which had the advantage of advertising Barclays and later Santander (and which were first announced in 2007 by Ken Livingstone, Boris's predecessor as Mayor). Boris did set up the Mayor's Fund for London, a charity to 'empower young Londoners from disadvantaged backgrounds'. But a lack of commitment became evident as the fund, despite decent leaders, failed to mobilise a substantial amount of money or a powerful agenda.

Every time I saw Boris he was admiring some lipsticked sycophant and I would shamelessly interrupt him to talk about the kids and the fact that nothing had been done for them. He would get flustered and tell me that Veronica Wadley was going to deal with it, Wadley being his £95,000-a-year colleague and 'volunteering tsar'.

I have a lot of respect for Veronica because I worked with her when she was at the *Evening Standard* and I knew her as someone who wanted to do the right thing. So, I felt hopeful when I turned up to a meeting with her at City Hall in her capacity as Boris's representative. She promised to address Kids Company's lack of funding from City Hall, but I never heard from her again. In the end, we did not receive the funding that we needed to work with the kids. Boris was, for sure, incredibly articulate about social mobility. However, unlike bikes or Routemaster buses, the subject was not worthwhile enough for brand Boris to address properly. Yet again, vulnerable kids lost out.

If political leaders are the heart and major arteries of brand management, there are also capillaries of influence. Think tanks will pick up the theme the Prime Minister declares as a priority and chew it over. Charities adjust their narratives to link themselves to the brand articulations of the government. This is primitive, affiliation-seeking behaviour to bring themselves, and their constituents, closer to the inner circle of power and make themselves more likely to be chosen for favours and better able to exercise influence. Before long, the intellectual life and diversity of the political system are compromised to fit into simplistic brand narratives. If you fit, you are accepted; if you do not, you are out.

What's missing, of course, is how they are going to evaluate and report back on achievement of the goals. As a substitute, new goals are generated to maintain the impression of being in charge. The voter is sustained on promises, as if constantly shopping for novelties can replace completing a difficult task. The need to refresh 'brand Prime Minister' and 'brand political party' means avoiding complex challenges. The large-scale maltreatment and mental health difficulties of vulnerable children in this country are among the complex tasks successive governments have avoided.

Instead, we were treated to lovely pictures of the leader with *his* children. The beautiful photograph of Cameron's daughter in his ministerial briefcase, the poignant images of him with his disabled son, the sweet stories of him dropping off the kids at school, all conveyed what the nation needed to know: David Cameron cared for children.

When Cameron was confronted with child protection scandals, from claims of sexual abuse and cover-ups to profound social services failures, he stepped up his brand rhetoric. He did not articulate a strategy or plan. Instead, he reacted to the immediate emergency because he had to, and then he made emotional announcements to position himself as an outraged and caring politician who finds abhorrent the harm to which children are exposed and the failures to protect them.

I knew I was being used as part of this branding game. In 2006, as the recently elected leader of the Conservatives, Cameron made the speech on social justice that came to be known, even before it was given, as his 'hug-a-hoodie' speech.[11] In it, he said teenagers who hide under intimidating hoods are trying to blend in rather than seem threatening and called for a more compassionate attitude to young criminals. He praised 'the deep understanding and patient work of Kids Company'. He even used the word 'love'.[12] The speech reads well, even now. It has truth, power and conviction. Unfortunately, the lines about teenagers needing love came from his speech writer. Cameron delivered them without conviction, leaving space for media sarcasm. If he had moral courage, he would have stood by his statement. It appeared to me that he abandoned the concept when it no longer suited him.

In contrast, his wife, Samantha Cameron, was one of the most genuine people I have come across. When she came to Kids Company you could see her authentic and thoughtful approach towards the children. She dealt with them with such tenderness.

People thought I was his Big Society 'poster girl', as they put it, but I was clear that I supported no political party except for the party that was going to help vulnerable kids. I knew Cameron's Conservative Party was not it, because they didn't have the stomach to do the gritty work that child protection required. In the later years, he acquired committed advisers on the child protection agenda, such as Eileen Munro, among others. But was the government prepared to do the root-and-branch redesign of children's services that was needed? I think the answer is no. They were prepared to put a plaster on the wound and respond to the media. When giving evidence during the parliamentary inquiry of 2015, Tim Loughton, who was the children's minister in the Department for Education, clearly articulated how within government systems the opinion of the media made a big difference: 'Well, on every submission I got there was a disclaimer that effectively said that Camila Batmanghelidjh has very close links with the *Evening Standard*, *Metro* and other people high up in the media, and that she would be in a position to create some uncomfortable press for the government.'[13]

I never threatened the government with the media; it was something they were worried about.

In 2013, they created Frontline following a realisation that the country had a crisis in child protection. It was supposed to be like Teach First – getting bright young people to go into social work. However, when you send an aspirational person into a depleted social work department, problems soon arise. Either the workers who have been there for years feel shamed by the enthusiastic newbie, or the newbie realises that they have entered a bog of dysfunction in which they cannot deliver the vision they are being encouraged to act on. In many ways, Frontline is an visionary programme like the Troubled Families programme, but the difficulty is that the delivery points, which are local authorities, end up killing off effective programmes because the structure they are asked to operate within is too depleted.

I knew Steve Hilton, the visionary behind Conservative strategy until 2012, before he went to 10 Downing Street. He was one of those unusual people who had the capacity to create brands but also to deliver on them. We had worked on a project together in the past and I was very sad to see him leave No. 10. I believe that if he had stayed, he could have stopped the government descending into brand entropy. Although I did not spend much time with him, I suspect Jeremy Hunt is another who takes up work with a commitment to see it through.

When Cameron came to power in 2010, his office invited me to No. 10. I was told it would be a private meeting to discuss the Big Society agenda. I arrived to find television cameras outside and within. The preparations extended to a printed table plan. On Cameron's left sat Martha Lane Fox, the founder of lastminute.com. My place was on his right. Opposite sat Nick Clegg, the Deputy Prime Minister. It was 18 May 2010, a week after the signing of the coalition agreement and the day the new parliament met for the first time. I had been hijacked for a brand agenda. What was I to do? If I sat where directed, I was seen as being his supporter. If I refused, would it mean we lost potential funding? I decided to take my seat, but to look down as a mark of disengagement.

The media took their photographs and when everyone left, Cameron and I were alone in the Cabinet Room. I never missed an opportunity on behalf of the kids. So I told him straight up, 'You are going to have two problems, David. One is child abuse on a large scale, and the other is radicalisation.' I had been watching the trends on the street and could see the drive to attract disenfranchised young men. The Nation of Islam, an organisation that framed the desire for black equality in a religious context, was recruiting kids in south London. Members wore black and were being told to attack people who showed un-Islamic behaviour. Girls were being assaulted for not covering up. In prisons, powerful and charismatic individuals were forcing inmates to convert. I heard all this from the kids.

Cameron then shared with me that he had yet to decide where to put the child protection department. Should he put it in health or education? There was a casual manner about it. He was also rather pleased with himself that he had chosen Tim Loughton as the children's minister. I told him I thought Tim, nice as he was, was weak and that the children warranted a first-class leader. This is what governments do: they put a strong minister in the education department to address literacy and numeracy attainment, and a half-baked minister on the child protection brief.

I knew that Michael Gove, who was Secretary of State for Education for four years until 2014 and before that the shadow spokesman on children, was not too interested in systemic child protection problems, because I had sat next to him at a small dinner. The meal was at the house of a multi-millionaire, and Gove laid out his vision just before the Conservative-led coalition came to power. I remember thinking someone had invited me to that dinner as a bad joke. The other guests were leaders of FTSE 100 companies.

I listened carefully to his passionate speech and was moved by it. He was determined to drive children along a literacy and numeracy conveyor belt. When he asked for feedback, I tried to say that behind a lot of underachievement is neglect or abuse, and that if children's hunger and fear were addressed, they could become ready for learning.

His response was telling. He told me he could only cope with a portion of education, and his chosen portion was to elevate skills. I do not feel outrage often. But I couldn't believe the arrogance of negating child protection. As it did not fit his agenda, he was unwilling even to talk about it. I responded by saying, 'Well, if you don't describe the whole cake, people will think you are thick.' Then I watched the political compromise on the welfare of children unfold.

Not knowing which government department should cover child protection was evidence that the Conservatives and their Liberal Democrat partners had given the subject no thought. They needed to be perceived as having a vision for troubled children, however. So, with Gove busy elevating literacy and numeracy, they came up with a clever trick called 'speeding up adoption'. This was a worthy cause, if not the central problem in the children's sector. It was also an attractive agenda because Michael Gove himself had been adopted so he could personalise the narrative and authentically present himself as passionate about it. This was a favourite trend among ministers picking up the children's brief. After Tim Loughton left, Edward Timpson was appointed. Wherever we went, we were told by him, 'I know all about it, my parents fostered children.' His parents were indeed gifted individuals who had made a genuine commitment and opened their homes to children in need of love and care. But I could not see how their good intentions were translating as political policy. But for brand 'I care for children', this was a great flag.

Speeding up adoption was a challenge the Department of Education could articulate and be seen to solve. They did it beautifully, and media attention would have stayed on this golden goose and not the other, more urgent, problem of so many children's lives being blighted by neglect and abuse, except that repeated scandals kept forcing the latter into the public consciousness.

Daniel Pelka, four, was starved and beaten for months before being murdered by his mother and her partner in 2012. Police were called twenty-six times to the family home for incidents involving domestic violence or alcohol abuse. Daniel was eating from school bins. A post-mortem found twenty-four injuries. Yet a serious case review found that he was 'invisible' at times and 'no professional tried sufficiently hard enough' to talk to him.

His fate echoed that of Peter Connelly, another beautiful, white, blue-eyed boy (also known as Baby P, Child A and Baby Peter). He was battered to death by his mother when he was seventeen months old. More than sixty professionals had failed to respond to the harm he was enduring.

To negate failure of political leadership over child protection, individual workers were identified to carry the burden of blame. Khyra Ishaq, seven, starved to death in 2008 in a house filled with fresh fruit, tins of sweets and shelves of groceries. She was denied them; a neighbour believed the little girl scavenged stale bread left out for the birds. After Khyra died weighing 16.8kg (2st 9lb), with her body mass index so low it was below the bottom of medical charts, sixty marks were found on her emaciated corpse. Three social workers were removed from frontline practice. But the problem was systemic, including the fact that she was being home-educated and no one was checking on her.

To be seen to act, Gove commissioned Eileen Munro in June 2010 to review children's social services. Like the Big Society meeting at Downing Street, this was a symbolic step by a new government.

Munro is a thorough, intelligent and experienced practitioner and academic, but after being appointed by the Department for Education she became perceived as an extension of the state. No one dared to tell her the truth about how bad circumstances are for child protection agencies, because it would contradict the glowing reports they have to submit to the same Department for Education to justify grants to carry on the work they do. As one of the leaders of these children's provisions told me, 'Camila, you don't think we tell them the truth, do you? We tell them what they want to hear. They know we're doing that. That is how they want it and we know that is what they want. So we all walk out of there happy.'

Munro produced a competent report, but who knows what she intended? I am told that before her report was released in 2011, the education department removed anything that was problematic, challenging or undeliverable. The result is that what remains as the task is a relatively minor ambition such as 'less paperwork for social workers' or 'better communication'. No one says what really needs to be said, which is that the child protection and child mental health system in Britain is fucked up. The kids are left to pay the price.

I am not against branding. I used it myself to get resources for our kids. As few people genuinely cared about the real subject, the children, I plotted multiple partnerships to get resources to redistribute to the kids, both in materials and experience. I am not against using branding to get the task done. I am against branding as a substitute for the task.

I approached politicians in the belief that they would want to do good for good's sake. I thought that if I could show the value of our model, they would want to embrace something that worked. I gathered the evidence, driven by the children's narratives. Soon I realised that most politicians do not care enough, and what really matters to them is their brand. Of course, there are exceptions to this statement and they act as beacons of hope. However, most politicians I have come across mobilise only if something complements their brand.

I yearned for moral leadership in the political system. Since this was lacking, I developed a parallel brand to ensure we met our children's needs.

Gordon Brown was committed to children but never got round to dealing with disturbed young people. Ed Miliband did not believe me at first when I told him how many kids are on the loose, not at school or engaged in anything else. A year later he apologised, saying that Labour, which was still in power, had identified 400,000. I respected him for that and I believed that he and his brother did care. Although I disagreed with Michael Gove's strategies to avoid dealing with the scale of childhood maltreatment, I always respected him because deep down, I believed he wanted to do the right thing but he regularly got hijacked by his own need to be at the centre of power for power's sake.

As for David Cameron, he had yet to decide which government department should cover child protection. After five years preparing for office, this basic step had not been settled. I was always grateful for the funding we received and he never failed to verbalise his commitment to children. However, I walked out of Downing Street that day knowing that the welfare of children was not a priority. Kids do not vote, and politicians do not really understand their problems. I knew I had to do something to make vulnerable children a political priority.

CHAPTER 11

FLASHBACK

I walked into the home of one of our children. There was a mattress on the floor surrounded by beer cans. This is where James and his little sister slept. It had no sheet or duvet and the stripes, which should have been white, were grey with dirt. The children's clothes were scattered on the floor. They did not have much to wear.

As I walked around I felt a crunch under my shoe and realised I had stepped on a crack pipe. The parents had removed their drug paraphernalia for my visit but left this by mistake. Assailed by the stench of urine, I felt so deeply sad that James, who had been attending our education unit for under-16s at Kenbury Street, was living in such rotten circumstances.

Looking up, I noticed on the wall the Kids Company certificate. There was something poignant about the lonely piece of card stuck to the damp wall. It had an air of resoluteness compared to the depletion weeping down the wallpaper.

Working with James, who had come to us at the age of fourteen, was taking our staff to their limits. He could not sit still. He threw furniture and tried to assault other pupils and his teachers. He had been excluded from multiple schools and pupil referral units. It was behaviour we knew well, as all the pupils placed with us by schools and local authorities had emotional troubles. By the time he finished with us, James was an apprentice mechanic who loved his work. His home circumstances were still difficult, but at least Kids Company had given him a secure base. His sister was training as a nursery nurse as we closed.

Many local authorities placed challenging pupils with Kids Company, although in the media frenzy of 2015 they all went quiet and failed to acknowledge that we coped with their extreme cases. They had government backing to use us. Ed Balls, Secretary of State for Children, Schools and Families, had described us in 2008 as innovative providers of education for disenfranchised young people.[1] Even after we closed, people who understood what we were about took inspiration for new ventures. David Holloway, for example, is the founder of a free school for creative teenagers in south-east London. He described his project in terms that will now be familiar to readers of this book. Most of the pupils had 'horrendous' backgrounds and their behaviour was a way to 'handle the world and keep adults away, because adults have been harmful to them', he told Schools Week, adding: 'We really liked that Kids Company never gave up on kids, and that's quite something.'[2]

During the great frenzy, the denial of Kids Company's role in education extended to Southwark Council, which talked about us as if we were a flaky, unregulated cult. The borough somehow forgot that it inspected and approved us as an education provider under a scheme called Southwark Guarantee, and that it sent us pupils it could not handle. Early on, the council had placed fifty children with us: then, to get out of paying the bill, it claimed the parents were home-educating them and had chosen to send them to Kids Company. Cherie Blair, QC, whose husband was then Prime Minister, offered to take Southwark to judicial review. I was reluctant to get into conflict with an authority we worked in and tried to negotiate, eventually accepting a part-payment.

On the north side of the River Thames we were a recognised provider for Westminster, Hammersmith, Kensington & Chelsea, Camden and Barnet councils. In south London we received pupils from Lambeth, Southwark and Wandsworth. As recently as February 2014, we had specialist permission from the Department for Education to provide education for a vulnerable pupil at Kids Company. Had we not been a respected provider, they would not have allowed the placement.

Teachers find it very hard to teach when there are challenging pupils in a classroom. According to a survey by ATL, the trade union, nine in ten staff in state schools have to deal with disruptive behaviour such as insults, threats, swearing, shouting, making accusations and rudeness. More than four in ten (43 per cent) had experienced physical violence from a pupil in the previous year. Of these, 77 per cent were pushed or shoved, 52 per cent were kicked, 50 per cent had an object such as furniture thrown at them and 37 per cent were punched – meaning that overall, one in five teachers is kicked or has something thrown at them each year.[3]

Unsurprisingly, schools respond with sanctions. The discipline works for children who have been well cared for, as they can use their frontal lobes to exercise self-control. Before generating harm, they re-member the sanction applied by the school and use it to inform their behaviour. This process encourages pro-social choices. Something quite different happens in the heads of children whose lives have been blighted by trauma and neglect. These students have an impoverished ability to control themselves. Many of them hate rules, because they experience the power conferred on adults by rules in the same way as the power enjoyed by an abuser.

The driver of bad behaviour in these children is chronic fear. The fright is disguised, however. It may not look like fear, and there might be no obvious abuse if the care failures happened years earlier. A delay in cause and effect is common: it can take as long as nine years for the repercussions of trauma to show. This is one reason why a child who is calm in primary school can turn into a troubled teenager, and the brain changes of adolescence are another. The frontal lobe rewires and relaxes its steadying grip on the emotions, leading even well-adjusted teenagers to become bafflingly impulsive. This makes the arrival of challenging behaviour even more difficult.

As with all Kids Company services, our ability to engage challenging teenagers in education was informed by what traumatised children taught us. Maltreatment generates chaos in mental wellbeing, which in turn produces inefficiencies in cognitive functioning, a combination that leads to educational failure. But the biggest barrier to children's learning is their sense of being constantly frightened.

The mistake the Department for Education has made over decades is to think that attainment can be raised without addressing the psychosocial difficulties children take with them to school. But even if, for the sake of argument, we imagine that nothing can be done about a child's home life – which would be a fallacy, of course, and a tragic failure of imagination – there are still strategies teachers can use to make teaching and learning more rewarding.

What are the troubles teachers see so frequently in front of them – even if they do not know it? They include flashbacks and other unhelpful surges of energy, dissociation, and problems with short-term or working memory. (We deal with dissociation in the next chapter.) Perhaps the most obvious challenge is anti-social behaviour, in the form of either bullying or a more general disrespect that disrupts the entire class.

Most maltreated children would describe flashbacks as their greatest challenge in educational settings. They might be sitting in class trying to listen when a teacher, without realising it, triggers one.[4] It is easily done. Children who have been abused are hyper-vigilant for patterns that suggest they are going to be harmed again.

Flashbacks occur after fear stimulates the hippocampus (the memory centres of the brain) and amygdala (a part that processes fright) to develop a high-speed pathway. The brain creates this short circuit as a survival strategy, to remember events that caused harm and react at any sign of a repeat. The amygdala then triggers stress responses in the body, readying the pupil to run, fight or freeze in the face of terror. For the maltreated child in a classroom, a flashback memory can recreate powerful biological responses, setting up an explosion or a feeling of being overpowered.

If a teacher repeatedly hits the palm of their hand with a ruler to emphasise a point, the ruler in the hands of an authority figure can be a reminder of belts and sticks. Because the brain goes into a state of emergency, it does not distinguish between ruler and stick, or between teacher and abuser. An animated teacher coming close to a child seated at a desk can recreate the size and position relationships of being forced into oral sex, compelling the child to disrupt the class by standing up and shouting to break the likeness.

A common flashback is when teachers whisper in a pupil's ear in a busy class, perhaps to give an answer they are struggling with. To a sexually abused child it can trigger the memory of being nibbled on the earlobe and neck.

Physical education is a bad class for flashbacks. A PE teacher who holds a boy's hip to show the right position for jumping over a hurdle will be unaware that this is what comes just before anal penetration. Sexually abused girls often resort to polarities: they disown their bodies and care so little that they do not bother to cover up, making the exposure of legs in PE kit no problem – or they dislike any flesh on show. The class is a tussle between past trauma and present school rules.

Abused children hate flashbacks. Often they have worked out ways to suppress them. Experience gives them a sense that something in their brain is 'kicking off' before the full flashback arrives, even if some flashbacks still take them by surprise. Although they do not have words for it, what they are experiencing is their limbic system (the emotionally driven parts of the brain) becoming dysregulated. Some scans show this state as excessive electrical activity, not unlike a seizure.[5]

If the child has experienced quality care and attachment, they can use the prefrontal cortex to talk themselves down and avoid a full flashback. However, teenagers in general, because the prefrontal cortex has weakened, are prone to being overwhelmed by emotion. The maltreated child, in particular, is at the mercy of the limbic system.

To avoid a full-blown recall of a terrible memory, most of these pupils use a distracting and evacuating technique. When the limbic system cannot be calmed by thought, the second-best thing to do is to evacuate the stress. This can be achieved by constant activity such as fidgeting or repeatedly shaking a leg. A more explosive and dramatic act is also effective. Most pupils try not to get to the point of explosion. Instead they regulate themselves by constant, low-level, irritating behaviour such as picking on other pupils.

They squeeze a ball of Blu Tack to expel some tension, then throw it at a fellow pupil. Understandably, teachers prefer to pre-empt such incidents by asking the student to 'sit still' or give up the Blu Tack. What the teacher does not realise is that prohibiting movement hurts the child's ability to get rid of limbic energy. Even if the pupil manages to suppress all movement, they have not discharged the tension and everyone in the class is likely to pay the price.

Some would argue that asking a child to be still is effective, since being calm reduces activity in the limbic system. If the dysregulation is mild, this is true. But if agitation is high, there must be an evacuation of tension before the child can even consider sitting calmly. If told, in effect, to let the stress build up, the inevitable expulsion will be more intense than if the child is allowed to carry on fidgeting.

A dilemma is created in the classroom. How do you allow tension relief without compromising discipline?

Letting children doodle during the lesson is often a good compromise. Drawing, scribbling and colouring keep tension relief confined to the desk and paradoxically allow the maltreated child to listen more. The doodling becomes the container for the anxious feelings, making a pupil less defensive and preoccupied. As a result, the brain can admit new information. Teachers can consolidate the learning by asking the pupil in private to repeat back the themes of the lesson, or can give the child a handwritten summary to help them remember the material.

In the United States, one teacher fitted bicycle pedals under the desks of her restless pupils and watched as their grades improved. 'They're not doing it to be defiant — it's just about being able to move,' said Bethany Lambeth, who teaches maths at Martin Middle School in North Carolina. Inspired by an article she had read about primary school pupils using pedals in a reading class, she decided to try it with her students, who are aged from eleven to fourteen.

Lambeth did not offer them any explanation when pedals appeared under ten of their desks. She said only, 'See what you think of this.' The small, gym-style pedal sets cost $180 each and are silent in operation. Her pupils could crank up the resistance if they needed to get rid of extra energy.

Within a week, the students seemed more engaged in class discussion. 'They were able to recall a lot more of what I was saying, and because they participated more they understood more and they did better in tests,' Lambeth said. Other teachers using the same room also reported an improvement in grades, and parents said their children were more interested in being in class.[6]

Some pupils have attention deficit hyperactivity disorder (ADHD), making them exhibit higher levels of agitation. It is thought in the UK that four in ten children who have been abused or are on the child protection register meet the criteria for ADHD disorders.

Children with ADHD can do well with stimulant-based medications, which activate the prefrontal cortex to calm the limbic system. But maltreated children do not respond well to stimulants, and those with high levels of dysregulation may require the reverse to calm storm-like limbic activity.

In fact, soothing can often be achieved without medical intervention. At Kids Company we used physical exercise and the arts to evacuate tension. Exercise was to the point of breathlessness. As for the arts, you can use any discipline, from drumming to drawing, that generates a repetitive rhythm. The aim is for the regulated pulse to reach the dysregulated activity in the limbic system and modify it. This is the principle behind most meditation and mindfulness techniques. When monks in the mountains breathe and chant in unison, it soothes them. If you ever come across a teenager bashing an object with a steady beat, the act is the opposite of mindless. Without even realising it, they are calming themselves.

By contrast, people who are afraid breathe in a shallow way. Their carbon dioxide levels rise, signalling an emergency. When oxygen replaces carbon dioxide, one of the brain's fear triggers is removed.

It is true that in severe cases, medication can reduce the impact of anxiety on the limbic system. Drugs that are used include the blood-pressure tablet Propranolol (which is a beta blocker that obstructs fright hormones), antihistamines and epilepsy medicine such as carbamazepine. Anti-psychotics can make a big difference in cases of violence arising from feelings of terror. With children, however, medication should be a last resort.

A great deal of research has gone into understanding the nature of violence and violent acting out in children. All children who have been violated and not helped appropriately go on to violate. Some will be internalisers who prefer to violate themselves while others will be externalisers and violate others. The internalisers self-harm or drive themselves mercilessly, adopting a callous attitude towards themselves. They might vent aggression through chronic self-neglect, either not eating or eating too much, not caring to wash, and not endeavouring to achieve. They trash themselves because they do not believe they are worthy of being cherished. The drive to take revenge goes within.

The externalisers include three groups. Children with oppositional defiant disorder (ODD) hate being controlled and will break rules, driven by a dislike of other people's power over them. Children with conduct disorder (CD) share the aversion to being controlled, but also enjoy damaging and hurting other people. They have moved on from defence to attack, and some will later develop personality disorders (anti-social and borderline). The third group are the exceptionally callous, often referred to as psychopaths. Children cannot be diagnosed with psychopathy until they are adults, but traces of the behaviour show up in childhood. These are the children who harm animals or exhibit exceptional cruelty to others.

Conduct disorder never has a single driver. Instead, it involves a feedback loop. The child behaves badly, so people treat him harshly and do not want him around, which in turn makes him more excluded and anti-social. However, we need to distinguish between small children who are unable to control their behaviour because they are far from mature, and the repeated transgressions of disturbed children. The difference is in frequency and severity.

Adrian Raine, a British psychologist who applies the techniques of neuroscience to probe the causes of – and cures for – crime, has reviewed the research on how genes can combine with the environmental narratives of our early experience to foster anti-social behaviour.[7] Some genes may become more active if a child is exposed to maltreatment, an example being MAOA.[8] Higher activity by this gene is associated with brain changes such as a shrinking of the amygdala (the fear sensors) and of structures in the prefrontal cortex that guide pro-social behaviours. The anti-social child then creates anti-social responses that feed back into the environment as further aggression. This can start as early as when a child is in nursery.

A three-year-old in a nursery in south London had a ferocious reputation. No one liked him. He would wear the hoodie of his jacket over his head and run around crashing into everyone like a demented mini superhero. He bit and kicked. Nursery staff constantly told him off. He started telling everyone that he was a 'bad boy'; what had begun as poor impulse control became a negative self-definition. As he perceived his caregivers to think of him as Bad Boy, it became his identity and he no longer had anything to lose by being 'bad' as everyone expected. Being seen, at least sometimes, as a good boy can open up a wider menu of behavioural and self-perception possibilities, but no one related to him as good.[9] As he did not exercise the pro-social parts of the brain, there was a risk that they would not develop.

Not all children who have been exposed to maltreatment externalise their reactions by being violent. Some develop a defeated response, born of a kind of neuro-biological shutdown.[10]

However, the arrival of a new teacher in the nursery changed the dynamic. Instead of constantly telling the little boy off, the teacher commented on good behaviour. At one point the little boy turned to the teacher and said, 'I'm a good boy, I'm not a bad boy,' almost wanting confirmation from her that he had the option to be good. This possibility was already in the mind of the teacher. Thanks to the boy's relationship with a single member of the nursery staff, he now had the choice of being good or bad, as opposed to his fatalistic earlier position of accepting that he was perceived as inescapably bad.

What evolved from here is that each time the teacher asked him to do something, he listened because he enjoyed her affection and attention. As other teachers saw his capacity to respond to praise, they began changing how they dealt with him. A more positive feedback loop was generated, helping to reactivate the moral networks of the brain. This little boy is still at the nursery, and he is doing well.

It is so important for a parent not to describe a child as bad, because the child will then feel lonely and separated from the regulatory capacity of the parent. Instead, the parent needs to come alongside the child and talk about how difficult it is to manage feelings, and how, when feelings are very strong, they can lead to bad behaviour.

This is a partnership. Adult and child agree to manage anti-social behaviour, sharing an understanding that poor impulse control is at the heart of it. Strategies can be planned to avoid the triggers for aggressive behaviour but also, when it happens, to put the brakes on it.

So the discussion between the parent and the child has a theme. Shall we think together about how these strong feelings can be managed when you have them?

If a seven-year-old is jealous of a new baby, the conversation might go: 'I understand what you're feeling. I had these feelings. And when they arrive, sometimes they stop you from being able to think good thoughts and they steal your good behaviour, leaving behind bad behaviour.

'So that strong feelings don't steal your good behaviour, you could ask for help when you feel very jealous, and we might be able to help you control the bad behaviour. Or you could try and change how you're feeling by leaving the room and doing something different for a bit. Let's think what kind of things you enjoy that you might want to do when you feel jealous.'

To be creative, a box could be made in the house called the 'I feel jealous – help me' box. Inside it could be distracting toys such as colouring books, play dough, a film or song that the child could switch on, or a picture of the trampoline waiting outside. The point is that these discussions need to take place with the parent being sympathetic to the child's struggles and partnering with the child to resolve them, while not labelling the feeling as bad. It is the negative behaviour the feeling produces that requires control and needs redirection.

I would argue that before a child can make a pro-social choice, they have to be able to regulate emotion. To do that, they have to be able to understand it.

Anyone who deals with children knows what happens when we explore with them why they behave badly. The justifications are heartfelt: 'It was his fault', 'She deserves it' and so on. American research has found a link between childhood abuse or neglect and criminal ways of thinking, suggesting that thinking styles may provide the psychological pathway for some maltreated children to turn to crime.[11]

The thought patterns include assigning blame externally, such as, 'If my wife hadn't argued with me earlier, I wouldn't have stabbed the neighbour.' Another is a feeling of entitlement: 'I've been abused, so someone else should be.' Then there are distortions in power and consequence. The abused individual, having been overwhelmed and disempowered in the past, feels weak and wants to have power over someone else. If not stopped, they become confident of their ability to get away with it.

These are 'proactive' criminal thinking styles, when someone actively justifies harm. The 'reactive' patterns include feeling cut off, not bothering to solve problems or even think about them, and having an impaired ability to hold on to doing good, with the result that good intentions are discontinued.

Kids Company encouraged children to question these thinking styles. But the endeavour is productive only when the child has been helped to calm down physiologically, allowing reflection to begin.

Kids Company addressed cognitive distortions around violence by running groups in schools and at our centres to consider anti-social behaviour and the role of stress in its genesis. Children and young people would engage in role play and philosophical discussions, watch films and be taught relaxation techniques. We liked to do this work in groups as well as individually: this was partly because we needed to create an alternative gang, but a good one. Through a shared under-standing and peer support, children and young people would cue each other into adhering to more pro-social functioning. We used former gang members to run many of these groups because they had a legiti-macy with the kids. It sends a powerful message when a big man says gangs are a dead end.[12]

We also organised prison visits to give the kids a sense of how unglamorous these environments were. One of the most powerful plays we brought into the schools and centres was put together by ex-prisoners, who shared with the children the oppression of being locked up for hours, deprived of freedom.

We visited young people who were in prison and tried to support them through their sentences. The majority had arrived at Kids Compa-ny with criminal cases outstanding. Once we became involved in their lives, few committed fresh crimes. Judges often suspended sentences if they saw that young people were with Kids Company; over the years, they could see our interventions were beneficial. I wanted the govern-ment to measure our effect on recidivism, and discussed this with Louise Casey, the director general of Troubled Families. Then we closed.

Oppositional behaviour in children who have been violated hap-pens partly because the dysregulated child is using a strategy to create an argument on which to hang his/her justification for an aggressive act. But it can also be because abused children dislike following other people's rules. Their aversion to being in a dyad where the other party has more power is born of a moment of powerlessness. During the abuse, memory systems in the limbic area of the brain store not only the violations but the feelings about it. A kind of fury that the abuser has power to harm them while they can do nothing. An unconscious pledge is made never to be in an encounter where the other party is dominant. It is not a conscious decision to refuse someone else's power.

When a head teacher instructs such a child to 'get in the queue', he believes he has the right to say it. But the child is not experiencing the teacher as an educator with benign intentions. He feels the presence of a perpetrator. He is driven to refuse entry into any construct where he takes up the role of the person with less power in the face of the head teacher's 'right to power'. It is as if the oppositional child thinks, 'I am not even remotely going there. I don't trust you to be more powerful than me. If I allow you to have power over me, that's the start of you abusing me.'

The head can pre-empt the oppositional child's defence by changing his strategy. He could say, 'Charlie, why don't I help you, and we'll together stand in this queue. God, it's boring having to queue up, but that's how we keep our lunch times fair for everyone.' After a little banter, the head could then ask Charlie nicely if he wouldn't mind waiting in the queue by himself while he goes to deal with something else. In standing with Charlie, the head has equalised the perceived power imbalance by being a participant in the act of queuing, rather than commanding it.

Of course, when one runs a community, whether a therapeutic institution or school, one cannot have different rules for disturbed children. Other children would experience it as an injustice. But there is no reason why the community cannot be informed by an understanding of how good control of behaviour is achieved.

Very young children get the point about using their prefrontal cortex to manage their limbic system better. We used to draw a large brain on the floor and get young children to sit inside the limbic system and plan naughty, emotional things. Then we would ask them to sit in the prefrontal cortex and work out strategies to manage the limbic system. Sometimes they would split into teams – one set of limbic children, another the prefrontal cortex. Soon they understood, and we could give them strategies through role play for regulating emotions and energy.

These workshops let us explore children's fears. What generated terror for them? By revealing child protection concerns, the exercise helped us make children safe. We delivered a similar seminar to parents so that they could use the same theoretical framework to help their children.

We also used a behaviour management technique we called Team Culture. All staff were trained in it. The idea was that if a child completely lost control, two workers would spend time with them, initially not talking to the child directly but pondering aloud what had gone wrong and verbalising it to each other. So, staff member Louis would tell staff member Elizabeth, 'I wonder what has happened to Fiona [the child]. Something seems to have really upset her.' Louis would describe what he had seen in a way that attributed no blame. 'Yes, it looks like Fiona and Muktar got into an argument and Muktar struggled to control himself, so he cussed Fiona's mother for drinking.' Elizabeth would then say, 'That must have been really hard for Fiona. Perhaps that's why she ended up punching Muktar.' The child hears the exchange while being given time to calm down. Either she will realise the staff understood the dynamic or, if they have got it wrong, she might jump into the discussion to correct the facts.

Once the narrative has been clarified, the two staff members ponder what should happen next. Louis says, 'Obviously, Elizabeth, we can't let any child get hurt when they are with Kids Company, and, where we can help it, outside Kids Company too. So I wonder what we need to do to protect both Muktar and Fiona.' At this point Elizabeth might check to see if Fiona has calmed down enough to engage in working out a reparation for Muktar, along with strategies to manage her behaviour in future. This technique makes children feel less attacked, minimises shaming, and involves the child in taking responsibility for what happened.

I was against restraint. In fact, we collaborated to bring a legal challenge against it, as so many children are harmed by it in custody settings. When a maltreated child is overpowered by adults they inevitably perceive it as if the abuse is happening again. The humiliation of being forcibly disempowered creates a need to take revenge and in the long run that means a cycle of harm for the child and staff. When we used restraint, there had to be a really good explanation. Just as important was the reparation after the restraint, because the child needed to feel cherished again and experience a restoration of dignity.

People working with children who show oppositional or aggressive behaviour often try to make them look an adult in the eye in the belief that they are not paying attention otherwise. This is not a good way of getting them to listen, particularly when they are distressed. Maltreatment gives children a disturbing relationship to the human glance. If there have been disruptions in maternal attachment, the child will have seen frenzy or coldness in the mother's eyes. For a baby who is reliant on the parent for sustenance, this dysregulated state creates a biological and emotional emergency. The child memorises the mother's disturbing eye quality. There is potentially the added dimension of cultural sensitivities where some children are taught that looking an adult in the eye is disrespectful.

If these children go on to be attacked by other people, the first thing they register is the abuser's eyes. It is not done consciously. If the child senses aggression before the violation, every detail of eye quality is captured as stress chemicals seal the glance in the memory centres of the brain. Over time, mistreated children develop an aversion to eye contact. When stressed, they find it even more intolerable.

Forced eye contact can send the brain into an 'emergency scramble', rendering the child unable to take in what the adult is saying, let alone process it. The preoccupation is with how risky the grown-up is going to be. Eye contact can also be shame-inducing if children feel looked at and disliked. Shame also triggers the threat pathways of the brain, because of the discrepancy in power between child and onlooker.

That is why, when sanctioning children, we did not make them hold eye contact and sometimes let them play with objects as we spoke. The Team Culture technique of using staff to talk about an incident meant that no one had to make direct contact with a child who was still emotionally very aroused. The child heard the workers trying to solve the problem until it was safer to engage.

The way children relate to school staff is determined by how much mistrust has been created for them by neglect and abuse. If a child's experience is that angry adults go on to hit children, why should a teacher be any different? Hearing shouting in another classroom, the maltreated child imagines a catastrophe in which the teacher they are scared of arrives to harm them. They can spend an entire lesson listening out for where this potential perpetrator might be in relation to their own class. What claims a child's attention is what they will remember. Abuse makes them prone to registering threat, not times tables.

Another aspect of memory that is affected in traumatised children is short-term or working memory. This is when you need to recall instructions or facts for only a short time. Abused children struggle with multiple instructions and cannot organise them in order. So, if you tell them to brush their teeth and fetch their school bag and put on their tie, they are likely to remember one but not all three and not in order.

Often carers conclude the child is disobedient. In fact, they do not have capacity in the hippocampus to see through such a memory task. As they fail and see adults getting angry, they become anxious and recall even less. It is important to give abused children one instruction at a time, or to write or draw instructions on a piece of paper. When you hand over the paper and tell them to carry out the requests one at a time, be prepared for the piece of paper to be lost too! Frightened children often have attention difficulties: they will put objects down and forget where. They exude an air of chaos. If a child has been abused at the age of two or three, or in adolescence from fourteen to seventeen, memory weaknesses are more likely. Some researchers have also linked poverty to poor memory.[13]

Of course, there are ways to help children develop a sense of agency, especially when they have been maltreated. At Kids Company we did this through a mentoring programme, which had older pupils mentoring younger ones. We trained some in basic listening skills and they would spend time in the playground identifying children who were being bullied and helping them.

We also had a project called Creative Leadership, in which older children in a number of schools created clubs for younger children. The leaders would be trained in behaviour management, which was our way of also training them to manage their own behaviours. Then they would set up the clubs, which were for art, drama, football, board games or cake decoration, among others. The clubs had child documentary makers and print journalists capturing their achievements while the Kids Company team leader in the school kept a distant eye. They would continue over a period of weeks while the film and news magazine were produced for the school by the children. The club leaders received a certificate of achievement, which I signed. They absolutely loved this programme, and we watched children with behavioural problems develop confidence both as club users and as club leaders.

At our street-level centres we had a group of children who were specialist advisers to Kids Company staff and would alert the team to any concerns. Our gang prevention mentoring programme had older kids helping younger ones. This is how we tried to change young people's perception of themselves as incompetent and bad. Seeing that they could be law enforcers rather than law breakers, they began to enjoy following rules.

With children of school age, it is never too late. A boy who had been raped as a four-year-old and worked as a prostitute at the age of eleven arrived at Kids Company as a ferocious sixteen-year-old hidden in a hoodie. At first, the best one could hope for was to receive his spit, which hit the face like a razor slashing the skin. His worst was to batter the person who had offended him uncontrollably. A few years of therapeutic intervention enabled us to get him to college. He was bright and wanted to study law. All seemed well until the day he arrived at my office panting. He had run for forty-five minutes.

This was a flashback. As a child prostitute, shorter than his punters, he would decide what to charge by looking at the punter's shoes. If they seemed expensive, the fee would be higher than if they were worn out. The transactions were complex moments. He was frightened yet in command. He set the fee but was scared. How much pain would he have to endure? How safe was it? Was he going to be humiliated by being spanked or beaten? However much the boy wanted to fool himself that he was in charge, the result was always humiliation and another scar for which he needed revenge.

On this day, the shoes were the first trigger. The young man was seated below the lecturer's feet, because the lecturer was standing on a podium. The lecturer was annoyed. A piece of work done by the boy, now seventeen, was not good enough. He dropped it onto the young man's table and said loudly, 'You can do better than this.' The whole class directed their glance, igniting humiliation. And with that, the boy erupted like a volcano of hatred. He lifted the table and hurled it through the air towards the lecturer, delivering a blow that contained layers and layers of ferocious revenge. The lecturer was struck by all the revenges the student had wanted to expel but had been too small, insignificant and frightened to deliver in the past, as a child prostitute.

Throwing the table was not enough to expel his pain. So, he continued to rampage through the room, boxing, kicking and hurling anything in his path. This was not a decision. In the face of overwhelming trauma, the brain relinquishes executive and emotional functioning. What emerge are instinctive survival behaviours embedded in the brain stem. At this point, when the primitive parts of the brain dominate operations, there is nothing to stop the cycle other than the resolution of the driving force.

Running from the college to my office absorbed the remainder of this ferocious force, and by the time he was opposite me, the breathless boy had tears streaming down his cheeks, as if the violator inside him had shocked not only his lecturer and classmates but also himself. He was astounded by his rage, full of remorse and sorrow, incomprehensibly moving his arms in the air as if looking for an explanation that he could grip for safety and ground himself with. The shame of what he had done meant he never wanted to go back to college. So much of our work was about helping these children repair not just the damage they caused, but the damage they carried.

Years later, this boy graduated from a Russell Group university. He works in the care industry.

In my eyes, this young man is a hero: the courage he exercised in overcoming his emotional and practical difficulties is equivalent to the courage needed by a soldier in war. Except that the battle he was fighting was a very lonely one. No one will be acknowledging it with a medal, but it is worthy of one.

He worked alongside Kids Company staff, planned his own recovery and in doing so ended up helping so many other Kids Company children and young people who'd been traumatised. Not only had he become an expert on the implications of childhood maltreatment, he knew what worked and what didn't work from experience. That's why the other kids trusted him so much. He could direct them towards all the treatments and solutions available within the charity.

For me, the greatest legacy of Kids Company is the knowledge and expertise our traumatised kids were able to share with peers. They helped to change so many lives for the better, in the process teaching us much of what we know about how to manage the repercussions of childhood maltreatment.

CHAPTER 12

GHOSTED CHILDREN

I sat in the dark recording studio at one of our centres. We had made it soundproof using egg boxes and scraps of carpet. It was the bane of my life because the teenagers kept trying to steal the equipment. They were ingenious. They would climb through the ceiling after hiding in the railway arch as we locked up at night, planning to take the equipment and escape via the fire exit.

Despite its nuisance value, and all the conflict over the young people's wish to smoke weed, I could see that repetitive rapping created an outstanding outcome. The 'spitting of lyrics' had an expulsive quality that let them release tension through the aggression of the words and the rhythm and movements that went with it.

Some of their deepest emotional pain was explored in this studio. A young man who would only grunt in a therapy session would transform into an eloquent wordsmith with a philosophical depth the equal of a textbook. I learnt to do most of the therapeutic work with gang members in that smelly studio.

When we saw that repetitive rhythm could soothe emotional networks of the brain, we introduced drumming. Expert teachers drummed with the kids in groups and individually. We even involved the staff and drummed as a community. Beating the skin of a drum releases stress, and when a group follows a collective rhythm, it generates companionship.[1] A study published after we closed found that six weeks of group drumming cuts depression, increases resilience and even helps the immune system.[2]

We also bought a then-new technology allowing children to touch a screen and watch as a computer program coloured a landscape according to the rhythm of their breath. If it was shallow the colours would be negative; with the right rhythm the landscape would begin to look beautiful. With younger children, we used bubble-blowing games. With this bio-feedback, the children learnt the importance of breathing appropriately as a way to calm themselves. We extended this practice to deliver yoga and other breathing techniques that helped regulate the limbic system.

Schools, too, could set up a small recording studio to enable pupils to create lyrics and then discuss why they have chosen certain themes. Finding new rhyming words increases vocabulary. As young people develop their music, they can perform for other pupils and set up a shop to distribute the tracks and other merchandise – exploring budgets, purchasing, record keeping, marketing and investment back into the studio. As pupils become less passive the power relationship with the teacher changes, diminishing one of the triggers of disturbance for maltreated children, namely their relationship to authority.

All such improvements are worth seizing. In the English language, the word 'empathy' is positive: it means the ability to see and share the feelings of others. The core of empathy is a mirrored understanding of another person's state, reached by feeling it too. But it works both ways. A disturbed child can synchronise other kids' brains to become dysregulated. Some teachers can dysregulate the whole class through agitation just as much as they can calm a class.

Even though some of the ideas about self-regulation were complex, the children and young people loved the logic of the science, because it gave them a sense of control and offered strategies to deal with the repercussions of maltreatment. In taking responsibility for their recovery alongside us, they stopped being passive victims of abuse. We often saw children who were more advanced in their recovery helping new members.

We used 500 plastic brains to teach self-regulation and how the brain works, including the emotional and biological repercussions of maltreatment. The children understood this material because they could evidence its truth by actually feeling many of the symptoms and challenges. One of the best moments for me was a presentation using the latest science in a secondary school, at the end of which more than 300 kids could not stop cheering and clapping. We gave parents a similar workshop and offered a facility to train teachers in the effects of maltreatment.

Some will wonder if the ovation was because I used science to take away blame. Did the joy come from being absolved of responsibility? The kids now had a licence to blame bad behaviour on their brains. They could walk away thinking that they did not have to work on themselves. I believe the opposite is true.

Knowledge gives young people tools they can use to take more responsibility for their behaviour, not less. Being told you are bad leaves you morally flawed, as if this is an intrinsic characteristic in the face of which you are powerless. To know something about the interface between maltreatment and biology helps a child understand the steps they can take to manage their own dysregulation and keep themselves pro-social. They stop feeling that their emotional reactions are bizarre, and comprehend the logic that drives their anti-social behaviour.

Hearing how the brain manages emotions and behaviour gave an explanation, possibly for the first time in these young people's lives, for why such difficulties arise in themselves and their peers. That is why they brought the house down. It is only when we know what we are dealing with that we can hope and strive for change.

Not all children who misbehave are aware of their challenging behaviours – some resort to dissociation. Take Tutu. To teachers, he presented as a thirteen-year-old who disrupted their classes. His parents beat him. He was placed in the care of an aunt by social workers who knew she was unsuitable but wanted to save money by using a family member. Tutu's school then decided to send him to Kids Company for education. When we learnt that he was being locked up and beaten by his aunt too, we tried to get social services to intervene more robustly. Feeling trapped and powerless, Tutu began dissociating, a common defence among maltreated children. It makes them less aware of their environment as they 'separate' from their bodies.

As a child is being hit, the networks involved in creating sensations of pain send messages to the brain. The brain registers the pain but simultaneously, as compensation, makes signalling adjustments so that the child feels it less powerfully. Opiate-like substances are released to manage the pain and diminish the recognition of it. This is a useful protective mechanism. However, we noticed that as a result of being more disconnected from his body and less aware of his environment, Tutu was becoming a risk to himself.

He shifted from provoking his peers to exposing himself to harm. He ceased to enjoy human contact and lost interest in play fighting, as if being out of touch with his body were leading to a form of self-exclusion. This had the consequence of people not seeking him out. Staff, who had instructions not to initiate contact with children unless they sought it, and only to respond if it was appropriate, now stopped engaging physically with Tutu, contributing further to his detachment from his body and environment.

Sadly, as is often the case with severely dissociated children, Tutu stepped in front of a bus and was run over, breaking his legs. In hospital, he would ring the bells and try to get out of bed against the wishes of the nurses, perpetuating the cycle of negative relationships with adults. Tutu accepted intensive key working from us as well as therapy, but we closed before we could see it through to a satisfactory resolution.

Some traumatised children disconnect so much from their 'core self' that they develop two personality expressions. One part of the personality, dealing with daily life, can become highly competent. The other is terrified and struggles with the repercussions of abuse. The first part wants to behave, the second to destroy.

A few develop dissociative identity disorder, popularly known as multiple personalities. This is a fragmentation of the self in which different parts come to the fore in different contexts, without being glued together by consciousness into one identity.[3] We had a boy at Kids Company who presented impeccably in everything he could. Every so often he would become monstrous in his behaviour. He assaulted others, then had no memory of it. We worked with him to 'own' the rage he experienced but could not accept in himself.

No two children's responses to trauma are the same. After the active ingredient of early trauma comes the compensatory reaction. The age, gender and care conditions of the child combine to create unique trauma syndromes.

Randolph was a fourteen-year-old boy from a middle-class background. He had been excluded from three schools and a fourth had refused to take him. He was exploding at home and was abusive to his mother. He got into fights, went off with local criminals, stole cars, shoplifted and chased after people to attack them. When his parents brought him to us they had already been to various psychologists who just described him as badly behaved and offered no strategies.

As a child, Randolph had had surgery on his forehead, so it was possible he had a damaged frontal lobe and was having trouble using it to manage his limbic system. The damage was always likely to show up in the teenage years, when the frontal lobe of teenagers rewires, making them less able to manage their emotional states.

We began by explaining to Randolph what we believed was happening in his brain. It was an immense relief for him and his parents to be offered a framework that did not portray him as evil. They could now take a clinical approach. We asked Randolph to do a lot of work in the gym to evacuate tension and release endorphins that would lift his mood. Exercise exhausts a young person, depriving them of the energy to work on a new outrage as a way of seeking evacuation and relief.

A key worker spent time challenging his social theories, including his negative attitude towards women, and helped him see his parents' perspective. He was encouraged to build relationships with kids who were more advanced in their recovery, who could help him sustain motivation. One of these boys helped Randolph to stop smoking weed.

Randolph gained qualifications through Kids Company courses and we negotiated with a new school to take him for GCSEs. As part of the planning, we explained how his conduct disorder manifested itself. One idea was that when Randolph felt a rise in limbic stress at school, taking him into the zone where he would seek to release the tension by misbehaving, he could put up a yellow card. The teacher would let him leave the room and he would use the nearest staircase to run up and down. The new school collaborated with him to regulate his emotional dysregulation and he passed his GCSEs.

It is important to realise that a child can get a build-up of limbic stress randomly. Something as simple as asking them straight away to run up and down a staircase or jump on the spot to the point of breathlessness can often avert bad behaviour. Reducing stimulus while getting on with an activity also helps. Headphones with calm music can shut out sound, or a child can be removed to a quieter space.

Above all, a kind and calm human being can use their frontal lobe to calm the child. Shouting or telling them off is likely to lead to greater aggression. Even if they freeze on being reprimanded, it does not re-solve the dysregulation. The child will evacuate the tension when the adult leaves.

Inside the Department for Education and the academies champi-oned by Michael Gove, there is not much room for Randolphs. The way success was conceptualised meant getting rid of children with emotional difficulties. The branding game demands that schools per-form. So, on the quiet, they dispose of under-achievers. The practice is so prevalent that head teachers have given it a name: 'ghosting'. They can make a pupil disappear from the school roll without expelling them. It is a backdoor exclusion.

The parent is called in and advised to remove the child to avoid a blemish on their record. Most parents are not legally or administratively savvy. They think the head is being kind. True, their child escapes exclusion – but now has no school place. When the head of the next school makes enquiries, they realise it is a 'ghosted' kid, not worth taking.

From 2012 to 2014, Maggie Atkinson, the then children's commissioner, published a series of reports on exclusion. She wrote:

> Whenever I speak to head teachers, educational psychologists or education welfare officers anywhere in England, all will admit, always in strict confidence, that these exclusions do sometimes happen. But nobody wants to go public ... for the sake of inter-school harmony, or the reputation of the system, this is a subject best left alone.[4]

At one academy we watched up to ninety pupils disappear. At another we were told of a similar exercise. Atkinson found that a black African Caribbean boy with special needs and who is eligible for free school meals was '168 times more likely to be permanently excluded from a state-funded school, than a white girl without special needs from a middle-class family'.[5]

There are other ways to hide inconvenient children. At a school in east London we were asked to remove pupils by the busload ready for an Ofsted inspection. We used our minibuses to take them for a day out. This was supposed to be an award-winning school with a super-head. In an 'extreme' case reported by the children's commissioner, a head teacher described his strategy for any Year 11 pupils who caused trouble between Christmas and May. 'We will get their parents in and ask them to keep their children at home for the rest of the academic year, otherwise it's a permanent exclusion. The pupils are coded as "C" [authorised absence] and slip under the radar.'[6]

In July 2015, Sir Michael Wilshaw, the Chief Inspector of Schools in England, wrote to the Education Secretary about the difficulty of identifying children who go missing from the system. He pointed out the safeguarding risks if schools have no duty to record the destination when a pupil is removed from the register.[7] The government showed its connivance in 2016 when it refused to act over claims that a primary school in Birmingham had excluded up to thirty pupils, many of them disabled, to improve its performance before becoming a self-governing academy. John Lines, a Conservative councillor who helped expose the exclusions, discovered disabled children not receiving an education eighteen months after the process started.[8]

All of this makes a mockery of official exclusion data. As a precaution against such abuses of power, a meeting akin to a child protection meeting should be called to make sure a pupil changing school is handed over to another educational setting.

It is a similar story with special educational needs (SEN). In 2013, 19 per cent of pupils in England had them, yet just 2.8 per cent had their needs recognised in formal statements. According to Jane Martin, the local government ombudsman, 'The percentage of pupils with statements has remained at 2.8 per cent of the overall school population for the last five years.'[9] Where do the other 16 per cent with special needs go? Their parents are on the other side of brick walls, banging their heads in despair as the authorities ignore them to keep their spending on vulnerable children within budget.

For an idea of what this means in human terms, look at the internet forums. 'Getting a statement is like going to war where the council has armour and machine guns and you have a popgun and a sheet of cooking foil,' wrote one parent, to which another, under the username Mumtopickle, replied:

> This is spot on and exactly what is happening to us. Eighteen months into his education, and even with a Statement of SEN my son has had to wait half a school year to get any appropriate support at his second school. Aged 6 with suspected autism, 2 fixed term exclusions, a part-time timetable, and being excluded from the good bits (school discos etc), and none of the support required by the Statement … is it any wonder he's now starting to refuse school?[10]

Working with a forensic psychologist, we assessed the pupils of a London primary school using standard tests agreed with the local authority. One in four children had emotional or mental troubles that merited a statement. When the council heard the results, it issued us with a 'gagging' order and told us to leave. Had we stayed, the council would have had to support the kids. Instead, their needs went unrecognised and the children lost our workers.

Many head teachers of academies do their best to help disturbed pupils. Faced with the aggression and school avoidance that arise from complex emotional need, however, they have no choice but to send students to alternative provision, including pupil referral units (PRUs). These often dysfunctional places are full of young people with entrenched problems, yet they cannot afford to create a proper care structure, as Kids Company was able to do.

An official report found that of 14,000 pupils in referral units, 79 per cent had special educational needs.[11] The annual cost per pupil was between £12,000 and £18,000, compared with under £7,000 for mainstream schooling, while the proportion of pupils achieving five or more GCSEs at grade C was 1.4 per cent compared with 53.4 per cent. They are the least monitored environments. I remember a disturbed young adult from Kids Company getting work in a PRU without anyone checking if she had a criminal record, which of course she did, much of it for violence.

In 2014, the government rushed through a new Children and Families Act, which was meant to be operational in September of that year, even before pilots had produced results. As part of this Act, the government issued the 'Special Educational Needs and Disability Code of Practice: Zero to Twenty-Five Years'. This changed the system of assessing children with special educational needs.

Statements of special educational needs were replaced with education, health and care (EHC) plans. It sounds as if the government is trying to coordinate the needs of vulnerable children. It is also fantastic that they have recognised that children with additional needs may require support in educational settings until they are twenty-five years old. However, in reality, it has become harder and more confusing for schools and parents to get the help their children need.

A special needs coordinator/inclusion manager in an inner-city secondary school described the challenges with a mixture of despair and commitment to the kids he represents. He is responsible for 110 students on his special educational needs register. He says that to prepare a report on one child under the new plan takes sixty-five to seventy hours. He describes himself as having turned into a full-time administrator.

The new EHC plans have led to approximately 140 additional pupils being removed from his register of pupils with special needs because their difficulties are not severe enough for the new plan. There is no additional money available to give these children the help they need.

The SEN teacher and an experienced educational psychologist speak of a secret queuing system to ensure that not all the children who have significant needs get support. This protects budgets. The only way to challenge these 'secret queuing systems' is to fight the local authority through a tribunal. There is a hope on the part of councils that parents will either not know their rights, or be frustrated by the prolonged and complicated process of getting an EHC plan. Again, this is not because staff in local authorities have ill intentions; it's simply their way of managing the discrepancy between resources and demand. My objection is that through this convoluted structure professionals collude in maintaining a dysfunctional system that betrays children.

In 2015/16, 88 per cent of tribunal decisions ruled in favour of the family. In a further 72 per cent, either the local authority conceded or parents were encouraged to withdraw, possibly because some kind of agreement had been reached. The implication is that the local authorities are either mistaken in their initial assessments at the rate of 88 per cent, or they string parents along, hoping they will give up.

It is in this context that Kids Company worked with more than forty schools a year. In many of these schools, we were inspired by the dedication of the staff and their commitment to the children, sometimes in very challenging circumstances. In theory, the schools programme was our least challenging client group. Parents functioned well enough to get their offspring to school, suggesting that family lives had not disintegrated. Yet even children in our schools programme endured shocking hardship. One measure was the Adverse Childhood Experiences (ACEs) survey, which is used across the world. It counts how many types of trauma a child has known, including divorce, abuse, homelessness and the imprisonment, substance addiction or mental illness of a household member. American research suggests that pupils with three ACEs have three times the rate of academic failure when compared to children with no known trauma. They are six times as likely to have school behaviour problems, five times as likely to have severe attendance problems, and have four times the rate of poor health.[12]

More than 40 per cent of children benefiting from therapy and social work in Kids Company's schools programme had *four* or more ACEs, a level of adversity found in only 12.3 per cent of the deprived and ethnically diverse British community that acted as controls.[13] High ACE scores are linked to poor adult health and shortened lives.[14] Within the schools were disturbed children needing intense intervention. Saddest to witness were the children exposed to chronic neglect: often they were carers for parents with addictions or mental illness, and many came to school not having eaten since lunch the day before.

In the majority of schools we had several therapy rooms, beautifully decorated with toys and art materials, and we let the children self-refer. In others we brought the children to our street-level centres and worked with them there. In one secondary school, where we were dealing with nearly half the 900 pupils, we were so short of space we put up sheds and converted a van into a therapy room. It had running water and a generator: it was called the therapy bus. Two full-time staff – one a mental health professional, the other a social worker – led forty-eight therapists and social workers; six were part-time staff and the others volunteers. This was an inner-London school that cared deeply about its pupils. We were an extra provision alongside its pastoral care team, yet we only just contained the pupils' troubles.

Our senior social worker would chase the local authority, which had failed an Ofsted inspection, over cases of neglect or abuse. At the same time, our mental health practitioner was chasing the NHS. To protect budgets, managers at the local health trust had urged psychiatrists not to diagnose adolescents with any disorder short of major mental illnesses. We could see it by reading the pupils' assessments. The clinicians would describe all the symptoms, then leave out the diagnosis. Not having one meant we could not take a case to judicial review, and had to pay a private psychiatrist before we could argue for the care the children needed.

Of course, many psychiatrists thought their failure to diagnose was unethical, so they signposted mentally ill children to Kids Company. They told families, 'Unfortunately at this moment in time we are unable to provide a service … We therefore suggest that Kids Company might be a suitable alternative.'[15] Hospitals did the same: doctors in A&E departments referred suicidal children to us by email. No one was paying us for this work, although the school with the therapy bus contributed £25,000 a year towards our eight staff there (and we were part of that school for about seventeen years). We asked head teachers to pay what they could afford: one paid £3,000 per annum, another £5,000 and so on, leaving us to subsidise the schools programme by about £1.5 million a year. We were outstanding value, yet many boroughs wanted to get rid of us because we could challenge them to have children safeguarded. Hackney, for example, put pressure on its head teachers for years – but they resisted, and we stayed in more than a dozen schools.

According to Charlie Taylor, a former head teacher who was appointed as the government's behaviour expert in 2011, some schools spend up to half a million pounds a year on alternative provision. He added: 'It would surely be a better use of resources for schools to use this money to build up their own capacity to improve and manage the behaviour of some of their more difficult children.'[16]

Indeed. Clusters of schools could set up a child trauma assistance programme, with a psychologist to make assessments and call on therapists, social workers and psychiatrists as needed. The schools could even have a pupil referral unit attached, to which they could send their most challenging pupils before integrating them as soon as possible back into some lessons, such as PE and art. If the referral unit is organised around the school, it can synchronise its timetable with the main provision. The child can build up to part-days in school, or can return to classes accompanied by one of the unit's staff.

Teachers would need training to identify the children who need help and to understand why they need to work with them differently. We used to give such training to all school staff. In the absence of robust political will to support these youngsters, we created a bespoke Kids Company intervention to enable them to learn.

The difference was captured by an interview given to the *Sunday Times* by Duza Stosic, who was deputy head of a big inner London primary school before moving to Kids Company to run an education centre, the Urban Academy.

On her first day [at Kids Company's Urban Academy], Stosic's instinct was to expel everyone she saw. But she was given pause by a friendly greeting from a girl she had excluded from primary school. Stosic reflected on the girl's hello. 'All people excluded from everywhere,' she said, in the accent of her native Montenegro. What had she learnt in 16 years of teaching? 'I don't care whether you are hungry, whether you are upset, whether somebody abused you last night. I as a teacher wanted you to sit, to behave and to achieve learning objectives. Because if you fail, I fail, and then I'm a failing teacher. It's a vicious circle. And in that one day I learnt from Kids Company more than the whole of my life.'[17]

In 2015, hundreds of qualifications were acquired by young people educated with us. All started out as reluctant learners, sometimes not even going to class. They responded because we combined education-al delivery with robust psychosocial intervention. We would stop at nothing. One teacher used to crawl under a car where a little boy had sought sanctuary, and she would teach him while they were both there, until he was ready to join the class.

A year earlier we had seventy-eight students from our two street-level centres in London at university and fourteen students who had graduated. They were on arts and humanities, social care and health, engineering, science, business and management courses. We had one at Oxford, one at Cambridge studying medicine, and many at Russell Group universities. Some were carers for mentally ill parents, others had parents who were substance abusers, and many parents were sur-viving their own childhood maltreatment.

It is important to be honest about how challenging these journeys can be, and how much they are about trial and error. The Urban Academy, our educational provision, was safe only because we were vigilant about risk. There were two powerful security guards at the door and black-belt judo specialists among the staff. Young people tried to bring in weapons and we had to guard against sexual exploitation, not to mention violent young adults who were not our clients but never-theless were in search of our kids. As we kept the premises drug-free, young people would try to smoke in the estates opposite, enraging our neighbours. Some people found it frightening that tall, impulsive boys and girls would hang outside the door on the pavement, but these were young people who wanted to improve and achieve.

There was such excitement at our graduation proms. We had to borrow clothes for many of our students from Topshop. Some had no parent in the audience and on occasion there were no parents present at all, but each pupil celebrated their peers' achievements because they knew what it had taken to overcome the barriers to learning. Without our teaching and therapeutic staff and exceptional head teachers, we could not have done it.

Disruptions in primary and secondary education take away the building blocks to university. As a response, we taught young people on our premises before feeding them into pre-university programmes. At the University of London, Goldsmiths has the Open Book project, which offers emotional and practical support to adults preparing to study for degrees. We were making similar arrangements with universities outside London just before we closed.

I remember being at the London School of Economics for the graduation of one of our young adults. She had struggled so courageously through childhood, and supported two brothers who were also deeply affected by maltreatment. She supported her brothers' children while negotiating her own bipolar illness. She was dedicated to her master's degree, even if there were times her moods would fluctuate, needing heavier medication, and she would drop into my office to lie on the sofa and be covered by a blanket.

Sitting at the back of the auditorium when she graduated, I screamed with such joy that the audience turned around. I was worse than a parent. Not only did she get her degree, but she won an award. The moment was tinged with sadness, as she had no mother or father to witness her achievement. Had we not helped her, and supported her brothers to reduce the load on her, the task might have been overwhelming.

We helped with grant applications, acted as referees for accommodation, drove young people to university, set them up in their halls of residence, helped them open bank accounts, budgeted with them and used our therapists to support them through their courses. For each student, we identified a mentor to help with assignments and to be on hand for advice. We partnered with the University of Oxford for this: some of their students mentored some of ours, while for business courses we used business people with degrees. Our kids struggled with structuring essays and completing tasks in sequence. Every one of them needed support.

During the holidays, we would go and pick the young people up and find them work experience or temporary employment. One of the most moving moments for me was watching a young girl we had as a five-year-old being taken to Manchester to start her degree. She said her role models were all her key workers over the years as she grew up at Kids Company.

Another student in the north of England was assailed by terrible night terrors that reminded him of being imprisoned as a child and sexually assaulted. He had arrived in Britain hanging onto the bottom of a truck. This terrifying journey would regurgitate in flashbacks. His limbic dysregulation involved a build-up of tension released through violence. Often he would crumble in despair and want to give up his degree, for which he is likely to get a first. We used long-distance calls with a Kids Company psychotherapist and worked with a local GP to help him sleep.

Childhood trauma generates enormous chaos, not least in personal agency. We tried to give young people the ability to create a narrative about their lives and to make decisions about the path they wanted to take. It is a transition from overwhelmed victim to mastery over one's destiny, to the extent that it is possible.

One of the challenges for maltreated children in ghetto neighbour-hoods is the lack of resilience around them. Everyone seems to be another survivor, barely managing. Often family members are causing harm or surviving it. This depletion extends into the neighbourhood. Shops are boarded up, youth provisions are shut, there are few leisure activities, community violence is high and children perceive keep-ing safe as a successful day. They do not get a chance to exercise the imagination or think freely about other possibilities, even if they are introduced to them.

We addressed that at Kids Company by holding careers fairs in our gym, while our Positive Experiences department followed up by negotiating for work experience in banks, medical institutions, media outlets, the fashion industry, interior design companies, garages, build-ing firms ... anywhere a young person wanted to go. We had young men from gangs employed in banks.

Neglected children fulfil their potential only when the stress on them is reduced. The education system has to adapt if the most vulnerable pupils are to flourish. We have to provide some form of re-parenting for children deprived of love. Unless that care is available, the brain's prefrontal cortex cannot be strengthened enough to organise learning tasks.

Ghosting children by denying their needs or making them disappear has, to date, not been a helpful solution. Left outside the school gate, these children will invariably target their peers who are being educated, in revenge and resentment. Exclusions foster hatred and we all pay the price for the injustice.

At Kids Company, we would use every technique we knew to get our kids through education and into university or employment. We wanted every child to be the best they could be.

CHAPTER 13

GANG WARFARE

I could not stop crying in the back of the car. The driver kept turning his head, then checking in the mirror. I tried to recover, but it was beyond my control. Tears came for days afterwards and even now, as I write, it is difficult.

My mobile had rung. It was a call to say that one of our young people had been machine-gunned outside a London nightclub. Jo Jo was eighteen years old. It was Halloween.

He was not involved in crime. Instead, Jo Jo lived in a dream world. It was as if his head were in a cloud while his body, which was extremely tall, remained clumsily on earth. No jumper or shirt was ever long enough for his arms, which still struggled to coordinate a knife and fork when he reached secondary school.

While cutting food into pieces for him, I would instigate conversations about his day. In the back of the car I had repeated flashbacks of one such moment. 'Why don't you buy me some parents, Camila?' I was lost for words, because in Jo Jo's world, this dream seemed a real possibility. He genuinely believed I could buy him love. A family that wanted him was all Jo Jo ever wanted.

Instead, he owed his existence to an elderly grandmother who could barely manage the basics because she was so frail. Jo Jo struggled with his behaviour, leading to his exclusion from several schools.

He was not violent but was often on the periphery of trouble, usually as a clueless bystander. Kids Company's social workers told him again and again to remove himself from problematic situations as he sensed them brewing. I said the same. He would nod down to us from his giant height and flash an enigmatic smile.

Flowers, candles, teddy bears, helium-filled balloons, and messages reading 'RIP Jo Jo' appeared on the pavement where he had been killed. The police asked for my help to get other young people at Kids Company to name his murderers. The word on the street was that it was a case of mistaken identity. Driving by in a car and spraying bullets in the dark, it was easy to mistake him for a gang leader. Echoing in my mind was a comment from another south London teenager: 'Camila, I am eighteen. It's my birthday today and I have survived this long in Peckham.'

Gang life in Britain's ghettos is not a chosen 'profession' or a pastime for bored children, as some politicians and bystanders suppose. Vulnerable young people are sucked in to violence. Some gangs are a loose collective of often maltreated children who support one another like a pseudo-family. Other gangs are highly organised and manipulate and threaten children into joining them. It is often safer to join the gang than to be attacked by it.

Police identified 259 violent youth gangs in London and 4,800 gang associates in nineteen gang-affected boroughs in 2012.[1] This figure is a gross under-estimate: police often do not acknowledge children under eighteen as being in gangs, and only if they come to their notice.

What is widely acknowledged is that gang life is dangerous and traumatic for its recruits and membership is largely determined by the roll of the dice at birth. Poverty, neglect and maltreatment are the underlying factors.

Perversely, Jo Jo was one of the lucky ones. At least his fragile grandmother had provided him with some semblance of a nurturing environment. Sometimes, grandparents made it possible for their sons and daughters to retain custody of children during periods of instability. They stepped in with food and babysitting and, crucially, they often had the respect of the children's fathers. This meant they could call on male relatives to support the children. Teens can only be kept safe on the streets if they are perceived to have a strong male backer capable of avenging wrongdoers. In the absence of family support, the only protection is the gang.

For some children, their families' criminality was their pathway to gang life. For six-year-old Denton, it began young. As a ten-year-old in my office, he fought back tears, his chin and upper lip quivering as he tried very hard not to cry. When I ventured that it must be hard to want to tell me everything and at the same time to be afraid to say anything, his shoulders eased back into the chair. He recounted how since he was very young he had been carrying drugs for his father, who would make him sit in the car as if they were on the school run. A flash of terror in his eyes was a signal of where the story went next. They had been stopped by the police, a stash of class A drugs under his feet. His father instructed him to get rid of them, but the boy froze and could not move. The father grabbed the package and saved the moment, but later beat his son close to death with his belt for not having acted on the command. It was sadly a familiar story. I knew that little girls in school uniforms were used, drugs stashed in their vaginas. Looking like a committed dad taking his daughter to school was part of the business. A kind of sick familiarity would develop between the dealers and young children. Eventually they were recruited as foot soldiers in the drug trade, and often sexually assaulted.

We managed to make Denton safe by housing him, his younger sister and his mother in one of the properties shown on the Kids Company documentary. Our social workers worked with the family, and Denton started to feel a sense of safety. He made me a little card to say thank you with a drawing of a happy family on the front. His father remains a risk in his life, but at least he now has a choice.

We were aware of many gangs. The police used to be shocked by the fact that warring factions were on our premises peacefully playing pool and bantering. We then had to protect them from being shot at or stabbed as they left. It was a ritual at our evening club for staff to escort young people out of the neighbourhood, but on one occasion, a fourteen-year-old was in a car, about to leave, when someone drove by and sprayed him with bullets. He survived because he curled up, protecting his organs.

Kings College Hospital were experts at dealing with this type of injury. However, when he left the hospital, no community nurse would visit him to change his dressings, for fear of being attacked. He had fourteen sites of injury. In the end, our nurse and one of our body therapists went to the house to help the boy and his single mum cope with the trauma, physical and psychological.

The situation was so challenging that we created a team in our safe-guarding department to deal with children and young people trapped in urban violence and gang warfare. The High Risk Outreach Team was led by some of the most tenacious and gifted staff, one of whom was Tony Wilkinson. Sadly, he lost his life in 2014 trying to save his young son from drowning on a Jamaican beach. Before he went on holiday, he brought me a copy of his university thesis. It was about gangs and his observations as a worker and a student of criminology. It was called, 'All about the Money or All about the Pussy'. Tony was committed to education and wanted kids from the gangs to have access to college and university because he believed that could change their lives. He often called me in despair, because he had taken a group of boys from an estate to register for college and they had been stopped by the police as suspected criminals. Eventually we had to issue him with a special badge to show the police.

Tony and the High Risk Outreach Team worked with many gangs, including ABM (All 'Bout Money) and PDC (Poverty-Driven Chil-dren). Each gang congregated in a particular neighbourhood and engaged in warfare with another gang. ABM inhabited the menacing streets around Stockwell Gardens and Stockwell Park, in south-east London. They had a long-running, violent dispute with the O-Tray Gang, which resulted in two murders. Sixteen-year-old Abu Kar

Muhammed was shot dead by a mob of youths on bicycles in 2007. An ABM member with the street name Shayzee was stabbed to death in a gang fight two years later. Each time one of the gang members died, we put out a white sheet at the Kids Company centre. The children would write messages to their peer before the sheet was taken to the funeral and put into the grave with the coffin.

Young blood was being spilled but politicians were not interested and police were under-resourced. A target culture encouraged some officers to turn a blind eye to young people with knives or firearms as long as they had not been used to kill someone. As one of our workers left our therapy house, the Heart Yard, he saw some young people who were not part of Kids Company with a firearm and alerted the police, who refused to interview him or record the incident. They had to be seen to reduce crime in the borough and if there was no record, the crime did not exist and targets were more likely to be met.

Children could be attacked by their peers and even family members if they were suspected of cooperating with a police officer.[2] Many kids perceived the police to be in cahoots with criminals. Kids Company heard stories about some officers who confiscated drugs from young people, gave them to other young people to sell on, on the street, and then took the profits. I was aware of an officer who had a reputation for recycling confiscated stolen goods through vulnerable young 'agents'. And children spoke of a female police officer who was allegedly having a sexual relationship with very dangerous criminals. She would spend the night with them before going out in her uniform. She was reported to be collaborating with the criminals. More worryingly, young people would occasionally speak of being beaten up by police, sometimes in the back of police vans. Such crimes are rarely reported.

Many mothers were committed to their children, sometimes working several jobs to make ends meet. They struggled to keep their offspring safe with such levels of normalised perversion in the peer group. Children would change, becoming aggressive as they went to secondary school and had to protect themselves against violence.

Other children had parents who made less commitment through struggles with addiction and mental ill health. One of our boys told Tony, his Kids Company key worker:

My mum was a single mother, I never really knew my father. It was a hard life really. My mum was young when she had me, she was only eighteen and I think she was, like, a gang member when I was young. There used to be a lot of activity going on in my house, there used to be a gang that chill in my house. I got to find out later on that she was kind of taking drugs, innit, and she couldn't really handle me.

One thing Kids Company was certain of was that there was rarely a father or father figure present. In 2013/14, a survey of 200 under-14s by our clinical psychologists showed that only 8 per cent of the children lived with a father. Mental illness and imprisonment were two of the reasons for their absence.

In 2009, about 200,000 children in England and Wales had an incarcerated parent.[3] This is double the number of children affected by divorce, yet there is scant specialist support for them.[4]

Liam was twelve when his father came out of prison. He was tearful in my office. He kept saying that the man he had hoped would be a father figure was not nice. After a little coaxing, the story unfolded. The child had been made to watch the punishment of a drug dealer who had stepped out of line: not only burning with lighters, but anal penetration with baseball bats and broken bottles. As the victim screamed, the perverse father figure remained impassive. It was then Liam realised he was trapped. The subliminal message to the boy was, 'If you don't obey me, this is the type of punishment I am going to subject you to.'

Children who are brutalised in this way transition from seeing themselves as largely decent to being part of a team that is evil but cool. The child starts to dislike himself. He struggles to reconcile the perception of himself as good with the harm he is causing. As one gang member put it, 'What I used as a mask, to fake being tough, took over me.'

In 2013, the psychiatrist Jeremy Coid began a study of violent gang members in the UK, who are thought to carry out half of all shootings. He describes gang violence as a 'core infection' that spreads through social contagion as violent individuals seek dominance to achieve safety, taking their cues from other gang members.

For a diagnosis of anti-social personality disorder, a young person must demonstrate violent characteristics before the age of fifteen that persist into adulthood. Gang members, however, showed a different kind of violence from other violent men. It was instrumental (purposeful) and repetitive: they used violence to get something done, such as a robbery. This was not loss of temper. As a result, violent gang members had more criminal convictions and tended to have more positive attitudes towards violence, as if they admired it as a trait, while being simultaneously terrified of becoming victims themselves.

Coid found a high incidence of psychiatric illness among violent gang members, even when compared to other individuals who were violent but not in gangs. There was a tendency towards anxiety disorders and psychosis, which he attributed to the prevalence of post-traumatic stress disorder (PTSD) in this group. He suspected that some gang members have undiagnosed psychosis, using substances to control it.[5] Mental health teams turn a blind eye to this group of young people because of the threat they pose.

When a parent is imprisoned, the child is available for exploitation. Young girls with no decent male role model are particularly vulnerable to sexual abuse and gang violence. They watch their mothers engage in exploitative and dangerous dating dances, and when it is their turn, they want to believe that the boys who profess love and flatter them with gifts are different. When the narrative turns out to be just as costly, they accept it as the norm.

Similarly, boys with violent and dominating male role models see little alternative. Sensitivity equals weakness. In fact, gang members need to score sexual points to 'bank' street cred. Girls who are familiar with violent men tend to disrespect kind males and perceive them as social failures. The subtext is that a kind boy will not protect them.

In gang culture, sex means power and dominance. The more girls a gang member has sex with, the greater his credibility. One boy described it as 'getting pussy and proving it'. A boy who expresses love and commitment is labelled 'pussy whipped', as if the girl has managed to dominate him.

Once in a relationship with a gang member, a girl sees it as a mark of trust and acceptance if she is asked to hide drugs or weapons. The boys leave their 'piece', 'thing' or 'shank' (guns) with them because they think the police are less likely to target the girls' houses for raids. [6] Defiance was unthinkable for the girls we counselled, because too many peers had been gang-raped. This practice had become so prolific that Kids Company was forced to start workshops warning young women not to enter homes where there were lots of boys and no adults. Even if girls failed to comply, other girls would entrap and kidnap them. Continued defiance usually meant rape. Over the years, we saw more girls carrying firearms and running their own drug lines. It was safer than staying on the periphery of gang culture. Sometimes boys were raped too.

High levels of sexual violence have complex origins. Many boys, as very young children, had witnessed their mothers being battered. They felt redundant and powerless: wishing to protect the mother, they simultaneously stored images of sexually aggressive behaviour by the man. When the mother continues in a relationship with this type of male, confusions arise in the child, fusing sexual attraction with violence and developing a distorted belief that this is what women want.

For many of the boys, their criminal fathers, or older lead gang members were the sole role models. At Kids Company we employed skilled youth workers, psychologists, psychotherapists and occupational therapists to unravel such mindsets.

Another dimension driving violent attacks on women in gang

culture is the unspoken hatred some boys develop towards their mothers. On the face of it, they are deeply loyal to their maternal carers and protect them at all costs. But as one boy disclosed, he also wanted to murder his mother for the abuse she had subjected him to as a child. Such relationships were complicated further when boys reached adolescence and began to resemble their fathers. Now it was the mother's turn to feel hatred as she was reminded of her abuser by the teenager in front of her.

Such pathology creates what I call a 'trauma switch', which is an altered brain state that can occur when traumatised young men or women are intoxicated through alcohol or drugs. Substances interrupt normal brain activity in the limbic system, a part of the brain responsible for emotions and memory, and the user becomes over-aroused and uninhibited. The frontal lobe, weakened by sedatives in the substances, cannot exercise the normal controls and keep the young person pro-social. You can tell when someone is in this altered state because their eyes have a glazed quality, as if the individual is ceasing to be in the here and now. The eye in the mind is viewing the past. In this altered state, a teenage girlfriend has the potential to morph into a mother and become a hated object, with dangerous consequences.

Sometimes the boys used to describe actually seeing their mother's features on an innocent girlfriend's face, or demonic features such as those of the devil. She could be repeatedly raped or beaten. Often these incidents would happen when the boy had been shamed. The girl may have hurled abuse or made him feel as if he had failed. A discrepancy in power was enough to tip him over into an enraged attack. These attacks were described as 'tearing up the pussy' or 'man beat that' and often captured on smartphones. To share the violation helped regain the power lost through shaming, but it also enhanced street cred.

Once the boy came out of the altered state, he would often be shocked by what he had done and maybe experience remorse. Boys described not comprehending what had come over them. They would even fall asleep with exhaustion as if their own brain had negotiated a brutal assault. Girlfriends knew not to provoke the boys; they survived by placating, and became experts at negotiating these incidents.

While some violence was secondary past trauma being triggered and acted out in an altered state, other violence was transactional and premeditated.

The thing about being in a gang, yeah, it gets you more pussy. That's the truth, it gets you more pussy. Seriously, it's all about the money and the pussy. You walk around and the girls are saying, 'Oh that's that guy there, that's that guy there,' and they're all whispering. The girl would never like you if she never knew who you are. I move to a lot of girls and they don't wanna give you their name, don't wanna give you their number. Then one of my friends call my name now, they look and go, 'Oh, you're him! I heard about you!' And they become a fan. I've fucked so much girls cos of that – and that's the truth. I tell you, pussy's the motivation.[7]

Many girls were left struggling with symptoms of serious trauma as a result of chronic violence. Often, they resorted to self-harm because they experienced themselves as dirty and disgusting. Some had used dissociation, a state that allows the mind to separate itself from the body in the face of extreme threat, to survive the rapes. A few described a sensation of hovering over their own bodies witnessing terrible violations.

Some of these girls, in the service of survival, would take on the identity of a 'hoe'. They no longer saw themselves as passive, but as actively providing sex to gang members. In part, this was to ensure their safety, but also to protect themselves from the corrosive impact of shame.

The psychiatrist Bessel van der Kolk, of the Trauma Centre in Boston, Massachusetts, is a world authority on trauma. In his book *The Body Keeps the Score*, he says:

Long after a traumatic experience is over, it may be reactivated at the slightest hint of danger and mobilise disturbed brain circuits and secrete massive amounts of stress hormones. This precipitates unpleasant emotions, intense physical sensations, and impulsive and aggressive actions. Feeling out of control, survivors of trauma often begin to fear that they are damaged to the core and beyond redemption.

We saw this bewildered hopelessness in our children. Our own research partner, Professor Eamon McCrory of University College London, concluded that many of them were showing the same vigilance and arousal displayed by soldiers with PTSD. The kids used to say to me: 'I'm a soldier, Camila, and we're in a war.'[8]

In extreme cases of untreated trauma, victims can develop serious illnesses such as autoimmune disorders because of the way such unbearable memories are stored. 'When no one wants to hear about a person's trauma, it finds a way to manifest in the body,' says Van der Kolk. Intervention to address maltreatment cannot separate the body from the mind.

Some young people cannot bear to remove any piece of clothing, after being burnt with cigarette lighters and battered with belts as small children. Our body therapists would begin by massaging them over their Nike caps and slowly progress to their hands. It might take six months to a year before the patient agreed to lie down. The kids respected and believed in the treatments. They would sob in the room, even while projecting ruthlessness and fear outside it as gang leaders. They loved the Morgan Stanley Heart Yard, which was the sanctuary we created for specialist trauma recovery work in partnership with the bank.

When Joanna Lumley opened it, the boy who escorted her to her car afterwards had gone the full cycle from traumatised child, to taking revenge as a perpetrator, to working through his trauma with therapy and then being able to help another child. He is now a qualified wellbeing practitioner with an understanding of emotional and physical recovery from maltreatment. This was a training we created with

London Metropolitan University. It attracted students of all backgrounds, but allowed those from traumatising neighbourhoods to promote recovery on their home turf. The media sometimes saw our work at the Heart Yard as frivolous, having failed to understand the interplay between emotional pain and physical health.

Just as children and young people were traumatised by chronic urban violence, so were the police who dealt with them. We had a very good relationship with the police. They showed many of the symptoms and reactions we saw in the kids: a propensity to explode, difficulty sleeping and engulfment by a sense of meaninglessness in the face of overwhelming stress. They were professional and dedicated, but it was evident they paid a price for the urban violence they were trying to protect everyone else against. Just before we closed, I wrote a model for a 'violence recovery programme' that treated Southwark and Lambeth Police alongside the kids, implementation of which was under discussion.

If violence was one dimension of the problem, another was the use of pregnancy as a weapon. Girls would consider themselves lucky if the worst outcome from gang life was a baby. The boys called it 'full dominancy'. Impending fatherhood still gave them shivers, however, and they would deny that the baby was theirs. It was a defence against the horror of taking responsibility for another life when they could barely keep themselves safe.

Some would encourage the girl, if they accepted that the child was theirs, to abort it. I found it amazing that the boy would pay for the taxi to the abortion clinic but not the return. Our workers were often at hospitals to support abandoned girls giving birth or having abortions. Sometimes extended families would soften after the birth: if the child looked like the father, the dad would be encouraged to take responsibility. Often I would notice hopefulness in these dads. They would tell me they wanted their child to have a better future.

So with great resolve they would go around to the girl's house to do their best, but not by changing nappies. If they wanted to prove themselves as fathers, they had to provide the baby with designer outfits. Adidas and Reebok baby shoes and minuscule Nike caps were needed, not by the pooing infant but by the mother, who now had to prove her status. If the baby's wardrobe fell short, the mum would be perceived as failing. Pressure to earn money to service such cultural expectations was a factor that attracted young men to deal drugs. As the mother walked the streets with her designer-dressed baby, the message to fellow gang leaders was that her partner, or the child's dad, was doing well in crime to afford the expensive clothes. The implication was that he must be capable of substantial violence to have 'maintained his business' on the streets, and have his baby mother and baby so well dressed. In this way, the girls endeavour to keep safe.

Against all odds, some of these teenage boys would maintain a commitment to their babies, but invariably they could not live with their partners. It was common to put the blame for the abandonment of children at the father's door.

They would be hated if they turned up with presents on Christmas Day or the child's birthday, because the child would be so happy to see them that often the mother would feel jealous and angry, punishing the child for looking forward to seeing their dad and repeatedly telling the child that what they should appreciate was the hard work the mother put in to care for them daily. Often the mothers did not have the money to buy lovely presents, and they would feel usurped. The child would think it better not to show any interest in Dad, because it was not worth the vengeful feelings the mother was going to hurl at them.

I tried to explain the complexity of fathers not committing to their children when I was asked to give evidence in parliament in 2008, as MPs tried to understand the over-representation of young black males in custody. Three-quarters of children in prison had an absent father and a third had an absent mother; two-fifths had been on the child protection register or had experienced neglect or abuse.[9] Fewer than 1 per cent of all children in England are in care, yet they make up 52 per cent of children in custody settings.[10] One in ten British prisoners are black, nearly four times their representation in the population.[11] Some 42 per cent of prisoners had also been expelled from school or permanently excluded.[12]

I gave no racial identity to my explanation, but the BBC, in reporting my evidence, added the word 'black' to the notion that one cannot simply blame men for failing to sustain their commitment to children, as mothers rejecting men contribute to this dynamic. For a while, I became a hate figure for black mothers, while black men came up to thank me for telling the truth.

In fact, I had an extraordinary experience. I was coming out of ITN, where I had been interviewed on the news for something to do with children. It was dark and suddenly a passing car braked sharply. Four tall black men got out, and I thought, 'Oh my God, I haven't been mugged in Peckham but I am going to be robbed in north London.' The men ran towards me and proceeded to shake my hand and hug me, expressing their gratitude for what I had said. However, if I turned up at a hospital appointment, the black female receptionist would invariably kiss her teeth and I knew she thought I had disrespected her race and the commitment of mothers. I had tried to explain a psychological dynamic that can exist in traumatised families, irrespective of race. We challenged the BBC about adding the word 'black' to my comment. It responded that this was justified because the inquiry was about over-representation of black young men in custody.

It is telling that the street name for drugs is 'food'. It was a desire to help their mothers, as well as a need to fit in with peers, that drove many young boys into crime.

• • •

In the south London neighbourhoods where Kids Company operated, there are leafy gardens with fences. Behind them you can find the middle-class households. Their children went to private schools or the local state school. Over the years, these families became rarer as they realised that peer pressure from disturbed children made life very difficult for children who were well cared for.

To survive, more prosperous kids picked up the street code. They would pull down their trousers, fake drug dealing and misogyny, and change their clothes before boarding a bus. If you travelled in a posh school uniform, you were a target. One boy from a loving environment was mugged six times in a month as he started secondary school. He resorted to carrying a knife.

There was a way to be mugged safely, and some private schools began teaching kids the strategies. They would tell them to put £5 in their wallet and hide the rest of their money in their shoes, not to look directly at the attacker, not to resist, and to hand everything over. In effect, the child was asked to facilitate the mugging to avoid assault. Empowered, the perpetrator would get what they wanted and refrain from humiliating the cared-for child.

However, many of the disturbed and poorly cared-for children confessed to feeling jealous of their nurtured counterparts. They often could not bear it that these kids had parents collecting them from school, and wanted to humiliate and belittle what they perceived to be the privileged child.[13] In turn, the private school children thought these predators were symbols of cool, especially since their negative behaviour was promoted in rap music. It became increasingly evident to me that violence was spreading as a virus, with 'initiators' generating it as a result of childhood maltreatment and 'imitators' mimicking it to survive in these challenging neighbourhoods.

Kids Company's safeguarding department took calls from middle-class parents across the country whose sons and daughters were trapped in the drug economy. A stranger stopped her Range Rover in the middle of the street in north London, begging me to help her son who, as a result of drug use, was now assaulting her. Our workers helped families who, despite prosperity, had nowhere else to turn when their children went out of control.

Part of Kids Company's role in trying to pull young people out of gangs and crime was to provide them with the practical means to break away, and that included financial support. Some 3,000 young people and families received some sort of financial assistance. For most, this was in the form of a travel pass or a Tesco voucher to buy food. For some, it involved cash to insert in electricity and gas meters or to buy food in the college canteen. Only when a full assessment had been carried out, and three senior practitioners had agreed what was needed, would the allowance be distributed. It was given in a brown envelope, with a receipt attached to the front so that the support could be audited. The allowances were counted at our head office and driven to the centres each week.

I am eternally puzzled by the notion that it is OK for well-off parents to give their children pocket money, but it was not acceptable for Kids Company to offer Britain's most needy children assistance with food, lighting and heating.

Critics suggested our kids were using their 'pocket money' for drugs. This suggestion was so preposterous it verged on the surreal. For most of our children, the only commodity that *was* plentiful in their lives was drugs. They did not need our help to get them: they needed our help to get away from them. A small allowance gave them a realistic way out. For many children, queueing for money was humiliating. It took courage.

The parliamentary inquiry quizzed me about a pair of trainers costing £150. I did not know what the MPs were referring to, as I do not buy £150 trainers. But on Christmas Day 2015, four months after Kids Company closed, I took Bobby and a group of other care leavers with no family out for lunch. In the restaurant, he put his knife and fork down. His eyes could barely meet mine. 'I need to apologise for something,' he said. 'I am responsible for the £150 trainers.'

Bobby had been a vulnerable child, living with his drug-addicted mother and two younger sisters. Now in his twenties, he is a remarkable young man, wise and profoundly kind. His early years were hellish. He was sexually abused by one of his mother's drug-addicted partners and became extremely disturbed. By the age of sixteen he had been in more than sixty care placements, and at eighteen he was in prison. I met him when he became destitute after his release.

There were never any presents at Christmas, but when he was eleven, there had been nothing to eat in the festive season either. He saw from his window a man on a street corner who looked as if he had money to spare. Bobby went out and asked for enough to buy a box of chicken and chips for the family to share. Instead, the bystander gave him little white balls wrapped in cellophane: 'Put these in your mouth and get them out one at a time when someone comes. Sell them for £15. That's how you make money.'

So while most kids were joyfully unwrapping Game Boys and Transformers, Bobby learnt how to deal crack. He did not choose this for fun, nor to acquire flash trainers. He did it because he and his siblings were hungry.

It transpired that his eleven-year-old cousin was being attacked in his children's home for not having trainers. The other kids were trying to burn him. A worker in the children's home then gave the boy a pair of his trainers, which were in poor condition and two sizes too big. This did not solve the problem and the boy was again attacked.

I had given £150 to Bobby's key worker to take him shopping for clothes. When the eleven-year-old cousin rang, desperate and upset, Bobby invited him to join them. He bought his cousin a pair of designer trainers with the money that was supposed to be for himself. Parliament is so far away from understanding the pressures these children are under. Meanwhile big sports brands target these poor communities, selling them an escape from humiliation through trainers.

I met Bobby when he had been left in a flat on his own for two years by the local authority after his prison sentence. Social workers were too afraid to visit him. They did not see that terror was at the heart of Bobby's disturbance. I fought tears as he described trying to stop his foster carer's dog touching his leg when he was a child, because he could not bear the fact that the dog made contact when no human being was prepared to touch him. All he had wanted was a hug.

I had to get past a trolley that was barricading the door to his flat. Everywhere was dark, because for the two years he had been living there, no one had bothered to connect utilities. He had no hot water, no heating, no cooker or fridge, but had managed to pull three sofas out of a skip and run a music set off a car battery. That's when I glimpsed that he is gifted. However, like most neglected children, he had no idea how to take care of himself.

When I asked him where his clothes were, he opened a cupboard. There were no railings or coat hangers; half a bin-liner of belongings rested on the concrete floor. There was something poignant about that bin liner and the image of it often replays in my mind.

When we were questioned by the Official Receiver about Kids Company's insolvency, we were asked if a £400 television in an ornate, hand-crafted cabinet was reasonable expenditure. On the one hand, it was not and I could understand why I was being quizzed about it. On the other, this TV was the first choice Bobby had been able to make when we did up his flat through our Colour a Child's Life scheme.

Annie and a team of workers kept asking Bobby what colour he wanted his walls; he could not choose. They asked him about sheets and towels; he could not choose. In fact, he could not make a decision about anything, a common characteristic of children who have been in residential care, where everything is settled for them. They often feel they have no right to choose in any case. So, the truth is that I chose everything for him until he decided on this television in an antique cabinet. It was miraculous progress: he now felt his home belonged to him. With the arrival of the TV, the transition took place and Bobby started taking pride in his flat. Symbolically, he had created a home when he chose the TV. I knew there was no point in explaining it to the Official Receiver.

When riots broke out in parts of south and east London in 2011, many politicians tried to understand the conditions that had precipitated the violence. It was an opportunity to review the young people's lives. Instead they were presented as greedy 'shoppers' in search of designer goods. The public saw pictures of angry young men smashing shop windows to take clothes and electronics. The truth is that they were also stealing rice, food and nappies. A lot of the stolen hardware would later be sold to pay for electricity and gas.

One of our girls who suffered from bipolar disorder was pictured sitting on three TV boxes she had stolen, calling for a cab. When I challenged her, she explained that she wanted to sell them because the electricity kept running out.

In 2010, I noticed a change that I communicated to Oliver Letwin, a minister close to David Cameron, in a meeting at Downing Street after the riots of 2011. I hoped it would lead to safeguarding rather than criminalising children. The drugs trade was moving into the countryside. This was referred to by the police as 'county lines'. The kids called it 'going country'.[14] The drug dealers would have London telephones, but also a set telephone line for the 'outside London' business. Dealers exploited children in local authority care, ex-offenders living in council accommodation, and local addicts. These people were given free drugs or a drug-based incentive such as sell one, earn one. Sometimes the dealers would arrange for a kid to be robbed, creating a debt to the dealer that had to be paid off to avoid being killed.

Dealers and their associates would write telephone numbers on pieces of paper that worked like business cards. Customers gave phone orders and little kids would deliver the 'produce'. Children were left waiting for customers on street corners with rocks of cocaine wrapped in cellophane hidden in their mouths, or pushed inside their vaginas or between the cheeks of their bottoms (boys called it 'balsing'). Often primary school kids were used because they could be terrorised more easily into compliance.

The drug dealers and kids travelled out of town by train or coach, using cars nearer their destination. Sometimes all the kids were piled into a car and taken up the motorway. They could be away for three days before being driven back. Eventually a house might be set up to grow industrial cannabis and serve as a local 'crack den' where people come to take drugs and have sex.

We noticed that some adult drug dealers were taking over the homes of care leavers. This is referred to as 'cooning'. Drugs as well as firearms would be hidden in these flats and if the young person used any of the stash, they would be hurt. Drug dealers often raped young people in their own homes but care leavers were too frightened to report them. They would also take over their bank accounts and launder money through them.

My worry about the 'county lines' drug dealing was time and distance. Police in rural areas did not have the experience of inner-city units. Nevertheless, they were facing extremely violent individuals. It also took longer to get to reports of trouble. Raids by armed drug dealers on provincial post offices became easy crime.

A Home Office report eventually acknowledged an attempt to recruit vulnerable drug mules from children's homes, or pupils excluded from mainstream schools. In just one small area of Essex, around Clacton-on-Sea, police estimated there were nineteen county lines running to Liverpool, London and Manchester. Lewisham Council has suggested that half its missing children may have been sucked into these gangs.

A report by the National Crime Agency found that 42 per cent of 'county line' drugs supply was in coastal towns. Communities near London, Reading and Southampton were favoured. Drug dealers worked from hotels before taking over houses in the area.[15]

Stephen Moore, a former senior detective with Merseyside Police, compared what was happening to the exploitation of centuries past. 'This is like mill owners using kids in Victorian times or sending kids down mines – cheap, easily replaceable labour.'[16] A lot is at stake when a countryside drugs franchise can make £5,000 a day. Most of this goes to the adult dealers. The kids might get a small payment or be given drugs to sell for themselves.

This type of threatening, coercive activity traps children. They need to be recognised as victims of abuse. To see them as criminals, as if they were some kind of vermin, shows no understanding of the terror behind the crime.

CHAPTER 14

CHARISMA

I

When a rock is thrown into a lake, there is the blow at the centre of the fall before rings emerge as reverberations. Emotional trauma operates on similar principles. After the original act come the repercussions.

Consider Charisma, a teenager we worked with at Kids Company. She had been brought to us by the local authority when it realised she was missing school. It was about to be inspected by Ofsted and needed to account for her.

I got to know about her when staff described a fourteen-year-old who was relentlessly kicking, biting and refusing to engage with education. She fought her teachers and other students, yet there was something likeable about her. Exasperated, the team decided I should meet her.

When I met Charisma, it was clear she had no faith in anyone's ability to engage with her meaningfully. I felt sarcastically undressed by her, which in view of the history of trauma she subsequently shared was a relevant communication. Her glance delivered a monumental blow, at the heart of which was the conviction that I was going to be completely useless. I found myself bowing to her power by acknowledging that we had all been too thick to understand her troubles, leaving her isolated and alone.

I started with an apology because before me, despite her aggression, was someone who needed to be elevated through dignity. I was going to symbolically accept the position of the adults in her life who should have taken the blame. It was an apology on behalf of Kids Company for having failed to understand her disturbance, but also on behalf of others I suspected had harmed her.

My confession seemed to hit a nerve, as loneliness and invisibility were indeed at the core of her experience. She sank into the chair in my office, her glance travelling across my table of trinkets. Then she looked up. 'You are different,' she said.

'Does that frighten you?' I asked.

'No.' But the eye contact ceased.

'I get the feeling you have a big secret and it is too big for the little girl who has had to cope with it.'

Slowly her eyes lifted until she locked her gaze into mine. This was the unveiling. I made a silent vow not to abandon her with whatever she was about to reveal. What I suspected then unravelled.

She described being pinned to the bed as a ten-year-old, her father on top of her. At first she talked of his hands 'creepily crawling' through her hair, as if the disgust of his desire were more tolerable if described through his perverted caress and not by the penetration that left her bleeding. The assault carried on, her shock fused with arousal. The arousal is a complication for which she continues to pay a price.

It had begun long before the rape. She described him treating her like a 'repulsive whore' when she was four years old, as he fondled her aggressively while keeping her pinned to his lap. It progressed to removing the bathroom door so that when she showered he could devour her with his 'sick gaze'. Her body belonged to him. He would say when she was to be washed and what she could eat. He would buy the sweets she liked for the little boys in the house, her brothers, but only they could eat them.

At nights she would sleep on a mattress soaked with urine that her younger brother had released in defiance. That was where she belonged, in a urine-stenched world with faded Walt Disney bedding covered in the dirt of ages.

Maths homework was punctuated by blows to her head. Sometimes her mother would intervene. Otherwise her mother's absence was so profound that her eyes were like dulled porcelain, expressionless in a body reminiscent of a battered fabric doll. Charisma did everything she could to get her mother to engage with her. She pleaded, at times she became angry but eventually she gave up. Her mother was present in body and absent in feeling.

Often, the pain of knowing or suspecting that your child has been sexually abused is so extreme that the parent resorts to disassociation. It reaches a point where the parent forgets the incidents of harm the child has endured, which if they had registered, would have helped them realise their child was at risk and led them to protect. At times, a parent can feel unconsciously angry with their own child, perceiving them as having somehow facilitated the abuse or allowed its continuation by not raising the alarm sufficiently. In some cases, this may be the mother's unconscious strategy to protect herself against the unbearable pain of having her husband, the father of her child, as the abuser.

A parent who has been sexually abused as a child may also have more complicated feelings. Paradoxically, in an unconscious way they may be relieved that their child is also damaged through abuse. This is because they experience such profound shame at having been harmed, and when their own children grow up unharmed, they perceive a power imbalance, with the non-abused child being seen as better than the abused child within the parent.

This of course is profoundly unconscious and not all parents experience it, but its power can result in a parent not intervening to protect their offspring's when they should.

In some households, a mother who may not want to engage sexually with her partner could be secretly relieved that the partner is having his sexual desires satisfied by his abuse of the child. Of course, some mothers are terrified of their partners and may not speak up, for fear they and the other children may come to harm. The abused child in the house is sacrificed to achieve pseudo peace.

Charisma described her grandmother as having witnessed atrocities in wars. When Charisma's mother was a child, her grandmother had dampened her pain with alcohol. Her consumption reached a point where her sense of self-preservation was potentially eroded. One dangerous man after another became her temporary companion and one of them began sexually abusing her first daughter, Charisma's aunt.

Charisma told me her mother had survived by pretending that nothing was happening. She was not the object of his desire. But she felt guilty and frightened and tried to hide as little children do. They close their eyes and believe that because they cannot see, other people cannot see them. The 'not seeing' may have become a life strategy for Charisma's mother. One generation on, when she realised Charisma had been sexually violated and precociously aroused, she could not cope.

Under these circumstances, a combination of maternal failure and a sense of disgust for her child's sexuality can leave a mother unable to tolerate her daughter. Every time she looks in her child's face, it reminds her that she has been, as she sees it, a bad mother. She may also see a sexual child who is more desired than she herself is, a rival who has stolen, as she sees it, her man.

Charisma loved her mother very much, but was deeply pained by her mother's inability to bond with her and protect her. She felt she had no option but to leave the house aged eleven.

Lack of food and shelter forced her into the arms of paedophiles on the street. They sensed her vulnerability and her aloneness. It was not long before she was being sexually exploited. She was beautiful and one pimp described her as a good money-maker. On one level, she was terrified; on another she felt empowered. They were looking at her, these men, and wanting her rather than rejecting her.

Some of the incidents she described were horrific. She was trapped in a public toilet aged twelve as more than thirty men took turns to penetrate her. I asked her how she had survived. She told me she could not feel. In fact, she was brutal, lethal and empty of compassion for the little girl in her who had endured so much. It was as if a combination of her mother and her father had been internalised as an attitude towards herself, abandoning and violating.

The trauma repeated itself endlessly. There was the sixty-year-old man who would force her into a school uniform and put her on a bed for his friends to look at. They were not allowed to touch her because raping her would be his trophy. She did not hate him; she called him Grandad. He was the best father she could have at the time, even if it meant he was having sex with her.

She went in and out of health clinics with sexually transmitted diseases. Then there were the abortions. No health worker seemed to wonder why such a little girl kept turning up with sexually transmitted diseases. Everyone did their job, but no one ended up doing the right thing.

The education authority and social services dipped in and out, on and off, clearly not realising the magnitude of what was happening to an eleven-year-old on the streets of London. Most of her nights were spent being shuttled by pimps between private homes and brothels where she serviced men. The pimp took the money but, as she saw it, there were some rules, she had some power. She was being perversely admired, rather than receiving blows randomly to her head because she could not do her maths homework.

As Charisma and I worked together, she was able to relinquish the attachment to the sixty-year-old man, and only when she did not need him could she see how violent and emotionally ugly he was. She was shocked by the fact that she'd been attached to him. She felt ashamed.

The second man got her when she was fourteen years old. He hid her in his room. She could not access the bathroom and had to wash in a plastic washing-up bowl as he looked on. She appreciated his wisdom and his ability to make music. He was exploiting her, but he also took care of her.

Our inclination is to believe that the people who harm such children are different from the rest of us. We reassure ourselves that in their difference they harbour risk against which it our duty is to safeguard. The frightening part is that these so-called 'evil' people, starting with Charisma's father, are just like us. Their development took a different course because emotional trauma deviated it.

Charisma told me her dad had scars on his back. He was beaten as a child, abandoned by his mother and left with an uncle's family. What does abuse do to a child to drive his compulsion to repeat it? Do all those who have been violated go on to violate others? Will Charisma be a perpetrator in the service of revenge?

The answer is that everyone who has overwhelmingly violating pain will pay a price for it. However, not all go on to exercise revenge towards another. Sometimes the revenge is towards the self. Charisma does have a 'perpetrator' in her: every day this internalised attacker exercises lethal revenge by having no compassion for the little girl who has been hurt, continuing to place her at risk.

The trauma has to be repeated by the victim, in part to acquire some mastery over it by exercising personal agency. It is also because the brain, having been shocked, requires the event to repeat itself so that perception can get a grip on it.

To be a neutral therapist is to be the dissociated mum. I must be upset and angry so that Charisma can experience a carer who is outraged by the harm the child is exposed to. I tell her the man she has met on the internet is an abuser and she cannot see him. I object to the fact that she has gone to the house of another man after meeting him at the gym, and then felt too frightened to leave. She had become too good at managing risk. She was an expert working out which men had to be obeyed and with which she could negotiate. That is how she kept herself alive.

Her Kids Company worker would walk down the street with her and tell her off each time she responded to the attention of passing men. She watched her key worker challenge abusing men, including the hostel worker who took advantage after she was placed there by social services. By watching us set boundaries, Charisma learnt what was appropriate and how she could protect herself.

I have to get the balance of outrage and acceptance right. If I show too much anger towards the perpetrators on her behalf, I risk making it unsafe for her to tell me about how she may be abusing herself or others. She may feel too ashamed to share the perverse steps she's had to take to protect herself against the worst harm. She would like to present herself as having heroically fended off the perpetrators, whereas she may have had to placate them.

She describes the patterns of prostitution. 'It starts with getting a high. I feel glamorous and powerful. I am in charge. We are in a transaction; they are going to pay me. But then that feeling wears off, and instead I want to die. I feel so suicidal, so rubbish. The darkness of it becomes intolerable. I take drugs and I am nowhere to be found. I have gone. They are having sex with a dead body.'

When you have died like that, how do you get back to wanting to live?

In her case, it was music. Secretly, she was writing songs. At first, she could not sing them. We sat together and it was as if her voice were a tiny child in her mouth and I was holding her hand and gently bringing her baby out of the darkness of her throat into the light. The sound came so tentatively it was excruciating. There was such a tightrope of delicacy between us as I invited this little voice to be heard.

It was something beautiful she could be in charge of and share, which had nothing to do with the perversions of prostitution and being seen as a whore. It was an invitation based on beauty and not perverted desire. Here was a paradox. A girl who could pole dance in front of crowds of aroused men had a voice that was too frightened to reveal itself.

II

Gaining some mastery over the effects of trauma requires sophisticated therapeutic interventions. Children who have been beaten and have lacked the protection of their parents often become hyper-vigilant. They experience the beatings as ferocious, random and arbitrary. The child is alone, not knowing when the perpetrator will arrive with the belt and the stick. Terror grows, but it is nebulous and it has no object to be its container, until the man with the belt enters the room. As the blows pound the skin, several things happen simultaneously that tattoo the trauma into the child's being.

The muscles, the skin and the flesh memorise the blows. The mind captures like a film the perversely exquisite detail of these horrific acts and seals them deep inside the brain, in the limbic system. The perpetrator is remembered with devastating clarity, even if the victim has a disorganised and episodic recall of events. The deranged quality of the perpetrator's eyes, the excitable breath, the clenched teeth, the sweaty upper lip and the words that deliver piercing hatred are all captured.

As humans, we have evolved to store traumatic experiences, helping us to avoid future risks. The child does not want to go near these memories again, but there is no escape. He is too small to get away and the blows keep coming. The fright hormones released from the adrenal glands on top of the kidney seal the memories, never to be forgotten, and in turn they send the emotional centres of the brain into overdrive so that the frightened boy is trapped in a terror loop he cannot escape.

Violence becomes an organiser of this terror, as the perpetrator transforms a vague, anticipatory dread into an encounter that, in the beatings, delivers a beginning, middle and end. The end is usually catastrophic exhaustion and depletion, fused with rage. But the child who has been beaten is perversely relieved, because instead of feeling an indistinct, limitless fright, they can now attribute their sense of terror to an event. Violence becomes a container and the battered child unconsciously learns to deal with indefinable fear by generating an exaggerated moment of harm, after which they are guaranteed a post-harm resolution perceived as rest, even if it comes courtesy of having been battered. In short, a terrifying episode is easier to manage than a vast, limitless dread of future violence.

Children who hurt others are often driven to manage distress like this, to get rid of pain they cannot name or otherwise address. If they do not expel it by hurting someone else, they will hurt themselves instead. Sometimes other objects can become the container. Relief can be through harming animals, damaging property, setting fires or, more positively, by using the rage in intense contact sports and arts activities. The point is this: the disturbed management of energy is secondary to chronic exposure to frightening circumstances. Charisma's dad may have used her to release emotional tension he could not soothe in himself because no one had soothed it in him. In victimising her, he needed to prove to himself that he was no longer the victim, but he had the power expressed in being a perpetrator. In explaining this, I am not condoning his violence.

The child who is being harmed often promises himself that one day he will be as strong as his abuser. He will come to understand that he is no longer the victim when he gets to victimise someone else.

In a morally perverse environment, the choice is not between good and evil but between victim and perpetrator. Quality resides with the person who does the harm because they are not passive and are not humiliated. It frees those with no capacity to act except as the container for another person's violence. Eventually, the victim-perpetrator has to compromise. If he cannot get to be 'good', he had better be very good at being bad.

All victims feel sullied. They ingest the perpetrator's hatred. They receive the message that when you are little and you are weak, you get to be hated. They also hate themselves because they could not fight back. The memory of this powerlessness fuels a lifelong disgust for the vulnerable.

The chronically violated child cannot tolerate vulnerability because he is disgusted by his own powerlessness. It is true of both sexes. When two girls in care, aged thirteen and fourteen, shocked Britain by torturing to death the harmless alcoholic Angie Wrightson in her Hartlepool home in 2014, it was likely her vulnerability that spurred them.[1]

The unspoken rule among violent gangs is: if you are attacked, never beg for mercy. They know a pleading victim conjures up in the perpetrator the memory of a pleading child, summoning up a double dose of hatred. There is hate for the victim before him and hate for the victimised child the perpetrator once was. The unbearable pain it ignites demands obliteration, sometimes by killing the pleading victim because he reflects a pain that could not be metabolised.

The emotional drivers of this violence are expressed in the desire of the diminished victim to have the power of the perpetrator, so that shame (passivity) is shifted to potency (activity). Parallel to this, and in part facilitating it, is an energetic force that presents itself as dysregulated electrical and chemical functioning in the emotionally driven parts of the brain.

Some children are traumatised but go on to achieve in their lives with minimal distress, because the architecture of self-regulation is afforded to them by virtue of having been loved and nurtured. This love not only teaches them behaviour strategies, but results in the development of appropriate neuronal networks in the brain, which have embedded in them the strategies to intervene and calm the self and also to calm others who may be agitated.

The loved child will still pay a price at times for being traumatised and overwhelmed, including night terrors, flashbacks that replay bad events, or aversions to experiences and objects that remind them of the trauma. But they are not at the mercy of it. The experience of being loved fosters resilience by equipping them to cope with frightening circumstances. These children's world view preserves the delusion of mastery over one's life.

Sometimes, the young person ends up hating themselves so much for having failed to prevent the abuse, or to forget it, that they end up hurting themselves, in part to self-punish but also to seek relief. When children cut or burn themselves, it expresses otherwise indescribable pain through the pain in their flesh. The act of harm can also balance the power of the emotional pain they are grappling with. Some describe watching the flow of blood as soothing, as if the red fluid acts like tears.

People wrongly see individuals who harm themselves as attention seekers. One only has to imagine the force of emotional pain a child is enduring that makes it worthwhile to cut into their own skin as an act of recovery. Even if it were attention seeking, the child would be in search of tenderness, because they feel that harming themselves is the only way to receive care.

III

When Charisma was referred to Kids Company as a troublesome truant, there was nothing in the referral to indicate sexual abuse by her dad. To have known this earlier would have enabled us to explore it sooner as a potential explanation for her aggressive behaviours. She had already been banned from two pupil referral units for violence.

Only years later did she reveal to me that a friend at school had disclosed to their teacher that Charisma was saying her father sexually abused her. At the time, both girls were ten years old. Social services intervened and the matter was taken to court. Inside the courtroom, Charisma's father was two seats away from her. Her mum sat with her dad.

She was asked whether her father had raped her. Charisma remembers him looking at her in the most terrifying way and her mum seeming to plead for her to say 'no'. She describes looking at her mother and father and thinking that she could not destroy their lives. He would end up in prison for a long time if she confirmed the rape. She was also very frightened of him. So she withdrew her allegation and instead he got a two-year prison sentence for beating her.

The professionals did not question this sudden reversal. The father was allowed to go back to the house, and it was not until I told social services that Charisma had disclosed rape by her dad and abuse by paedophiles that the social work teams began to intervene again in this family's life. We ensured that the father was banned from the house, restoring to the children some sense of safety.

Charisma believes that from the age of eleven until she arrived at Kids Company aged fourteen, she was forced to have sex with more than 200 men. My job was to find her, and not to let her be lost among perverse companions. I could not be like a dissociated mother. Each time I managed to catch her at an act of self-harm, she smiled in delighted relief.

The traumatised child is always lonely: they have to be found. They do not want neutrality. They want someone to seek them so that they can know that they are wanted. The seeking has to be delicately balanced. If it is too intrusive, the child will see the therapeutic worker as a devouring monster pursuing them for personal consumption.

When Charisma was not actively placing herself in situations of harm, she would become the victim to her persecutory fright. She would beg me to remove the terror from her, but at the same time frustrate any attempt to soothe her. She was convinced she had gone mad. Eventually, the repercussions of what had happened to her were no longer containable and she wanted to die.

There was no point to living. We were tussling: she wanted death and I had to keep reflecting back to her the side of her that could live. I could feel the power of her fright because as a repercussion I had a parallel paralysis of efficacy. I felt useless, as if her despair was going to be more powerful than my hope.

All the secure givens by which we organise our lives had been taken away from her. For her, the delusions of order through which we reassure ourselves were irrelevant. She felt that anything she built could be taken away from her through the malevolent intention of someone else. It was simple. If your father wanted to rape you, he could. There was nothing that a ten-year-old could have done, alone in the house with him. Powerlessness was a truthful and intrinsic experience, and here I was telling her that she could make a go of her life. I kept reminding her that her music was beautiful and that it was worth living for.

Her singing voice became powerful. It had a rich, exotic, bellowing and spiritual quality to it. In 2016, I took her to a record company as I wanted someone else to reflect back to her the value of her extraordinary talent.

An astute music producer identified what was wrong. She needed no music lessons, he told me; her singing was perfect. Yet she didn't exist. She lacked presence and the embodiment of passion. She lacked the will to be Charisma and until she acquired it, he could not sign her on.

For Charisma to regain a sense of identity, and the legitimacy to express it powerfully, she needs to be helped through the developmental trauma she has endured. She starts at the bottom of a well and has to make her way to the top of a mountain. With Kids Company's help, she reached flat land. She was no longer terrorised by the darkness of her anxiety.

Post Kids Company's closure, I continued working with her. Since social services were not housing her appropriately and no one would take proper responsibility for her care, we were left with no option but to get her a solicitor, who challenged the local authority through a judicial review. The judge acted to protect her, and Charisma now has her own home and a job.

For the first time in her life, she is in a routine which is not perverse or abusive to her. There is more work to be done to help her integrate and achieve a cohesive identity. Sometimes, going back to prostitution feels attractive. The money is quicker and better.

She is compelled to repeat the trauma, but at least she has gained awareness of how her psychology can hijack her.

For many traumatised children and young people, Kids Company workers were islands of safety. Children could turn to them to be validated and replenished. As time went on, the child internalised the key worker's goodness, and forgave their shortcomings. Charisma benefited from brilliant workers, each helping her on her journey to achieve mastery over her trauma.

By caring for her and helping her understand the havoc child-hood maltreatment can cause, Charisma was also able to persuade her mother to seek help. As her mother relinquishes the defence of dissociation, she can acknowledge the existence of her daughter. In the process, she is building the relationship she had always wanted with her child, but could not because of how damaged the child within her was.

Kids Company never intended to replace the children's biological carers; we recognised that bond as sacred. However, we embraced the truth that at times parents cannot take care of their children the way they would like to, because of the childhood harm they have endured. Some parents were less resilient. Our role was to strengthen the bio-logical carer, supplement their care and sometimes substitute it. Our priority was to help children and parents reunite in love.

Some children and young people could not return to the family. For them, Kids Company had become a substitute family setting. Over the years, I watched an informal network of care develop among the kids. As adults, they turned to each other for support. It made me deeply happy. We helped reduce the loneliness of maltreated children and, in loving them, helped them love others. We couldn't do it perfectly but we did it well enough.

CHAPTER 15

CIRCLES OF REPAIR

Drowned today in tsunami of Technicolor blancmange, oozing psycho-babble, emotional blackmail & verbal ectoplasm. Beware Batmanghelidjh.

TWEET SENT BY PAUL FLYNN MP, A MEMBER OF THE PUBLIC ADMINISTRATION AND CONSTITUTIONAL AFFAIRS COMMITTEE OF THE HOUSE OF COMMONS, 15 OCTOBER 2015

The outside world often described me as a charismatic leader. This idea has a shallow hue, because it assumes an organisation run on charm, exotic dress and the wing of fickle chance. The positive side of the premise is the arousal of inspiration, but on the back of inspiration rides the follower's sense of personal inadequacy, which eventually will deliver the sour fruit of envy.[1]

The power of my 'charisma' was articulated on the day Kids Company closed by an unnamed Whitehall source who said I had 'mesmerised' David Cameron into handing over millions. 'We were all overridden by No. 10,' this 'senior figure' told the BBC.[2] I thought, 'If only you knew what a complex and structured task leading Kids Company was.'

The other narrative was the 'mother figure': Kids Company was led by a woman who loved children. The implication was that I could not have any business sense and that men were needed to run the organisation, leaving the woman to love the children. Even when I was raising £2 million a month, they still said it. Interestingly, the people who never thought like this were the entrepreneurs. They thought I was like them.

Even our trustees, who relied on me to 'pull the rabbit out of the bag' to keep the charity going, were amazed by how structured everything was. When staff presented their work at trustees' meetings there was often a feeling of shock. Of course, there are things I cannot do because of my learning difficulties. Yet something about my character makes people think I am incapable of order, and what I *can* do gets negated. Is it my appearance, or the fact that, like many women, I achieve without fuss?

These questions were always in the background, and did not endanger the charity until 2015. Successive governments saw our value; the problem was money. 'In an ideal world, every neighbourhood should have a Kids Company,' said a report commissioned by the Home Office in 2003. The ink was barely dry when the Home Office cut back on grants. Responsibility for us moved to the Treasury, which tried to solve the funding challenge caused by the kids self-referring. A fantastic civil servant called Michael Jacobs, who had seen our work in one of the schools, took over the brief. I took him and some colleagues from the Cabinet Office to the house of two boys; the party included David Halpern, then the chief analyst in the Prime Minister's strategy unit. The parents were severely ill with mental health difficulties and the brothers, both under fourteen, attended Kids Company. The poverty and bleakness shocked the visitors, hardening their resolve to help.

They also met an older sister who, as a teenage mum, had developed psychosis and nearly killed her own baby. I remember going to see her in a psychiatric unit. The anti-psychotic medication had made her very big, but she had no one to buy her clothes and she begged for some leggings. Her delight when I returned with a Marks & Spencer bag of colourful garb was beyond price. The family lurched from crisis to crisis, its members surviving as best as they could, and like us they hoped the kind government representatives they met would change things for the better. I was really hopeful.

In October 2006, Prime Minister Tony Blair wrote to me to say he felt 'very strongly' about social exclusion and would work 'relentlessly' against it. He went on: 'I agree entirely with the need to create structures which protect quality of delivery at street level ... We are often reliant on frequently overstretched frontline practitioners taking the initiative to adopt best practice, which isn't fair or sustainable.' Responding to my suggestion of a new centre of excellence for children and families, he wrote: 'The government will also consider the case for a centre of excellence for children's and family services to identify, evaluate and disseminate best practice ... Your continued support, expertise and input into this agenda are very much appreciated.'

As politicians picked over our bones ten years later, a pet theme was that we had absorbed millions in public funds without proper assessment of what we were achieving. Even the National Audit Office (NAO) succumbed to this. 'Until 2013, the government relied heavily on Kids Company's self-assessments to monitor its performance,' it found, reporting that the Department for Education 'oversaw the grant funding of Kids Company until summer 2013 but has limited records of monitoring activities before 2011'.[3] What this hasty investigation failed to say was that comprehensive records of our evaluations were conveniently 'lost' by the education department until after the NAO report, when they were magically found again after it became clear we had copies. By then, however, MPs were confident they knew the story. Paul Flynn, a member of the committee of MPs that examined our relationship with Whitehall, accused our auditors of overlooking 'misuse of large amounts of public funds, possible fraud going on everywhere ... looting of the public purse of millions ... [money] wasted on a gargantuan scale,' adding:

You did your audit, gave it a clean bill of health, picked up your fee and they still carried on in what was I believe not far off a confidence trick … The money was being wasted and much of the work the charity had done was damaging and not beneficial.

He even accused us of 'neglect of children'.[4]

The notion that grants were based on self-assessment until 2013 was nonsense. The government was intimately involved in our audits and evaluations. As long ago as the Blair years, the Home Office placed a forensic psychologist in our clinical audit department to help us generate outcome reports for the Treasury. The reports measured the children's progress using psychological tests. At the same time, Treasury auditors came down to Kids Company and went through our accounts. When the Treasury proved unable to solve our funding problems and the brief was moved to the education department, the scrutiny continued. 'To monitor performance, DfE asked Kids Company to provide twice-yearly self-assessment reports during this period,' says the National Audit Office. 'The documents have been annotated, suggesting that DfE officials reviewed their content. Although DfE told us that it challenged Kids Company on any issues arising, it could not provide evidence to support this.'[5] The reason there is no record of challenge is that there was no challenge to make: they were satisfied with the reporting. There was plenty of external scrutiny too.

Between 2005 and 2008, one of the independent organisations who evaluated Kids Company's work was the University of London Queen Mary. Researchers randomly turned up on the premises and carried out quantitative as well as qualitative research with approximately 1,500 participants. The research was peer-reviewed by Professor Towel, head of psychology at the National Offender Management Service of the Home Office, as well as Dr Bostock, senior research analyst from the Social Care Institute for Excellence and Dr Sarah Johnston from the Centre for Housing Policy, University of York. The research team was made up of a researcher, who had a Master's in social policy and planning at LSE, and another research consultant who used to work with Accenture as part of their strategy and business consultancy. The funding came from an independent research body which London University accessed directly. Their ethics committee oversaw the research process.

At the time, 83 per cent of the Kids Company client group were found to be suffering from complex trauma but 77 per cent of them, while with Kids Company, returned to education, training or employment. Ninety-seven per cent of children accessing Kids Company street-level centres believed that they were helped with their difficulties. In the schools, teachers considered 89 per cent of pupils to have experienced positive outcomes because of the therapy they had received, with 83 per cent of them being considered by teachers to have engaged more with education, improved overall concentration and reduced disruptive behaviour as well as improved grades.

The research found that 89 per cent of the children were self-referring and 89 per cent did not experience any stigma when accessing Kids Company. Professor Towel observed that there was a 50 per cent reduction in arrest rates among the Kids Company children and young people, which he described as a 'dramatic reduction'.

The evaluation discovered that Kids Company children and young people were presenting with more risk and adversity than prisoners. During the research, Strengths and Difficulties Questionnaires, an independent psychological assessment, were used to capture data on 1,242 children, with teachers and teaching assistants completing the questionnaires as well as the children.

You can therefore imagine my sense of injustice when civil servants stood up in Parliament and said we didn't have independent evaluations demonstrating outcomes and outputs.

However, one brave civil servant demonstrated great integrity. Chris Wormald, the permanent Secretary for the Department for Education, when giving evidence to the parliamentary inquiry led by Meg Hillier in 2015, said the following: 'If you look at the total volume of what we give to the voluntary sector, you see that it comes to a bit over £200 million a year, and Kids Company was receiving about 2 per cent of what we gave to the voluntary sector over that period.'

This shows that Kids Company did not 'take' the bulk of the money depriving other voluntary sector organisations of grants as had been wrongly suggested by MPs and some Cabinet Office civil servants. Nor was the charity favoured over others; we submitted applications which were subjected to scrutiny and we often scored the highest points. Chris Wormald states:

It is of course true that the money went up, mainly because Kids Company was extremely successful in a series of bidding rounds, where its bids were measured against the criteria of those schemes...

Certainly the view we took at the time was that the outcomes we were getting – I do not think there is any disagreement about this – for some highly innovative work with some extremely vulnerable people was value for money. I can only tell you what we thought at the time, which was that, that did represent value for money.

He also confirmed that the Department for Education reviewed the charity's outputs and found them to be a 'reasonable set of outputs for that sum of money', adding:

Certainly, until very recently, very few people have been doubting the quality of what Kids Company has been achieving ... We did have a set of evidence on the table that those interventions were being successful ... You were saying there was no evaluation evidence. That is not correct ... I have already quoted the evaluation that we did in 2011, and there was also the LSE study, the UCL study, et cetera. There were proper studies writing up this work.[6]

In 2013/14, we had over thirty independent research protocols, the majority of which were funded by the universities and academic institutions. The research teams included UCL Developmental Risk and Resilience Unit, Kings College London Institute of Psychiatry, University of Cambridge Department of Developmental Psychiatry, UCL Anna Freud Centre, University of Portsmouth, University of Leeds, Southbank University, University of Bristol, the Tavistock and Portman NHS Trust, Centre for Social Work Research, University of East London, University of Sussex, Lancaster, Brunel and the London School of Economics, among others. The majority of this research was shared with government departments but barely any mention of them was made during the disruption of 2015 as there was an effort to present Kids Company as a ramshackle, unaccountable, ineffective organisation working with no kids.

Even when the Department for Education was audited by the government, it was stated by the auditors that the grant Kids Company received from the Department for Education in 2008–11 'is helping Kids Company to become a centre of excellence, enabling them to disseminate informed educational packages for service users and providers'.[7]

Confusion seems to have been created via the Cabinet Office, which hasn't always represented a straightforward story regarding Kids Company. In 2015, senior civil servants from the Cabinet Office claimed we did not report back appropriately.[8] They even claimed that we hadn't reported back to them on a grant payment. However, the report on Kids Company by the National Audit Office shows a different picture.

In November 2014, the government internal audit agency reviewed the Cabinet Office's oversight of the Kids Company grant. It focused on the ongoing oversight of payments and delivery, not the original award decision. The review concluded that the Cabinet Office had satisfactory reporting and assurance arrangements in place for administering the Kids Company grant. The review included looking at a sample of quarterly performance reports, and Methods validation reports. It concluded that there were no issues to indicate the grant was being misused.[9]

None of our research data was reflected in any of the reports the government produced for Parliament. Kids Company was made out by civil servants in the Cabinet Office to be unaccountable and without effective outcomes for children.

Of course, it was hard to measure Kids Company against any other organisation, given the complexity of our case work on the front line of deprived inner-city communities. When the National Children's Bureau evaluated us, they decided the closest comparison was with Harlem Children's Zone in the United States, a non-profit organisation committed to breaking the cycle of poverty. But how could anyone assess our value for money when no figures exist for the cost of a maltreated child to the public purse? A young person's impacts on education, health, mental health, social care, police, justice and welfare budgets are counted separately or not at all, and that is before you start costing the lost economic output of a troubled life, or the effect on other people of an anti-social one. No one has the faintest idea what value for money looks like. I wish they had, as there is evidence we were it. In 2013, we provided for the education department an analysis by Martin Knapp, professor of social policy and director of the personal social services research unit at the London School of Economics and Political Science (LSE). His team calculated the impact of a government grant we received to help 750 young people, concluding: 'Total potential cost savings and economic benefits generated from Kids Company were estimated to range from £8.767 million to £9.501 million over a period of up to ten years.'[10]

We got grants because no one would pay for the kids. Public money represented about 30 per cent of our income; the rest came from voluntary donations. We collaborated with civil servants, they evaluated us properly and no favours were done. To suggest that we owed our income to the arm-twisting of Prime Ministers is to deny both the degree of private support and the extent of official scrutiny. We had excellent relationships with thoughtful civil servants, who were committed to finding a solution.

In February 2010, in the dying months of Labour's final administration, the civil servant responsible for Kids Company – Antony Hughes, a deputy director of what was then called the Department for Children, Schools and Families – wrote to say: 'We remain determined to support you in finding a long-term solution to the financial sustainability of Kids Company.' He urged us to continue applying for local authority funds in the hope that at some point we would get proper money. Referring to an evaluation of our three-year £12.7 million grant under the Youth Sector Development Fund, he said he hoped this would 'provide a strong evidence base for the support that Kids Company are providing to young people', adding that 'it was great to meet such committed and friendly staff, and also look at the great systems and plans that you have in place at Kids Company'.[11]

Not a word of it in the NAO report.

The grant, equivalent to £4.2 million a year from 2008 to 2011, was intended to help Kids Company become a centre of excellence, delivering care to 14,000 vulnerable young Londoners at the same time as developing training packages for other voluntary and community organisations. We were audited by Ecotec, a consultancy appointed by the government to manage the grant programme. It made site visits and carried out random checks, asking for case files to trace the financial and clinical activity relating to individual children. A typical Ecotec report, in June 2010, found 'good' governance systems and controls, 'good' documentation to show delivery of the programme, and a 'good' level of assurance regarding financial controls. In addition, the Department for Education examined the accounts we submitted, as did the accountants who audited Kids Company as a charity. For one grant we went through three types of audit, as well as having independent researchers from universities work alongside us to evaluate the provision for the children. Civil servants were in and out of the charity all the time.

By 2011, despite the goodwill, Kids Company's funding was still unresolved. Troubled young people were continuing to present themselves.

Officials asked KPMG to identify streams of government funding we could access. At the same time, two civil servants were seconded to the charity full-time to help us find pots of public money. They worked hard; we were hopeful.

KPMG reported back that Kids Company and local authorities had different ideas on how to help a group of young people that was hard to reach. 'Kids Company believe that not all children and young people fit one model,' it said, accurately, while councils 'find it difficult to unpackage the service delivery model Kids Company seeks to implement and where this starts and finishes with respect to their statutory obligations'.[12] In other words, the charity took a holistic approach, the public sector a gate-keeping one. We did receive some disturbed young people from councils and youth offending teams, but each child was paid for on an hourly basis. It did not cover the cost of the psychologists, special needs teachers and social workers we made available.

The two civil servants were doing no better. After submitting more than eighty applications for public money, the total they had raised was zero. It was powerfully evident that a systemic barrier was preventing Kids Company becoming sustainable. Reporting back to her bosses at the education department, one of the civil servants told of the tension with local authorities. 'Unlike other charities [Kids Company] are committed to taking on the most troubled cases,' she wrote. 'As well as providing services themselves, Kids Company acts as an advocate for the child in accessing statutory services. This has led to Kids Company taking Local Authorities to Judicial Review on several occasions and even to a change in child protection law.'[13] She included five case studies. One was a bright child viewed by social services as not at risk of significant harm; aged fifteen, he was 'shaking with fear and had been sleeping rough'. Another was a girl aged fourteen who had been raped at three by her stepbrother and raped again at eight by a friend of her father, and was also neglected and physically abused. 'Subsequently the client was placed on a short child protection plan and then downgraded to Child in Need status,' the civil servant reported. 'The client started self-harming and sadly became an in-patient and lost all trust in social services ... The girl was put in her father's care and allegations of abuse continued.' When finally taken into care, she 'ran back to Kids Company as the only place she felt she could be heard'.[14]

As our three-year grant from the education department was coming to an end in 2011, I started to see immense restlessness in the inner city. Levels of violence were rising. Gangs were kidnapping and stabbing young people and there were horrific sexual assaults. John Sutherland, the police commander in Southwark, went off on sick leave, shocked by the rape of a boy of fourteen by another the same age.

I remember being in a car with a group of kids. The coalition government led by David Cameron had been in office for a year. A boy sitting in the front turned round and said quite randomly, 'Camila, this government hates us.' His depth of feeling sent a chill up my spine.

It prompted me to write to Oliver Letwin, begging him to pay atten-tion. It was June 2011 and he was minister for government policy in the Cabinet Office. 'I hope you don't mind me being very straightforward with you, but I wanted to make you aware that the risks at street level have enormously escalated,' I wrote.

Now fourteen- and fifteen-year-olds are carrying firearms ... I am also aware that the drug dealers are actively exporting the business into the countryside and into wealthier areas. We are going to see an increase in car jackings around Kensington and Knightsbridge and areas such as St John's Wood. The countryside is also being actively targeted, with crack houses being set up and kids being given drugs for free initially, then forced into an addiction ... There's a real sense of despair amongst young people who feel that legitimate structures within society have abandoned them, and in effect the drug dealers are offering them perverse solutions. Against this background is also

[a] movement which is radicalising young people, using pseudo-religious constructs. There is a clear link between vulnerable young people being pulled into these gangs and the failure of child protection agencies in intervening in their lives robustly and early. What's very clear is that the current status quo can no longer be sustained, because it could be interpreted as racism and the abandonment of vulnerable children in the ghettos of Britain.

Oliver kindly offered me an appointment in September 2011, but by then the August riots had shown the rage and despair felt in some communities. They were triggered when police in north London failed to explain why they had shot Mark Duggan, a young father who had taken possession of a handgun fifteen minutes before being killed by an officer from Trident, the Met's unit for tackling gun crime. During the riots, the kids in Peckham stole sack-loads of rice and other food from shops, but this was not reported. Instead, they were presented as materialistic for also breaking into Foot Locker for trainers. Interestingly, they left the bookshop alone; the owner had never banned children, and for this he had their respect.

I was later told privately that car jackings had risen as I predicted, while radicalisation and the spread of drug-dealing using 'county lines' became recognised concerns.[15] Five years after my letter, more than eight in ten police forces in England and Wales faced an established or still-emerging pattern of urban criminals, mostly from London, using the homes of vulnerable people as a base for provincial drug deals. They also reported the exploitation of children to deliver the drugs, as the result of control through grooming, intimidation, violence and debt bondage.[16]

When I met Oliver in Downing Street, he was visibly shaken by the ferocity of the riots. The coalition knew it must do something meaningful for dispossessed young people. He promised to bring together the heads of government departments to create a fund to make Kids Company sustainable. I was convinced he was serious, because he picked up the phone in front of me to talk to Theresa May in the Home Office. She wasn't in.

I left Downing Street in 2011 full of hope that perhaps now we would get some sustainable income and could concentrate on the children and their needs. I was starting to tire of promises that, despite their sincerity, never materialised into anything meaningful. Yet it was the positive intentions of ministers and civil servants that kept us going. At no time did anyone suggest Kids Company was failing. Everyone was trying to remove the barriers to sustainability.

Just before the two civil servants left, I wrote a project which secured a £2 million grant from The Big Lottery Fund as the result of a project involving Channel 4 and the fashion expert Gok Wan, who was filmed with some of our most challenging teenagers for a documentary series called *The Secret Millions*. The T-shirts they created sold out in Sports Direct. The grant outcomes were outstanding: more than seven in ten young people ended up in employment, education or training.

Oliver failed to find the funding he had hoped for. For 2011/12 and 2012/13 we were back to receiving a government grant of about £4.5 million a year, awarded by the Department for Education to improve outcomes for 750 disadvantaged young people by providing health, social care and educational support. This time the department's head of research and evaluation for children's social care became involved. He was convinced, despite the findings of the KPMG report, that if we could show all our wonderful results then local authorities would fund us.

It was written into our grant requirement that we replicate our service using funding from a local authority. Bristol at the time was seeking a partner to take over some of its education. The city seemed to be in a rush after the previous provider hit a funding crisis. For us, it was an opportunity to build a portfolio that would give confidence to local authorities, just as the Department of Education was urging. It did not seem a substantial risk, as the city council would pay for the education of the children and also hand over some teachers. We could not see exactly what we were taking on, however, because most of the negotiations took place over the summer. It was an expansion for which we would be much criticised, as if we were trying to build an empire instead of striving to sustain ourselves as instructed.

So, by 2012 we were in Bristol. The reality was an absolute shock as the children were so disturbed. I remember walking into a pupil referral unit for under-11s to find a teacher we had inherited sitting on a stool. Her eyes were glazed with exhaustion and despair. She had locked the door to her classroom: I had to knock on the glass to get in. The kids in her charge were crawling around on the ground, poking a cardboard box and climbing into it to squeeze their eyelashes through the holes. There was no exchange of normal speech among the children.

The carpet was disgusting. The walls were bleak and dirty. Then I noticed a child climbing a filing cabinet and crawling into a foetal position inside a doorless kitchen cupboard that was hanging off the wall. It was terrifying: I thought it was going to break. I coaxed him down, but could not get any of the children to sit long enough to talk to them for a few minutes. The manic fragility was gut-wrenching. These were eight- and nine-year-olds who looked five or six.

I raised my voice above the mayhem and calmly explained that I wanted to give them my heart and look after theirs. 'What colour would you like it to be?' I then pulled out some paper and felt tips and started to engage with the first of the kids to respond. Eventually they all snatched a piece of paper with a different heart for each child. I promised them I would be back.

As I left the site, a little girl aged nine, but who appeared no older than six, ran to the tall metal gates and stretched out her hand. The locked gate separated us and she looked like she was in a cage. She shouted, 'Please, please don't leave me!' and burst into tears. Still weeping, she pressed two fingers into her eyes and started talking to herself: 'I have to control myself. I have to stop crying.'

The sight of her profound sorrow and attempt to control it broke me. I promised her that I would be back and that I would not leave her. Then I got into the car and wept for the two-and-a-half-hour journey back to London. The driver, Devan, kept looking in his mirror. He had taken me in the past to appointments all over the country; in the back of the car I would be on the phone, negotiating for funds with government departments and philanthropists. In between, he would hold my mobile to answer emergencies from crazed kids as I was speaking at a conference or dealing with other children. Devan knew everything. On this car journey I could not bring myself to string two sentences together, such was the power of what that child had projected.

We all knew it was going to be a challenge to stabilise these children. The budget allowed a single class teacher. It took play therapists, psychologists, a psychiatrist to work with the parents, and several teachers to do it. Every child had been abused. The little girl was supported by our team to give evidence in court; her father had been sexually abusing her since she was a baby. He was imprisoned for fifteen years.

We managed to advocate on her behalf so that she could go to a therapeutic community. When I next saw her, a couple of months later, she was carrying an art box our team had given her with all sorts of little trinkets in it. She had also been writing poetry, for which she later won an award. The relief that the right kind of help had arrived and the bond with Kids Company, along with her foster carer's support, had transformed her. Before me, even after such a short time, was a little girl capable of sitting and chatting. Her temper tantrums remained furious, but there was a glimpse of potential brilliance. It was for children like her, in their thousands, that our workers carried on. However frustrating the task became and however hard it became to pay for it, encounters with such kids renewed my determination too.

It was also in Bristol that one of our staff supported a thirteen-year-old in our schools programme to give evidence against a Somalian gang taking vulnerable girls to hotels. No one had thought to ask why a slight young girl slept in the same room as an adult who was obviously not a relative.

For the girl to feel safe, our worker had to go into hiding with her for a week while she gave evidence. Another underage girl was found crying in her underwear in the cupboard under her sister's kitchen sink. This was after a rape. It is the casual lack of concern for children that allows such exploitation.

I thought I had seen the worst of it, until one of our workers called from Bristol to say that they had done a home visit and found a little boy sleeping on a urine-drenched mattress on the floor. We trained our workers to look inside household cupboards when they did home visits, so that they could discern if there was enough food, or the children's clothes were sufficient and looked after. When the worker opened the wardrobe, the paedophile who was abusing the child was standing naked.

Bristol was one of the most caring local authorities we came across. They behaved with integrity and wanted a partnership to solve problems. Just before Kids Company closed, we were given an NHS contract as a pilot which, if we had seen through, could have become a big source of funding in the future. They were also the local authority who worked with us to make sure post-closure that the young people in our care transitioned appropriately into their systems.

Thirteen men were jailed for up to thirteen years for a campaign of abuse, rape and prostitution of teenage girls. The police commended the Kids Company worker, but I heard no mention of this at the parliamentary inquiry in 2015 as Bernard Jenkin and his colleagues fretted over whether we had bought the kids trainers.

By August 2012, a year after the riots, David Cameron realised that Kids Company's uncertain finances remained a problem. 'Firstly let me make clear how much your work is valued,' he wrote to say. 'I know that you are transforming the lives of many young people, and I am pleased that a substantial grant from the Department of Education is helping you to do this. I also understand how hard the constant battle for resources must be in a time of austerity.'

He then suggested a solution.

I am therefore very happy to ask that a senior official from the Department for Education convene a discussion with senior colleagues from other departments, in order to improve understanding of Kids Company's contribution to agendas across government ... Discussions will explore opportunities to unlock barriers to the commissioning of Kids Company's services and identify possible paths to funding.

The result was a new cross-government grant of £4.5 million in 2013/14 and 2014/15, put together with contributions from four government departments. Under the grant offer made by the education department in July 2013, we were required to submit quarterly self-assessment reports on our performance. We exceeded the targets by a handsome margin, a fact verified by Methods Consulting Ltd, which was given a £200,000 contract by the government to audit our reports. Methods took random samples of the kids' records from the computer system and traced the key workers' paper entries. It had unfettered access to our venues and staff.

'A key finding of the Q2 report is that all targets set in the Grant Offer document have been met or exceeded,' the consultancy reported.

Having examined the definition of the targets and the underlying data collected by Kids Company staff, we confirm that this is true. The Grant Offer specified a number of interventions to be carried out in each quarter for a given number of clients. We can confirm that not only are Kids Company meeting the specified numbers of clients and interventions, in some cases they are achieving three or four times the number of target interventions.[17]

The education department commissioned Professor Stephen Briggs of the University of East London to report on how Kids Company worked. He tracked in depth a small sample of 'extremely deprived and traumatised' young people, finding positive outcomes that were impressive educationally, practically and in terms of emotional well-being'. We also submitted standardised psychological tests and reading tests showing the progress of 300 other young clients. By now, responsibility for Kids Company had passed to the Cabinet Office. Richard White, the head of research in the DfE, forwarded the Briggs report to his colleagues there, saying that it 'brings to life vividly the needs and development of the young people supported'.[18]

The email was dated 18 October 2013. We did not know it, but time was running out. Soon came a series of events that unnerved me so much I started logging the evidence with a top human rights barrister and a former Archbishop of Canterbury.

• • •

When I was a child in Iran, I used to look up at the big turquoise mosques with their beautiful domes. I realised the ornate designs could be broken down into the repetition of a circle. Something complex and exquisite had emerged from a single geometric shape.

I became fascinated with whether organisations could be structured to have the mosque's complex harmony while keeping the confined intimacy of a circle. Could a charity function with multiple delivery points, at the same time making people feel valued and significant as individuals?

We aimed to foster resilience in our young clients by first solving practical problems such as hunger, poor housing and inadequate clothing. Then came therapeutic recovery programmes. After that we looked for a talent in each child that would allow them to join the wider community, be valued by it and add something of value in return. We wanted our young people to become citizens who recognised their membership of society. We expected them to use the collaborations we organised for them to work towards economic self-sufficiency. Kids Company would always be their safety net but we wanted them to connect more and more with the outside world, according to their abilities.

We explored this vision in regular staff meetings. Every month, senior managers came together for what was known as a 'Can Do' meeting, in which we discussed what we wanted to achieve and why, then turned it into a plan. We were a collective centred on the children. We learnt from them how best to care for young people by addressing the repercussions of the maltreatment they had endured.

By now I had worked out that what the government of David Cameron cared about, and in some ways Tony Blair's, was branding. If something had a high brand value, they wanted to be affiliated with it. If it had a low brand value, they saw no potential to elevate their own brand and paid no attention.

I set myself two goals, which were to run the charity using a spiritually informed leadership style and to create a parallel brand that would act as an interface with the brand-driven political world we were having to deal with. The moral and spiritual drivers required to run a good charity were not on their own going to mobilise resources in a brand-conscious world. At the same time, it was important that the shallowness of branding did not interfere with the day-to-day running of the organisation. I did not want to create a brand narrative around Kids Company that was inauthentic or emotionally vacuous.

The fusion I arrived at was an aspirational brand that had at its heart an emotional agenda promoting the value of doing good for the most disadvantaged children. It came back to the circles on the mosque. We were not looking to be liked or admired, except to motivate the delivery of practical and emotional help for the kids. There was no merit in the charity unless it delivered quality to them.

I recognised that I was in a complex and dual position, because on the one hand the children and the staff needed a strong, maternal, value-based leader, who could tolerate distress and not be overwhelmed by it, keeping everyone on the path of acquiring mastery over their traumas and going on to flourish. But in being a present maternal object, I did not want to be idealised.

I would make my PAs hide any awards I received. I did not allow pictures of me with celebrities or Prime Ministers. I had an open-door policy so that everyone in the organisation could contact me. Seeing myself as one of the workers, I cleaned the floor and helped out as much as possible. I made sure that we never had pictures or newspaper articles about Kids Company stuck anywhere on the walls in the centres; only three or four people in the charity knew I was receiving a CBE. I tried to keep the branding world, and the idealised view of me in the media, out of the organisation. We refused photo shoots with famous people that had no deeper meaning. I called it 'rent a poor kid syndrome'; if anyone wanted to collaborate with our children, they had to contribute by making things better for them.

The trustees in turn held me accountable. They were serious people, and from time to time they asked external consultants to review my leadership. The deputy chair was Richard Handover, a former chief executive of WH Smith. He does not have a record of tolerating waste. Commissioned by Ed Balls to assess the spending of the Department for Children, Schools and Families, he called for 40,000 teaching assistants to lose their jobs.

By this time we had arrived at a point where the organisation had robust enough structures for the clinical work with the kids to be safe and monitored. Internally we had created a culture where the child was at the centre of our decisions, and staff framed their activities as doing their best to encourage resilience and hope. The turning point came two or three years into Kids Company's existence. It involved a twelve-year-old girl called Daisy, who had tried to jump from her bedroom window as the fire brigade gathered below. She did not always turn her death wish onto herself, and on this day, in a ferocious tantrum, she was being held by a staff member to stop a spree of destruction. He was gentle and kind, but she spat at him and verbally assaulted him when she could not deliver punches. What was striking was how the other children allowed the incident to happen without winding her up further or claiming that she was suffering an injustice. They had come to recognise these tantrums, which they all had, as part of the 'switching' that creates wounded beasts ready to kick, bite, punch, gouge out eyes, stab or kill.[19]

Once the brain's limbic system is agitated, it needs only three or four further cues that match a child's original trauma to trigger a loss of control in which they end up operating through the brain stem. The stem does not 'think'; it reacts in a programmed way as if this is a moment of life or death. A tall, male staff member who looks like he could be your father is not an abusing dad. But in the transference, the traumatised child reacts as if he is. He in turn, through counter transference, may inadvertently do something to increase the danger, hooking him into the enactment of the trauma.

The worker with Daisy was called Jason. I watched for half an hour as he managed Daisy's ferocious assault. Not once did he raise his voice, retaliate, or behave aggressively. He was in charge, and he knew that she was out of control and not evil. This was the moment I knew we had arrived. We were a therapeutic community, including the child who had lost her temper, the peers who did not intrude and the worker who was allowed to contain it all. Kids Company's provisions had synchronised, organised by a theoretical underpinning that came from our training and our modelling of appropriate behaviour.

While the outside world saw me as a charismatic leader, I aspired to be a transformational one. The drive of such a leader is to help people develop transformational autonomy by recognising their own capacity to do good. I loved our workers as much as the children. I wanted each to flourish, even if it meant that personal growth would lead them to go out and seek other adventures.[20] Although conscious of the needs and character of each member of staff, I wanted the workforce to organise itself around a central philosophy so that this diverse and complex community could be bound together in the service of the children, and I was absolutely uncompromising in defining the priority. Everything was subservient to the delivery of loving care to vulnerable children.

In this respect I exercised authority, at least until workers could see for themselves the transformational power of love. When they came to believe in it, they would work with it without a need for policing. I saw my power as the ability to carry a worker, sometimes against their will, into the deployment of love until the results showed the validity of the intention.

The truth is, had I not been strong in intention and delivery, we would have given up early on. At virtually every trustee meeting there was debate over how long the charity would survive and whether we should close it. These meetings were robust. I argued for an entrepreneurial approach and the trustees for less risk. If it had not been for the risks we took, Kids Company would have shut in the first year.[21]

Often the strength of a founder's determination is seen as a symptom of 'founderitus' or 'founder's syndrome'. This is a condition in which the founder remains dominant and typically makes all the decisions. I did not perceive myself as the founder of Kids Company: instead, I was the catalyst who facilitated the collective creativity of staff, children and supporters to generate a sanctuary for the most vulnerable.[22] My role as a leader was to encourage everyone to make self-sacrifices, putting the interests of the children above personal interests without feeling that they were being depleted. I wanted to help people experience the transformational potency of their own moral courage in keeping Kids Company alive for its kids.[23] Workers could have individual strategies, but the non-negotiable priority was to put children first and to exercise compassion in all their dealings.

Some perceived Kids Company as a cult. I prefer the concept of tribal leadership, which assumes that there are five stages of development in any group of twenty or more people and that the leader's task is to raise performance by changing the culture.[24] At Stage 1 are alienated workers who think that 'all life sucks'. They act out in despairingly hostile ways and are thought to represent 2 per cent of the workforce in any organisation. At Stage 2, the workforce experiences itself like an apathetic victim needing rescue. A quarter of the workforce is at this stage: lacking passion, quietly sarcastic and waiting for tasks to fail as they have in the past. At Stage 3 (49 per cent), workers see themselves as warriors, competing for individual greatness while finding many colleagues a disappointment. Collaboration is minimal. Only at Stage 4, thought to represent 22 per cent of the workforce, does tribal pride emerge as the group works together against a common adversary. This stage pits one tribe against another, such as a commercial rival. It is the top 2 per cent of the workforce who are at Stage 5: they experience themselves as people who are making history. They push against the limits of possibility and not against another tribe.[25]

There is no point cajoling people into a disciplined and emotionally generous approach. When workers are required to exercise continuous self-control, their capacities and vigilance diminish over time. Executive function, the control ability of the brain, is exercised through inhibition, which uses up a limited resource. Refraining from behaviour requires an act of self-control. As energy is expended to do it, resources deplete. At Kids Company, staff had to exercise great self-control as the children and families often provoked them.

Research shows that if control is achieved on the first task, by the second task the individual's functioning is impaired. Self-control is like a muscle that can become fatigued and needs to be replenished. People need rest and resources. If balance is not achieved, workers may acquire a depressive, learnt helplessness or function as bystanders.[26] They will not help a child in difficulty as they believe someone else will do it; and if others fail to react, the worker will not either. Through this defence mechanism, groups can become dysfunctional by unconsciously cueing each other into doing nothing.

But the dysfunction that most terrified me was moral disengagement. I knew that human beings were capable of reframing inhumane conduct into worthy behaviour. For example, one of our long-serving staff members began to struggle with the more difficult kids, so she started to disengage from them, describing one mentally ill young man as 'lazy'. I found him demanding too; conversing with him was hard. I could understand what she was trying to avoid. What I could not accept was presenting a wish not to see the young man as his fault.

She did engage with boys who were charming and chatty. I challenged her several times, explaining that the kids were not there to entertain her and that just because she had been with Kids Company for some time did not mean she could work less rigorously. After one of these challenges her face cleared, as if I had helped her to return from her defence mechanism to her decent core.

At times, I also felt the risk of disengagement. Some young people were described as my 'favourites' because they had stayed with Kids Company for years and I was involved in managing them. The Charity Commission, in the statutory inquiry it held into Kids Company for two years until mid-2017, took an interest in these cases as some were expensive. They had earlier been described by a witness who gave written evidence to MPs. 'One particular group of young adults – many of them in their late twenties – were known throughout the organisation as "Camila's kids" and inordinate amounts of money and resources were lavished on them; creating envy and resentment among others,' said this anonymous former member of the charity's staff.[27]

The reason I handled the so-called 'favourites' was that nobody else could face them. I knew their behaviour was driven by trauma and I had set myself the standard of never giving up, even on the most difficult. Some were so violent, disturbed and difficult that there were moments when I absolutely hated them. A legacy of abuse made them do and say the vilest things. They smashed up my office, tried to strangle me and sent emails threatening my mother with rape. They threw fire extinguishers at my door and overturned my PAs' computers or hurled them across the room. In the middle of the night I would then get a call to say they had been arrested; I really did not want to get out of bed to go to a police station and be with them while they were interviewed. But I got up because I realised how alone they were and I didn't want to let them down. I genuinely cared for them.

A consultant psychiatrist at the Maudsley told me to forget a client who was then nineteen. This girl will try to harm you, the psychiatrist said. She might destroy you. I knew it was true: she told the police she wanted to kill me, and described to journalists her crazy fantasies about a lesbian affair with me, which they believed. Still I would not walk away. Had it not been for a moral standard, I would have given up on these kids, because the horror of spending time with them was sometimes unbearable.

Culturally, we were surrounded by a dehumanising approach to disturbed young people. They were described as animals, criminal and 'feral', and thus unworthy of care. Workers, perhaps wanting to align themselves with mainstream society, could define the children as flawed and the public as victims.[28] I knew that morality could not be demanded from them. It had to be experienced emotionally and kept alive by self-regulation and space for staff to reflect.

It was not just the children I wanted to protect against poor moral choices. I was afraid for the workers' self-esteem if they became aware of a discrepancy between their aspiration to do well and poor delivery. I did not want them to condemn themselves and be shamed.[29] As Kids Company matured, we introduced systems to improve communication and accountability, but I did not want people to hide behind pseudo-professional functioning and insulate themselves against personal, moral responsibility. I wanted them to enjoy the good they could generate, and to avoid the self-exoneration of being seen to have followed procedures without honouring psychological truth.[30]

It was a leadership tightrope between managing workers' personal challenges, born of the complexities of transference and counter transference driven by the unconscious dramas of their childhood wounds, and trying to maintain high moral standards.[31]

The British psychoanalyst Wilfred Bion believed that if a group is functioning well, it keeps its focus on the task.[32] But the group can deviate from the task, avoiding it unconsciously by engaging with one of three destructive behaviours. He identified these defences as dependency, fight/flight and pairing.

In dependency, the group turns to the leader as a rescuer, wanting the leader to carry out the task for the group. Eventually the group will decide to take down the idealised leader and replace them with another.

In fight/flight, the group can either be hostile or exercise 'flight' through gossip, lateness or simply failing to do the work. This kind of group requires the leader to attack an outsider or collude in avoiding the central task.

In pairing, the group avoids the constructive task and two people emerge who hope to undermine the leader, presenting themselves or another leader as a replacement. The promise of a change in leadership gives the group relief and they eagerly await this pseudo-transformation as a rescue.

There was a risk that these unconscious ways of operating would sabotage the work of Kids Company. In the first five years, I experienced all three, because I was insisting that we work in a different way. As the brain research was not yet available to us, the staff were stuck on wanting to punish the kids, believing loss of control was just bad behaviour. When the kids got better, however, the key workers could see our method was effective. By the fifth year, I understood how the defence mechanisms worked in the staff, too.

The children, meanwhile, would have ambivalent feelings towards the staff. They were desperate for the workers' tenderness and their ability to bring to life a child's emotional experiences. But there was an internal tussle for worker and child. Children felt desperate, satisfied, and then resentful that the meeting of needs was coming from a stranger and not a parent. However good a worker was, it was never enough to answer the maltreatment the child had endured. As the British psychoanalyst Donald Winnicott would say, we tried to be a good enough substitute parent and recognised that we could not be an ideal one.

The worker was also exposed to the parents' ambivalent feelings. They were grateful for the help their child received but resentful that we had the power to create solutions they would have liked to provide. Some were jealous of what the children received, having had depleted childhoods themselves. They would turn up at the gate begging to be let in, or angry that their child was receiving clothes and they were not.

In turn, our workers sometimes felt rage towards the children and their carers for making impossible demands. They experienced themselves as failures for not meeting their needs. They felt guilt and sometimes jealousy while also being moved by the children's courage and fortitude.

I was at the top of the substitute parental ladder, trying as a leader to contain all these complex feelings. At times it felt as if bolts of electricity went through me delivering powerful energies, not only from the workforce but from trustees and funders. Even the public, wanting me to be an idealised mother who offered the care they would have wanted to give vulnerable children, including the child within themselves, used me as a psychological container.

In challenging the dysfunctional parts of the child protection and child mental health systems, I was experienced as someone who championed children while also being hated for aspiring to do better. Social workers and some psychiatrists admitted privately to feeling bad because they had given up on trying to improve their agencies. They knew they were letting kids down and I reminded them of that. They had similar feelings about trainees, whose enthusiasm and hope shamed them. Meanwhile the trainees were telling me that they would hear: 'We'll soon knock it out of you.' It was as if some professionals needed to make the students as spiritually dead as they had become, so that the student would stop reflecting back at them the aspiration they could no longer sustain.

In trying to represent a higher standard, I may have unwittingly triggered shame for those who felt they fell short, and envy for those who felt they wanted to occupy my position. Either way, it was inevitable that I would become a target to be despised. Yet the fatal challenge to Kids Company, which came from inside the organisation as well as outside, did not emerge until 2014.

• • •

The trustees and I knew that no charity could survive by delivering complex therapeutic programmes in response to self-referrals. Sooner or later it would die from donor fatigue. We created a strategy to keep the project alive.

Most supporters are not interested in funding long-term services. They prefer short-term projects that create no commitment to salaries, which made up 73 per cent of our costs. Therefore, survival of the Kids Company model would depend on persuading the government to fund us fully, either through a special grant or by seeing the model adopted in local authorities.

We were not invested in charity for charity's sake; Kids Company was an innovation hub. The aim was that its work would transfer to and transform the public sector, and the charity would cease to exist.

That is why we encouraged academics to measure the harm the children had endured and the effectiveness of our response to it. The idea was not just to reassure ourselves that our clinical practices were sound, important though that was. It was to persuade the government that something different was needed to obtain beneficial results with disturbed children and families. A 2010 symposium at the Royal Society of Medicine, at which scientists and academic institutions agreed to partner with Kids Company to explore the lives of our kids, was part of a strategy to inform political decision-making as well as to enhance the understanding of those who work with young people. The research programme was also about informing the public. I wanted people to understand that these children were struggling with neuro-developmental assault rather than being morally flawed. We created 'Peace of Mind, One Neuron at a Time', with the public sponsoring a neuron so that we could fund some of the research alongside charitable trusts who were also contributing. The results of the research came in post Kids Company's closure, demonstrating how trauma had affected our children's brains, making it difficult for them to manage their emotions and reactions.

Once we had developed a robust clinical intellectual property, we planned to campaign to change the system to create proper provision for children with no functioning parent in their lives. The Kids Company model would be offered to statutory agencies on a national scale. As a charity, we would make ourselves redundant.

This was the mission, articulated to anyone interested. I doubt I could have raised £123 million from private supporters if the message was that Kids Company was a self-perpetuating charity helping generation after generation of vulnerable children. It was always time-limited. At some point we would make our value so visible that we would no longer be needed.

This journey and its destination were known throughout the organisation. The message was important, because it meant the role of the staff went beyond confronting the repercussions of childhood misery. They also experienced themselves as pioneers working towards national improvements in children's services. We did not see ourselves as the only people who were doing this, but we knew that Kids Company was accumulating experience in the specialised area of urban, traumatised families.

When the LSE and the University of Heidelberg examined staff morale at Kids Company, they found it to be very high: 97 per cent of our staff were proud of their work.[33] Business schools and companies including Superdrug, B&Q and Unilever took an interest in our management strategies. Aviva asked me to give a talk at Saïd Business School, part of the University of Oxford. I also spoke at Cass Business School, part of City, University of London. I hope our staff really felt that they were in that top 2 per cent of the workforce, pushing against the limits of possibility.

Every half-term the staff met to hear about the research portfolio and the most recent findings. We also discussed the precariousness of our funding, as we never knew from month to month where our money would come from. We were quite open about this. Kids Company could not sustain itself using traditional funding streams because no commissioning agent was prepared to pay for the children who referred themselves to us. Most organisations solve this by stopping self-referrals and only taking commissioning contracts. We could not follow their example. It would mean turning away kids who asked for help, while accepting those who had been already taken into statutory systems.

As a result, every year we would start with no more than a third of our funding confirmed. We never made false promises and the staff knew the risks. It is a measure of their commitment and passion that they stayed. This will be familiar to most small and medium-sized charities. The big charities have larger reserves, courtesy of legacies and consistent donations.

In these large staff meetings we would lay the plan for the next few months. Then, after lunch, people could submit anonymous notes, highlighting what worked in the organisation and what not. They ranged in subject from the plumbing to the number of records workers were asked to keep on the kids, which created a tension between frontline engagement and administration. We shared the contents of this feedback the same day, acting on what could be dealt with immediately and agreeing to follow up the rest and report back.

There was a culture of encouraging staff to see the organisation as their own space within which to innovate, provided they kept the therapeutic focus on the children and the social focus on the agenda to transform public provision for the most vulnerable. We gave creative freedom but asked for rigour. Workers had to report back on their innovations, evidence the outcomes, and keep their focus on enhancing quality rather than personal promotion.

The organisational model in my head was based on the circles I had seen in the mosque designs as a child. I broke down this big charity, with some 11,000 volunteers, staff and trainees working for it in 2013/14, into small teams. At the centres, they were identified by colour and called a yard. So the red yard, for example, was a small team of social workers, psychologists and key workers who met weekly to support each other, discuss the organisation and ensure peer supervision. Expert advice, from psychiatry and nursing to housing or education, was on the premises for immediate access. Our workers did not get stuck with challenges.

In addition, every day people met twice in their large teams. They also had clinical supervision once a week as well as weekly or bi-weekly supervision from line management. The supervisors were senior people in social work and mental health, and this was an important part of how we worked. If we were practising poorly, they could have raised the alarm.

It was not perfect and we were constantly refining it. But I was certain that every worker could seek help, could blow the whistle on any dubious practice and could innovate. To avoid burnout, compassion fatigue and boredom, we created new jobs and moved staff around to give them the chance to regain resilience.

We looked for people with passion and talent. I interviewed the rollerblading champion of Italy; we created a therapeutic job that used her skill. Our recovery model was to restore to the children a love of life, using healthy attachments in a loving community. Whether that came through football, art or rollerblading did not matter.

Once we had embedded the working philosophy and clarified what we were doing, we began communicating with the outside world through campaigns. This was the interface between Kids Company the service-delivery agency and Kids Company the campaigning agency.

Using the same principle of the circles on the mosque, I mapped British society. It has theme-driven groups that operate within their own spheres but coexist with other spheres, and where appropriate these spheres communicate.

So, taking fashion as a sphere, one has to identify the key power player or visible leader. And in fashion at the time Alexandra Shulman, the editor of *Vogue*, was a highly respected and much-admired leader. I really liked her and sensed genuine compassion in her. Within each sphere are sub-circles; in fashion, the leader in the group of models was Kate Moss and later Cara Delevingne. The most-wanted celebrity was Gwyneth Paltrow. The art sphere was led by Tate Modern and Nicholas Serota. Music had the record company heads and then the circles of talent: one was led by Adele, another by Coldplay, and so on. Each sphere also had its elite venues. And as well as mainstream leaders, each had quirky, underground leaders. One had to operate with the emerging as well as the established brand leaders.

Having defined the main spheres, my problem was to engage those leaders to support maltreated children and effective child protection. I had to work out how to get the children highlighted in these spheres so that their affiliates, as members of the public, could glimpse the challenges the kids faced and have an emotional reaction that would trigger their desire to help. At the same time I was clear that would we would not use any of these relationships in a manipulative way. It had to be genuine, and that is why I grew incredibly fond of the leaders of these spheres and all the celebrities who helped us. When Kids Company closed without warning, Nicholas Serota wrote me the most moving email, which I shall always treasure. Unfortunately, the Official Receiver is now in possession of it and I no longer have access.

Let us take two spheres, fashion and art, as examples. We created an exhibition in 2006 at Tate Modern called Shrinking Childhoods. There was no space inside the gallery, but walking around I saw a square of grass outside and begged Serota and the Tate team to allow us to build a mock council estate there. My thinking was that the children could have their own 'flats' to express a dimension of their lives. Then the visiting public could go into the flat and experience the child's perspective.

A firm of builders with the most fantastic Irish foreman agreed to help. They are now called ISG and are big property developers. So we built the 'estate' and the children created moving experiences. The public spontaneously started writing on the walls of the estate, recounting their own childhood experiences. The result was an interactive, poetic and poignant set of communications about childhood. People wrote on the walls about their humiliations, about being sexually abused, and above all they expressed gratitude for the sharing of lives and the courage of the kids.

For the children, it was a transformative experience. One group recreated the drug den they lived in with their parents. The mother slumped in a chair, her crack paraphernalia scattered on the table in front of her. The father was asleep in his own vomit on a mattress on the floor. When they finished creating him, collectively they spat at him. Looking back, it was in part hatred for fathers who had failed to protect them, but also a hatred for themselves as males. Then there was a little girl weeping in the corner of this room, separate from either parent. When the kids made her, they wanted her to have the best clothes. They searched the scrap boxes we had brought to create the collection, looking for spotless socks to give her some dignity in this rotten place. All over the floor they had tipped pots; half-open baked bean cans spilled onto the floor, the windows had ripped bin liners for curtains, the wallpaper was peeled into shreds, the place was dark. In the background played a loop of the children's voices as they described what it was like to live on a violent estate with drug-addicted parents.

Over time, real mice and rats also entered the exhibition, enticed by the baked beans. One night I got a call from the Tate: a local addict had burgled the 'drug den'. He had broken a television while stealing it and had ended up bleeding all over the exhibit. The kids were elated that the realities of their lives, the repeated intruders, the drug addict's spouted blood on the walls, the vermin, had also come to the exhibition, making their dark secrets visible. They could not believe that I was going to show their lives to the public. Before the exhibition opened, they had said to me, 'Are you really going to show this stuff?' It was as if I were exercising a daring they had been denied. They had been trained from infancy not to say what goes on at home, especially to social workers, teachers and police. We were taking ghetto Britain into legitimate Britain, before 'reality' TV started showing deprived urban lives.

In another flat was a perfect image of a child's bedroom, with an immaculate girl sleeping on a bed made from papier-maché. The kids dressed her in a little girl's outfit of white lace. Her legs were astride. Dangling over the bed, above the vagina, was a mobile of men's shoes with the soles facing the ceiling. The subtlety of it was overwhelming. Then I noticed that everywhere, including the doll's house and the Barbie car, there were dolls in inappropriate positions: being raped, having oral sex – the room was a child's dream, a pink and beautiful playroom, but up close it was perverted.

The exhibition was the start of a relationship with the Tate, the Royal Academy and artists such as Damien Hirst, the Chapman Brothers, Antony Gormley, Grayson Perry and Tracey Emin, who auctioned works for us or collaborated with the kids. The Royal Academy put on an exhibition called Childhood: The Real Event. We saw its power when Mariella Frostrup tweeted: 'Just sobbed and ran from Kids Company exhibition at Royal Academy. Powerful images of abuse and fear turned by kids into inspired art. Genius.'

In recognition of our artistic collaborations and the delivery of therapeutic arts to traumatised children, Kids Company received the Royal Society and Public Health Arts and Health Award in 2012 for it 'innovation and outstanding contributions to the field of arts and health practice with children and young people'. Kids Company could not have had a better group of artists and arts psychotherapists working daily with the kids.

The fashion sphere opened up when Alex Shulman asked Gwyneth Paltrow to interview me about child protection. As it was *Vogue*, Bryan Adams took the photographs. I had to turn up at his house with a suitcase of clothes. He could not believe the array of mad outfits and wanted them all in shot. The result was several pages on child protection, and the photograph.

I would not do anything if the children were not represented, and refused any project that was only about me. In the background of the *Vogue* shoot was a council estate made up of shoe boxes piled on top of one another like flats. In each box a child had created an expression of their bedroom. We called it Shoebox Living. One in six of the primary school children who made the rooms needed child protection investigations because of what the art revealed. Inspired by the children, famous artists then created shoeboxes of their bedrooms when they were little. At auction they fetched about £187,000. Next the Style section of the *Sunday Times* came forward with an idea for a magazine photo shoot in which our kids modelled the clothes. At the end of the article we mentioned that the children lacked winter coats. The campaign yielded 5,000 new coats.

By 2013, we had a warehouse full of donations from companies, designers and brands. It was run by the philanthropist Sunetra Atkinson. We had a name for the redistribution of goods and volunteers' time from legitimate Britain to ghetto Britain: the Poverty Busting programme. Samantha Cameron launched it in Downing Street in 2011, and in four years it mobilised over £40 million worth of goods and volunteering. 'I have been to see what they do at Kids Company and it's brilliant because it is so simple,' Mrs Cameron said. 'They give children all those vital things they are lacking at home, from the practical things like help with their homework, to the emotional things like a cuddle or proper chat about how school is going.'

Of all the spheres, our relationship with Coldplay was probably the pinnacle. One day I arrived in my office to find Chris Martin sitting there. I had no idea who he was, but I knew he must be important because my PAs were freaking out with excitement. I walked in to find a man who could not stand still. He said his band had been collecting money for about ten years and wanted to invest it in vulnerable children. Wherever they went, people had told them to take it to Kids Company. 'I wanna hang out with you and find out what you do,' Chris said. I thought, 'Oh no. How am I going to manage this bouncing ball of a man, hanging out for a while?'

I took him to our centre at Kenbury Street. The dining room was packed with kids eating. The little ones would finish at 6 p.m.; we would clean up and serve a second dinner at 8 p.m. for the teenagers. Chris took a chair, sat slightly back and watched as the kids were fed. The tenderness in his eyes was extremely moving. He is one of the most genuine people I have ever encountered; Coldplay's manager, Phil Harvey, also had an understated manner, kind and highly competent, and soon I had met the rest of the band. Jonny Buckland, Will Champion and Guy Berryman were just as committed and generous. There is something about Coldplay. From the backstage team to the accountants, they were authentic. This is what I call real philanthropy, as opposed to narcissistic philanthropy.

They did what they intended. They spent quite a long time visiting our programmes, doing due diligence, and decided to create a centre for kids on the north side of the Thames. Before long, we had opened the Treehouse in West Hampstead. Chris would call in as we painted it; I remember the care with which he went around pushing down the switches on the sockets. The band bought musical instruments for our centres on both sides of the river, and the Treehouse became a creative hub.

When Kids Company closed, Coldplay continued funding the Treehouse. By then they had spent more than £10 million. We share an embarrassing joke. In 2012, Coldplay, along with Tinie Tempah,

Emeli Sandé, Steve Coogan and Rob Brydon, held an event at the O2 for Kids Company. Chris urged me to go on stage and speak about child protection to 20,000 people. The glare of the lights triggered what must have been a mini seizure, so in the middle of the speech I thought I was thanking Chris Martin but in fact I was saying Steve Martin.

The crowd was shouting back 'Chris!' while I carried on with Steve, knowing that something was wrong but that I could not get out of it until the seizure completed its cycle. Then, at the end of the concert, every drunk at the O2 came up to hug me and shout 'Steve Martin!' What made it worse is that Gwyneth, Chris's wife at the time, started calling him Steve, and then Chris ended up on a plane next to Steve Martin.

Whenever he sees me, he still introduces himself as Steve Martin.

CHAPTER 16

CIRCLES OF DESPAIR

I

January 2014

I used to think that Britain was a country of fairness and justice. I love this land and its people. The gratitude I felt as a seventeen-year-old receiving political asylum has not faded. It was personal, too: over the years, I came to associate my asylum with a Conservative politician called Douglas Hurd. This is actually an example of my trouble with dates and sequences, because I thought Hurd was the Home Secretary who had signed my asylum papers; in fact, he did not take charge of the Home Office until I was twenty-two. But for years I felt a sense of loyalty towards him, and he must have been baffled when he came to a concert for Kids Company and I sent him a message of thanks for accepting me as a refugee.

So you can imagine the significance I attached to working with his son, Nick Hurd, to try to achieve something meaningful for maltreated children. Nick was minister for civil society in the coalition government led by David Cameron. When responsibility for Kids Company moved from the education department to the Cabinet Office, he became the minister who was going to solve our problems.

Nick wrote to me in January 2014 to say we were going to be audited by PKF Littlejohn, a firm of London accountants. This was not a normal audit; we had statutory auditors already. It was a review of our financial and governance controls, specially commissioned by the Cabinet Office, and came as a total surprise. Nick was also pleased to inform me that Methods, the consultancy with an existing £200,000 government contract to verify our performance, would now engage with us 'to develop an outcome framework for demonstrating the impact of [Kids Company's] work'.

We were comfortable being audited. Since 2003, we had had not only annual audits of our finances but quarterly evaluations of our government grants. We were also scrutinised by every major bank. The last bank to carry out due diligence on Kids Company was Barclays; a team led by Kathleen Britain, its head of citizenship, took three months. Then Sir David Walker, the bank's chairman, wrote on 25 November 2014 with the result:

> I am very pleased to be able to tell you that the Kids Company proposal was approved by our global investing committee last week ...
> I wanted to write to you personally to add my congratulations. The work that you do is indeed inspirational and I am so pleased that Barclays can be a part of it.

Another audit just added to the conveyor belt of information going into Whitehall. But I could not understand why we were being audited a second time, at taxpayers' expense, after all the scrutiny we had received since 2003. Was the government genuine in its desire to help? I had a feeling they would use the review to find an excuse not to give us money.

On the table was an additional £500,000, which had appeared for two reasons. The *Evening Standard* was campaigning to highlight the plight of young people in gangs. And I had been to see Laura Trott, the Prime Minister's political adviser on women, education and childcare, to say that we could not cope for much longer without proper funding.

I told her that we had too many children and families in extreme need, including cases of hunger, homelessness and mental illness. Our team had proved that the Kids Company model worked and now we needed to be sustainable. Either that, or local authorities would have to take responsibility for our caseload.

After years of being passed from department to department and promised a solution that never came, I was growing assertive. There was a reason for the firmness. By 2013, the philanthropists who supported Kids Company were getting fed up. They had been happy to fund a charity they saw as an innovator, but seventeen years down the line they were tired of covering for government failure. They could also see that we were overwhelmed by the levels of need. For the first time, Kids Company had waiting lists.

Trott told me there was no extra money. She had the smugness of someone in power, concealed by a pseudo-warmth. Sitting opposite her in Downing Street with one of our trustees, I said, 'No problem. I am not fundraising any more, because you are abusing our moral commitment to absolve yourselves of taking statutory responsibility. You can come and take over.' She looked shocked, and her immediate reaction was to offer £500,000. I thanked her but was furious at the casualness of it all. I could easily have walked out without the cash injection, believing her to have nothing to offer.

Sitting in the corner was Helen Tabiner of the Cabinet Office, a member of a team we would later have much trouble with. She kept mouse-quiet. The new audit followed.

The auditor concluded that Kids Company was properly run but lacked sustainable funding. I could not have agreed more. It seemed that this was not the result the civil servants expected, because then something interesting happened. A senior policy adviser at the Cabinet Office, tried to get the auditor, Alastair Duke, to change his report. He appeared to want a darker tone. He asked for the review to recommend a minimum level of reserves and suggested that 10 per cent would be appropriate. The auditor felt uncomfortable and refused: reserves are for trustees to decide. Perhaps to his surprise, Nick Hurd conceded that the audit presented no problems and we received the £500,000.

The auditor told our finance director, Ruth Jenkins, about the pressure from the Cabinet Office. I think he was also surprised by the discrepancy between the order he had found at Kids Company and the disorder he had been led to expect. He was even planning to use Kids Company as an example of good practice: 'Kids Company's processes are better than most organisations I see,' Ruth reported him as saying. 'I will be using Kids Company as a case study in a presentation I am giving next week on governance.'[1] But he toned down his enthusiasm in the report, apparently because this was not what the Cabinet Office wanted. Ruth was very concerned by what looked like an attempt to influence an accountant's professional judgement, and repeated what the auditor had said to a lawyer. I called a Conservative in Cameron's circle and told him what had happened. He replied, 'If you go public with this, we will deny it.' The auditor himself, however, chose to draw a veil over the episode when he later gave evidence to a committee of MPs.[2]

Also in January 2014, we received a call from Lambeth Police to say they had had a man on the phone called Miles Goslett, whose attitude they did not like. Apparently he had suggested that Kids Company could not possibly have had 4,000 people at the Oval cricket ground on Christmas Day. Soon afterwards we had a call from the Oval to say that a Miles Goslett had called in an accusatory way.

The police knew our numbers because they always sent two officers: Christmas brought all our disturbed people into one place. The Oval, too, told the sceptical reporter that about 4,000 people had been to the event, as its security team had witnessed. The police must have marvelled to see adolescent boys from rival gangs playing football on Christmas Day next to kids jumping on bouncy castles. We had 250 staff and volunteers there, and any of them would be able to vouch for the crowds, especially the queue to get into the dining hall.

I had never heard of Goslett, a freelance journalist who had won scoop of the year at the London Press Club for a story about the BBC and its former star presenter Jimmy Savile. The article revealed that the BBC had suppressed a *Newsnight* investigation into whether Savile was a paedophile. Goslett helped bring the scandal to light and there is no doubting his determination as a reporter.

I wrote to him saying, 'Kids Company is an open door. I would be delighted to welcome you here, answer anything you wanted to ask me and you would be able to see for yourself how rigorously we account for what we do.' The award-winning investigative journalist refused, telling our communications team that he feared being 'charmed'. To this day, I have neither met nor spoken to the reporter who has written the most damaging stories about Kids Company. Journalists always look shocked when I tell them that for his first mainstream article about Kids Company, printed in *The Spectator*, no one approached us to seek a response before publication. Instead, the magazine relied on answers given to Goslett when he was trying to get an article into the *Daily Mail* three months earlier.

That was not all. In January 2014, at the same time as the new audit and the appearance of Miles Goslett, a detective from the Metropolitan Police came to see me. He had written first to say that he had watched me over the years and that I had not wavered from trying to protect children and standing up for their rights, and he needed to impart something important. When he came, he named a few recognisable individuals and recounted a horrific story about a house in Hampstead where boys had apparently been murdered after being sexually assaulted. The detective said his own investigations into child abuse had repeatedly been blocked. He also mentioned the child abuse scandal in Jersey, centred on a children's home that had closed in the 1980s called Haut de la Garenne, where he believed the bones of murdered children had been swapped with animal bones to halt further inquiry. This was interesting, because I was approached at much the same time by a female GP from Jersey who spoke of systemic abuse there. She had taken her files and left the islands in fear. She struck me as a sensible and experienced doctor who had become despairing, frustrated and afraid after successful efforts to suppress her.[3]

The detective asked if I would meet some of his colleagues and returned as part of a group, including another serving officer who held a sensitive and senior position. I met them several times. One of the party showed me a list of 147 people suspected of child abuse. There were serving politicians, police officers, judges, members of the House of Lords and celebrities. I was careful not to ask questions, as I did not want to interfere with due process if a prosecution followed.

One of the most alarming stories related to Jimmy Savile. A social worker in the group said that Savile had abused a young man in his care. The boy had stolen one of the TV presenter's possessions during a sex session and had taken it to his hostel, and Savile wanted the item back. The celebrity informed the social worker that he had kidnapped the boy and proposed a swap in a car park, where the young man was duly handed over in exchange for the item, which had been retrieved from his room. In short, a former social care worker was claiming to have been fully aware of Savile's activities with a young person in his care. His body language during this part of the meeting suggested he was telling the truth: he acted out the encounters as if repeating the experience, but for the rest of the time kept still. Again I asked no questions, thinking that I would share the information with the independent inquiry into child sexual abuse once it was established.

I was aware of the political tension in all this. On the one hand, the establishment now communicates a seemingly open approach to investigating so-called 'historic' child abuse. On the other, it closes down investigations that have the potential to expose the secret harm suffered by generations of children, as my police visitors knew from experience. And it was clear to me that the government, in the run-up to the 2015 election, was keen to contain any narratives that could discredit senior politicians.

I had an intuitive sense that I was surrounded by murky waters and needed to take precautions. I called Amber Melville-Brown of the law firm Withersworldwide to report the Cabinet Office attempt to tamper with our audit. We met in my office and Ruth recounted what the auditor had told her. I was right to be concerned. It would not be long before the Cabinet Office started leaking information and briefing against Kids Company.

II

Summer

When I went to 9 Downing Street in July 2014 to meet Oliver Letwin, the conversation followed an unlikely course. I was ready to argue the case for Kids Company to be properly funded. There was no need. Oliver got there first.

He promised to find us £20 million, which he said he would achieve by allocating some of the money set aside for the Troubled Families programme, a £448 million scheme to turn around the lives of people in 120,000 households. He justified this by saying that we were a substitute family for children who were not being taken into local authority structures. Oliver seemed confident and determined, and £20 million was his figure, not mine. We had been struggling for so many years, he said, but were now a proven programme that needed proper resourcing.

I was so pleasantly shocked that I captured the conversation in a letter, phrasing it carefully as we would be required to submit formal applications for the funds. I did not want to compromise him by suggesting the £20 million was already agreed, turning the applications into a farce. 'You acknowledged that we should be accessing £20,000,000 of funding a year to make us sustainable, and to enable us to continue the work with this group of children who have complex needs,' I wrote. 'I appreciate that the creation of this fund, for which there will be a competitive tender, will take time to formulate. As you suggested, it would be created either alongside or, potentially, through the Troubled Families budget.'[4]

In 2015, after Kids Company closed, Oliver would deny the conversation. An official said I had never written a letter and then, when I produced it and the email confirming that he had received it, the narrative changed to 'Camila misunderstood'.

I did not misunderstand. I was so sure of Oliver's offer that I called Louise Casey, the outspoken civil servant who ran the government's Troubled Families initiative. 'Louise, Oliver is saying we could get funded from your budget.' She was outraged. 'He is chatting rubbish, there is no money for him to allocate,' she said, promising to pay him a visit because she, too, thought our predicament unfair and that Kids Company needed to be funded properly. She went to see him and reported back that he was genuinely trying to help.

As far as the trustees and I were concerned, from July 2014 onwards the government was going to come up with a substantial grant and in our twentieth year we would be sustainable. This was the point at which I thought I should step down as founder and hand over the running of the organisation to a new chief executive. For the first time we could appoint someone of calibre because we would have the money to pay them. We started recruiting psychiatrists to join our board for the same reason: we believed we were to have proper funding. We even brought in Lynn Alleway for what became a BBC documentary on Kids Company's final days. That was not the original idea at all. The film was to mark twenty years of the charity, including my stepping down and a new chief executive taking over now that we were to have consistent funding.

Up until this point, finding a good CEO would have been next to impossible. As soon as potential candidates realised that we did not know where our money came from, they backed off, often because they had family commitments and needed security. I wanted to increase my clinical work with the children and train other agencies in dealing with traumatised kids. For the first time, it was possible.

For the rest of the year, I tried to get an update on the £20 million from Oliver. I wrote to him in July. I wrote again in September. I asked Philippa Stroud, Iain Duncan Smith's special adviser when he was

Secretary of State for Work and Pensions, to speak to Oliver on my behalf. Louise Casey spoke to him. So did Sir Nigel Crisp, the former chief executive of the NHS and the uncle of Ruth Jenkins, our finance director. I also communicated with Nick Hurd and Chris Grayling, the Secretary of State for Justice, to try to get the grant confirmed. I was told repeatedly in calls and emails, 'It's coming', 'We are trying to put it together', 'It's difficult, but we are committed to it'. Not one of them said it could not be done. Every so often, Philippa would ask, 'Can you take less?' or 'Can you take less now and more later?' and I would make it clear the answer was no.

The mood music coming out of the education department was also supportive. 'I was very glad to read that the external audit was successful and that Kids Company has secured further funding from the Cabinet Office,' Michael Gove, the Education Secretary, wrote to a philanthropist in May 2014. 'The inspirational work that Kids Company do with young people in our cities is a credit both to them and our country.' At no time had Michael suggested that he had any difficulties with Kids Company's functioning, so I was surprised in 2015 to read his comment in *The Times*:

> One of the reasons I got into trouble so often in the government is that I disagreed with some of the things that we were doing, and normally people would say, 'Well, it's not really your department, so shut up.' But because I knew, because I had some evidence that things weren't working, like the troubled families programme, which was not achieving what it was supposed to achieve, or other stuff, I would get into scraps. I would say it's wrong, it's wasting money, we shouldn't be giving money to Kids Company, we should be giving it to the troubled families programme. But I'm not in government now, I don't have access to all that material.

Nick Hurd, when he left the Cabinet Office in July 2014, wrote with particular honesty:

I have so much to thank you for: not least for taking me out of my comfort zone and confronting me with a very uncomfortable truth about our failure as a society to meet the needs of vulnerable children … We have always been frank with each other and I know that your patience with the current funding model is being tested to the limit.

You can imagine my amazement when Oliver sat at the parliamentary inquiry a year later claiming that Kids Company could not show 'outcomes'. This is not something he even hinted at when I met him in Downing Street. He could not have been more positive.

Meanwhile, the group including the two police officers came back to ask if I would chair the independent inquiry into child sexual abuse announced in July by Theresa May, the then Home Secretary. At the time, Baroness Elizabeth Butler-Sloss, a former president of the family division of the High Court, was to fill the role. I like Elizabeth very much, and never doubted her integrity. Whenever she and I speak at the same event, she is passionate about vulnerable children. But the group was worried about some of her family connections, and my role was to be neutral and not to have an opinion.

I was clear with my visitors that I lacked the ability to lead an inquiry, and offered instead to help them identify a candidate they could trust. Acting as an advocate for this group of concerned individuals, I recommended Baroness Helena Kennedy QC to the Home Office. The official at the Home Office listened carefully as I said that if Helena proved unacceptable they should consider a foreign judge. I made this proposal because of the 147 names on the list: it was hard to envisage a senior British judge remaining free from suggestions of a link to child abuse suspects.

My understanding is that Baroness Kennedy, a Labour member of the House of Lords, was turned down by Downing Street. Instead May appointed Fiona Woolf, a lawyer who was then Lord Mayor of London. She lasted two months before resigning after scrutiny of her social contacts with Leon Brittan, a former Home Secretary targeted by Operation Midland, a £2.5 million police inquiry into the alleged sexual abuse and murder of children, which was later abandoned with everyone discredited except for those under investigation. Only after losing Woolf did May turn to Dame Lowell Goddard, a judge from New Zealand, who led the inquiry for eighteen months before resigning 'with immediate effect' in a two-sentence letter that offered no explanation.

The visiting police officers also told me about the prolific abuse of children in Lambeth children's homes. When Lowell Goddard – at this point still in charge of the inquiry into child sexual abuse – announced twelve priorities for investigation in November 2015, number one was 'Children in the Care of Lambeth Council'. A year after that, in December 2016, Lambeth Council made an unreserved apology to the thousands of children it had put at risk in just one of its homes, Shirley Oaks, and announced proposals to pay 'tens of millions of pounds' in compensation.

The government acted after a report by the Shirley Oaks Survivors Association revealed that sixty suspected paedophiles had operated at the home or were linked to it, and that forty-eight children had died in the care of the council between 1970 and 1989. Twenty of the deaths were linked to Shirley Oaks. The report also claimed that corrupt policing in south London had allowed the abusers to escape justice. Not all the abuse had been sexual. Former residents said they had been beaten with bamboo, belts and fists and that it was common to punish children by putting them in coal bunkers, sometimes without clothes. Six new police investigations into abuse at Shirley Oaks were prompted by the disclosures.[5]

If the group that visited me is right, there is much more of this scandal to come, including the role of the police in covering up abuse. I have also been told of links between corrupt London detectives and organised criminals making child pornography.

III

Christmas

The beginning of the end for Kids Company came three days before Christmas 2014 in a letter from Downing Street. 'Firstly, thank you for the incredible work you do every day with children in great need,' wrote Oliver Letwin. 'We have all been working to make sure that these children get the support they require on a longer term basis.' Then came the killer.

> To this end, following cross departmental discussion, we have agreed to offer Kids Company a single fund of £4.265 million for 2015/16. However, we all agree that we need to put the services you provide on a more sustainable basis, without the need for ad hoc Government assistance. I have asked officials to work collaboratively with you and relevant Departments early in the New Year to develop these plans further.

That was it. There would be no £20 million. There was not even a reference to the sum we had agreed just five months earlier. Oliver added in a handwritten note: 'P.S. We had a very useful discussion with two of your trustees today, as I'm sure you will be aware. We look forward to working with them and you to establish a more sustainable way forward for 2016/17 and beyond.'

Now, I always pay attention to what a minister writes by hand at the bottom of a letter because the real message often lies there, outside the typed script that goes into civil service files. But this was ambiguous. I took it to mean that Oliver was still committed to proper funding for Kids Company. But a 'more sustainable way forward' without 'ad hoc government assistance' could mean something else entirely. Was there a plan to reduce the charity's size and scope? The truth depended on the understanding Oliver had reached in his 'very useful' talks with the two trustees, Alan Yentob and Richard Handover. If there was an agreement at that Christmas meeting, tacit or explicit, to cut down Kids Company, they did not say.

I was grateful to my trustees, and I tried not to burden them. Trustees are unpaid. They do not get public recognition, except when things go wrong, yet they are ultimately responsible for the fate of a charity. Alan Yentob was visible as Kids Company's chairman partly because he was already a public figure as creative director of the BBC; the other trustees were not. They gave their time, and accepted the risk to their reputations if Kids Company ran into any sort of trouble, for the best of motives. That is why I tried to keep the burden on them light. Alan always responded to emergencies and was as committed as a person could be. But when staff presented their work at trustees' meetings, I saw their surprise at the sophistication, scale and depth of the organisation for which they were responsible.

Trustees are necessary and powerful because they allow a charity to exist and they subject it to scrutiny. Their role is a legal requirement. But I felt throughout the nineteen years of Kids Company that I was asking too much of them, even as I protected them, because in the end the task is too great.

However, you could not have asked for a more cohesive, committed and caring group of trustees. They intensively scrutinised Kids Company. We had monthly finance and risk committee meetings. They were always at the end of the phone. The trustee meetings were either monthly or bimonthly. Practically everyone attended. Some of them supported Kids Company on a daily basis. They did their best to help Kids Company survive. They always had a contingency plan in the event that we would not be funded. They asked me in December 2014 to prepare one just in case the government did not come through with further promised funds.

On 21 January 2015, I wrote to Philippa Stroud. The email was short.

Dear Philippa,

I hope you're well. Just wanted to say that my trustees have instructed me to draw up redundancy plans to make over 300 staff redundant and shut our street-level centres. Once that goes public I think potentially other donors will not give us money and it will lead to Kids Company completely folding.

Please can we talk on the phone? I know Alan Yentob was also trying to make contact with you.

With love,

Camila

On one level, it seemed obvious that we should close our street-level centres. They were the source of our highest costs. The centres were expensive for a reason: the security in them was subtle, but it was carefully conceived. We avoided the violence common in young offenders' institutions by having the right staff levels. No worker was ever in a room on their own. It was the only way to survive in an environment in which young people had access to firearms, and gang feuds could mean life-changing injury or death. We owed safety to everyone, worker, visitor, client or volunteer. But the centres were also at the heart of the self-referring model. Without them, Kids Company would move closer to conventional provision: yes, we can help you, but someone must refer you and pay for you first. In other words, the same, flawed model of delivery would be regenerated in the service of organisational survival, and vulnerable clients would be betrayed.

People imagine that questions such as the reach and role of a charity are factual and objective. In fact, the decisions are often driven by psychology. This is complex territory. It is risky to set it out in a book, because readers might think that I am trying to blame others for the closure of Kids Company. Alas, I have no choice. I cannot convey to you the truth as I understand it unless I include the psychological truth. This means describing the part played by my own, unusual psyche in the charity's closure.

Very few people can get a grip on me, because I am more of a psychological force than I am a person. It seems an absurd thing to say, I know. But it is true. Imagine a therapist: you can see a therapist, and be helped by one, without any need to understand the therapist's character. My role in people's lives is similar. But if they cannot get a grip on me, they start constructing me according to their own perception of why someone would behave as I do. It is a natural mental shortcut. And as soon as this process starts, communication is lost.

Keeping Kids Company alive required vision and courage. As soon as one or the other was lost, so was the charity.

A flavour of the bravery everyone needed to stay focused on the vision, and not to fall into line with the anti-task, came in an exchange at the parliamentary inquest into Whitehall's relationship with Kids Company. Oliver Letwin is a politician who understood Kids Company. He accepted the vision, because it had touched him once, somewhere near the core of his being, and he was moved by its truth. Then he got himself into a state of irreconcilable conflict over what he understood. This is the first question he was asked when he appeared before the committee of MPs to give evidence.

Paul Flynn: I confess that I am a great admirer of your work as a Minister because of your intellect and your integrity, which are not attributes shared by all Ministers. That is why I find it very surprising – the Committee met for three hours with Ms Batmanghelidjh and some formed the conclusion that she was an obvious confidence trickster with little to offer, except the emotional blackmail and psychobabble that she produced in great reams in the time we saw her – that you have been a long supporter of Ms Batmanghelidjh and Kids Company, and that you named her as your hero of the year in 2002. Why?

Rt Hon Oliver Letwin: I can certainly explain that. When I was shadow Home Secretary – I think you and I had encounters at that time about various issues – in 2001, 2002 and 2003 I visited Kids Company I think on three, but perhaps two, separate occasions for some hours. They were then operating in a small way in, I think, four arches that they had converted for use. I met a large range of the kids and also the people who were helping them. I was immensely moved by what they were doing for those kids who had been deprived almost every kind of emotional support that all of us would take for granted as children and indeed as parents. They were trying to do some of the things we subsequently tried to do with Troubled Families – to knit together the statutory agencies. Partly they were trying to get people over drug and alcohol dependency; partly they were trying to provide just the simplest kinds of love and simple help. I thought that was a very valuable thing for the voluntary sector to be doing. I continue to believe that, notwithstanding all the many things that have come out that are very much less than good and that no doubt we will be talking about, underneath that there was something very valuable being done.[6]

That is a man trying to stay true to himself while under pressure to agree that something in which he once believed has no basis in fact.

At the same time as my bond was broken with the trustees, it broke with several senior managers who began to gather in one of the group's offices. From March 2014 I noticed that they were regularly huddled there.

I knew something was wrong, but as there had been no animosity, I assumed that these senior managers were simply supporting one another. We all felt the strain from the uncertainty of our funding, and we were a cohesive group. Then I noticed a vast amount of photocopying taking place outside that office. I talked to one of them, who had been with us for some years, to see if she would open up about what was troubling her. I explained that I loved her very much and that we had worked together for a long time; I wanted the best for her, and I needed her to be candid. I said that if she found her job difficult, I would be happy to change her role to something less stressful. Her reply seemed fake, prompting the insight, which felt as if it came from nowhere, that she was preparing to claim constructive dismissal. We agreed that she would let me know her wishes, and I contacted one of the trustees to say that I felt a need to lodge a record of the conversation. The trustee said not to bother.

After Christmas, she did not come back to work. I wrote to her saying, 'I am a bit concerned about your wellbeing, we had a discussion about future roles for you here if you wanted a change. You agreed to get back to me after Christmas and I haven't heard back from you, is everything OK?'

Days later, her letter claiming constructive dismissal arrived, including the absurd reason that I was going to get the kids from one of the centres to come and beat her up at head office. The allegation was so outrageous it left me in giggles. She did mention that she was worried about our sustainability, but then we all were. I wanted to go to a tribunal: I did not see why the charity should pay out for such a case. However, the trustees decided to settle. I refused to have anything to do with it.

This was in January 2015. The law firm dealing with the settlement was Freshfields, which worked on the case *pro bono* because one of our trustees was a valued client. I did not feel at ease being railroaded by the lawyer and the trustee into a compromise I thought was morally wrong.

All four senior managers then left at once. Two resigned amicably, explaining by email that they were worried about their personal circumstances. One gave no explanation.

Then the unexpected happened. Just as the settlement was being negotiated, someone sent the solicitors a bundle of printed emails through the post. I never saw these messages, but I heard about them after a trustee was called to the law firm to read them. They appeared to be personal communications involving the departed staff. When the police later asked to see the emails, Freshfields claimed they had been 'lost'.

In these exchanges, one of the staff members purportedly claimed to her boyfriend of the time that another was taking information about Kids Company to the Mail newspaper group via a friend. She appeared to believe that publication of a negative article about Kids Company was imminent.

Also in these purported emails, as I understand it, was talk of poisoning the medical drip in my office. This was a drip I used every two weeks, as I am unable to absorb some nutrients as a complication of my premature birth: it hung from the ceiling, where it was pinned into place by a carving of four letters made by a troubled client and reading LOVE. The drip would be left in my arm for a few hours as I continued with my meetings, and was a normal feature of office life. The *Daily Mail* later made a big deal of it, claiming that I had a private nurse on the Kids Company payroll to administer to my needs every morning, which was entirely untrue.[7] Another email, to a friend who worked on the business affairs of Damien Hirst, said that I was 'bonkers' and the artist should support the charity no longer. Damien had been one of our most generous and visionary funders, and I genuinely loved him. I felt great sadness to imagine his sense of betrayal on receiving this information, believing the charity he had supported to have been a sham. I asked the trustees to contact Damien, but they were unwilling to act on the emails. Neither did they challenge any of the departed quartet.

The trustee who read the emails summarised their content at a meeting I was asked not to attend. It was the only time this happened, except for three occasions in two decades when it was decided to give me a pay rise. Perhaps the trustees decided the exchanges were harmless shows of childish feeling – just the private letting-off of steam. When material stolen from Kids Company started appearing in the *Mail*, however, it became obvious that journalists possessed the personal data of vulnerable young people for whom we were responsible. The seriousness of what was happening dawned on the trustees, and now they listened when I insisted that the theft be reported to the police. This was when Freshfields revealed that the emails had been lost. I was outraged that a firm of solicitors had not kept them safe. How could a thick pile of evidence disappear?

But that was still some months ahead.

IV

February 2015

After hawking his investigation into Kids Company around newspapers and getting nowhere, Miles Goslett found a mainstream publisher in February 2015. His article, published in *The Spectator*, had a tone that came to seem moderate compared with the frenzied allegations that would emerge a few months later, including from his keyboard, as the questions about Kids Company caught fire. Miles reported that a 'number' of people believed that the charity had 'perhaps grown too quickly and would, despite its undoubted achievements, benefit from a review of its operations and controls. They worry that Kids Company has become too famous, untouchable, and now acts as a drain on well-meaning donations that might otherwise go to better causes.' He added: 'Having investigated the charity for several months, I'm afraid I agree.'[8]

Goslett had been interested in Kids Company since 2013, when an unnamed contact helped him to meet a few disgruntled staff in a London pub. What they said convinced him that I was his next Jimmy Savile. He believed that, like the DJ whose reign of abuse he had helped to expose, I was 'untouchable' because I used celebrity to deter scrutiny. On the day Kids Company closed, he wrote an account of how his pursuit had begun.

They insisted we sit in the quietest corner available, and spoke in hushed tones of serious financial irregularities and 'serial exaggerations' about its clients. They said it had spent vast sums of money from private donors and the public purse irresponsibly and believed that this ought to be exposed. Strikingly, they were genuinely concerned about the consequences of speaking to me. One said: 'What you don't understand – what most people don't understand – is that you do not cross Camila.' Another said: 'Camila is basically pretty impossible to work with. And she's giving the charity sector a bad name. People need to realise that Kids Company is her personal empire. I am not aware of her having anything else in her life. I'm not aware of her having any friends with whom she can just go and have a cup of coffee. That is not healthy. The charity is her and she is the charity.'[9]

Of course, our staff satisfaction was among the best in any organisation. None of the independent evaluations suggested I was difficult to work with. But Goslett had, if not his facts, then his quarry.

His *Spectator* article threw a spotlight on the dissatisfaction of a single donor, Joan Woolard, who had sold her house and given us the proceeds. Now she wanted her money back. Woolard later told MPs that her reversal in attitude was driven by Goslett. A widow in her seventies, she had been impressed by Kids Company 'as a genuine work of love' until the reporter telephoned, demanding to know how she could be sure that her money had been properly spent.

'Did I know where my money had gone? How had it been spent? He found it hard to believe that I had not asked for any details or been sent any,' Woolard told MPs in a written statement. 'I told him I had trusted Camila implicitly … Resistant to his assurances that all was not what it seemed, I was very reluctant to believe ill of Camila. However I said I would volunteer to work at the charity in order to find out the truth.'[10]

This was the coming together of an aggressive reporter and a donor who, unsettled by his scepticism, developed a grievance. We had thanked Joan profusely for her generosity with a painting, a poem, a page devoted to her in our newsletter, a formal letter and a section in our annual report. Goslett made no mention of this. Instead, he quoted Joan as saying: 'I never received a personal letter from Camila thanking me for making my donation.'

Two years earlier, Joan had tried to give us her four-bedroom house in Lincolnshire. I refused out of concern that she would become homeless. But she had heard me on the radio and was determined. She moved into a council bungalow and sold her former show home herself, sending us the £200,000 proceeds, and it seemed disrespectful to continue to refuse her. I had asked Joan to bring a friend with her to my office; the friend confirmed that her intention was genuine, and that there was no risk to her wellbeing. Her solicitor had said the same. From then on, Joan, her friend and I used to meet regularly whenever she was in London.

Joan certainly was a character. She was appalled by banks, and had bought five shares in several to get the right to go to their annual meetings. She got herself into the *Daily Mail* when she travelled from Lincolnshire to denounce directors of Barclays as 'greedy bastards' who should be in jail. Mocking the new Barclays motto as the 'go-to bank', she had declared to applause at its AGM: 'Go-to? Go to hell, Barclays! A lot of people regard Barclays and its board as a bunch of crooks … Banks have brought us down – brought the entire global economy down. Yet none of you have gone to jail. I don't understand how you can sleep at night.'[11]

She was delighted when this performance won her Heckler of the Year from *The Oldie* magazine.

When she came to do the sniffing around at Kids Company that she had promised Goslett, there was no sign of anything amiss. She asked if she could have a bed in one of Kids Company's units for vulnerable young people, an impossible request for someone with no police check, but stayed with her brother in Hertfordshire when I offered to find a hotel room instead. At the end, I wrote to thank her and apologised for not being able to see her, and she replied to say how much she had enjoyed herself and how wonderful the project and staff were. Then, out of the blue, a letter arrived to say that her friends thought I had treated her terribly by not offering her somewhere to stay, which baffled me since I had attempted to make arrangements for her. 'The off-peak journey to Blackfriars took two hours and involved much walking in one of the hottest weeks of the year,' she later told MPs. 'Camila, however, was conspicuous by her absence ... I was mildly surprised by her lack of interest in my work experience, not even a phone call to ask about my travel in such a hot week.'[12] She also noted: 'Others conspicuous by their absence were children,' and reported her findings to Goslett, who quoted them at length in his *Spectator* piece. The article recorded that Joan had 'complained to the Charity Commission and is demanding back her money', but made no mention of the fact that the commission had already assessed Joan's complaint with some care. It had verified that the information in Kids Company's accounts was consistent with what we had reported to Joan. The commission stated: 'We saw no evidence to suggest the donations made were not applied for the purposes for which they were given.'

Undeterred, or more likely unaware that the Charity Commission had reached this judgment, Goslett referred instead to an earlier interview with Joan, published in *The Oldie*. Writing now in *The Spectator*, he approvingly quoted himself as having observed in *The Oldie* a year earlier: 'What is perhaps most bizarre about this tale is that Joan has no idea what has become of her money. The charity has never informed her how it has been or will be used, despite her being its largest individual donor.'

Joan, for her part, had found herself a creative outlet for her disenchantment. She sent limericks to some of our most prominent supporters, who were listed in our annual report. 'There's a cunning fat stunt called Batman / who collects more cash than the VATman / takes kids off the streets / but shows no receipts / that cunning old stunt called Batman,' was one. 'Kids Company is a lucrative scam / run by an Iranian mam / in African dress / who should confess / it's all a very big sham,' ran another.

The *Spectator* article raised proper questions about Kids Company, but it was carelessly executed and it had an immediate effect. A pledge of £300,000 was withdrawn, and our fundraising became more precarious than ever. When I sent Fraser Nelson, the magazine's editor, a correction of 300 words to use as a letter, he refused to print it because it implied a lack of professionalism from his reporter.

One interesting question is what motivated such an article in the first place. Goslett had tried to publish his piece the previous November, in the *Daily Mail*; after we contacted its lawyers and provided the evidence that the story was not true, the newspaper killed it. When a version finally reached print in Fraser Nelson's magazine, the article opened:

> In 2006, when David Cameron was leader of the opposition, he made an infamous speech that is remembered as an exhortation to hug a hoodie. Feral youth, he said, should be helped rather than demonised. He was reaching towards what he hoped would be a new, 'compassionate' conservatism inspired in part by the charismatic social activist Camila Batmanghelidjh. She was the perfect lodestar for the young Tory leader.

Here was a piece of journalism built around Joan Woolard and raising the perfectly proper question of how many children we supported. Yet it started with a reference to the Prime Minister. Cameron had once used me to rebrand Conservatism; he embraced me, to my discomfort, as a symbol of his Big Society. Now I was being used to undermine him. If I could be revealed as flawed, a little damage would touch him too. Every political party is in a permanent state of inner conflict as people fight to define what it stands for, and Cameron was perceived by some Conservatives as too left-wing. Kids Company gave them an opportunity to administer a kicking.

Working in parallel with Miles Goslett was Harriet Sergeant, a research fellow at the Centre for Policy Studies, a think tank dedicated to 'freedom and responsibility' that was founded by Sir Keith Joseph and Margaret Thatcher in 1974. She submitted evidence to the parliamentary inquiry into Whitehall's relationship with Kids Company that included hearsay and outright fantasy from troubled young people. It can be seen on the House of Commons website. Harriet was honest enough to mark some of her more dubious evidence as 'unconfirmed' – but not all of it. She quoted at length a Kids Company client, 'Jermaine', who developed a theme that I had 'favourites' among the clients. For them, the troubled young man noted jealously, anything was possible.

> Nor are we talking about the odd designer hand bag here and there. Camila's favourites 'get serious money every week, all in cash in envelops [*sic*]'. This is spending money, travel money, clothes money. She even gives them money for cars. 'They pull up in serious cars, BMWs. They demand £9,000 for a car and she will give it to them' … Unlike many of the staff and kids, 'The favourites never complain about her. They rely on her and she likes to feel like a mother to them.' She makes them dependent, 'and then keeps them like her children.'[13]

In her written evidence, Sergeant goes on to give Jermaine's account of how I prepare for a speech. She follows this with a false assertion about my supposed wealth (this, at least, is marked 'unconfirmed'):

> He describes what happens when she makes her annual speech, 'It is rehearsed over and over again,' so she is able to work up the emotion. 'There she goes,' Jermaine overhears her head office staff say, 'She's going to cry for the 16th time.' Jermaine went on, 'She's a good actor. She looks at you, everything sweet and a tear rolls down from her eye. Tears been rolling down from that eye for years now.' She owns three mansions and Jermaine has visited two of them. (unconfirmed)

To sum everything up, Jermaine is quoted as saying:

> I am not going to lie, Camila shatters lives, trust me. Because of her certain people are in jail, some are doing serious time. Some are

taking drugs. She's broken lives. That's why a lot of staff tell kids who come to Kids Company for help, 'Leave while you can.'

For the record, I have lived in the same ground-floor flat for twenty-five years. There are no mansions. I do not cry when I give speeches and neither do I rehearse them. The notion that I bought cars for favourite clients should have been too ridiculous to submit to a parliamentary inquiry, let alone record as evidence on its website, but this is what happens when a firestorm consumes an individual in the public eye. The truth ceases to have any power, and time must pass before anyone is willing to hear it. By then, powerful ideas have taken hold, such as having 'favourites', and they become very hard to shake off. By late 2015, people who saw me in the street were demanding to know what I had done 'with the fucking money'. It is important to show where these ideas come from.

Opponents of Conservatism, or Cameron's strand of it, seemed to find it useful that Kids Company was in difficulties. Here is Oliver Letwin again, being baited by Paul Flynn, a veteran Labour MP.

> Paul Flynn: Do you think now that the concept of Big Society will be buried with the remains of Kids Company?
>
> Rt Hon Oliver Letwin: Absolutely not. You and I never agreed about Big Society. I believe it is alive and flourishing in our country, and that there are thousands – perhaps tens of thousands – of voluntary groups and social enterprises the length and breadth of our country that are part of the fabric of society and do an immense amount of good.[14]

Was Kids Company collateral damage in a contest to define Conservatism? Being linked with the Prime Minister certainly gave us extra value as a target. A former Cabinet minister says there was no conspiracy against Kids Company:

> To have a conspiracy like that you have to be pretty well organised.

And my general view about government is, most times there isn't really a conspiracy. There may be amongst politicians, but generally government would have to be incredibly tight to be able to conspire on that sort of scale.

But perhaps the real problem was that Kids Company grew too big to tolerate. In December 2016, a mutual acquaintance asked a minister why Kids Company had closed. This man knows powerful players in politics and the civil service, thanks to his business life. After speaking to a senior political source, he reported back:

> I asked around for feedback ... They told me, when Kids Company had 300 and then 3,000 kids, it was fine. When it got to 30,000 kids, it became a movement and a problem. We try to keep the numbers low, because we don't want to go to the public for the tax and we don't want people to realise the scale of trouble we have with children. With Camila being around, it was something the public were becoming aware of. She was getting too powerful, with too big a following, so we had to shut it all down.

He then went on to say that 'they' had told him that 'if there was an island in Jamaica where they could ship them all to, they would'.

This is hearsay, of course; it has the same status as Harriet Sergeant's use of Jermaine to say that I have three mansions and buy young people cars.

But which, I wonder, is more likely to be true?

CHAPTER 17

PERFECT STORM

I

I n the run-up to the 2015 general election, senior Conservatives were under stress. Nobody expected the party to win outright and cracks were emerging in the airbrushed world of the Tories.

David Cameron's team was jumpy. I was told by a well-placed source that Sir Lynton Crosby, the Prime Minister's election guru, was extremely annoyed that I had been on LBC saying that the Conservatives had strengthened the middle and upper classes but damaged the poor. He was furious that I was challenging their record despite all the help I had received, as he saw it. Of course, this was actually money that belonged to the public, not the government, and along with a bigger sum raised privately it funded work that was not being done by the state.

Crosby had been generous to Kids Company on a personal level and I was grateful. After I had briefed him on child protection and gangs during a private dinner at the five-star Bulgari Hotel, he had given us a four-figure sum. He is a thoughtful man and I liked him. But I see a similarity between what happened to us in 2015 and the attempt a year later to discredit Sadiq Khan when he campaigned to be Mayor of London. Khan, a former government minister, is the first Muslim mayor of a major Western capital. For three years he had chaired Liberty, the human rights group, and for eleven he had been an MP. He was not exactly unknown. Yet, when he presented himself as 'A Mayor for All Londoners', the Conservatives smeared him. Observers suspected Crosby's hand.

'[It was] real gutter stuff,' recalls Sam Butler, a Labour activist. 'Writing to the Sikh population claiming Labour's candidate, the Muslim Sadiq Khan, would tax family jewellery, playing fast and loose with divisive language, culminating in an utterly outrageous piece in the *Mail on Sunday* titled: "Are we really going to hand the world's greatest city to a Labour Party that thinks terrorists are its friends?" against a photo of a London bus destroyed in the 7/7 bombings.'[1]

This was a calculated attempt to deflect attention from the real questions facing London, and something similar happened to Kids Company. The difference is that Khan and his team had an election machine, whereas we were a charity struggling to cope with the numbers of children and families who were with us.

Inside government, they had failed to resolve the problem of how to fund us. After the news from Oliver Letwin, three days before Christmas 2014, that we were to receive an annual grant of £4.265 million and no more, I really felt I could not continue like this any longer. We could not live with such stress and uncertainty while keeping provision consistent for children and staff. I told the trustees that we would struggle to fundraise to make up the difference.

We had known this truth for some time. Three months earlier I had gone public, telling the *Sunday Times* that without proper government funding Kids Company would close at the end of the year. The reporter, Nicholas Hellen, understood the impact his story would have and read me the text before publication, giving me a chance to correct any errors of fact. No one warned me about the headline, which suggested we were going under.[2] We were not insolvent; that would not come until news broke of the police investigation into unfounded sexual abuse allegations broadcast by *Newsnight* nearly a year later. But time was running out, and the *Sunday Times* story made some big donors hesitate. Our fundraising challenge was now even harder.

Letwin agreed to give us the money as a lump sum at the beginning of April 2015. I now had to work out a way of getting Kids Company to survive from December until April, keeping everyone stable while negotiating with a government whose position was completely unclear in the run-up to the election.

I also met Labour's Jon Cruddas, who was co-ordinating party policy under Ed Miliband. There was every possibility that Labour would come to power, and the word from the Labour leadership was that it was interested in the Kids Company model and might adopt parts of it in future initiatives. When I spoke to Miliband at the leaving party for Alan Rusbridger, editor of *The Guardian*, he was outraged that we were not being properly funded by the Conservatives. In the meantime, I had to demonstrate to the Cabinet Office that we would be able to raise money in future. This was to meet one of its conditions for receiving any help at all, so I presented them with a list of prospective funders.

The list included a fantastic deal involving a telecommunications company and a globally famous rock band. But the plan to stream a concert, creating an income for us of as much as £3 million, was put back a year because of scheduling problems. That was the nature of the business. I could not dictate to funders when they should give their money. I was transparent with the Cabinet Office, dividing my list into 'income' and 'prospects' to identify what was confirmed and what was uncertain but likely.

This was the sort of precariousness that I felt was no longer tenable. We were not some pony riding club where one could say to the kids, 'There are no more rides on Wednesdays, as we need to adjust our services to match our income.' We were a substitute social work and mental health provision with serious commitments to children and staff, all framed by the absolute need for consistency, as that is the basis of trust. Without trust there cannot be clinical efficiency.

For the government, the final irritation may have been a demand I made in the feverish pre-election atmosphere. From December 2014 until April 2015, I tried to persuade civil servants at the Cabinet

Office to come to Kids Company to review our caseload. I believed we needed an external consultancy such as KPMG to record the number of clients we served and their levels of difficulty. Then we could have an evidence-based discussion of unmet need and the extent to which statutory services should pay the bill.

This was just the latest attempt to base discussion of our funding on something real. Call me naive, but I still hoped to anchor a sense of moral obligation on the correct side of this struggle over public funds. Bringing in the Centre for Social Justice, a think tank sympathetic to the Conservatives, had failed despite its explosive 2014 report based on our case files, 'Enough Is Enough'. 'Some [councils] are flagrantly disregarding, circumventing and contravening the very legislation and statutory guidance which provides for the protection and/or support of vulnerable children and young people,' the CSJ report had said, concluding: 'We have been astounded by the number and nature of legal failings and missed opportunities which were identified by the legal professionals' review of Kids Company cases.'[3] These were failings by statutory services, of course – not by us. Perhaps a new review in business speak from KPMG would make our value for money obvious.

The civil servants had done a whistle-stop tour of Kids Company, face painting with the kids on one of our fun days. The place was packed. I felt outraged that none of them spoke up later that year when it was claimed we had no kids. I also invited two senior Cabinet Office officials, Helen Tabiner and Sian Joseph, to meet Kids Company staff to go through 300 of our high-risk cases. They agreed to this and I chased them, but nothing happened. It seemed they did not want to engage with any real investigation of need.

The £4.265 million was duly handed over. Letwin promised the trustees that if the Conservatives were elected, he would resume meetings with a view to finding more funding for Kids Company. He had even identified a pot of post-election money in the child mental health budget.

Naturally, the Cabinet Office resisted the KPMG idea, but nothing prepared me for what was coming.

II

It was probably inevitable that Miles Goslett and the departed directors would find each other. If he did not know them already, his *Spectator* article in February 2015 was a shining neon sign to attract discontent.

Wherever it came from, internal Kids Company information was soon in wider circulation. It included a list I had presented at trustees' meetings of the twenty-five most expensive clients. This stolen document would provide the basis for a series of challenges to Kids Company exposing our supposed extravagance. Journalists used it freely, an MP on a parliamentary committee waved it around in a public session and as this book goes to press I am still being questioned on it two years later by investigators from the Charity Commission and the Official Receiver.

The list was the innovation of a former auditor, Peter Gotham, to improve our internal controls. On one piece of paper were our most costly cases. It was an open invitation for the trustees to scrutinise every decision we had made about them. The sheet showed the person's name and the total spent on the family, including clinical fees, housing, clothing, education and any living allowance. Top of the list for 2014/15 was Dave, an adult for whom we paid private psychiatric hospital charges when he was psychotic and the NHS would not accept him. In a year he had cost us £73,364.12, including hospital admissions, a stay at a spa when he was on anti-psychotic medicine and no hospital bed could be found, time in rehab clinics and a deposit for a rented flat.

We had known Dave since the age of eleven: he is the troubled young man who was caught by police as he threw himself off a bridge. For years we could not do anything consistent with him as he was in and out of prison. Then a judge suspended Dave's latest sentence to allow us to work with him properly, and we helped him to stay out of trouble. After Dave, costs on the 'Top 25' list fell rapidly. The median figure – the annual spending on no. 13 on the list of twenty-five – was £25,455.

It was so unfair. To this day, the narrative even from people who should understand Kids Company is that we exaggerated the levels of need. The deep disturbance and mental anguish we accidentally uncovered over nineteen years did not really exist. What happened to the truth in all this?

In March, an article by Goslett appeared in the *Sunday Times* stating that three directors had left Kids Company over concern about its funding and 'high levels of stress within the workplace'.[4] The new story took more funding away from us. But its real significance was that it was now obvious that at least one of the former directors was briefing against Kids Company. Before long I would have the *Mail on Sunday* on the phone, armed with the list of clients and expenditures relating to them. I could see for the first time how this ugly game would work out. And in the midst of all this, I was still struggling to get a substantial grant from central government to ensure our survival.

III

In May 2015, a general election brought the Conservatives to power. They were able to govern alone, albeit with a narrow majority, for the first time in eighteen years. Our trustees negotiated with Oliver Letwin for an additional £3 million. The civil servants claimed David Cameron had turned us down. It took just seven weeks after the election for the charity to be on the brink of closure.

Ministers will argue that we had been given a year's money at once, before the election, and that they were shocked when we came back for more. This is nonsense. Everyone understood that the funding of Kids Company was still unresolved. The salaries were due to go out on 27 June 2015. We needed the £3 million. I gave Philippa Stroud, the special adviser to Iain Duncan Smith as Secretary of State for Work and Pensions, a piece of my mind as politely as I could after hearing that a civil servant had called local authorities in secret to warn them that Kids Company was closing and to be prepared for an influx of young people. I told Philippa that to shut a charity abruptly like this was irresponsible. No one had told me anything. I found out by chance that the government was planning for our closure. It seemed to me that we had been kept sweet with money before the election only to be treated as an intolerable irritant after it.

Much later, while researching this book, I discovered that the Cabinet Office had carried out a post-election review of us, an internal assessment by civil servants that I knew nothing about and therefore could not challenge. The report caused even sympathetic ministers such as Duncan Smith to lose faith. It claimed that we were not fulfilling what we had agreed with the Cabinet Office.

'The civil servants had finally got their boot in the door,' a former Cabinet minister told us in 2017, 'because if you're spending public money and you mis-spend it,' – as the report apparently alleged we had – 'they will walk straight in and take the process over … making a very strong recommendation that the other monies should not be paid, no matter what.' The report, the minister added, had been 'pretty damning' about the organisational weaknesses of Kids Company and its trustees.

The real story now seemed clear. The Cabinet Office had tried and failed to get an independent auditor to find weaknesses in our charity and when that did not work, it drew up the report it wanted itself. Civil servants and ministers were engineering the closure of Kids Company. They were so confident that this was the end that they had made a quiet round of calls to councils advising them to be ready for large numbers of vulnerable children at social services. I found out only because a social worker from one of the local authorities called our safeguarding director to ask what was going on.

But I was ready for them. By now I had stopped trusting Letwin and as a safety net I had been talking to Stuart Roden and John Frieda, two long-term supporters. Roden is the chairman of Lansdowne Partners, one of London's oldest hedge funds, and Frieda is a celebrity hairstylist who founded the School of Confidence at Kids Company. They stepped in with the money to meet our commitments and took over negotiations with the government. This had a transformative effect. Not only did it stop Kids Company from closing in June 2015 but, as Roden and Frieda were part of a little group of philanthropists that included Conservative donors, they were listened to immediately.

Stuart, Alan and sometimes Richard Handover went to the meetings. They did not want me to attend and I regret not going, as I might have been more challenging towards ministers and less worried about the consequences. I had no doubt that all three men would fight for the kids. But Alan was in a difficult position because talks over the BBC licence fee were at an advanced stage, and Stuart is an enigmatic character. I believe he wanted to do the best for the kids.

The next I knew, as a result of these meetings, it was decided that Kids Company had to shrink from a £24 million organisation to £10 million. I was told I had to find £11,650,000 in three weeks to seal the deal. If I raised the money, the government would put in £3 million and Stuart's group of philanthropists would add £3 million. Alongside my £11.6 million this would allow us to make staff redundant and have a year's money ahead and three months' reserves. It was equivalent to being asked to find £555,000 every day without fail, Sundays included, for twenty-one days.

I tend to be pragmatic and task-focused in emergencies. Some people misread me, thinking that as I display no anxiety I do not care. This is not the case. I felt calm but hugely burdened by the realisation that if I failed to raise the money, the staff I loved would lose their jobs, the children and families would lose their sanctuary and our collective attempt to create an efficient model of care would be lost. Thousands of workers, volunteers and children over nearly two decades had helped create Kids Company. The trustees had worked hard alongside them. I felt as deep a loyalty towards the woman who had sent us her £10 benefit money as to the millionaires who had given to us over the years. But I am disciplined about not wasting energy on anxiety while trying to keep a team hopeful and focused.

I picked up the phone to individual donors. It was the only way to do it. My policy was always to be honest with them about the challenges and the opportunities. One of my first conversations was with an amazing self-made man. He had visited our Bristol provision, and I liked him very much because he was one of those rare individuals who responded to teenagers and showed empathy for them. He was also astute, with a no-nonsense approach. At our meeting in Bristol he had asked searching questions which I followed up by submitting our accounts and annual reports. He had given us £600,000.

In the conversation I explained that if I raised the £11,650,000 we would be restructuring, and he poignantly shared a story with me of how his father's business had gone through a similar transition. He understood the predicament facing the trustees and me. This man pledged the first £400,000. When I put the phone down, I cried at his generosity on every level – for his understanding as much as his money.

When the unfounded sexual abuse allegations emerged two months later courtesy of *Newsnight*, the sense of betrayal in his voice was palpable. It was as if I had let him down by not keeping my promise to honour his decency. All he had wanted from me was that his original £600,000 would not vanish into a hole, with no good coming of it. In effect, however, that is what happened. He felt so let down, and even though the cause was beyond my control I felt terrible for not being able to keep things safe as I had promised.

After the abuse allegations aired on *Newsnight* turned out to have no substance, he would not respond to my calls. It made me realise how painfully deep the betrayal felt for him. It also made me very sad.

My second phone call was to a man who can only be described as exceptional. I met him at a dinner at which we were seated together. Within minutes, never having met me before, he told me I should go for a gynaecological check-up. This man claimed the ability to see through a human body, and it was not a normal fundraising conversation. However, I genuinely cared for all the people who gave us money. It was often a deep, inexplicable bond, and conversations frequently became intimate. People would talk about their childhoods, sometimes breaking down as they recounted how frightened and alone they had felt. The disconcerting part of all this is that the man warning me about my innards at a posh dinner was absolutely right. I went for a check-up and was told I needed an operation.

Our next encounter was when he came down on Christmas Day into my makeshift grotto, and then he went into the dining room to serve food for the 4,000 clients who had arrived for lunch. He was on the other side of the world when I called, waking him up. Half asleep, he pledged £20,000 and instructed his charitable representative to confirm it in writing.

My third call was to an equally unique man who had made a fortune in pharmaceuticals and has spent the rest of his life fighting for social justice. He, too, was on the other side of the world, where he was getting out of a cab. As I trusted him, I explained that we were in a precarious situation and that I could not be sure what I was dealing with. I said that among our challenges was a potential child protection problem in which important people, including politicians, had been found to be abusing children, and that this information had been brought to us by a police officer. I wanted him to know that there were multiple layers to our troubles. He pledged £50,000. He was one of the remarkable few who continued to help after Kids Company closed. He enabled us to stabilise the children and young people whom the local authorities pledged to support after the closure but in fact did not.

The bottom line is that every philanthropist I called pledged money because they really did care and wanted Kids Company to survive. Before each call, I took a deep breath. It is not easy to beg. I was just very lucky that the people I begged were kind and generous. As I cannot read small spreadsheets, my PAs printed a large sheet and as donors confirmed their pledges, we wrote the sum and a brief record of the evidence we would need for the Cabinet Office. By the day of the deadline I was short by just £350,000, for which I offered my home as a substitute. The Cabinet Office took signed paperwork in which I promised to sell my flat and hand over the money if I failed to raise the final sum.

As part of this deal I was required to step down, a fact I learnt from a letter hand-delivered by Alan. Mark Fisher, director of the Office for Civil Society and Innovation – then part of the Cabinet Office, but now in the Department for Culture, Media and Sport – had asked for me to leave my post immediately. Stuart Roden, however, felt this was untenable. They did not think they could run the organisation without me, so the deadline for my resignation was extended to October 2015.

No one gave me an explanation as to why this decision had been made. There was no complaint from any government department on my file, or disciplinary action, or indeed a formal letter suggesting I had fallen short. Stuart Roden told me the demand for my resignation had come from the Cabinet Office. Alan was also to step down as chair of trustees so that Stuart could take over. My lawyers advised me to resist, but I agreed to go – and even to offer my flat – so that Kids Company would get its money. Just to make sure I went, the Cabinet Office leaked my resignation to *Newsnight*.

I was sad about Alan, as I knew he genuinely cared for the kids, but I felt I could work with Stuart. As for the redundancies, I believed we were destroying an amazing programme that after two decades should be going mainstream, not being cut.

It killed me that I could not discuss it with the staff. Job losses involve a formal legal consultation and I was not allowed to speak. I planned to campaign and change the decision; I did not want to give up. I loved our workers and was not prepared to lose them. For each worker lost, at least fifteen families would be affected. The negative cascade of these decisions would create great toxicity and sadness. I sometimes think, as devastating as closure was, at least we were spared the ugliness of having to choose among staff in a redundancy process.

IV

In July 2015, Kids Company had enough money pledged by philanthropists to restructure the charity, meet all liabilities, have three months' reserves and have confirmed income for a year ahead. It did not feel like a success. We would have to let go of three-quarters of our staff, with a huge impact on how we delivered to the children. I knew this was an attempt to save the charity. But I saw it as a failure, because for nearly twenty years I had fought alongside the trustees to use Kids Company to inspire the changes that were needed nationally in children's social services and mental health.

I held on to some hope because Stuart Roden, who was going to take over as chair of trustees, had promised to bring in consultants to look at the systemic problems stopping the state from protecting vulnerable children properly. He had in mind McKinsey & Company and I knew he had the intelligence and determination to see through such a project. He was a curious mix, able to focus single-mindedly on making vast amounts of money, yet committed to the children. I believed in his empathy for them.

Stuart probably thought that if the organisation shrank, he could use McKinsey's evidence of systemic failure to get proper funding out of the government. That was the strategy I had pursued for years, until I realised that actually government does not respond to evidence; it is run according to PR. But I was still happy. As Stuart had managed to get the government to be a major contributor to this new phase of Kids Company, perhaps he and John Frieda could go further than I had been able to. The struggle I had embarked on nineteen years earlier was not over yet. In any event, there was no choice: if the children had been brave enough to seek help and manage the effects of the maltreatment they had endured, the least we owed them was to be inspired by their courage and not to give up in the face of adversity.

The unfounded sexual abuse allegations reported by the media on 30 July 2015, and broadcast on *Newsnight* one week later, led the whole edifice to collapse. The philanthropists withdrew their £3 million. The Cabinet Office also wanted its money back, dishonestly claiming that its £3 million, which had gone into our bank account minutes before news of the police investigation broke, had not been for salaries.

The police indicated to me that *Newsnight* had been aware of these allegations for some time. This was part of a pattern. The charity was under sustained attack, but from unofficial sources. If the *Newsnight* team really thought young people were being abused at Kids Company, it should have contacted the police to prevent more children being harmed. Instead, it waited until its broadcast was nearly ready for transmission. On 30 July, we were totally unprepared. We knew absolutely nothing about the allegations. Never in a million years did I imagine hearing that a charity I had founded was supposedly covering up the abuse of young people. On 6 August, one day after we shut, *Newsnight* aired with the story that Kids Company staff had failed to report to the authorities complaints of violence and sexual exploitation involving its clients. The incidents were said to have occurred between 2008 and 2012. We closed the day before the broadcast because the damage had been immediate: the decision to shut was taken within hours of police confirming that an investigation, prompted by *Newsnight*'s belated approach to the authorities, was underway.

The police assigned to the investigation seemed outraged by the BBC's behaviour. One detective told me there was cheering in the office when I challenged Kirsty Wark, who presented the programme, over its evidence. I was lucky that the serious complex case team of the Metropolitan Police sexual offences, exploitation and child abuse command took every claim and investigated it thoroughly. Some of it bordered on silly, including two teenagers having an argument when neither wanted to empty a bin as part of their chores. One had turned to the other to make a threat. The police took a statement from the individual who was threatened. He laughed about it, stating: 'In what household don't kids argue?'

But it was a shock during the months of police inquiries to be given a copy of an email from David Quirke-Thornton, the director of children's services in Southwark, to Chris Cook, the reporter who made the *Newsnight* film that shut us down. Dated 13 October 2015, it referred to 'very serious' sexual abuse allegations against Kids Company:

Dear Chris,

I hope you are well. The child protection and criminal investigation being undertaken by Police and Local Authorities continues – it is a complex investigation involving a number of alleged victims and perpetrators, and concerns about the culture and leadership of Kids Company in regard to child protection. Several alleged victims have come forward directly to Police, Local Authorities and via the NSPCC helpline that was established for this investigation. The allegations are very serious and will take some time to investigate fully.

This was inexplicable. It was inaccurate and inappropriate. This was the lead director of children's services in a police investigation. His duty was to keep any material related to the inquiry confidential. Instead of exercising propriety, he was sharing information with the media and exaggerating it. My understanding of the darkness we faced deepened.

It was also Quirke-Thornton who played down the number of children and families Kids Company worked with. I believe he misrepresented information on purpose. Had he and the government acknowledged the scale and severity of Kids Company's caseload, they would have had to explain why the state left such a serious level of need to a precariously funded charity.

At least the police had a sane perspective, telling me as they reviewed the accusations: 'You have done well if this is the sum total of all the allegations against your organisation over nearly two decades.'

What was the role of the departed directors in bringing about the destruction of Kids Company? If any whistleblower really believed young people, staff and donors needed protection from my leadership of Kids Company, they could not only have gone to the trustees, but the local safeguarding board, the Care Quality Commission, the police, Ofsted, the NSPCC or the Charity Commission before involving the national press. There was no dearth of watchdogs if it was felt I was failing or, as it has subsequently been represented, I had too much power.

Instead, the destination was the media, with the immoral consequence of sharing confidential information about vulnerable children and young people. The Charity Commission was only contacted on 16 July. Did this show a belated awareness that leaks to the media would expose the leakers to liability for breaches of confidence? On the day Kids Company closed, one of the departed directors posted a picture of herself on Facebook holding the Olympic torch, which she had been passed while running with the Kids Company team before the opening ceremony in 2012. She used a slogan, taken from a campaign to get women into sport, at the top of this triumphant image. 'I love playing. I just love winning slightly more. THIS GIRL CAN.'

She apparently felt so sure of the moral worth of what she had done that she posted for her friends a little boast, on the day it shut down, of her association with a charity that was a lifeline to destitute children – children for whom she had cared, handing out living allowances over a six-year period.

V

With the closure on 5 August, everything stopped. Carefully nurtured relationships between worker and child were severed. Some staff carried on without pay to support vulnerable adults, but for the children nothing could be done. We could support the families through a food bank for their parents, but could not make contact with a child. When the schools reopened in September, our workers were not allowed even to say goodbye to pupils they had grown in some cases to love, because they were viewed as a child protection risk.

How could we have continued? It would have taken £12 million to stay open, paying staff who were unable to work with children for the six months that passed before the police announced that 'detailed and extensive inquiries' had found no evidence of criminality at Kids Company.

I had sympathy for Alan Yentob, who initially could not speak up in public. He could not be seen to challenge the government while the new BBC licence regime was being negotiated. I cried when he resigned as its creative director, feeling the searing injustice.

The first person to reach out to me was a QC. I had never met Ian Wise, but as an experienced barrister he, before anyone else, suspected that the assault on Kids Company had the whiff of political mischief. He was well placed to make the judgment. Described by Chambers UK, the guide to the country's best lawyers, as 'a force to be reckoned with in public law litigation' and by Legal 500 as 'the driving force in all the landmark test cases for children in recent years', he was at the end of a phone throughout the turmoil to give support. He was shocked by the lack of help from most of the people who had claimed to be my friends and supportive colleagues when the charity was a going concern.

Bindmans, the law firm, generously agreed to wait for its fees as we worked together to protect young people from the media. Other supporters disappeared from view or distanced themselves. The first to speak up publicly was Tony Simpson, a partner in an international consultancy who had been in care himself and was one of our trustees before moving to the Middle East. Bella Freud, Jemima Khan and Laura Bailey, the model and writer, also defended us.

Kids became media targets. Asking newspapers not to pursue young people who had been violated as children did not work. Tamsin Allen of Bindmans worked with me to have the Independent Press Standards Organisation, the industry regulator, issue a reminder that they should not photograph the kids or pursue them outside their homes. Two boys we had managed to get into a private school without having to pay fees pretended not to know Kids Company for fear that they also would be targeted.

Vulnerable children and young adults alike were left without our help. Some who were at university were at risk of losing their accommodation because we helped them, care leavers especially, with rent.

I had no access to money of my own. Hour after hour, calls were coming through from devastated young people. One boy tried to throw himself onto a train track. He had been left by the local authority in a hotel, but lacked capacity, under the Mental Health Act, to look after himself.

At times like this you see the people who are genuine and have moral courage. Straight away, a few of them stepped in. Through a grant from them, we managed to stabilise approximately 150 of the most high-risk kids and vulnerable adults.

The co-founder of a Muslim-led charity took over the support of one of our mature students, paying his fees so that he could keep studying and stay away from gangs. This was for a man in his twenties whose parents were drug addicts. His father had died of an overdose and his mother was as fragile as girl aged five. He had no one else to rely on.

A restaurant chain in London immediately organised the delivery of food to a railway arch so that we could hand it out to 500 of the most destitute. A record company stepped in straight away to help with stabilising the food and housing of another group of kids and families.

A well-known musician took over funding of the food bank as well as supporting the Christmas event, at which 1,500 children and family members received a food bag and attended a party at Oasis Academy South Bank, a school in Waterloo. Steve Chalke, the founder of the academy, courageously hosted the party. Many of our former staff greeted the families, comforting them after the abrupt closure. It was brave of Chalke because of what I call 'brand terror', or the fear of being tainted by association. At a party for the Garden Bridge, the proposed public garden and pedestrian crossing over the River Thames, a whisper went round when Mervyn Davies, the former banker and government minister, announced that an ex-client of Kids Company was going to perform. 'What is Mervyn doing getting a Kids Company kid to dance?'

In Bristol, a team of staff continued to support the children with the help of transitional funding from the city council. A skeleton therapy programme and a food project survived, while individual workers counselled the most disturbed young people. But I would describe one pharmaceutical owner as the most heroic supporter. Without him, it would have been chaos and the children and families would have been completely devastated by lack of ongoing support. He took over from a couple in the arts to ensure that young people kept their places at university and did not lose their homes.

I had no income and used all my redundancy money, which was about £11,000, on the kids and their families. I was lucky that friends stepped in and supported me. I was supposed to use the money to pay my service charges, as I was due to contribute £6,500 to a new boiler in my block of flats. When I could not do this, my heating and hot water were cut off.

I made friends with the cold tap. The challenges I faced were nothing compared with the 100 or so Kids Company workers who had been self-employed. I begged for them to be paid, but was told it was not possible. The man who ran our security faced losing his business. Other people who worked with us scraped by, and I was acutely aware of the damage non-payment had caused them.

Meanwhile, inaccurate briefings from the Cabinet Office that the final £3 million had not been intended to pay staff salaries resulted in a perception that I had personally stolen the money. Van drivers and random members of the public shouted, 'Where the fuck have you hidden the money?' or 'You fucking thief.' One evening I was invited out to dinner by two scientists. A passer-by shouted into the restaurant that I was a thief. I wanted to explain that he had got his facts wrong, but the waiters intervened.

Kind neighbours handled the media camped on deck chairs outside my flat.

The Landmark Hotel, a five-star hotel in Marylebone, were brilliant. They let me use a public area with comfortable sofas to see the kids for support. We would huddle up under an ornate staircase for birthday parties and counselling sessions. The sight of tall boys from gangs appearing for a chat raised no eyebrows and the waiting staff could not have been kinder.

I cannot hide from the truth, however. Even though I tried to find solutions, the number of children and families we failed to protect against our abrupt closure was painfully large. There were so many I could not help, and because of it some felt betrayed and did not want to talk to me any more. The whole experience was profoundly confusing and disturbing for young people already devastated by a conveyor belt of disrupted relationships.

I felt sad for my brothers, to whom I am close, and my nieces and nephews. They were so worried about my welfare and felt paralysed by the fact that they were unable to protect me. As the drama around me unfolded, I was grateful for the innate sense of peace I have always had. My commitment was to secure the children's welfare as much as I could.

Of course, I also had to fight for justice.

When the destruction of Kids Company started to unfold, I was at an immediate disadvantage. It is easy to criticise spending when you know only what was spent. It is harder to defend the decisions, because they make sense only in the context of people's life stories. No clinician is at liberty to reveal a client's history. But without the history, who can make a fair judgement?

In April 2017, nearly two years after Kids Company closed, I confronted this question with the official whose job was to say what punishment, if any, he would recommend as a result of Kids Company's collapse. Yet another leak suggested that the trustees and I faced being banned as company directors for up to fifteen years. It is the Official Receiver, a civil servant in the Insolvency Service, who decides whether to recommend this to the government.

Trustees carry the legal responsibilities of running a charity. They do it without pay. Just as I put up my flat, some of our trustees had lent Kids Company six-figure sums as well as giving their time and risking their reputations on the judgements they made about the operation and survival of the charity. The internal processes they oversaw were benchmarked against the guidance issued by the Charity Commission.

It should be obvious that even to threaten committed trustees with the removal of their freedom to run companies will deter anyone with business experience from getting involved in charities for years to come.

It is also the Official Receiver who takes possession of a failed company's records. Investigators look through the files for signs of wrongdoing. In our case, eyes came to rest on Client 10. Shorn of context, this seemed an open-and-shut example of favouritism and lax controls. Kids Company had spent £2,250 to send a boy on holiday to Lanzarote, after spending £200 to buy him photography equipment and a jacket the previous year.

I had found this young man as a six-year-old, standing in the snow in his underpants with no shoes on. He started talking to me as I left my block of flats. The NSPCC has estimated that for every child on a register or subject to a child protection plan, another eight suffer abuse and neglect without support. This boy was one of the invisible eight.

I took him back to his house and waited nearly half an hour until the mother responded to the doorbell. It was obvious she was on drugs. Afterwards I called social services.

I was not the only person to report this. The boy was often without food as his mother was driven to prioritise her addiction. The neighbours who fed him when he turned up on the doorstep also raised the alarm. Schools and the local police were worried about his wellbeing.

As I understand it, the boy's father was a street beggar who had died from the effects of drugs and alcohol when the child was four. For a while, social services placed the boy in foster care, but his carers abused him and he was returned to his mother.

At primary school his attendance was poor. At secondary school he was rarely seen because he was worried about drug dealers hurting or raping his mother. He had witnessed her screaming as dealers and other drug users assaulted her; a dealer who carried a firearm particularly frightened him. Anxiety disrupted his sleep. He would keep himself awake at night and rest during the day: in his mind, he needed to stay awake to protect his mum.

When the Official Receiver's team read the file, it found a 2005 letter from Camden social services expressing concern that my involvement with the boy, known as Client 10, 'may undermine Client 10's mother's role as a parent'.

On its own, without context, this letter presents me as interfering with the quality of care a mother provides for her child. When I learnt that this letter was part of the case being built to disqualify me from being a director of any company, I wrote to the Official Receiver.

What your team failed to identify is that the reason I received this letter was because I had gone to social services in West Hampstead to meet with the manager in charge of Client 10's case. I was worried about his welfare. During the meeting, I had asked social services to do a hair test so that the level of substance misuse the parent was engaged in could be identified. Social services' approach in relation to this case was that they had 'no evidence' of the mother being a class-A drug user. My assertion was that they didn't want to find the evidence, because if they did the status of this child within social services structures would have to be elevated to a child protection concern, as opposed to 'child in need', which permitted them to select a very low-level intervention.

During this meeting, the manager stated that the reason the child had survived the challenges within his home is because of the protective factors my involvement was facilitating. They promised to look into the case, including drug-testing the mother. The next I knew, I received the letter that you mentioned and the mother was encouraged to ban the child's contact with me. This will explain why there is a gap in our records for him beyond this period, and why I received the above-mentioned letter from Camden social services.

Camden social services were identifying the means by which Kids Company could be removed as an advocate for this child and a challenge to their poor care.

I knew the mother was using Class-A substances because her child, at the time aged eight, had found crack pipes, rocks of cocaine wrapped in cellophane and syringes in the house. He thought his mother was dying and that is why he asked about his discovery.

He was one of the young people at Kids Company whose history of being failed by statutory services was examined by the Centre for Social Justice in its 2014 report, 'Enough is Enough'. 'Throughout my whole childhood, [my mum] couldn't look after me. I had to look after myself but at the same time I was looking after myself, I was the one supporting her and not social [care],' he told the researchers.

I made plans myself for how I could help my mum. I tried a sympathetic plan, I tried an aggressive plan, and I tried a runaway plan – for example, when I was 15 and went to [stay with a relative]. That was one of my plans – to run away and tell her I'd never see her again – and for her to be clean for a year at least before I would see her again. Another plan was to give my mum the choice: me or the drugs. I said that to my mum. As heartbreaking as it was at the time, she chose the drugs. She didn't say it but her actions told me that. I can understand it's an addiction but an addiction can be broken with the right support.[5]

He also said social workers 'kind of gave up and disappeared'. A neighbour told the Centre for Social Justice that when she reported that a very neglected child was appearing at her house almost daily for food, 'I was told that if he had no bruises there was no reason for social care to [get involved].'[6]

When Client 10 was in his teens, a drug dealer threw another out of the second-floor window of the mother's house. The man who fell was taken to hospital and the one who threw him claimed it was the child who had pushed the dealer out of the window. When the police arrested the boy, they asked me to follow their car and act as an appropriate adult.

As he recognised me, the desk sergeant did not put Client 10 in a police cell: we were allowed to sit on a bench opposite his desk. This boy who had never committed a crime gave his DNA, was made to wear a white jumpsuit and fought tears throughout the twelve hours we were at the police station. There was no sign of a social worker to support him and he had no family friends or relatives. He was on his own facing serious allegations. I knew from the desk sergeant that the drug dealer was dangerous.

Despite all this, no child protection meeting was held to discuss the safety of this boy in the family home. He was released into his mother's care. I was not contacted by social services.

Shortly afterwards, the mother burnt the flat down in a drugged state. The boy did his best to rescue the neighbours. The accommodation was uninhabitable but social services again did not step in and Kids Company paid a private foster carer to take him on. Camden did not contest the placement but did not pay for it either, although it should have.

The Official Receiver seized on a file note. 'An intervention record dated 18th February, 2009 stated that a two-week holiday to Lanzarote had been booked for Client 10 at a cost of £2,250.00 with Miss Batmanghelidjh agreeing the holiday and the cost. Client 10 also due to commence weekly piano lessons,' the Insolvency Service noted.

On its own it looks like a casual holiday. I authorised this trip because the boy's new foster family was going away. They could not afford to take the boy, who was now seventeen, with them. Neither did they feel he was well enough psychologically to be left at their house on his own. I weighed up this decision with our team. If we had kept him in England we would need to pay for alternative accommodation and a carer. This would cost more than the holiday. So, both psychologically and financially, sending him to Lanzarote with his foster parents was the best decision.

I wrote to the Official Receiver: 'I am surprised your team were unable to identify the communications which led to this decision as the foster carer had written to me requesting this intervention.' Also unnoticed by the Insolvency Service was the risk posed by a paedophile who had befriended this vulnerable young man on a bus.

And there, in microcosm, is the one-sided battle I have fought for two years to restore the reputation of the charity I founded. I wrote to the Official Receiver myself as I have no money to pay for legal letters. The Official Receiver is in possession of all the files and I do not have access. Disturbingly, many of the records appear to have been mislaid. Just as the education department lost the records showing Kids Company's performance at the time of the National Audit Office investigation before magically finding them again after the NAO report was published, the Official Receiver has been unable to locate important clinical records. In the end, the quest for justice is all about the audit trail of clinical decisions. Without knowing why a decision was made, I'm just a fat beggar sending a boy on holiday, who has now been found out.

Clinical decisions were made under a process we called 'Right to Health'. 'I am aware that the Insolvency Service were not able to find the Right to Health meeting notes where clinical teams on a weekly basis were discussing complex cases,' I told the Official Receiver in my letter in April. 'This is despite the notes to these meetings being robustly kept and distributed. When [the former clinical director of Kids Company] provided the code for his laptop so that your team could access the notes, your team were unable to open his laptop. So, you can appreciate the apprehension I feel.'

I also noted that the Official Receiver's summary of the case does not refer to Client 10's weekly psychiatric appointments, for which Kids Company paid the invoices. He suffered depression, was on the autistic spectrum and had a pronounced obsessive compulsive disorder that resulted in his pulling out his eyelashes, eyebrows and body hair. 'Your records do not indicate the severity of his difficulties and instead suggest that he had "no incentive" to sustain employment,' I wrote.

Kids Company never gave up on this boy and all the others. We alone recognised that his behaviour was not a 'refusal to engage' but a product of the challenges he endured. But I now have to accept that the world will be told a new story about Kids Company; the narrative is changing from 'We had no kids' to 'The kids had no needs', and the committed individuals who signed off Kids Company's support for children such as Client 10 are to be barred from running companies because they supposedly authorised spending on kids who did not need it.

Was all the furore about the money spent on these children motivated by genuine concern, or by a different agenda? Steve Hilton, former adviser to David Cameron, suspects the latter. As this book went to press, he was quoted in the *Sunday Times* as saying of me:

> She was seen as a poster child for the Big Society, and that was a conscious decision on our part. As a result, she became a victim of attacks on the Big Society from the civil service and the media, especially *Newsnight* ... I do think there was a conspiracy. Not an organised one, but among parts of the Establishment that she threatened.'

In the public sector, things will carry on as before, as if Kids Company never existed.

Perhaps I should explain another bullet in the Official Receiver's loaded pistol. 'A file note dated 19th May 2008 recorded Miss Batmanghelidjh authorised £200 to buy photography equipment and a jacket for Client 10,' the Insolvency Service stated.

These were entirely reasonable expenditures for a boy who did not have a jacket, did not go to school, and who had shown an interest in photography at a time when he was spending days in bed because of depression. We were hugely encouraged that he wanted to take up photography. He pursued this interest with his key worker, then started to think about going to college.

Similarly, we used a personal trainer to minimise his isolation, reduce his dissociation, address his depression through the release of endorphins secondary to exercise, and provide him with a male role model. He reduced his use of computers and started attending the gym, where he built relationships and became interested in rock climbing, through which he identified a community where he might belong.

I should like to ask the reader of this book a question. You are the founder of a charity that identifies serious failures in state provision, then tries to cover for them by acting like the family a youngster does not have.

You care about Client 10. You are an extension to the family he wishes could have looked after him. 'There was no fun in my childhood. To be honest, there was no childhood … I literally feel like I was born an adult, just … smaller,' he told the Centre for Social Justice, adding:

> If I didn't have Kids Company, I would be on a wrong path … I wouldn't have the educational potential without them … Everyone needs support in some way … I think I would be homeless without them … Even though I am doing well, they still … care to send someone to see me once each week – it's a constant thing – it's not some random person every couple of weeks – it's a set plan.[7]

The question is this.

What would you have done?

In that same month, April 2017, I went to the assembly of a seven-year-old receiving a star. He had no one else that day to witness his moment of recognition. His pride that I would be there, as if I were an A-list celebrity appearing at assembly just for him, made me profoundly sad.

One day he will learn that the world is a little more complicated.

CONCLUSION

'Where there is ruin, there is hope for a treasure'

Rumi

I

The image in my head is of a circular junction into which many roads feed. Each route carries an anxiety and as they join up to form the intersection, a toxic cocktail forms, leading to the destruction of Kids Company.

Along one road flowed the need to silence our campaigning role. A second carried confusion about who deserves help and what form it should take. A third was the need to suppress child protection failings, contemporary and historic. A fourth arose from my role as a woman, a foreigner in a position of relative strength, as a maternal object within Kids Company and outside it. The fifth was about the need of powerless people to feel powerful, and I put the journalists who disrupted Kids Company into this category. A sixth, perhaps, was Kids Company as collateral damage from efforts to undermine David Cameron in the run-up to Brexit.

Repeated governments in Britain have avoided dealing with the child protection scandal blighting the country. One Prime Minister admitted it. He told me after leaving office: 'We know children's social services are not fit for purpose but none of us want to go near it.'

It is not worth their while. Vulnerable kids and their parents rarely participate in politics. An abused child is unlikely to approach the media and as long as the government looks like it cares, everything is fine.

This was particularly true when Michael Gove led the Department for Education in David Cameron's government. Gove was a visionary minister with a focus on attainment. His understanding of how children succeed in education was framed by the notion that they should be rigorously taught. Perhaps he was right in the case of the well-adjusted child, but his perspective lacked subtlety.

We now know that a child's ability to learn is hugely influenced by the care conditions sculpting their neurological capacities. If toxic stress damages the centres of the brain responsible for memory and attention, that child is going to come into the classroom with a hidden disadvantage that rote learning cannot fix. Gove could not see it. Instead, he carried the youth and child protection agenda within his department reluctantly. Eventually he opted to put his reforming spirit into something he knew as a result of personal experience, which was adoption.

Gove defined the national task in relation to the care of vulnerable children as speeding up adoption. He was assisted by Edward Timpson MP, whose parents had fostered a lot of children. Together, these men crafted a journey on which they took the public. Charities and think tanks joined in, and a relatively small concern in the national childhood crisis, with 4,900 children needing to be adopted, became central because this was something relatively small as a project, which the government could demonstrate outcomes against.[1] At the same time, some 600,000 children a year were being referred to child protection departments, 80 per cent of which the National Audit Office described as 'failing'.[2]

However, this agenda was hijacked in 2012 by revelations of child sexual exploitation across the country.[3] Some 2,245 children who were being exploited in Rotherham, Bristol, Rochdale, Oxford and Newcastle had tried for years to draw attention to their plight, but the powers that be were not interested. Fourteen-year-olds forced into prostitution were described by police and social services as 'making lifestyle choices'.[4] When Her Majesty's Inspectorate of Constabulary (HMIC) reviewed 384 police investigations into child sexual abuse cases, it found that three-quarters were substandard. According to Matt Parr, lead inspector for HMIC, one in ten was so poor there was a continuing risk to children.[5]

The child protection system in Britain has been structured around traumatic events. No great minds are applied to it or top ministers put in charge of the brief. It is the afterthought given to some low-key minister, whose role, it seems, is to run it without fuss.

But the endeavour to keep child protection out of the headlines is always disrupted by a tragic new case. In 2000, it was Victoria Climbié, who died in a bathtub with 128 injuries after years of horrific abuse. She had been in contact with numerous professionals including being taken to hospital twice, but the abuse was not discovered.

Her death led to Every Child Matters and the Children Act 2004, which asked professionals to collaborate in support of a child. This was a good idea but hard to realise because the professionals dealing with children were in different settings, including health, education, social services and the police. Time was often wasted making appointments, communicating on paper, and passing the child back and forth like an unwanted football as tighter budgets discouraged the different settings from taking responsibility for complex cases. However, things did improve.

In 2002, Jessica Chapman and Holly Wells went missing from their home in Soham and it transpired that Ian Huntley, their school caretaker, had killed them. An inquiry led to the vetting of people who work with children. Why did no one think to check people who choose to work with children until 2002? It is an example of Britain's 'child blindness'.

In 2008, a toddler called Peter Connelly (Baby P) died of injuries sustained over nine of his seventeen months. This prompted another inquiry and new guidance. The government set up the Social Work Taskforce and the Social Work Reform Board to overhaul the profession. From this emerged the College of Social Work, which was supposed to train new social workers with leadership quality. That was soon deprived of funding and shut. In between, other children were killed while under the care of local authorities.

Throughout the period of the reforms, the children who were being sexually exploited in Rotherham, Rochdale, Oxford, Bristol, Newcastle and elsewhere continued to plead for help and received none. It was only after the uncovering of Jimmy Savile's abuse of perhaps 500 people that the nation woke up to the fact that for decades children had been abused in institutions such as churches, boarding schools, sports facilities and hospitals.

Initially, I thought the government was reluctant to address the child protection problem because it did not understand life for vulnerable children in the ghettos of Britain.

Let's face it: political leaders were usually white, middle- or upper-class men, the majority educated in private schools, where there might be child abuse, but not the street violence and chronic poverty that children in the ghettos knew. In 2013, I was still hopeful that if the government saw the facts they would do something, because I believed that deep down they must have cared about children. David Cameron's tenderness towards his own children gave me hope. I was even cheeky enough to think that if he had such a caring and authentic wife, there must be something really good in him that she recognises. I had only goodwill towards them and genuinely wanted to be helpful.

Kids Company partnered with the Centre for Social Justice to carry out a piece of research showing how local authorities were failing to protect the children who were self-referring. We selected this organisation, a think tank created by Conservative supporters and Iain Duncan Smith, as we thought the government would not shoot it down. The resulting report, 'Enough is Enough', was damning and described local authorities operating 'unscrupulous and illegal practices' with 'overwhelmed' systems perpetuating 'grotesque failures for vulnerable children'.[6]

The report recommended a Royal Commission on children's services, but we did not want to repeat the pattern of producing reports instead of reforms. So, in 2014, we started work on See the Child. Change the System, a campaign to redesign children's services from first principles, with economic modelling by the University of Cambridge. My thinking was that once we had produced a new structure we could hand it over to the state. I approached the National Lottery to propose a child protection lottery that could pay for pilots of a new model of care for vulnerable children. Kids Company was trying to assist the government by presenting a new possibility.

See the Child. Change the System was not about Kids Company. It had an independent funder and board, to be chaired by Sir Keir Starmer, the former director of public prosecutions who became shadow Secretary of State for Exiting the European Union. He was joined by the then Children's Commissioner, Maggie Atkinson, Tessa Jowell MP and Dr Peter Green, a consultant forensic physician and consultant in safeguarding for the borough of Wandsworth. The project had support from all the lead organisations in the children's sector, including the royal colleges of GPs, paediatrics, psychiatrists and nursing, the College of Social Work, teachers' organisations, universities and unions as well as many large children's charities.[7]

I believe See the Child. Change the System was the final straw for the Cabinet Office and the government in general. As one minister said (off the record), 'When she had 300 kids in a railway arch, we could cope. When it became 3,000 kids, we were just about able to tolerate it. When it got to 30,000, it became too much.' He then went on to say that if there was a boat we could put them on and send them back to where they came from, we would. What could he have meant? The ethnic minority children and families that Kids Company was caring for?

In reality, Kids Company had a balance of boys and girls, blacks and other ethnic minorities on the one hand and whites on the other hand in more or less equal numbers. The most destitute and traumatised were on the whole the children who came from the black community.

Following See the Child. Change the System and my putting pressure on the Cabinet Office to review Kids Company's case load, I believe some political operators within government decided to diminish my voice by discrediting me. The British do reputational assassination to perfection. Plan number one was to starve the charity of funding and close it down. The government refused the charity a grant when they knew it was essential for our survival. Behind our backs in June 2015, civil servants in the Cabinet Office warned local authorities to expect lots of Kids Company kids at their doors. There was a complete disregard for the vulnerable children we cared for.

Plan two emerged when two Conservative donors, John Frieda and Stuart Roden, and their friends made clear they were prepared to take over the charity. The plan (not theirs) was to shrink Kids Company so that it would fade into the background. As part of this I was pushed into a position where I had no choice but to resign as chief executive. The Cabinet Office told Alan Yentob that if I did not resign, it would not give Kids Company £3 million we expected. I had not been the subject of any disciplinary action in nearly two decades running the organisation. There had been no letters of complaint from the government about Kids Company's reporting or management of its services and finances. Mysteriously, the request for me to resign leaked from the Cabinet Office to BBC *Newsnight*. When the charity closed, reports demonstrating its efficacy disappeared from the Department for Education, I believe as part of an agenda to present Kids Company as dysfunctional.

In 2017, as I write the conclusion to this book, I look back at the charitable sector. I never believed that complex social and therapeutic work should be done by charities. Ultimately, the paymaster determines the job. They have the power to determine clinical models and decisions by virtue of what they choose to fund. This leaves the least qualified people driving clinical models and decisions.

No matter how brave charities are, in the end many just change shape to fit the money. Through this process, children and young people who cannot produce quick results or good enough results for the 'outcome seekers' start to be excluded from provisions.

I want to highlight a pattern in British politics of a drama covering up a truth that the system wishes to keep buried. In many ways, the scrutiny and destruction of Kids Company by the political system was a drama. The public were encouraged to worry about whether I owned mansions, had mesmerised the Prime Minister, had stolen public money and gone to expensive restaurants with it – while no one would focus on Britain's incapacity and unwillingness to cope with childhood maltreatment.

One of the dynamics I have discovered is that there is a risk in being an advocacy and a service-delivery provision in one. If you challenge politicians and it does not suit their agenda, they retort by shutting down the services of the organisation. In this respect, I very much regret the price the children paid. A former minister in the Cabinet Office disclosed to a Kids Company director that the charity's closure was planned by some ministers and civil servants who used key journalists to achieve what they wanted.

The economics of children's services are decades behind in Britain. Until recently no local authority could capture the cost of a child because each time a young person turned to services for support, they would be counted as a new child with a new cost centre. This made a mockery of the civil servants in the Cabinet Office suggesting that Kids Company was expensive and there were cheaper provisions to which our funding could be redirected. One wonders who they were comparing us to.

Our resources went mainly to the most challenging group of young people. The comparatively less challenging we supported through volunteers. The children for whom we needed the most money should have been in the care of local authorities or supported by mental health providers, but were not. Kids Company was their informal holding space and the government knew it. We received about £41 million from government over twelve years through statutory grants while privately raising a further £123 million up to 2015. This money was focused on vulnerable children living in Britain, nearly all of whom should have been cared for by child mental health services and social services. Some 17,000 of our cases were the responsibility of the state, child protection and child mental health services. By working with them therapeutically, we saved the state money.

Professor Martin Knapp at the London School of Economics demonstrated this. Reviewing expenditure on 750 young people who were funded by a grant from the Department for Education of nearly £9 million over two years, he calculated that the work with these clients would produce a 'net benefit' of between £8.7 million to £9.5 million over ten years as the wider economy gained from higher employment and the NHS, social services and criminal justice system made savings because vulnerable young people had stabilised their mental and physical health and improved their prospects. In other words, the true cost to the taxpayer of every pound spent on 750 disadvantaged teenagers would eventually fall to zero.[8]

To put our £41 million into context, the government's flagship Troubled Families programme, despite the visionary leadership of Louise Casey, was found to have failed because it relied on delivery by local authorities which optimised data and outcomes in order to get the money promised for each family.[9] It cost £448 million to provide services for 120,000 families which were thought to cost the state £9 billion a year in the disruptions they caused.

When resources are seen to be limited, invariably a hidden hierarchy develops of who deserves help. In this framework, the influence of racism is powerfully played out, as are confused notions of equality.

The premise by which British culture understands equality is equally distributing goods and services between people. The idea is that they should all receive the same, which means that fairness has been exercised. Embedded in this doctrine is the negation of the individual. It does not really matter what the individual's need is and whether provision for them is sufficient to bring about meaningful change. So, long as there has been material distribution done equally, all is well. In this context, there is 'need blindness' and 'colour blindness'.

Colour blindness emerges from the idea that irrespective of cultural and racial background, everyone is the same and should be treated the same. It assumes that everyone has the same opportunity and therefore those who do not achieve are failures.

It is a reassuring argument. But the truth is that race and colour are relevant, because whether we like it or not the black community is disproportionally disadvantaged in Britain. Proportionately the largest number of prisoners are black. Black prisoners make up 15 per cent of the prisoner population but 2.2 per cent of the general population.[10] The pupils most excluded from London schools are black. According to research published by the Department for Education in 2012, black Caribbean pupils 'were nearly four times more likely to receive a permanent exclusion than the school population as a whole and were twice as likely to receive a fixed period exclusion'.[11]

It cannot be the sole moral responsibility of these individuals; disturbed behaviours are their attempts to survive within a socio-political structure that is failing to deliver safety and genuine opportunity. In 2017, Britain divides itself into ghettos where there is urban youth violence structured around gangs attacking predominantly white wealthy neighbourhoods as well as their peers. Then there are white ghettoised communities where there is nothing for young people to do apart from drink alcohol and smoke drugs. Both groups of kids are condemned to hopelessness fuelled by isolation and lack of political care.

Some would argue that white journalists, civil servants and politicians saw the black children and families Kids Company supported, especially those who were recent immigrants, as not worthy of British care and money. I was struck by the image in August 2015 of predominantly black children and families opposite Downing Street pleading for services to be saved as white police kept them away from the gates.

Many of the young people the white journalists used for their agenda were children, in the care of local authorities. No one from the state stepped in to protect them at a time when they were at their most vulnerable and without any parental support while being set up by the media. Kids were chased while walking by journalists in their cars who would shout out their names and question them in the middle of the street. The kids could be tracked through their mobile phones. The young people felt terrified and humiliated. Their personal details in the hands of the media were plastered all over the papers. Journalists were forcing their way into these young people's homes. Which government ministers, politicians or local authority heads spoke up to protest and protect?

As well as 'child blindness' and 'colour blindness', a powerful role in discrediting Kids Company was played by 'need blindness'. I was described as having 'favourites' who received more resources. There was unease about the money spent on individual children. When I was questioned by a parliamentary committee about a pair of trainers costing £150, I did not know what it was about or who they were for; all I knew is that I had not bought them. The young man who did know experienced horror and guilt as he watched me being interrogated on live TV. He told me later that his eleven-year-old cousin was being burnt with lighters at a children's home and had called him crying. The older boy was out shopping with one of our key workers at the time, with £150 to buy clothes for himself. He decided to use it to buy his cousin a pair of the latest trainers, so that the other kids would not burn him. This young man knew what it felt like, because when he was in a children's home he too had been attacked for not having the right clothes.

There was also disquiet over money in brown envelopes. Try living every week on £57.35 (Job Seekers Allowance) to cover your food, travel, laundry, toiletries, phone, clothes and TV licence. If your fridge breaks down you need a loan to replace it and eventually it becomes untenable. Just one day's travel is £4.50, not to mention the need for internet to look for jobs and turn up to interviews. One family of four who received a brown envelope with money and food vouchers were living on £28 a week because of loan deductions at source.

What happens to the child whose mother is an addict and goes through the household budget in one smoke? Of course, they should be supported by social services, but a report from Action for Children released in 2017[12] will tell you that there are just under 270,000 children living with either alcoholic[13] or opiate dependant parents.[14] 118,000 children are homeless or in temporary accommodation.[15] They are not getting proper help because thresholds of intake in social services are too high and by 2020 there will be a £2 billion gap in funding for local authority child protection departments.[16]

I remember Nick Hurd MP coming down to Kids Company as part of the *Evening Standard*'s Frontline London campaign 2014, highlighting the plight of vulnerable young people in gangs. He was faced with a hall packed with kids who wanted to talk to him. One of them turned around to him and said, 'If this was your child being attacked every day, you would do something about it, but it is okay for us black kids to be attacked.' Another said, 'If it's your job to know about our area, but you have never been down, how can you judge whether you spending enough on the problem? How much did you lot spend on Boris bikes? It is all about priorities ... down here, people are stabbed every day and there are kids with no food what is important?'. A third gang member butted in, 'We are the bottom of the pyramid. It is quiet up your side. No stress ... nice clean air. Your children have a different life.[17]

Nick was visibly shocked, although he was very thoughtful and appropriate in his responses to the kids. He saw that his government had not understood the intelligence of these black children or how much they were being let down.

This meeting and the *Standard*'s campaign prompted the government to release £2 million for work with gangs.[18] If the money existed, why did it take a newspaper campaign facilitated by Kids Company to make the government hand it out? The government then complains that I 'blackmailed' them through the media. What kind of confused thinking is this? If you care and you think it is right to do something about kids in gangs then release the money. Don't wait to be coerced into it to protect your brand.

II

When I was considered a 'politically desirable' product as part of the Big Society agenda, I was described as a British business woman and charity leader. In 2015, as my status changed to one of a 'mesmerising witch' I was being described in newspapers and online as a 'foreigner' who should be 'sent back to her country'.

Thurstone Furlong: 'Batmanandrobin's a foreigner, and we all know that foreigners can basically do what they want, when they want to, without fear of any comebacks, the rules only apply to the English Indigenous population.'[19]

Mike, London: 'This woman has no respect for UK law, for what is right and for ordinary decent and honest behaviour. Is there any chance at all that we can deport her back to Iran?'[20]

I was accused of using Kid's Company as cover-up for trafficking Iranian children into Britain and carrying out clandestine Iranian activity. A reporter from Sky News confirmed receiving the allegations along with the false suggestion that I ran a brothel in east London from which I was collecting money. The *Sunday Times*, apparently fed a similar narrative, made inquiries at the UN as to whether I was favouring Iranians. I had absolutely no dealings with Iran since I was twelve years old and had received political asylum in Britain. Kid's Company had fewer than five Iranian clients in the context of 36,000 and some six Iranian staff in the context of 650 employees.

Kids Company was described as dysfunctional and the existence and needs of the children were negated. It was claimed that we did not deliver services to 36,000 clients annually and only had 1,900 clients or so. No one stopped to think: how could this be possible? Our 650 staff, 10,000 volunteers, 500 trainees, their supervisors, practice teachers, universities, research institutions and 140 companies would all need to have been colluding in a fiction if there had been that number of kids at Kids Company. What were our staff doing working with some forty schools?

The media didn't have the gumption to scrutinise the false allegations against Kids Company. However, some lawyers who had been working with us over two decades stood up for the kids in a letter to *The Guardian:*

> The young people we represent are abandoned without food or shelter and sometimes turn to crime and gangs to meet their needs. Justifying inaction, authorities disbelieve these children and accuse them of 'not engaging with services'. The Children Act 1989 expresses the will of society that these conditions should be prevented and authorities should intervene to protect children. Despite this, local authorities ignore the law.[21]

Neither the Charity Commission nor the Official Receiver showed any curiosity about who made the unfounded sexual abuse allegations that ultimately closed the charity. They failed to ask other important questions such as why children and young people were self-referring to Kids Company, leaving it to deal with serious mental illness, childhood maltreatment and poverty when the state should have carried that burden. They showed no interest in the fact that statutory agencies signposted their clients to Kids Company without taking financial responsibility by paying for them. The two bodies described their reluctance to see any of this as relevant by saying, 'It's not in our remit'.

There is much that the staff of Kids Company can be proud of. We created an effective community, focused on the needs of the most vulnerable. We innovated social care solutions in a context of limited resources. We drove changes in the law. We shared our scientific partners' brain studies with the Law Commission to inform a new understanding of mental incapacity in criminal cases.[22] We helped change the law on restraint in youth custody and supported a case that compelled the government to take responsibility for housing 16–18-year-olds when local authorities were denying these homeless young people access.[23] Kids Company was recognised at the Liberty and Justice Human Rights Awards for 'ground breaking and inspirational work in helping this country's most disadvantaged children and young people.'[24]

Kids Company's volunteering, and its care for the trainees who annually did their work experience with us, were exemplary, and were recognised through a quality Kite Mark, by Volunteering England in 2013. The charity was the biggest employer of psychotherapists outside the NHS.

The children's art was exhibited at Tate Modern, the Royal Academy and the Saatchi Gallery. Their fashion designs under the label 'Bare Thread' sold out at Selfridges, John Lewis and Liberty. Kids Company's innovative approach to using the arts with very traumatised children was recognised by the Royal Society and Public Health award in 2012. Everything we did was about the children, like this one:

> I sleep on the floor. I am watching my baby brother so he doesn't fall out of bed. My mum is not lazy she is just teaching me. I like sleeping on the floor anyway. I make rice for us and if my mum goes out I change my brother's nappy – Boy, aged 8[25]

One thing I regret deeply is that I became the focus of the Kids Company story as opposed to children like the eight-year-old above. As a figurehead, perhaps within the charity and in the public space, I functioned symbolically as a maternal archetype.

I tried to prevent my idealisation in this role by creating a collegiate culture where everyone's innovation was embraced. I refused to have pictures of me in annual reports and instead used the children's cartoon drawings to represent me. I would not allow positive media articles about me displayed in the charity.

Even so, I was described as 'Mother Camila of Camberwell', 'our own Mother Teresa' and 'the Angel of Peckham'. It terrified me because I knew that one day the archetype would be attacked. Internally we kept this risk under control for a long time. Externally, some of the public projected onto me their need for a healing, maternal experience, which was presented in the media in an idealised, almost saintly form. For many members of the public I was doing the work they would wanted to do, but it wasn't possible, because of their personal life commitments. I was happy to carry out the task on their behalf and with their support.

I tried to reduce the intense public focus on me, hoping to dilute the maternal disappointment that I knew would be acted out. I wanted to protect the organisation against being damaged on account of my leadership.

We provided media and communications training so that staff and young people who were interested could become spokespeople. But as a BBC radio presenter and trainer explained, these staff could not operate under pressure because they were preoccupied with how they came across and froze. They could not recall information quickly enough to use it in debates. Some staff would have been brilliant at representing the children and their needs, but they did not want to deal with the media. If we offered them for interview we would be told, 'No, we want Camila.' I remained in a space that I knew would eventually be attacked.

I never set myself up to symbolise the perfect mother. I took up a substitute maternal task in an endeavour to help developmentally traumatised children and young people acquire some mastery over their difficulties. My intention was to lead the delivery of pragmatic love and ordinary kindness with all its vicissitudes. However, my public role as a fundraiser and campaigner left me exposed to the effects of a national wound, which is the absence of good quality maternal care in some people's lives. This also applies at a political level. There was an unconscious hope on the part of some that I would be able to effect repair of damage caused by lack of love. It was inevitable that I was going to get attacked because motherhood, while good enough, is also never good enough.

III

The denigration of the maternal is driven partly by disappointment that she cannot deliver the imagined perfections, and by an infantile hatred for the mother who is perceived to have all the power. I became, sarcastically, 'Lady Bountiful'.[26] There is also the fantasy that the mother will destroy through her capacity to give and the potential to withdraw that giving.

In some commentators' minds, generosity and kindness became toxic, as if they would ruin the recipient. Anything the children had received was considered to be indulgence, which should be vomited back out as toxic 'food'.

The children were perceived as 'greedy' and 'manipulating' the mother so that they could get more. The clients of Kids Company were transformed in public narrative from the destitute individuals they were into greedy, tricky, manipulative, unworthy recipients of riches that should have been distributed elsewhere.

The other side of being perceived as the mother who gave too much is the mother who took too much. With my 'mother witch capacities', I was accused of taking government money by tricking and mesmerising politicians. In this context, the politician is seen as my victim child.

When I had my interview with the Official Receiver, with a biro he pointed to some expenditures which included pizzas and a Coca Cola drink. I could see in his eyes that he thought I had eaten them. I hadn't.

As the records named the family we were working with, I could give him an explanation.

We used to have a family of three children and a single mother who came for therapeutic and social work support once a week. A fourteen-year-old child in this family had a tumour in his neck and was dying. The case had been referred to me by key workers because the mother could not bring herself to acknowledge that her child was going to die. The result was that the child, who knew he was dying, was unable to talk to his mother. The key workers felt unable to confront the mother and could not work out if the boy was aware he was dying. They were afraid.

I began work with the boy and we arrived at a point where he acknowledged he was going to die. Together we worked out how to awaken his mother to this reality, which we did. Then the boy and I made a list of what he needed to do before his death, part of which was preparing his two younger siblings who were aged under nine. He also wanted me to buy his mother a Dyson vacuum cleaner after his death. So, if the Official Receiver sees an 'expensive' cleaner on the list of my crimes, this is the explanation.

At all our centres, staff and children used to eat together because it was an important part of the substitute family model. At head office, we fed the kids who did not attend the centres because they were too vulnerable or too disturbed. Some of the best conversations I have had with teenagers were over these meals. My Persian culture of being a generous host is also relevant. I used to have fruit on the table in my office and a cupboard with sanitary towels and toiletries for the girls. Kids, staff and visitors would take the fruit. When the Cabinet Office asked me to resign, the manager who was placed in to the charity as my replacement would make a point of not having any of the fruit and he would comment on its indulgence. Looking back, I understand that his moral rigidity would not allow him to take a piece of fruit. Yet he and his colleague were charging the charity £19,000 a week for the work he did.

Events are framed in a particular context to serve a purpose. The risk is that we are not going to have a fair scrutiny of Kids Company by the Official Receiver and the Charity Commission because a landscape of concern has been created, driven by the disturbing archetype of the greedy mother who is going to deprive her children of resources.

The reality was the reverse. I mortgaged my flat to pay the staff. I later offered my home as security so that a restructuring deal could be agreed with the Cabinet Office. The Cabinet Office accepted the pledge of the flat. I worked seven days a week to raise funds. I took no holiday and never asked for money in lieu. For a long time my salary was lower than the chief executives of other charities of similar size. After years at £40,000 it rose when Kids Company appointed other senior directors and the trustees felt that I could not be paid below them. In the final three years it rose again, to £90,000, because a philanthropist thought it was too low and told the trustees that he wanted to fund it.

I have pondered what I could have done differently. I now realise that running an organisation on maternal principles of care – which can be delivered by males or females – has huge benefits, but also harbours a shadow. The benefits flow from the ability to nurture another human being and return them to a sense of strength and resilience. Communicating unconditional positive regard enabled children and staff to embrace their individuality and develop respect for what they could contribute to the community. People felt worthwhile and cherished.

The shadow of this is that the recipients of maternal care can end up terrified that on their own they will lose these good feelings and sense of empowerment, because the symbolic mother gave it to them. They fear it will be withdrawn by her, incapacitating them. A maternal leader risks turning bad in the recipient's head.

The maternal drama that was acted out publicly in 2015 always had the potential to be re-enacted internally. Kids Company protected itself against potential implosion by giving each worker a therapeutic supervisor to help them untangle genuine organisational problems that needed to be confronted from the psychologically-driven 'anti-task'.

However, the attack on the maternal in the media frenzy of 2015 meant that some staff lost sight of the good they had been part of. Some described even losing memory of the quality of the work they had delivered. They began to doubt. It also gave opportunity to a comparatively small group of staff who had disturbed relationships with their own mothers to reflect that disturbance onto me. From their perspective, it appeared that I had become yet another mother figure by whom they felt betrayed. Envy and resentment of what the children were receiving was also given an opportunity to surface. Hence the false narrative of me allegedly having favourites.

I now realise that I needed to pay more attention to the 'mother drama' that was brought to life with varying levels of intensity in different people based on their personal backgrounds. I had expected the once-weekly therapeutic supervision to have contained that drama. However, what I needed to do, was to talk about its potential manifestation in the staff meetings we held regularly. Had I done so, perhaps those in the grip of a toxic transference would have been more aware of their own potential destructive acting out. Some took distorted and false information about Kids Company to the media. Journalists took the material at face value, not realising that an emotional wound was driving this destructive behaviour. For other journalists, their informants served a useful purpose. The media had helped create a 'damaged mother image' which generated repulsion in unsettled staff members and some children, who on a very primitive level, went for the 'kill'.

Kids Company had some eleven senior directors on a management level. It also had outstanding staff satisfaction and well-being ratings of above 90 per cent.[27] The handful of disgruntled staff had every opportunity if there were legitimate concerns to raise them within Kids Company or with the Charity Commission. But in two decades there had been no complaint to the Charity Commission or local authorities about Kids Company's practices prior to the destruction of 2015. The presence of the external clinical supervisors, academics, researchers, government auditors and consultants did provide the organisation with the safety net if staff and clients had wished to raise concerns. That is not to say that there wasn't room for improvement; we endeavoured to constantly work towards quality.

Kids Company's campaigning role had to be politically silenced while the disappointing mother had to be punished. So, I was asked to apologise and to give back the honorary CBE. My portrait was taken down at the National Portrait Gallery. Cartoons were created of me losing all colour as if I had been publicly disrobed.[28] People feared communicating with me, just in case their brand became tarnished by association.

For the children and young people, the experience of having their substitute symbolic maternal carer attacked publicly was confusing, painful and perhaps exhilarating. One of them, frustrated by the fact that I could no longer help her, shouted down the phone, 'Don't let me believe what they say about you.' Seeking help from someone who has the power to give it is disempowering and at times humiliating. The person who takes the help wishes they did not have to. There are also times when young people need to bring about a separation from their maternal carers and they can only do it by turning the attachment object into something bad so that they can leave it with ease. There may also be an attempt to deny need by presenting the carer as the person who needs them and from whom the young person must escape. The carer is hated for having in their memory recollections of how vulnerable the child was when the young person wants to forget and recraft their identity. In this respect, the carer has to be banished so that the memory will not interfere with the rewrite.

There are such complex dynamics at play in an attachment relationship with those who have experienced ruptures in family love. These intimate and private struggles with dignity were now becoming an uncontained toxic football, exploited in the hands of some unaware and ambitious journalists.

Kids Company was about the transformative power of ordinary kindness, helping maltreated children and families regain resilience and hope. Thousands of workers, clinicians, volunteers, scientists, lawyers, supporters and funders collaborated to create an effective community. Over two decades the charity learnt from traumatised children and families the most effective methods of helping them. It came down to providing a consistent attachment experience informed by specialist medical and psychological expertise. Our collective aim was to help children and families who were devastated and excluded to become valuing and valued citizens.

The courageous children and families we worked with remain an inspiration and because of them, the dedicated staff and our generous supporters, my smile is not for stealing.

When staff saw the results of their own efforts, they internalised the potency of love and I was no longer needed to convince them. Kids Company would have clinically run without me and I was attempting to make it independent of me as a founder, but the fact that it was reliant on me as a fundraiser was the problem. We attempted to solve this difficulty by accessing consistent funding so that a chief executive could take over without worrying about their own livelihood. It was unethical to get rid of the kids so that the charity could survive. That is not why we were set up in the first place. I also did not accept that the government did not have the money to meet the children's needs. Evidence demonstrated that they always came up with the funds as it suited them. Some 17,000 of the children and young people who were with us should have been cared for by Statutory services. The government knew this but wanted to deny it.

Kids Company changed lives for the better, and that change will have implications for generations to come. The twelve-year-old homeless boy who self-referred to the charity and whose parents were street drug addicts is now employed and due to complete his degree. His wife also received a degree and was given a scholarship to complete her master's degree because the charity made it possible. Their children will have employed and educated parents.

When this twelve-year-old became an adult, he encouraged his mother to relinquish her addiction while continuing to live with the trauma of losing his father to drug abuse. Kids Company interrupted the cycle of harm and helped maltreated children live with the psychological and physical compromises abuse created in their lives.

Even though we dealt with human sorrow and abuse, Kids Company was not a miserable charity. It was filled with joy, because every day we could see how compassionate companionship reduced maltreated children's loneliness and generated healing and enthusiasm. We helped staff and volunteers acquire a deeper understanding of children's needs. We cherished all those who worked with and supported us.

I am sorry for the sense of betrayal generated in our donors and the distress caused to our staff. Our trustees worked really hard and did not deserve the unjust attack they were exposed to. They were at the top of their professions, extremely rigorous and profoundly committed to the cause. They were being punished because they cared enough to fight for what is right and not give up.

Many people found it hard to accept that I would not apologise. I was not prepared to apologise for a false story created by the media. Neither was I prepared to be seen as, symbolically, another 'battered mum' in our children's lives. That is not the same as not experiencing sorrow for what happened. To this day, I well up at the thought of the hurt our kids experienced at the hands of media and politicians. I also regret the self-employed not being paid even though the money was there to pay them, but the Cabinet Office had created anxiety through their false claim of a misspent £3 million which prohibited the trustees from making the payment.

I never claimed personal or organisational perfection. Instead, we got on with the ordinary business of overcoming difficulties. I was being advised to wear black, take off my turban and apologise publicly for something. The professional PR agencies who volunteered their advice used to tell me that the public love 'a repentant sinner' and I should just fake it. As a matter of principle, I refused to play the apology game because the reality is that running an organisation is a complex task. I am against creating a drama out of challenges and I do not believe in apologising to placate and to simplify narratives into fairy-tales and Greek tragedies.

I hope that some good will come of the ruin that is Kids Company. The jewel awaiting discovery is the need for a fifteen-year plan to redesign children's services with all political parties signed up. This warrants its own government department under a committed senior minister and advisers who have clinical experience of working with a diverse range of vulnerable children in different settings, as opposed to high-end academics only or those who have worked solely in conventional clinical settings. We must widen the delivery of reparation within the community using all societal resources. But volunteering cannot be a substitution for professional intervention. We must create a model that is informed by the emerging science on how maltreatment affects children's development. Ultimately, it is about delivering unrelenting love, with an unwavering resolve to help any child, no matter how challenging their difficulties. This is important for individual children. It is also an important moral message to reclaim the worth of a human being and stop the cheapening of lives. If we allow the erosion of standards in care, we will someday be at the receiving end of the same rot.

Kids Company developed the beginnings of a model that not only worked but engaged wider society in caring for vulnerable children. By 2015, we had the worlds of fashion, the arts, sport, business, finance and the general public engaged with delivering powerful, ordinary kindness, each according to what they could share as opposed to what they could spare.

Mary Carpenter, the Victorian social reformer, had the vision decades before. She tried to reflect back at society a catastrophic institutional failure in managing the needs of 'destitute and juvenile offenders'. Her recommendation for turning around the lives of 'moral orphans' was to love them. In her book, *Juvenile Delinquents: Their Condition and Treatment*, she analysed what was wrong and suggested a rethink. If Carpenter looked at Britain today she would probably despair at the fact that the rotten situation has not changed much.

Today's neuroscientists would also marvel at her insight and her daring to recommend love as the potent ingredient of healing in 1852. Much of what she had to say is now being evidenced through developmental neuroscience.

> These are perhaps delinquents, not only perishing from lack of knowledge, from lack of paternal care, of all that should surround childhood, but they have positively become dangerous. Dangerous to society ... such a condition is one of grievous moral disease. It needs a moral hospital and requires a treatment guided by the highest wisdom of those who learnt the art of healing from the physician of souls.
>
> Christian men and Christian women must become the fathers and mothers of these 'moral orphans'. They must restore them to the true condition of childhood, give them a home, open their souls to good and holy influence. If need be, correct them but with a loving severity.[29]

I feel sorrow for the pain the closure of Kids Company caused, creating yet more injustice in the lives of vulnerable children and families. The sight of our families grabbing potatoes on the last day from our kitchens and weeping outside the gates will always remain a source of searing pain for me.

Children found their beautifully decorated centres taken over by squatters and drug addicts. One of these centres became an animal hospital. Kids had to walk past knowing that an animal would be allowed in but they wouldn't. Children were locked out of a haven. Families and passers-by left notes on the gates. As our Urban Academy closed, young people wrote on the walls how grateful they were. These are the people I feel accountable to, because despite their ordeal, they had more integrity than the government who claimed to manage them. To them an apology is owed and I give it unreservedly.

As for the misogynists, saboteurs and racists, I refuse the tango of damage they want me to dance. I can't sing it for them as Edith Piaf did, but here it is: 'Je ne regrette rien.'

NOTES

Introduction

1   http://www.bbc.co.uk/ethics/animals/defending/legislation_1.shtml, accessed 16 September 2017; http://www.legislation.gov.uk/ukpga/1889/44/enacted, accessed 16 September 2017

Meet the Kids

1   https://www.nao.org.uk/wp-content/uploads/2015/10/Investigation-the-governments-funding-of-Kids-Company.pdf, accessed 16 September 2017

2   Miles Goslett, 'Now Kids Company Camila faces being stripped of CBE', *Daily Mail*, 7 November 2015, accessed 16 September 2017 at http://www.dailymail.co.uk/news/article-3308717/Now-Kids-Company-Camila-faces-stripped-CBE-Chief-scandal-hit-charity-lose-honour-police-continue-probe-alleged-illegal-activity.html

3   Tim Loughton, oral evidence, 'Whitehall's relationship with Kids Company', Public Administration and Constitutional Affairs Committee, 19 November 2015, accessed 16 September 2017 at http://data.parliament.uk/writtenevidence/committeeevidence.svc/evidencedocument/public-administration-and-constitutional-affairs-committee/kids-company/oral/24967.html

4   Sue Berelowitz, oral evidence, 'Whitehall's relationship with Kids Company', Public Administration and Constitutional Affairs Committee, 17 November 2015, accessed 16 September 2017 at http://data.parliament.uk/writtenevidence/committeeevidence.svc/evidencedocument/public-administration-and-constitutional-affairs-committee/kids-company/oral/24766.html

5   Oliver Dowden, oral evidence, 'Whitehall's relationship with Kids Company', Public Administration and Constitutional Affairs Committee, 15 October 2015, accessed 16 September 2017 at http://data.parliament.uk/writtenevidence/committeeevidence.svc/evidencedocument/public-administration-and-constitutional-affairs-committee/kids-company/oral/23222.html

6   Charles Mackay, *Extraordinary Popular Delusions and the Madness of Crowds* (1841)

7   Quentin Letts, 'He looked like a pudding waiter sitting next to a bowl of fruit salad', *Daily Mail*, 16 October 2015, accessed 16 September 2017 at http://www.dailymail.co.uk/news/article-3275138/He-looked-like-pudding-waiter-sitting-bowl-fruit-salad-QUENTIN-LETTS-sees-charity-chiefs-face-MPs.html

8   The same family is described in Chapter 8, Innocence.

9   Adele Eastman, 'Enough Is Enough: A report on child protection and mental health services for children and young people', Centre for Social Justice, June 2014, p. 35

10 Ibid, pp. 362, 390

11 http://moderngov.southwark.gov.uk/documents/s57291/Report%20on%20Kids%20Company.pdf, accessed 16 September 2017

12 Ibid., pp. 113–14
13 Oral evidence, 'Whitehall's relationship with Kids Company', Public Administration and Constitutional Affairs Committee, 15 October 2015, op. cit.
14 Adele Eastman, 'Enough Is Enough', op. cit., p. 25
15 Metropolitan Police statement, 'Update: Investigation into children's charity', 28 January 2016, accessed 16 September 2017 at http://news.met.police.uk/news/update-investigation-into-children-s-charity-148142?utm_campaign=send_list&utm_medium=email&utm_source=sendgrid

Suzy
1 Patrick Butler, 'School holidays leave 3 million children at risk of hunger, report says', *The Guardian*, 24 April 2017, accessed 16 September 2017 at https://www.theguardian.com/society/2017/apr/24/school-holidays-leave-3-million-children-at-risk-of-hunger-report-says

Ghetto Britain v. Legitimate Britain
1 To this day, the disorder is not recognised in the DSM. Bessel van der Kolk, a renowned traumatologist and psychiatrist, and other experts in childhood trauma have been trying to have the condition accepted as 'developmental trauma'. It seems as if the world is not ready for it, despite the evidence.

The Origins of Violence
1 Teicher, Martin, 'Scars that won't heal: The neurobiology of child abuse', *Scientific American*, Vol. 286, No. 3 (March 2002), p. 70
2 When you know what behaviour patterns signify, it is surprising how often they come up. For example, in August 2016 an IT consultant in York went to court to challenge an order requiring him to give twenty-four hours' notice to the police whenever he intended to have sex. The order was imposed after he was cleared of rape but assessed as 'very dangerous'. He allegedly told health professionals of an inability to climax during sex unless his partner was frightened, and that he had thought about killing his girlfriend 'a lot' and had choked her unconscious several times. A community psychiatric nurse told the court that he was deliberately getting into fights so that he would be beaten up and injured.
3 The source for this is Connor's mother, who was very depressed. I spent quite a lot of time with her. I used to see her in the arches for therapeutic support because she had been struggling.
4 McCrory, E., Gerin, M., and Viding, E., 'Annual Research Review: Childhood maltreatment, latent vulnerability and the shift to preventative psychiatry – the contribution of functional brain imaging', *Journal of Child Psychology and Psychiatry*, Vol. 58, No. 4 (2017), pp. 338–57; McCrory, E., and Viding, E., 'The theory of latent vulnerability: Reconceptualizing the link between childhood maltreatment and psychiatric disorder', *Development and Psychopathology*, Vol. 27, No. 2, pp. 493–505; Li, Fenfang, and Godinet, Meripa T., 'The impact of repeated maltreatment on behavioral trajectories from early childhood to early adolescence', *Children and Youth Services Review*, Vol. 36 (2014), pp. 22–9. See also Pollak, Seth D., 'Early adversity and mechanisms of plasticity: Integrating affective neuroscience with developmental approaches to psychopathology.' *Development and Psychopathology*, Vol. 17 (2005), pp. 735–752
5 Center on the Developing Child (2007). The Impact of Early Adversity on Child Development (InBrief). Harvard University, accessed at http://developingchild.harvard.edu/resources/inbrief-the-impact-of-early-adversity-on-childrens-development/
6 Lee, Vivien, and Hoaken, Peter N. S., 'Cognition, emotion, and neurobiological development: Mediating the relation between maltreatment and aggression.' *Child Maltreatment* Vol. 12, No. 3 (2007), pp. 281–98; Dackis, Melissa N., Fred A. Rogosch, Assaf Oshri, and Dante Cicchetti, 'The Role of Limbic System Irritability in Linking History of Childhood Maltreatment and Psychiatric Outcomes in Low-Income, High-Risk Women: Moderation by FKBP5.' *Development and Psychopathology* Vol. 24, No. 4 (November 2012), pp. 1237–52

7   Heim, C., 'Decreased Cortical Representation of Genital Somatosensory Field After Child-hood Sexual Abuse', *American Journal of Psychiatry* Vol. 170, No. 6 (June 2013), pp. 616–23

Prince of Intuition

1   Ouellet-Morin, Isabelle et al., 'Blunted Cortisol Responses to Stress Signal Social and Behav-ioral Problems Among Maltreated/Bullied 12-Year-Old Children', *Biological Psychiatry*, Vol. 70, No. 11 (2011), pp. 1016–23; Jaffee, Sara R.; Caspi, Avshalom; Moffitt, Terrie E.; Taylor, Alan, 'Physical Maltreatment Victim to Antisocial Child: Evidence of an Environmentally Mediated Process', *Journal of Abnormal Psychology*, Vol. 113, No. 1 (February 2004), pp. 44–55

2   Hart, H. and Rubia, K. (2012), 'Neuroimaging of child abuse: A critical review', *Frontiers in Human Neuroscience*, Vol. 6, No. 52 (March 2012)

3   Misselbrook, David, 'What is it with kids these days?', *Journal of the Royal Society of Medicine* Vol. 104, No. 10 (October 2011), pp. 392–393, accessed 22 September 2017 at http://jrs.sagepub.com/content/104/10/392.full

4   Cecil, C. A. M., Viding, E., Barker, E. D., Guiney, J. and McCrory, E. J. (2014), 'Double dis-advantage: The influence of childhood maltreatment and community violence exposure on adolescent mental health', *Journal of Child Psychology and Psychiatry*, 55(7), 839–848

5   Pincham H. L., Bryce D., Kokorikou D., Fonagy P., Fearon R. M. P., 'Psychosocial Intervention Is Associated with Altered Emotion Processing: An Event-Related Potential Study in At-Risk Adolescents', PLoS One, 11(1), (2016).

6   Ibid.

7   Siegel, D. J. (2012) The developing mind: How relationships and the brain interact to shape who we are. 2nd edn. Guilford Publications. pp. 175–7. See also Cozolino, L. J. and Siegel, D. J. (2010) *The neuroscience of psychotherapy: Healing the social brain.* 2nd edn. Norton, W. W. & Company, pp. 213–36

Narcissistic Philanthropy

1   Andreoni, J. and Rao, J. M. (2011) 'The power of asking: How communication affects selfish-ness, empathy, and altruism', *Journal of Public Economics*, 95(7–8), pp. 513–520

2   Hoffman, M. L. (1996) 'Empathy and moral development', *The Annual Report of Educational Psychology in Japan*, 35(0), pp. 157–162

3   Smith, A. and Rosenbaum, S. E. (2000) *The Theory of Moral Sentiments*, edited by Robert M. Baird. Prometheus Books, p. 3

4   Brosig, J. (2002) 'Identifying cooperative behavior: Some experimental results in a prisoner's dilemma game', *Journal of Economic Behavior & Organization*, 47(3), pp. 275–290; Bohnet, I. and Frey, B. S. (1999) 'The sound of silence in prisoner's dilemma and dictator games', *Journal of Economic Behavior & Organization*, 38(1), pp. 43–57; Small, D. A., Loewenstein, G. and Slovic, P. (2007) 'Sympathy and callousness: The impact of deliberative thought on donations to identifiable and statistical victims', *Organizational Behavior and Human Decision Processes*, 102(2), pp. 143–53; Andreoni, J. and Rao, J. M. (2011) 'The power of asking: How communi-cation affects selfishness, empathy, and altruism', *Journal of Public Economics*, 95(7–8), pp. 513–20; Small, D. and Loewenstein, G. 'Helping a victim or helping the victim: altruism and identifiability', *Journal of Risk and Uncertainty* 23:1 (2003), 5–16

5   Moll, J., Krueger, F., Zahn, R., Pardini, M., de Oliveira-Souza, R. and Grafman, J. (2006) 'Human fronto-mesolimbic networks guide decisions about charitable donation', *Proceedings of the National Academy of Sciences*, 103(42), pp. 15623–15628; De Dreu, C. K. W., Greer, L. L., Handgraaf, M. J. J., Shalvi, S., Van Kleef, G. A., Baas, M., Ten Velden, F. S., Van Dijk, E. and Feith, S. W. W. (2010) 'The Neuropeptide Oxytocin regulates parochial altruism in intergroup conflict among humans', *Science* 328(5984), pp. 1408–11

6   Schwartz, C. E. and Sendor, R. M. (1999) 'Helping others helps oneself: Response shift effects in peer support', *Social Science & Medicine* 48(11), pp. 1563–1575; Taylor, J. and Turner, R. J.

(2001) 'A longitudinal study of the role and significance of Mattering to others for Depressive symptoms', *Journal of Health and Social Behavior*

7 'Children in care missing out on right to a mentor', *The Times*, 8 August 2016, p. 2, accessed 22 September 2017 at http://www.thetimes.co.uk/article/children-in-care-missing-out-on-right-to-a-mentor-szlmckfhq

8 Cozzarelli, C., Wilkinson, A. V. and Tagler, M. J. (2001) 'Attitudes toward the poor and attributions for poverty', *Journal of Social Issues* 57(2), pp. 207–27

9 Omoto, A. M. and Snyder, M. (1995) 'Sustained helping without obligation: Motivation, longevity of service, and perceived attitude change among AIDS volunteers', *Journal of Personality and Social Psychology* 68(4), pp. 671–86; Brown, S. L., Nesse, R. M., Vinokur, A. D. and Smith, D. M. (2003) 'Providing social support may be more beneficial than receiving it: Results from a prospective study of mortality', *Psychological Science* 14(4), pp. 320–27

10 'Determinants of help seeking behaviour: The effects of helper's similarity, task centrality and recipient's self esteem', *European Journal of Social Psychology* 17(1), pp. 57–67; Newsom, J. T. (1999) 'Another side to Caregiving: Negative reactions to being helped', *Current Directions in Psychological Science* 8(6), pp. 183–7; Statman, D. (2000) 'Humiliation, dignity and self-respect', *Philosophical Psychology*, 13(4), pp. 523–540

11 Warner, L. M., Schuz, B., Wurm, S., Ziegelmann, J. P. and Tesch-Romer, C. (2010) 'Giving and taking – differential effects of providing, receiving and anticipating emotional support on quality of life in adults with multiple illnesses', *Journal of Health Psychology*, 15(5), pp. 660–70

12 Galdas, P. M., Cheater, F. and Marshall, P. (2005) 'Men and health help-seeking behaviour: Literature review', *Journal of Advanced Nursing*, 49(6), pp. 616–23; Fangen, K. (2006) 'Humiliation experienced by Somali refugees in Norway', *Journal of Refugee Studies*, 19(1), pp. 69–93; Lee, F. (1997) 'When the going gets tough, do the tough ask for help? Help seeking and power motivation in organizations', *Organizational Behavior and Human Decision Processes* 72(3), pp. 336–63; 'Determinants of help seeking behaviour: The effects of helper's similarity, task centrality and recipient's self esteem', *European Journal of Social Psychology*, 17(1), pp. 57–67

13 Exley, C. L. (2015) 'Excusing selfishness in charitable giving: The role of risk', *Review of Economic Studies*, 83(2), pp. 587–628

14 Andreoni, J. (1990) 'Impure altruism and donations to public goods: A theory of warm-glow giving', *The Economic Journal*, 100(401), p. 464

15 Exley, C. L. (2015) 'Excusing selfishness in charitable giving: The role of risk', *The Review of Economic Studies*, 83(2), pp. 587–628

16 Harbaugh, W. T. (1998) 'What do donations buy?', *Journal of Public Economics*, 67(2), pp. 269–284; Harbaugh, W. T., 'The Prestige Motive for Making Charitable Transfers', accessed 22 September 2017 at http://harbaugh.uoregon.edu/Papers/Prestige.pdf

17 Kasper, C. and Mulder, M. B. (2015) 'Who helps and why?', *Current Anthropology*, 56(5), pp. 701–732

18 Batson, C. D. and Moran, T. (1999) 'Empathy-induced altruism in a prisoner's dilemma', *European Journal of Social Psychology*, 29(7), pp. 909–24

19 Saito, K. (2015) 'Impure altruism and impure selfishness', *Journal of Economic Theory*, 158, pp. 336–70; Schulz, A.W. (2016) 'Altruism, egoism, or neither: A cognitive-efficiency-based evolutionary biological perspective on helping behavior', *Studies in History and Philosophy of Science Part C: Studies in History and Philosophy of Biological and Biomedical Sciences*, 56, pp. 15–23

20 'Neuroeconomics of Charitable Giving and Philanthropy'. Ulrich Mayr, William T. Harbaugh, and Dharol Tankersley; Mayo, J. W. and Tinsley, C. H. (2009) 'Warm glow and charitable giving: Why the wealthy do not give more to charity?', *Journal of Economic Psychology*, 30(3), pp. 490–99; 'Self-signaling and diagnostic utility in everyday decision making', Ronit Bodner, Drazen Prelec, May 2001 (final version); Trivers, R. L. (1971) 'The evolution of reciprocal altruism', *The Quarterly Review of Biology*, 46(1), p. 35

Love in Action

1 The types were defined by Lenore Terr in 'Childhood traumas: an outline and overview', *American Journal of Psychiatry*, vol. 148, issue 1 (January 1991), pp. 10–20

2 'Kidnapped by ISIS', *The Times*, 6 August 2016, accessed 22 September 2017 at http://www.thetimes.co.uk/article/kidnapped-by-isis-8tjrkg20f

3 'Freedom is like a prison, says Natascha Kampusch', *The Times*, 13 August 2016, accessed 22 September 2017 at http://www.thetimes.co.uk/article/freedom-is-like-a-prison-says-natascha-kampusch-khmnzgtsw

4 Allen and Lauterbach (2007): 'Personality characteristics of adult survivors of childhood trauma', *Journal of Traumatic Stress*, Volume 20, Issue 4 (August 2007), pp. 587–95

5 Komarovskaya, I., Maguen, S., McCaslin, S. E., Metzler, T. J., Madan, A., Brown, A. D., Galatzer-Levy, I. R., Henn-Haase, C. and Marmar, C. R. (2011) 'The impact of killing and injuring others on mental health symptoms among police officers', *Journal of Psychiatric Research*, 45(10), pp. 1332–6; Maguen, S., Luxton, D. D., Skopp, N. A., Gahm, G. A., Reger, M. A., Metzler, T. J. and Marmar, C. R. (2011) 'Killing in combat, mental health symptoms, and suicidal ideation in Iraq war veterans', *Journal of Anxiety Disorders*, 25(4), pp. 563–7

6 Telles, S., Joseph, C., Venkatesh, S. and Desiraju, T. (1993) 'Alterations of auditory middle latency evoked potentials during yogic consciously regulated breathing and attentive state of mind', *International Journal of Psychophysiology*, 14(3), pp. 189–98; Van der Kolk, B.A., Stone, L., West, J., Rhodes, A., Emerson, D., Suvak, M. and Spinazzola, J. (2014) 'Yoga as an Adjunctive treatment for Posttraumatic stress disorder', *Journal of Clinical Psychiatry*, 75(06), pp. e559–e565; Cuthbert, B. et al. (1981) 'Strategies of arousal control: Biofeedback, meditation, and motivation', *Journal of Experimental Psychology: General* 110(4), pp. 518–546

7 Rodenburg, R., Benjamin, A., de Roos, C., Meijer, A. M. and Stams, G. J. (2009) 'Efficacy of EMDR in children: A meta-analysis', *Clinical Psychology Review*, 29(7), pp. 599–606; Lansing, K., Amen, D. G., Hanks, C. and Rudy, L. (2005) 'High-Resolution brain SPECT imaging and eye movement Desensitization and Reprocessing in police officers with PTSD', *Journal of Neuropsychiatry and Clinical Neurosciences*, 17(4), pp. 526–532; Nardo, D., Högberg, G., Looi, J. C. L., Larsson, S., Hällström, T. and Pagani, M. (2010) 'Gray matter density in limbic and paralimbic cortices is associated with trauma load and EMDR outcome in PTSD patients', *Journal of Psychiatric Research*, 44(7), pp. 477–485; Cahill, S. P., Carrigan, M. H. and Frueh, B. C. (1999) 'Does EMDR work? And if so, why?', *Journal of Anxiety Disorders*, 13(1–2), pp. 5–33; Devilly, G. J. and Spence, S. H. (1999) 'The relative efficacy and treatment distress of EMDR and a cognitive-behavior trauma treatment protocol in the amelioration of Posttraumatic stress disorder', *Journal of Anxiety Disorders*, 13(1–2), pp. 131–157; Elofsson, U. O. E., von Schèele, B., Theorell, T. and Söndergaard, H. P. (2008) 'Physiological correlates of eye movement desensitization and reprocessing', *Journal of Anxiety Disorders*, 22(4), pp. 622–34; Levin, P., Lazrove, S. and van der Kolk, B. (1999) 'What psychological testing and Neuroimaging tell us about the treatment of Posttraumatic stress disorder by eye movement Desensitization and Reprocessing', *Journal of Anxiety Disorders*, 13(1–2), pp. 159–72

8 Van der Werff, S. J. A., Pannekoek, J. N., Veer, I. M., van Tol, M.-J., Aleman, A., Veltman, D. J., Zitman, F. G., Rombouts, S. A. R. B., Elzinga, B. M. and van der Wee, N. J. A. (2013) 'Resilience to childhood maltreatment is associated with increased resting-state functional connectivity of the salience network with the lingual gyrus', *Child Abuse & Neglect*, 37(11), pp. 1021–9

9 Graham, S. A., Nilsen, E., Mah, J. W. T., Morison, S., MacLean, K., Fisher, L., Brooks, B. L. and Ames, E. (2014) 'An examination of communicative interactions of children from Romanian orphanages and their adoptive mothers', *Canadian Journal of Behavioural Science / Revue canadienne des sciences du comportement*, 46(1), pp. 9–19

10 Martin H. Teicher and Jacqueline A. Samson, 'Annual Research Review: Enduring neurobiological effects of childhood abuse and neglect', *Journal of Child Psychology and Psychiatry*, 57:3 (March 2016), pp. 241–66

11   Sartre et al., *Nausea*. New Directions Publishing, 1969.

12   Target, M. (2007) 'The interface between attachment and Intersubjectivity: Another contribu-
     tion from Karlen Lyons-Ruth', *Psychoanalytic Inquiry*, 26(4), pp. 617–21

13   Rogers, Carl R. 'Client-centered Approach to Therapy', in I. L. Kutash and A. Wolf (eds),
     Psychotherapist's Casebook: Theory and Technique in Practice, Jossey-Bass, 1986

14   *Juvenile Delinquents: Their Condition and Treatment* by Mary Carpenter. London W. & F.G.
     Cash, 1853

15   *Juvenile Delinquents: Their Condition and Treatment*, ibid., pp. 15–16

16   *Juvenile Delinquents: Their Condition and Treatment*, ibid., pp. 15–16; Marshall, P. J., Reeb, B.
     C., Fox, N. A., Nelson, C. A. and Zeanah, C. H. (2008) 'Effects of early intervention on EEG
     power and coherence in previously institutionalized children in Romania', *Development and
     Psychopathology*, 20(3)

17   Lemma, A. (2010) 'The power of relationship: A study of key working as an intervention with
     traumatised young people', *Journal of Social Work Practice*, 24(4), pp. 409–27

18   Winnicott (1956) 'Primary Maternal Preoccupation', accessed 22 September 2017 at https://
     manhattanpsychoanalysis.com/wp-content/uploads/readings/Woldenberg/Winnicott,%20
     Collected%20Papers%20Ch24%20Primary%20Maternal%20Preoccupation.pdf; Stein, H.
     (2010) 'Steven Tuber: Attachment, play, and authenticity: A Winnicott Primer', *Clinical Social
     Work Journal*, 38(2), pp. 248–249

19   Taken from interviews for 'The Odd Couple', News Review, *Sunday Times*, 6 December 2015,
     pp. 1–3, accessed https://www.thetimes.co.uk/article/the-odd-couple-qglgxwv3f0f.

Innocence

1   In the early days, when I had 400 young people, three-quarters were run by gangs. Later, when
     we had thousands, about half were involved with gangs or drug dealers on arrival. Bristol had
     a massive drugs problem. A taxi driver told us there was more water boarding in Bristol than
     in Guantanamo Bay.

2   Main table D4 in 'Characteristics of children in need in England, 2014–15', Department for
     Education, 2015, accessed at https://www.gov.uk/government/statistics/characteristics-of-
     children-in-need-2014-to-2015, combined with child protection register and plan statistics
     for Northern Ireland, Scotland and Wales.

3   Bentley, H., O'Hagan, O, Raff, A. and Bhatti, I. (2016) 'How safe are our children? The most
     comprehensive overview of child protection in the UK 2016', London, NSPCC, p. 8

4   'How Safe Are our Children? Data Briefing', NSPCC, April 2014, p. 2. Accessed at https://
     www.nspcc.org.uk/globalassets/documents/research-reports/how-safe-children-2014-data-
     briefing.pdf

5   Hood, Rick, et al. 'Exploring demand and provision in English child protection services',
     British Journal of Social Work 46.4 (2016): 923–41, accessed at https://www.ncbi.nlm.nih.gov/
     pmc/articles/PMC4986093/. The 2016 report revealed 'a filter-and-funnel process ostensibly
     designed to reserve child protection interventions for high-risk cases, but which over time
     seems to be increasingly using those interventions to manage demand'. 'As a result,' it con-
     cluded, 'the sector needs to question whether its current indicators are really serving the right
     purpose, namely the purpose of services as users see it. While it is useful to know how local
     authorities manage demand in their communities, it would arguably be more useful to know
     whether services are meeting their communities' needs.'

6   'Three quarters of children's services weak, Ofsted says', BBC News, 28 June 2016, accessed at
     http://www.bbc.co.uk/news/education-36652997

7   Some professionals in social care disagree with this statement, because, to arrive at it, Ofsted
     used attainment in school as a measure, which is thought to be an inappropriate benchmark
     for overall wellbeing.

8   Ofsted Social Care Annual Report 2016. http://www.trixonline.co.uk/website/news/pdf/
     policy_briefing_No-176.pdf

9   Alan Wood, 'Wood Report: Review of the role and functions of Local Safeguarding Children Boards', Department for Education, March 2016, pp. 5–6

10 McFadden, Paula (2015). 'Measuring burnout among UK social workers: A Community Care study'.

11 'Shoesmith: culture of blame has to stop', in *Professional Social Work*, December 2014/January 2015, pp. 20–21

12 'Baby P: born into a nightmare of abuse, violence and despair, he never stood a chance', *The Guardian*, 16 August 2009, accessed at https://www.theguardian.com/society/2009/aug/16/baby-p-family

13 'Shoesmith: culture of blame has to stop', in *Professional Social Work*, December 2014/January 2015, p. 22

14 'Social worker launches petition to stop Cameron's proposal to jail social workers', *Community Care*, 5 March 2015, accessed at http://www.communitycare.co.uk/2015/03/05/social-worker-launches-petition-stop-camerons-proposal-jail-social-workers/

15 'Shoesmith: culture of blame has to stop', in *Professional Social Work*, December 2014/January 2015, pp. 20–21

16 Bentley, H. et al., (2016) 'How safe are our children? The most comprehensive overview of child protection in the UK', NSPCC, p. 63, accessed at https://www.nspcc.org.uk/services-and-resources/research-and-resources/2016/how-safe-are-our-children-2016/

17 Jütte, S., et al. (2015) 'How safe are our children? The most comprehensive overview of child protection in the UK', NSPCC, p. 8, accessed at https://www.nspcc.org.uk/globalassets/documents/research-reports/how-safe-children-2015-report.pdf

18 Written evidence from David Quirke-Thornton to the House of Commons Public Administration and Constitutional Affairs Committee, accessed at http://data.parliament.uk/writtenevidence/committeeevidence.svc/evidencedocument/public-administration-and-constitutional- affairs-committee/kids-company/written/25929.html

19 Written evidence from David Quirke-Thornton to the House of Commons Public Administration and Constitutional Affairs Committee, accessed at http://data.parliament.uk/writtenevidence/committeeevidence.svc/evidencedocument/public-administration-and-constitutional-affairs-committee/kids-company/written/25929.html

20 Jütte, S., et al. 'How safe are our children?', op. cit., p. 7

Voices

1   'Anti-extremism tsar fights bid to gag her', *Sunday Times*, 9 October 2016, p. 2, accessed at http://www.thetimes.co.uk/edition/news/anti-extremism-tsar-gagged-tvn32nnt5

2   'PM announces new taskforce to transform child protection', Prime Minister's Office, 10 Downing Street, 24 June 2015, accessed at https://www.gov.uk/government/news/pm-announces-new-taskforce-to-transform-child-protection

3   'Children's social care reform: A vision for change', Department for Education, January 2016, accessed at https://www.gov.uk/government/uploads/system/uploads/attachment_data/file/491968/Childrens_social_care_reform_a_vision_for_change.pdf

4   Howard League for Penal Reform (2006) 'The Carlile Inquiry: an independent inquiry into the use of physical restraint, solitary confinement and forcible strip searching of children in prisons, secure training centres and local authority secure children's homes'

5   Mohr et al., 'Adverse effects associated with physical restraint', *Canadian Journal of Psychiatry* Vol. 48, No. 5 (June 2003), pp. 330–37

6   Nunno, M. A., Holden, M. J. and Tollar, A. (2006) 'Learning from tragedy: A survey of child and adolescent restraint fatalities', *Child Abuse & Neglect*, 30(12), pp. 1333–42; Steckley, L. and Kendrick, A. (2008) 'Physical restraint in residential childcare: The experiences of young people and residential workers', *Childhood* 15(4), pp. 552–69

7   Bell, L. (1997) 'The physical restraint of young people', *Child & Family Social Work* 2(1), pp.

37–47; Steckley, L. (2011) 'Touch, physical restraint and therapeutic containment in residential child care', *British Journal of Social Work* 42(3), pp. 537–55

8   'The Carlile Inquiry 10 years on', Howard League for Penal Reform, 20 June 2016, accessed at http://howardleague.org/wp-content/uploads/2016/06/Carlile-Inquiry-10-years-on.pdf

9   C, R (on the application of) v Secretary of State for Justice [2008]CO/6174/2007 (Supreme Court of Judicature Court of Appeal (Civil Division) on appeal from the Queen's Bench Divisional Court)

10 'Boris Johnson "has done virtually nothing to tackle youth violence"', *The Guardian*, 23 April 2012, accessed at https://www.theguardian.com/politics/2012/apr/23/boris-johnson-youth-violence

11 'Cameron softens crime image in "hug a hoodie" call', *The Observer*, 9 July 2006, accessed at https://www.theguardian.com/politics/2006/jul/09/conservatives.ukcrime

12 For the text of the speech, see http://news.bbc.co.uk/1/hi/5166498.stm

13 Tim Loughton, oral evidence, 'Whitehall's relationship with Kids Company', op. cit.

Flashback

1   Balls (2008): 'Taking Back on Track Forward: Response to consultation and next steps'. Department for Children, Schools and Families

2. Fleming et al. (2016): 'Meeting the needs of "pushed out" learners: education for students with additional social and emotional needs (Commissioning Plan)', Bristol Learning City

3. Evelyn Grace Academy's Inclusion, accessed 8 September 2017 at http://evelyngraceacademy.org/inclusion

2   'Alternative provision school for "gifted" pupils seeks riverside flat', *Schools Week*, 27 May 2016, accessed 8 September 2017 at http://schoolsweek.co.uk/ap-school-for-gifted-pupils-wants-riverside-apartment/

3   'Education staff facing physical violence from pupils', 21 January 2016, ATL Media Office, accessed 8 September 2017 at https://www.atl.org.uk/latest/press-release/education-staff-facing-physical-violence-pupils-atl

4   Bourne et al. (2013) 'The neural basis of flashback formation: the impact of viewing trauma'. *Psychological Medicine* 43, pp. 1521–32

2. Turim, 'The trauma of history: flashbacks upon flashbacks'. *Screen* Vol. 42, No. 2 (Summer 2001), Reports and debates

3. Duke et al. (2008) 'The sensitivity and specificity of flashbacks and nightmares to trauma', *Anxiety Disorders* 22 (2008), pp. 319–27

5   Pechtel et al. (2014) 'Sensitive periods of amygdala development: the role of maltreatment in preadolescence', *NeuroImage* 97 (2014), pp. 236–44; Teicher et al. (2003) 'The neurobiological consequences of early stress and childhood maltreatment', *Neuroscience and Biobehavioral Reviews* 27 (2003), pp. 33–44

6   Annie Flury, 'Pedal power boosts N Carolina pupils' performance', BBC UGC and Social News team, 20 September 2016, accessed 8 September 2017 at http://www.bbc.co.uk/news/world-us-canada-37420834

7   Laura A. Baker, Serena Bezdijan and Adrian Raine, 'Behavioral Genetics: The Science of Antisocial Behavior', accessed 8 September 2017 at https://www.ncbi.nlm.nih.gov/pmc/articles/PMC2174903/

8   Lee, S. S. (2011): 'Deviant Peer Affiliation and Antisocial Behaviour: Interaction with Monoamine Oxidase A (MAOA) Genotype', *Journal of Abnormal Child Psychology* 39 (2011), pp. 321–32

9   G. Fairchild, N. Toschi, K. Sully, E. J. S. Sonuga-Barke, C. C. Hagan, S. Diciotti, I. M. Goodyer, A. J. Calder, and L. Passamonti, 'Mapping the structural organization of the brain in conduct disorder: replication of findings in two independent samples', *Journal of Child Psychology and Psychiatry*, Vol. 57, No. 9 (September 2016), pp. 1018–26

10 B. Perry, R. Pollard, T. Blakley, W. Baker and D. Vigilante, 'Childhood Trauma, the

Neurobiology of Adaptation, and "Use-dependent" Development of the Brain: How "States" Become "Traits"', *Infant Mental Health Journal*, Vol. 16, Issue 4 (Winter 1995), pp. 271–91

11 Lorraine E. Cuadra, Anna E. Jaffe, Renu Thomas, David DiLillo, 'Child maltreatment and adult criminal behavior: Does criminal thinking explain the association?', University of Nebraska, Lincoln, accessed 8 September 2017 at http://digitalcommons.unl.edu/cgi/viewcontent.cgi?article=1652&context=psychfacpub

12 Hannah L. Pincham, Donna Bryce and R. M. Pasco Fearon, 'The neural correlates of emotion processing in juvenile offenders', *Developmental Science*, Vol. 18, No, 6 (2015), pp. 994–1005

13 Dunn et al. (2016): 'Does developmental timing of exposure to child maltreatment predict memory performance in adulthood? Results from a large, population-based sample', *Child Abuse & Neglect* 51 (2016), pp. 181–191; Irigaray et al. (2012) 'Child Maltreatment and Later Cognitive Functioning: A Systematic Review'. *Psicologia: Reflexão e Crítica*, 26(2), pp. 376–87; Cicchetti et al. (2010): 'The effects of maltreatment and neuroendocrine regulation on memory performance'. *Child Development*, Vol. 81, No. 5, pp. 1504–19; A. Danese, A. Caspi, B. Williams, A. Ambler, K. Sugden, J. Mika, C. M. Pariante, H. Werts, J. Freeman, T. E. Moffitt and L. Arseneault, 'Biological embedding of stress through inflammation processes in childhood', *Molecular Psychiatry*, Vol. 16, No. 3 (March 2011), pp. 244–6; 'How Early Experiences Get into the Body: A Biodevelopmental Framework'. The Center on the Developing Child, Harvard University; B. Perry, R. Pollard, T. Blakley, W. Baker, D. Vigilante, 'Childhood Trauma, the Neurobiology of Adaptation, and "Use-dependent" Development of the Brain: How "States" Become "Traits"', op. cit.

Ghosted Children

1 Yehuda, N. (2011) 'Music and Stress', *Journal of Adult Development*, June 2011, Volume 18, Issue 2, pp. 85–94. See also Hüther, G. (2009) 'The significance of exposure to music for the formation and stabilisation of complex neuronal relationship matrices in the human brain: implications for the salutogenetic effects of intervention by means of music therapy', in Haas, R. & Brandes, V. (2009) *Music that works: Contributions of biology, neurophysiology, psychology, sociology, medicine and musicology.* Springer Vienna, pp. 119–30

2 Fancourt D., Perkins R., Ascenso S., Carvalho L. A., Steptoe A., Williamon, A. (2016) 'Effects of Group Drumming Interventions on Anxiety, Depression, Social Resilience and Inflammatory Immune Response among Mental Health Service Users', PLoS One 11(3), accessed at http://journals.plos.org/plosone/article?id=10.1371/journal.pone.0151136

3 Davidson and Foa (1991) 'Diagnostic Issues in Posttraumatic Stress Disorder: Considerations for the DSM-IV', *Journal of Abnormal Psychology* Vol. 100, No. 3, pp. 346–55

4 'Always Someone Else's Problem', Office of the Children's Commissioner, 2013, p. 4, accessed at https://www.childrenscommissioner.gov.uk/sites/default/files/publications/Always_Someone_Elses_Problem.pdf

5 'They never give up on you', Office of the Children's Commissioner, Executive Summary, 2012, p. 9, accessed at https://www.childrenscommissioner.gov.uk/sites/default/files/publications/They%20never%20give%20up%20on%20you%20summary.pdf

6 'They Never Give Up on You', Office of the Children's Commissioner, Executive Summary, 2012, p. 16, accessed at https://www.childrenscommissioner.gov.uk/sites/default/files/publications/They%20never%20give%20up%20on%20you%20summary.pdf

7 Advice letter from Sir Michael Wilshaw, Her Majesty's Chief Inspector, on the latest position with schools in Birmingham and Tower Hamlets, 14 July 2015

8 'Primary school's exclusion of disabled pupils "an utter disgrace"', *Disability Today*, 17 April 2016, accessed at http://www.disabilitytoday.co.uk/primary-schools-exclusion-of-disabled-pupils-an-utter-disgrace/

9 Dr Jane Martin, Special Educational Needs: preparing for the future, Local Government Ombudsman, 2014, p. 2, accessed at http://dera.ioe.ac.uk/19600/1/SEN-focus-report-final.pdf

10 Comments under 'Ombudsman warns children with SEN not always treated "fairly" by

councils, http://www.localgov.co.uk/, 4 March 2014, accessed at http://www.localgov.co.uk/Ombudsman-warns-children-with-SEN-not-always-treated-fairly-by-councils/35760

11 Charlie Taylor, Improving Alternative Provision, Department for Education, 2012, p. 5, accessed at https://www.gov.uk/government/uploads/system/uploads/attachment_data/file/180581/DFE-00035-2012.pdf

12 Jane Ellen Stevens, 'Spokane, WA, students' trauma prompts search for solutions', ACES Too High, 28 February 2012, accessed at https://acestoohigh.com/2012/02/28/spokane-wa-students-child-trauma-prompts-search-for-prevention/

13 Kids Company Q1 Report: Demonstrating sustainable impact and outcomes for children, young people and families, May 2015. This was a private report to the Cabinet Office.

14 Surtees, P., Wainwright, N. 2007 'The shackles of misfortune: social adversity assessments and representations in a chronic-disease epidemiological setting', *Social Science and Medicine* 64(1), pp. 95–111; Kelly-Irving et al. 'Adverse Childhood Experiences and premature all-cause mortality', *European Journal of Epidemiology* 28, pp. 721–34; Bellis et al. 'Adverse childhood experiences: retrospective study to determine their impact on adult health behaviours and health outcomes in a UK population', *Journal of Public Health Advances* 36(10), pp. 81–91

15 Letter from South London and Maudsley NHS Foundation Trust's Southwark Specialist Adolescent Service to parent

16 Charlie Taylor, Improving Alternative Provision, Department for Education, 2012, p. 13, accessed at https://www.gov.uk/government/uploads/system/uploads/attachment_data/file/180581/DFE-00035-2012.pdf

17 Tim Rayment, 'The odd couple', *Sunday Times*, 6 December 2015, News Review, pp. 1–3, accessed at http://www.thesundaytimes.co.uk/sto/newsreview/features/article1641276.ece

Gang Warfare

1 http://www.publications.parliament.uk/pa/cm201415/cmselect/cmhaff/199/19904.htm

2 'Snitches get stiches', one youth mentor reported. 'Stab victims "paying vets to stitch up their wounds"', BBC News, 3 March 2017, accessed at http://www.bbc.co.uk/news/uk-england-nottinghamshire-39127090

3 Wilks-Wiffen, S. (2011) 'Voice of a Child', Howard League for Penal Reform

4 There were 94,864 children aged under sixteen in families where the parents divorced in 2013, a decrease of 38 per cent from 2003 when there were 153,088 children. 'Divorces in England and Wales: 2013', Office for National Statistics, accessed at https://www.ons.gov.uk/peoplepopulationandcommunity/birthsdeathsandmarriages/divorce/bulletins/divorcesinenglandandwales/2013#children-of-divorced-couples

5 'Children at Kids Company have experienced insecure attachment security' (Cecil, preliminary research findings, unpublished, 2012). Jeremy W. Coid, MD; Simone Ullrich, PhD; Robert Keers, PhD;Paul Bebbington, MD; Bianca L. DeStavola, PhD; Constantinos Kallis, PhD; Min Yang, MD; David Reiss, MD; Rachel Jenkins, MD; Peter Donnelly, MD. See also Raine, A., 'From Genes to Brain to Antisocial Behavior', *Current Directions in Psychological Science*, 2008, 17:5, pp. 323–7; and Coid J. W. et al., 'Gang Membership, Violence, and Psychiatric Morbidity', *American Journal of Psychiatry*, 170 (2013), pp. 985–93

6 http://www.standard.co.uk/news/crime/jailed-gang-member-who-stashed-guns-at-homes-of-vulnerable-people-in-southwest-london-a3397461.html. See also http://www.standard.co.uk/news/crime/jailed-young-mother-who-was-paid-to-store-deadly-weapon-under-babys-cot-at-southwark-home-a3413921.html

7 Tony Wilkinson, 'All About the Money or All About the Pussy'

8 http://www.bbc.co.uk/news/health-35595086

9 Jacobson J. et al (2010) Punishing Disadvantage: a profile of children in custody, London: Prison Reform Trust

10 Redmond, A. (2015) Children in Custody 2014–15, London: HM Inspectorate of Prisons

11 Table 4, Office for National Statistics (2011) Population Estimates by Ethnic Group 2002 – 2009, London: Office for National Statistics
12 Ministry of Justice (2010) Compendium of reoffending statistics, London: Ministry of Justice
13 See 'Wealthy Balham residents targeted in air gun drive-by spree "for being rich"', *Evening Standard*, 1 March 2017, accessed at http://www.standard.co.uk/news/crime/wealthy-balham-residents-targeted-in-air-gun-driveby-spree-for-being-rich-a3479621.html
14 http://www.itv.com/news/2016-09-29/going-country-itv-news-reveals-the-scale-of-children-being-exploited-and-sent-around-britain-to-carry-drugs/
15 National Crime Agency. County Lines, Gangs and Safeguarding. 12.08.15. pp 3.
16 http://www.itv.com/news/2016-09-29/going-country-itv-news-reveals-the-scale-of-children-being-exploited-and-sent-around-britain-to-carry-drugs/

Charisma

1 Tim Rayment, 'Killing like it's child's play', *Sunday Times*, 10 April 2016.

Circles of Repair

1 Gebert, D., Heinitz, K. and Buengeler, C. (2016) 'Leaders "charismatic leadership and followers" commitment – the moderating dynamics of value erosion at the societal level', *The Leadership Quarterly*, 27(1), pp. 98–108; Margolis, J. A. and Ziegert, J. C. (2016) 'Vertical flow of collectivistic leadership: An examination of the cascade of visionary leadership across levels', *The Leadership Quarterly*, 27(2), pp. 334–48; Mittal, R. (2015) 'Charismatic and transformational leadership styles: A cross-cultural perspective', *International Journal of Business and Management*, 10(3)
2 'David Cameron "mesmerised" by Kids Company boss', BBC News, 5 August 2015, accessed at http://www.bbc.co.uk/news/uk-politics-33787201
3 'Investigation: the government's funding of Kids Company', National Audit Office, 29 October 2015, p. 8
4 'Oral evidence: Whitehall's Relationship with Kids Company', Public Administration and Constitutional Affairs Committee, 17 November 2015, pp. 26–44
5 Ibid., p. 19
6 Chris Wormald, oral evidence to the Public Accounts Committee, 2 November 2015, accessed 19 September 2017 at http://data.parliament.uk/writtenevidence/committeeevidence.svc/evidencedocument/public-accounts-committee/kids-company/oral/24013.html
7 Ibid.
8 https://www.nao.org.uk/wp-content/uploads/2015/10/Investigation-the-governments-funding-of-Kids-Company.pdf, para 4.17
9 Ibid., para 4.14
10 Ariane Buescher, Monique Ferdinand, Marija Trachtenberg, Sara Evans-Lacko, Martin Knapp, Kids Company Impact Analysis: Economic Impact Analysis for Kids Company's DfE Grant Response, London School of Economics and Political Science, 9 September 2014, p. 8
11 Hughes, A. (2010), letter on 24 February 2010
12 Kids Company: Accessing future government funds, KPMG, 29 March 2011, p. 2
13 Alison Culshaw, 'Accessing Local Authority funding for Kids Company', draft, 30 April 2012, pp. 5–6
14 Ibid., pp. 8–9
15 The patterns of radicalisation are considered in Chapter 12.
16 'County Lines Gang Violence, Exploitation & Drug Supply 2016', National Crime Agency, 17 November 2016, accessed at http://www.nationalcrimeagency.gov.uk/publications/753-county-lines-gang-violence-exploitation-and-drug-supply-2016/file
17 Methods Consulting Ltd report
18 Richard White, 'Subject: re. Kids Company', Children's Social Care Analysis & Research Team, Department for Education, 18 October 2013

19 The process of 'switching' is explored in Chapter 4: The Origins of Violence.
20 Mittal, R. (2015) 'Charismatic and Transformational leadership styles: A cross-cultural perspective', *International Journal of Business and Management*, 10(3); Kipnis, D., Castell, J., Gergen, M. and Mauch, D. (1976) 'Metamorphic effects of power', *Journal of Applied Psychology*, 61(2), pp. 127–35
21 Brandstätter, H. (1997) 'Becoming an entrepreneur – A question of personality structure?', *Journal of Economic Psychology*, 18(2–3), pp. 157–77; Kisfalvi, V. (2002) 'The entrepreneur's character, life issues, and strategy making', *Journal of Business Venturing*, 17(5), pp. 489–518
22 English, L. and Peters, N. (2011) 'Founders' syndrome in women's nonprofit organizations: Implications for practice and organizational life', *Nonprofit Management and Leadership*, 22(2), pp. 159–71; Adler, Carlye, 'Is it time to replace yourself?', *Fortune Small Business* Vol. 17, Issue 4 (May 2007), pp. 70–78; Carman, J. G. and Nesbit, R. (2012) 'Founding new nonprofit organizations: Syndrome or symptom?', *Nonprofit and Voluntary Sector Quarterly*, 42(3), pp. 603–21
23 Mittal, R. (2015) 'Charismatic and Transformational leadership styles: A cross- cultural perspective', *International Journal of Business and Management*, 10(3); Margolis, J. A. and Ziegert, J. C. (2016) 'Vertical flow of collectivistic leadership: An examination of the cascade of visionary leadership across levels', *The Leadership Quarterly*, 27(2), pp. 334–48; Gebert, D., Heinitz, K. and Buengeler, C. (2016) 'Leaders "charismatic leadership and followers" commitment – the moderating dynamics of value erosion at the societal level', *The Leadership Quarterly*, 27(1), pp. 98–108
24 Logan, D., King, J. and Fischer-Wright, H. (2008) 'Corporate tribes: The heart of effective leadership', *Leader to Leader*, 2008(49), pp. 25–30
25 Ibid.
26 Muraven, M. and Baumeister, R. F. (2000) 'Self-regulation and depletion of limited resources: Does self-control resemble a muscle?', *Psychological Bulletin*, 126(2), pp. 247–59
27 A8 – written evidence, 'Whitehall's Relationship with Kids Company inquiry', Public Administration and Constitutional Affairs Committee, October 2015, accessed at http://data.parliament.uk/writtenevidence/committeeevidence.svc/evidencedocument/public-administration-and-constitutional-affairs-committee/kids-company/written/24390.html
28 Bandura, A. (1999) 'Moral disengagement in the perpetration of inhumanities', *Personality and Social Psychology Review*, 3(3), pp. 193–209; Morton, T. A. and Postmes, T. (2011) 'What does it mean to be human? How salience of the human category affects responses to intergroup harm', *European Journal of Social Psychology*, 41(7), pp. 866–73; Bandura, A. (1999) 'Moral disengagement in the perpetration of inhumanities', *Personality and Social Psychology Review* 3(3), pp. 193–209
29 Strack, J., Lopes, P. N. and Esteves, F. (2014) 'Will you thrive under pressure or burn out? Linking anxiety motivation and emotional exhaustion', *Cognition and Emotion*, 29(4), pp. 578–91
30 Bandura, A. (1999) 'Moral disengagement in the perpetration of inhumanities', *Personality and Social Psychology Review* 3(3), pp. 193–209; Taylor, S. E. and Brown, J. D. (1988) 'Illusion and well-being: A social psychological perspective on mental health', *Psychological Bulletin* 103(2), pp. 193–210
31 Parish, S. M. (2014) 'Between persons: How concepts of the person make moral experience possible', *Ethos* 42(1), pp. 31–50
32 Bion, W. R. (1948) 'Experiences in groups', *Human Relations*, vols. I–IV, 1948–1951, Reprinted in *Experiences in Groups* (1961); Bion, W. R. (1952) 'Group dynamics: a review', *International Journal of Psycho-Analysis*, Vol. 33. Reprinted in M. Klein, P. Heimann and R. Money-Kyrle (eds), *New Directions in Psychoanalysis* (pp. 440–77), Tavistock Publications, 1955. Reprinted in *Experiences in Groups* (1961); Bion, W. R. (1961). *Experiences in Groups*
33 Sandra Jovchelovitch and Natalia Concha (September 2013): 'Kids Company: A Diagnosis of the Organisation and its Interventions'

NOTES

Circles of Despair

1 Email from Ruth Jenkins to Richard Handover and two other trustees, 11 February 2014
2 Oral evidence, Whitehall's Relationship with Kids Company, House of Commons Public Administration and Constitutional Affairs Committee, 17 November 2015, Q350–Q357
3 As I have been writing this book, a report was released by Frances Oldham QC confirming systematic child abuse at Haut de la Garenne. It seems as if some 553 alleged offences were reported by adults who had been in children's homes in Jersey between September 2007 and December 2010, of which 315 were committed at Haut de la Garenne. The police officer who had been ridiculed for raising the alarm was now exonerated. Jimmy Savile was one of the people who had been visiting this children's home.
4 Letter from Camila to the Rt Hon Oliver Letwin at the Cabinet Office, 14 July 2014
5 Sandra Laville, 'Lambeth Council to pay tens of millions to child abuse survivors', *The Guardian*, 16 December 2016, accessed at https://www.theguardian.com/society/2016/dec/15/lambeth-council-pay-tens-of-millions-pounds-child-abuse-survivors-shirley-oaks
6 Oral evidence: Whitehall's relationship with Kids Company, Public Administration and Constitutional Affairs Committee, 19 November 2015, p. 24
7 Paul Bentley and Katherine Rushton, 'Kids Company founder used charity nurse for her own medical care: Whistleblowers claim chief had daily appointments with staff member who was meant to look after underprivileged children', *Daily Mail*, 24 August 2015
8 Miles Goslett, 'The trouble with Kids Company', *The Spectator*, 14 February 2015, accessed at http://www.spectator.co.uk/2015/02/the-trouble-with-kids-company/
9 Miles Goslett, 'How I blew the whistle on Kids Company – and Camila Batmanghelidjh', *The Spectator*, 6 August 2015, accessed at http://blogs.spectator.co.uk/2015/08/the-inside-story-of-how-the-spectator-broke-the-kids-company-scandal/
10 http://data.parliament.uk/writtenevidence/committeeevidence.svc/evidencedocument/public-administration-and-constitutional-affairs-committee/kids-company/written/24467.html
11 James Salmon, 'You bunch of crooks! Widow, 75, speaks for millions as she stands up at Barclays' AGM to attack "greed" of bankers pocketing sky-high pay packets', *Daily Mail*, 26 April 2013
12 http://data.parliament.uk/writtenevidence/committeeevidence.svc/evidencedocument/public-administration-and-constitutional-affairs-committee/kids-company/written/24467.html
13 Written evidence from Harriet Sergeant (KCI 09), Whitehall's Relationship with Kids Company inquiry – publications, October 2015, accessed at http://data.parliament.uk/writtenevidence/committeeevidence.svc/evidencedocument/public-administration-and-constitutional-affairs-committee/kids-company/written/24321.html
14 Oral evidence: Whitehall's relationship with Kids Company, Public Administration and Constitutional Affairs Committee, 19 November 2015, p. 25

Perfect Storm

1 Sam Butler, 'It's Lynton Crosby who made Zac Goldsmith's campaign so nasty – and now he's being knighted', *The Independent*, 6 May 2016
2 Nicholas Hellen, 'Stars' backing "cannot save" kids' charity', *Sunday Times*, 21 September 2014
3 Adele Eastman, 'Enough Is Enough', op. cit., pp. 288, 362
4 Miles Goslett, 'Kids Company directors quit over stress and funding concerns', *Sunday Times*, 8 March 2005
5 Adele Eastman, 'Enough is Enough', op. cit., p. 14
6 Ibid., p. 37
7 Ibid., pp. 12, 25

Conclusion

1 http://www.telegraph.co.uk/women/mother-tongue/11222574/Adoption-crisis-in-numbers.html

371

2   Action for Children, 'Revolving Door Part 1: Are vulnerable children being overlooked?'; https://www.gov.uk/government/publications/childrens-services-innovation-programme

3   http://www.telegraph.co.uk/news/uknews/crime/11057647/Rotherham-sex-abuse-scandal-1400-children-exploited-by-Asian-gangs-while-authorities-turned-a-blind-eye.html

4   http://www.bbc.co.uk/news/uk-england-31708492

5   https://www.theguardian.com/society/2016/nov/25/met-police-martin-hewitt-apologises-for-failing-to-protect-children-at-risk-of-abuse

6   'Enough Is Enough', op. cit.

7   http://www.theresident.co.uk/london-culture-events/local-people/child-change-system/

8   Kids Company Impact Analysis Economic Impact Analysis for Kids Company's DfE Grant Response (Buescher, Ferdinand, Trachtenberg, Evans-Lacko, Knapp, 2014)

9   https://www.theguardian.com/commentisfree/2016/oct/18/troubled-families-programme-ministers-data; https://www.nao.org.uk/wp-content/uploads/2016/10/The-troubled-families-programme-update.pdf

10 https://www.theguardian.com/society/2010/oct/11/black-prison-population-increase-england

11 https://www.gov.uk/government/uploads/system/uploads/attachment_data/file/183498/DFE-RR190.pdf

12 https://www.actionforchildren.org.uk/media/9363/revolving-door-report-final.pdf

13 Pryce, R; Buykx, P; Gray, L; Stone, T; Drummond, C; Brennan, A (2017) 'Estimates of Alcohol Dependence in England based on APMS 2014, including Estimates of Children Living in a Household with an Adult with Alcohol Dependence: Prevalence, Trends, and Amenability to Treatment', Public Health England, accessed at http://www.nta.nhs.uk/uploads/estimates-of-alchohol-dependency-in-england[0].pdf

14 Public Health Institute, Liverpool John Moores University Public Health England (2012) 'Estimates of number of adults with opiate dependence that have children living in the same household and the number of children in 2011/12', Public Health England, accessed at http://www.nta.nhs.uk/uploads/ljmu-opiate-and-children-estimates.pdf

15 Children's Commissioner (2017), op. cit.

16 LGA (2017) Councils face £2 billion funding gap to support vulnerable children by 2020. https://www.local.gov.uk/about/news/councils-face-2-billion-funding-gap-support-vulnerable-children-2020

17 http://www.sodiumhaze.org/2015/10/14/kids-company-spoke-truth-to-power-was-it-silenced-nicholas-sebley/

18 https://www.standard.co.uk/news/dispossessed/the-dispossessed-fund-1m-to-help-charities-fight-gangs-8956995.html

19 https://www.express.co.uk/news/uk/600311/Kids-Company-scandal-founder-used-charity-nurse

20 Twitter

21 https://www.theguardian.com/society/2015/aug/06/kids-companys-demise-speaks-volumes-about-how-britain-is-run

22 http://www.lawcom.gov.uk/app/uploads/2015/03/Unfitness_to_Plead_Symposium_Programme.pdf; http://www.lse.ac.uk/researchAndExpertise/researchImpact/caseStudies/peay-establishing-a-test-of-fitness-to-plead-in-criminal-court.aspx

23 http://www.crae.org.uk/news/high-court-issues-damning-judgment-on-%C3%A2%E2%82%AC%CB%9Cwidespread-unlawful-use-of-restraint-in-child-prisons-run-by-g4s-and-serco/; https://publications.parliament.uk/pa/ld200809/ldjudgmt/jd090520/appg-1.htm

24 https://www.liberty-human-rights.org.uk/previous-award-winners

25 Kids Company Newsletter, Issue 11, Spring/Summer 2010, p. 8

26 https://www.thetimes.co.uk/article/fine-talk-big-staff-but-where-are-the-children-lady-bountiful-xx65k9fvv23

27 https://shoobuy.files.wordpress.com/2017/02/kids-company-research-and-evaluation-re-

port-c-gaskell-queen-mary-university-july-2008-1.pdf; 'Kids Company: A Diagnosis of the Organisation and its Interventions'. Final report. Sandra Jovchelovitch and Natalia Concha (September 2013), p. 7; 'Experience in Social Systems Questionnaire (EXIS)' from the data acquisition at Kids Company in November 2012 and January 2013, Julian Geigges, University Hospital Heidelberg
28 https://twitter.com/simon_pegg/status/629206326611152896
29 Mary Carpenter, *Juvenile Delinquents: Their Condition and Treatment* (1852)

INDEX

INDEX